CANNABIS NATION

CANNABIS NATION

CONTROL AND CONSUMPTION IN BRITAIN, 1928–2008

JAMES H. MILLS

OXFORD

UNIVERSITY PRESS

OXFORD
UNIVERSITY PRESS

Great Clarendon Street, Oxford, OX2 6DP,
United Kingdom

Oxford University Press is a department of the University of Oxford.
It furthers the University's objective of excellence in research, scholarship,
and education by publishing worldwide. Oxford is a registered trade mark of
Oxford University Press in the UK and in certain other countries

First Edition published in 2013

Impression: 1

British Library Cataloguing in Publication Data

Data available

ISBN 978-0-19-928342-2

Printed in Great Britain by
MPG Books Group, Bodmin and King's Lynn

For my loves, Rebecca, Constance, and Beatrice

Preface

When I wrote the preface to the predecessor of this book, *Cannabis Britannica: Empire, Trade, and Prohibition, 1800–1928* (Oxford: Oxford University Press, 2003), David Blunkett had just announced that as Home Secretary he would be seeking to reclassify cannabis in order to alter its legal status. That news sparked a fresh set of controversies about the plant and preparations made from it in government, in scientific and medical circles, in the media, and among law enforcement agencies. These controversies rumble on today. This book seeks to bring a historical perspective to these events and controversies. The history of cannabis and the British stretches back over two centuries and, while *Cannabis Britannica* looked at the period before 1928, this book considers the story since then and up to 2008. In that year Jacqui Smith, one of Blunkett's successors as a New Labour incumbent at the Home Office, reversed his decision to reclassify cannabis. The twin themes that shape the narrative are control and consumption, as tracing these provides explanations for the growth in the market for cannabis in the UK of the twentieth century and for the forms that efforts to control users have taken. The book argues that a historical perspective on recent events and controversies is vital as it can reveal how current positions have been arrived at, and can show how well founded they are. Its conclusions are that the story of cannabis and the British has been shaped by the wider history of twentieth-century Britain. Current positions among both those that advocate consumption and those that insist on control have been formed by the prejudices, misconceptions, and politics of the past.

A wide range of people are owed a debt in the making of this book. Archivists and librarians at the University of Strathclyde, the National Library of Scotland, the British Library, the Wellcome Collection, and the UK National Archives have been crucial in locating relevant material and deciphering obscure catalogues, the greatest challenge of which was the League of Nations series. Jan Usher, Francine Millard, and Kevin Halliwell at the National Library of Scotland, and Ross Macfarlane at the Wellcome Library have been good enough to become colleagues in various enterprises beyond this book for which I am particularly grateful. Most of the research completed was funded by the award of a three-year ESRC (Economic and Social Research) Research Fellowship (RES-000-27-0018), and the later stages of writing were enabled by a Wellcome Trust Enhancement Grant (WT085432/Z) to the Centre for the Social History of Health and Health-care Glasgow (CSHHH). I am very grateful to both organizations for their encouragement and the imagination shown to support work in this field. The University of Strathclyde has provided both funding and time for me to bring this project to completion and I consider myself fortunate to be employed by what is an exemplary institution in terms of the support that it offers historians in their work.

Many others have played a part in shaping my thinking and preventing my settling for easy conclusions. Caroline Coon, Anthony Gifford, Robin Corbett, David Watson, and Rob Clarke were kind enough to allow themselves to be interviewed for this book, and Free Love Cannabis and Robert Kilroy-Silk helped out through correspondence. Colleagues at the CSHHH Glasgow are a constant source of inspiration and wisdom, and I am particularly grateful to Tricia Barton, Emma Newlands, Arthur McIvor, Matt Smith, Ryan Johnson, John Stewart, and Chris Nottingham, for insights and alcohol. Thanks are also due to members of the Scottish Oral History Centre (SOHC) at the University of Strathclyde who equipped me to conduct the interviews on the project. David Brown, now at the University of Southampton, endured the poor jokes and provocation with which I disturbed his work when I found myself in need of distraction from my own. That Satadru Sen at City University of New York (CUNY) uses my work to shock his students has always driven me to produce more of it, and some useful comments and questions by Alex Mold, Joe Spillane, and David Courtwright at the Alcohol and Drugs in History Society conference of 2010 at Buffalo enabled me to fine-tune some of my conclusions. I thank them all! Stephanie Ireland, Assistant Commissioning Editor for Academic History at Oxford University Press, deserves special mention. She found herself cursed with the goal of getting me to deliver this book, and despite having her patience and endurance tested outrageously, has remained patient and polite throughout her ordeal.

If a lot has happened in the story of cannabis and the British since this book's predecessor appeared in 2003, then it is safe to say that the same is true of life in the Mills family. In part this is down to the arrival of Beatrice May, who in 2004 joined her mother Rebecca Jane and her sister Constance Verity in the task of keeping me on my toes. All of my work is for them, with love.

Contents

I

Introduction

History, control, and consumption

> No government should take unilateral measures without considering the
> impact of its actions and ultimately the consequences for an entire system
> that took governments almost a century to establish.[1]

In 2003 David Blunkett, then Home Secretary, sought to reclassify cannabis to ensure that those caught in possession of it in the UK could not
be arrested. He was immediately scolded by Philip Emafo, who used the
argument above to condemn the action. At the time the latter was president
of the International Narcotics Control Board of the United Nations, the
most senior drugs official in the world. At the heart of Emafo's rebuke to
Blunkett was history.

This book answers the question raised by Emafo's response, namely was
he right to be confident that history supported his case? In other words, was
it safe to assume that the century of concerted action on cannabis had been
one of sensible decisions made for sound reasons that had resulted in a
coherent and well-thought-out approach to controlling the drug, that no
wise government could contemplate improving upon? This book's predecessor, *Cannabis Britannica*, started from a similar position. It was first
published in 2003 in a period of frantic posturing on the issue of cannabis
by politicians, journalists, and a host of other interested groups and individuals. Like Emafo, they had used fleeting allusions to the past to claim that it
bolstered their positions, whether they were for or against change in the
control regime related to the drug. The introduction to *Cannabis Britannica*
reviewed a number of their publications before concluding that none
offered a satisfactory account of the history of the drug in Britain.[2] This
raised two issues. The first related to the misuse of history, and the way in

which advocates for a variety of positions on cannabis felt able to blithely claim that the past vindicated their arguments despite the fact that they knew so little about it. The second was the question of what a satisfactory account of the relationship between cannabis and the British might look like. Addressing these issues amounted to a challenge to come up with a more informed overview of that history. *Cannabis Britannica* covered the period until 1928 in order to begin the task of providing just such an account, and this volume takes up the story in order to complete it.

Providing a detailed history of the relationship between cannabis and the British promises more than just greater amounts of detail, however. A clear and factual account has the potential to undermine current arguments and stances, or to validate them, by exposing their origins to scrutiny. If the historian can claim a place in contemporary drug debates it is in order to provide a sense of how today's consumers and those responsible for control regimes find themselves in the positions that they do and with the arguments that they advance. In doing this the historian can often reveal flaws in previous decisions or in earlier reasoning that suggest that contemporary positions need not be so entrenched or have become so for reasons that no longer make sense now that political or cultural circumstances have changed. Whether this then offers new ways of working out how to move on from those positions is for others to establish, but at the very least it should demand that assumptions are re-examined and approaches placed in historical context. After all, as *Cannabis Britannica* demonstrated, the history of the drug and the British stretches back over two centuries or more.

The book focuses on the twin themes of consumption and control as these are at the heart of the controversies and debates about cannabis. Some clues are already available as to how to make sense of the story. The international drugs regulatory system alluded to by Philip Emafo is an important part of the UK's story as the country has been a signatory to treaties that included controls on cannabis since 1925. Historians such as William McAllister and William Walker have drawn out the competing national agendas and the diplomatic wrangles behind its evolution.[3] Others, like David Courtwright and Richard Rudgeley, have taken a similarly international framework but have looked beyond control mechanisms to include investigations into changing markets for psychoactive substances and evolving consumer demands and practices.[4] Indeed, important revisionist accounts of particular drugs markets and efforts to control them in other countries have recently refocused attention on consumers and the importance of understanding their drives and demands rather than accepting often dismissive generalizations about them. For example, the work of Frank Dikötter, Lars Laamann, and Zhou Xun, and also of Yangwen Zheng, in this direction has been particularly important in demanding fresh ways of thinking about the opium trade in Asia.[5]

In the UK itself a number of histories have been written of psychoactive substances other than cannabis. Virginia Berridge and Alex Mold, for example, have pointed to factors that include changing approaches to public health and to the contested nature of concepts such as addiction in the context of tobacco and opiates.[6] While all these studies provide useful insights it remains the case that the relationship between the British and cannabis has been relatively neglected. Martin Booth's *Cannabis: A History* did include episodes from the UK but these were intermingled with those from the USA. His conclusion, that when it comes to cannabis 'it is now time we stopped blinding ourselves with our narrow-minded bigotry and started, as the hippy jargon of the Swinging Sixties would have put it, to "get real"',[7] suggests that his book was shaped by particular sympathies. His book also failed to fully engage with the wide range of sources available, focusing largely on newspaper and literary accounts and neglecting government archives and scientific sources. Other books that have touched on the story of cannabis in the UK have tended to engage with its cultural history rather than with the history of markets for the drug and the controls imposed upon them.[8] There is much more available on the story of cannabis in the USA.[9] On the one hand there are the conspiracy theories which argue that the industrial giant Du Pont sought to protect its interests in oil, coal, and wood pulp by campaigning in the USA in the 1930s to have cultivators of the hemp plant heavily taxed for fear that it would become a rival source of energy and paper. The outcome was the 1937 Marihuana Tax Act.[10] Other historians prefer to tell the story of a vigorous American government official, Harry Anslinger, who was appointed head of the new Bureau of Narcotics in 1930. By 1937 he had succeeded in stoking a media outcry against hemp drugs and had forced the issue into Congress where legislation designed to combat consumption of cannabis was eventually passed despite the opposition of the legislative counsel for the American Medical Association.[11] There are also those that argue that Anslinger's personal activities would have come to nothing had it not been for the wider context of the United States in the period. A suspicion of intoxication was common there in the early twentieth century and had developed into a dominant theme in the 1920s when agitation for post-war moral reform resulted in the prohibition of alcohol.[12] Cannabis itself became closely identified with Mexican and African American migrant populations that the white legislators of 1930s America feared. By placing restrictions on the drug it was hoped that greater control could be exercised over those suspect populations.[13] The politics of the 1930s may also have been important, as this was the period of the New Deal Congress government in the United States, an administration that was convinced that vigorous state action was the means of solving anything identified as a national evil. As such, it was a government that was receptive to Anslinger's appeal for legislation and for centralized control.[14] Taken together then, the history of the USA's first legislation aimed at curbing the use of cannabis preparations is one of the activities of an entrepreneurial bureaucrat against the backdrop of white America's racist and moralistic attitudes in the context of a control-happy government. The legislation had no grounds in science or medicine and indeed it has been argued had no grounds in real issues of social order or of crime and punishment.[15]

Studies of cannabis in other countries also provide useful perspectives. In Mexico the ambitions of the nation's Sanitary Council in the nineteenth century to assert its authority over medical practice eventually ensnared cannabis in a regulatory framework as the plant was used there in preparations of therapeutic substances as well as for recreational purposes.[16] In Canada, controls on cannabis consumption became a divisive issue in the 1960s which was caught up in tensions between federal and provincial government, within the medical profession, and among various bureaucratic agencies. The range of competing voices and agendas ensured that the legislative framework changed little despite significant opposition to it.[17] In Australia, efforts to control the market for cannabis in the 1970s resulted in police corruption on a wide scale.[18] When taken together then, the range of studies in drugs history point to a number of factors that have shaped the consumption and control of psychoactive substances in modern societies that include the changing demands and desires of consumers, the interests and ambitions of medical professionals, the agendas of politicians, police officers, and bureaucrats, and the role of the media in selecting and disseminating ideas about such substances to those that have little contact with them. This volume will establish how far these factors were among those that shaped the story of cannabis and the British since 1928.

Cannabis 1928–2008

Before taking on the task of exploring and explaining this story it is worth summarizing its key features. This book's predecessor set the scene for the period before 1928 and it established that the story stretched back beyond the nineteenth century. It found that, while few in the country used the substance before the 1920s, millions in Britain's colonies were consumers spread across territories in Asia, Africa, and the West Indies. In many societies and communities in these places the use of preparations of the cannabis plant had long histories that pre-dated the arrival of the British. There these preparations were used for purposes of intoxication, but also for therapeutic and medicinal reasons.

Imperial administrators adopted a number of responses to these consumers. For example, in Egypt outright prohibition of use of the drug was attempted, while on the other hand in India officials allowed consumption and simply taxed trade in the substance. When the opium trade in Asia between British India and China became a matter of political controversy in the second half of the nineteenth century this taxation policy in South Asia became entangled in these debates and eventually the subject of an official enquiry, the Indian Hemp Drugs Commission in 1893/4. At the same time scientific curiosity about the drug focused on the hunt for the active ingredient, a venture that was to end in an explosion that killed a member of the team at Cambridge that was leading the field. When cannabis came to be debated at the League of Nations in the 1920s, British delegates there led the opposition to the proposal that the drug be included in the international controls considered at the Second Opium Conference at Geneva in 1924/5. They failed to prevent this, and the UK found itself in a position where it was obliged to ratify agreements to regulate access to cannabis products that its representatives had opposed.

This book is organized into chapters on a chronological basis. It is structured in this way partly to make it easier to follow the narrative of key events, characters, and decisions and partly in order to trace trends as they began to emerge and to identify points of the story where certain aspects ceased to be important. However, the structure has further significance as it is designed to draw attention to the observation that chronology is important in the history of cannabis and the British. That control came before consumption in the UK is highly significant, as is the fact that encounters with the drug stretch back into the time of Empire. Indeed, a sense of chronology is also important in grasping the idea that neither control nor consumption have been unchanging or isolated phenomena, and that both have been regularly reshaped by wider historical circumstances.

Chapter 2 takes up the story in the 1920s where *Cannabis Britannica* left off. An early media scare about the drug and an example of ham-fisted policing of North African migrant workers in London propelled cannabis into the Poisons Schedule at much the same time as it was inserted into the international drugs regulatory system at Geneva. There remained little domestic consumption of preparations of the plant in the UK in the period before the Second World War save among the itinerant workers of the imperial ports. There was certainly limited medical application of substances containing the drug, which was omitted from the British Pharmacopoeia in 1932. However, in these years the control regime was being carefully assembled. Ambitious bureaucrats at the recently established Home Office Drugs Branch primed police forces around the country to be on the lookout for cannabis, even where few were ever likely to encounter the drug.

In the same period Britain's approach to the substance abroad was riddled with contradictions. On the one hand the issue of cannabis was kept alive at the League of Nations by Thomas Wentworth Russell, a colonial policeman who made his career in Egypt enforcing a prohibition on the drug. On the other hand, the British administration in India persisted in selling the substance to colleagues in Burma and the West Indies with an utter disregard for the restrictions imposed by the international drugs regulatory system. Chapter 3 explores the tangled relationships with cannabis of the British Empire in its final years. It shows how imperial administrators shaped the approach of the League of Nations to the drug and ensured that the inhabitants of many of the country's colonies lived in some of the world's most thriving markets for preparations of the plant.

Some of these inhabitants were to make their way to the UK in the immediate post-war era in order to answer the country's call for manpower to rebuild its cities and economy. Chapter 4 explores the years between 1945 and 1962, in order to look at the dynamics of a period in which a permanent domestic market for the drug was established in Britain. The migrant workers arriving from the colonies introduced new forms of music, distinctive styles of dress, and tastes that would have seemed exotic to the

locals. Cannabis was among the indulgences imported to satisfy these predilections and the more curious members of the UK's population took to
experimenting with it as well as with the new food, clothes and music of
the migrants. The less curious and more reactionary met the migrants with
racism and rejection. Discussions of cannabis in this period were often
nothing of the sort as cases like the murder of Joseph Aaku linked the drug
to anxieties about race and immigration against a backdrop of the end of
Empire. They were often about more than that too, as the period's Cold War
tensions and increasingly uneasy relations between generations were voiced
when the drug was debated by colourful characters like Donald McIntosh
Johnson, the failed doctor turned hotel proprietor and publisher who served
as Conservative MP for Carlisle. Such debates were increasingly common in
this period as more stories about the drug were circulating, largely thanks to
the fact that the enforcement mechanisms that had been carefully put in place
in the pre-war period were primed to deal with the small numbers of migrants
who brought cannabis from the colonies with them.

While Britain's colonial past began to shape the UK's experience of
cannabis in these years, other overseas contexts were similarly important
and Chapter 5 considers them. There was a flurry of interest in British
medical circles about the therapeutic potential of synhexl, or synthetic
cannabis, early on in the period of research into antibiotics sparked by the
wartime development of penicillin. However, events at the United Nations
(UN) and the World Health Organization (WHO) were to kill off any
chance of a revival of therapeutic applications of substances based on the
plant in the 1950s. A determined campaign against cannabis was waged by
the WHO and the UN Secretariat in this period which was to ensure that
little doubt was left in the mind of medical experts and drugs bureaucrats
that it was a useless and dangerous material. However, the intervention of
British delegates and their colleagues from newly independent India served
to prevent an even more radical position on the drug being adopted in the
1961 Single Convention on Narcotic Drugs.

Chapter 6 begins to assess the events of the last half-century in the UK as
markets in the country for cannabis became larger and more complex and
control mechanisms expanded and attracted ever greater time and resources.
Stories from the 1960s are familiar, as Keith Richards of The Rolling Stones
went to prison for cannabis offences under controversial new laws, The
Beatles paid for protests in *The Times*, and pro-cannabis campaigners rallied
in Hyde Park. The chapter seeks to get behind the headlines, however, and

to examine exactly what was significant about the decade. While cannabis consumers found their voice in legal and policy circles in this period it is important to understand that it was a particular type of consumer that chose to speak up, one for whom use of the drug was a political gesture. Not all users shared their commitments, and the chapter explores just how far the drug was adopted by the country's youth outside of London's fashionable elites. Indeed, the real significance of the decade may lie in the other voices that were given a place in the system of arriving at cannabis policy and the content of what they were saying. Despite the controversies over the Report on Cannabis of the Hallucinogens Sub-Committee of the Advisory Committee on Drug Dependence in 1968 which was chaired by Baroness Wootton the place of scientific, academic, and professional experts in the processes of determining drugs policy was secured when the Advisory Council on the Misuse of Drugs was established as a statutory body in 1971.

Chapter 7 takes on the story of what happened when the experts gave their advice. It seems that they advocated what R. D. Laing called 'the British compromise' where the law did not change but enforcement of the law did. This approach was to dominate the next three decades as a new generation of consumers emerged. For those growing up in the emerging multicultural communities of the UK's cities the drug seemed less exotic than to previous generations and as familiar a part of the routine of youthful recreation in the inner cities as Asian shopkeepers and reggae music. Nevertheless the drug remained a controlled substance and possession was illegal, so consumers continued to fall foul of the law. As such they became caught up in the civil liberties controversies of the period, and figures as varied as Lord Gifford and Robert Kilroy-Silk sought reform of cannabis legislation. At the same time, however, these reformers were opposed by a phalanx of scientists marshalled by Griffith Edwards who felt that the perceived public health perils of cannabis consumption should be the key concern for government. Chapter 7 explores the clashes over cannabis between what were fundamentally different views of government between 1971 and 1997, and investigates how far they were actually of any real relevance to those controlling and consuming cannabis. In a period when the Advisory Council on the Misuse of Drugs could take eight years to come up with a statement on cannabis which was subsequently ignored, 'the British compromise' ensured that policemen and magistrates found themselves free to make decisions about consumers and consumption on a daily basis.

Chapter 8 considers the decade or so before 2008 in order to explain some of the features of a period that stands out in the story of cannabis and the British as one of remarkable activity. By the late 1990s there were more cannabis consumers than ever before in the UK, and greater numbers of them finding themselves in trouble with the police than had previously been the case. This despite attempts to focus enforcement agencies on other drugs under the Conservative Government of the period 1979–97. In the years immediately after the New Labour administration came to power in 1997 many of these consumers again found their voice and began to make various demands, for access to medicines based on the plant, for changes in sentences for cannabis consumers, and, indeed, for the legalization of cannabis consumption itself. Newspapers and political parties took up their concerns as never before and a number of expert bodies rushed to offer their opinions. When David Blunkett assumed office as Home Secretary in 2001 he broke with the policy of his predecessor and took the decision to reclassify the drug. However, his successors quickly back-pedalled and, ignoring the advice of the experts appointed to inform the government's decisions, Jacqui Smith reversed the classification decision in 2008. The chapter explores these events and argues that they are best understood in the wider context of the history of the period, as the nature of the New Labour administration and the agendas of the police served to frustrate those that sought change to 'the British compromise'.

2

'Frost is the only thing which kills it': Lascars, the Drugs Branch, and Doctors, c.1928–c.1945[1]

Introduction

A flurry of activity in the mid-1920s had seen cannabis briefly become a matter for the authorities in the UK. The Pharmaceutical Society included the drug on the Poisons Schedule in 1924 and the League of Nations incorporated various preparations of the plant into the international system of drugs treaties early in 1925. Obligations imposed by these treaties were finally implemented in the UK under the Coca Leaves and Indian Hemp Drug Regulations of 1928. Few in Britain would have noticed that the legal status of cannabis had suddenly changed. Amidst this regulatory activity officials at the Home Office wrote:

> There is no evidence of the abusive use of Indian hemp amongst the inhabitants of this country. Very occasionally haschish [sic] has been found in the possession of oriental seamen who have brought a small quantity for their own use.[1]

The only group to voice any concern about the new restrictions on cannabis was the UK's corn-plaster manufacturers. It turned out that some of them included preparations of the plant as an ingredient in their products, although none could remember why this was the case.[2]

What is most surprising given this calm about cannabis in the middle of the 1920s is the size of the Home Office file which holds the document from which the above quote is drawn. Found in the National Archives in

Kew, it is nearly 10 inches thick and is stuffed with thirty-four folders relating to cannabis products in the period 1923–6 alone. This seems to be an awful lot of information-gathering and memo-generating on a subject that the Home Office did not perceive to be a problem. This is the core issue to be explored in this chapter, the way in which cannabis became a concern of the authorities and the medical profession at a time in the 1920s and the 1930s when it was hardly a concern for any of them.

To understand what lay behind this, the chapter returns to the title of the book and addresses the reason that it lists control before consumption. There is little evidence that cannabis users became significantly more numerous in the UK between the middle of the 1920s and the end of the Second World War. However, there is plenty of evidence that in this period police officers, customs officials, pharmacists, doctors, and medical scientists all had the opportunity to form opinions on a drug that they rarely encountered, and to construct ideas about consumers that few would ever actually meet.

Consumption: Lascars, corn plasters, and 'soul-murderers'

In the immediate aftermath of the Geneva Opium Conference of 1924/5 the Home Office felt compelled to establish an accurate picture of the domestic trade in preparations of the cannabis plant. A member of staff was sent out into the City of London to research the topic among the brokers and agents of the pharmaceutical companies. He discovered that the trade dealt in three different types of material. The first was called 'Bombay Tops' and turned out to be the ganja of India transported 'green and of the size and shape of large raisins'. Its price was about 25s. per lb and it all came from Bombay. The second type was known as 'African hemp' and the man from the Home Office established that it 'look[s] very similar to the hemp given to canaries' and that it could be traced back to Natal in South Africa. Finally, 'American Hemp', at 1s. 9d. per lb, was found to be even cheaper than the African product which sold at 3s. per lb and was thought to be 'not liked by British manufacturers'. The Home Office met with two of the directors of the company British Drugs Houses in 1925 and found out that the imported cannabis was used to manufacture extracts and tinctures based on recipes included in the British and North American pharmacopeia. They expressed the opinion that 'the use of medicinal preparations of cannabis in this country appears to be rapidly diminishing; but the BP extract and tincture are still, in their view, a necessary part of a stock of the dispensing chemist'. Investigators also established that the corn-plaster industry was coming to terms with the new situation, reporting that 'cannabis Indica was used as the colouring matter in corn paint and corn plasters, but owing to the fact that the drug has been scheduled as a poison under the Poisons and Pharmacy Acts, this use of the drug will probably disappear'. This was confirmed by the directors at British Drugs Houses who thought that 'this use has been practically killed by the inclusion of cannabis in Part I of the Poisons Schedule'.

The Home Office also turned up a suspicious link with Russia. While interviewing the brokers in the City of London an official discovered that most of the cannabis imported into Britain was subsequently re-exported rather than used by domestic drugs companies. Foreign buyers were typically pharmaceutical concerns on the Continent such as Merck and C. F. Boehringer, but there had been unusual developments recently: 'two brokers told me that a surprising demand in the last two years has arisen from Russia and quite large consignments have been shipped there, having been exported by Arcos Ltd. One broker said that although he had no evidence that it was used in Russia for illicit purposes, the demand from that country was so unusual (he had been dealing in Indian hemp since 1896) that "if anything was wrong he would suggest looking in that quarter"'. The Home Office took the hint and investigated Freudentheil Smith and Co, drugs importers of Mincing Street in London, and their agent concluded that 'these people evidently know more than they told me, especially with regard to the Russian and Continental trade'. For all his concern, the Home Office seemed content with the general tone of the findings and it was decided that 'no further action is now required'.[3]

Once statistics began to be gathered on the legal trade in cannabis later in the decade it became clear that the brokers and pharmaceutical companies continued to trade in cannabis for legitimate medical products in modest quantities. In 1929, the first year for which records are available, 1,313 lb of the plant were imported and added to stocks, from which 1,990 lb were used in the manufacture of cannabis extract and 29 lb were used in producing cannabis tincture. A further 2,410 lb were exported as raw cannabis while smaller amounts were sold abroad as extract and tincture. This contrasted in scale with the legal trade in opium; 113,017 lb were imported in that year, with 78,844 for conversion into morphine and 6,022 for medicinal opium, while almost 10,000 lb were exported in a raw state.[4]

Establishing a picture of the illegal trade in cannabis in the UK in this period is not so easy. There were occasional glimpses of it in the news-papers. The *News of the World* of 16 June 1935 carried a 'Special' report with the headline 'Growing Menace of Drug Trade: "Doped" Cigarette Perils in West-End'.

> The closing months of Lord Trenchard's command of the Metropolitan Police will be marked by an intensive drive against drug traffickers—'soul-murderers' they have been called—whose nefarious trade has recently been growing apace in the West-end . . . Two aspects of the new drug menace are causing grave concern—the increase in the smoking of doped cigarettes, particularly by white girls in the West-end, and the ease with which drugs can be obtained in the heart of the Empire's capital.

The story went on about 'young and pretty girls, butterflies of the metro-polis . . . [who], jaded and weary after sleepless nights and hectic days, fall easy victims to the plausible temptations of the "snow" and hashish seller'. It conjured up tales of motorboats connected with the cannabis trade appearing off the South Coast, of airports being watched, and of 'gangs who attempted to Americanise crime in this country'. However, it never strayed too far from the central image of the 'innocent girls . . . ruined body and soul as a sequel to that first "whiff"'.[5] Despite considerable embellish-ment the story did have a basis in real events. It referred to a trial at Marlborough Street in which Detective Sergeant Keen had spoken for the prosecution. Keen was a member of the Criminal Investigation Department (CID) of the Metropolitan Police and he reported to superiors on 4 June that he had been told by an informant 'that a drug known as Hashish was being sold to drug addicts in various clubs in the West End. This drug is apparently being mixed with tobacco and made up in the form of a cigarette for the purpose of smoking'. He persuaded the informant to return to the club and to purchase some evidence, and on receiving the required cigarette he sent it for analysis in order to confirm that there was cannabis in the contents. On 6 June the Metropolitan Police Laboratory reported that 'the sample in the cigarette paper consists of a mixture of cigarette tobacco and Hasheesh (Indian Hemp)'. Armed with this news Keen was true to his name and arrested Max Fisher 'a seaman . . . for being in possession of a quantity of Indian hemp (hashish) and two hand made cigarettes containing a mixture of tobacco and hashish'. He then obtained a search warrant and took off for a premises on West India Dock Road, where he found more cannabis. As a result of this he arrested Simon Perera, a 45-year-old café proprietor.

The cases went to trial and Max Fisher pleaded guilty on 12 June to being in possession of three packets of hashish as well as a handful of cigarettes containing the drug 'he not being so duly authorised'. He was sentenced to four months' hard labour. Simon Perera argued through his solicitor, the unfortunately named Mr Fail, that 'the drug had been left at his address by some other person unknown to him'.[6] This clearly did not impress the magistrate who, on 17 June 1935, sentenced him to a fine of £50 and three months' hard labour.[7]

The *News of the World* report promised that 'the police have no illusions about the task confronting them' and that 'the Dope Squad will meet and destroy the gangs who are seeking to promote the drug trade in this country'. However, the discussion of the case contained in the Home Office report contains nothing to suggest that the newspaper's excited assertions had any solid foundation. In fact, subsequent correspondence suggests a curiosity about an unfamiliar substance and an unusual haul rather than anything more urgent. Dr Davidson of the Police Laboratory wrote on 25 July 1935 that 'I should like the whole of this sample for instructional and experimental purposes', and his request was quickly granted. On 7 August Keen of the CID found himself once more in possession of the hashish that he had done so much to secure, as he was given the job of taking it up to Hendon to present it to Dr Davidson.

Despite the newspaper prophecies of the 'growing menace' of cannabis the Metropolitan Police do not seem to have concerned themselves with the drug again until 1938, when a report in the *Sunday Referee* brought the issue back to the public's attention. 'New Drug Peril Sweeps Britain' was the headline on an article which claimed to have traced a trading route in cannabis that ran between the cottage gardens of rural England and the cafés of London's Soho. The newspaper urged readers to 'communicate with the police at once if you see growing in any country gardens a straggly plant from three to eight feet tall, with dark green leaves hanging in bunches of seven, each leaf having saw-toothed edges. You may save hundreds of people from wrecking their lives'. It went on to argue that Scotland Yard was concerned that a 'syndicate' had been buying up country cottages that included a few acres of land in order to grow cannabis for 'reefers', and the report worried that 'frost is the only thing which kills it'. According to the author of the article 1 acre of land could produce a crop worth £3,500, and profits on this scale promised a grim future where 'in the East End opium dens have been replaced by reefer dens, where for an entrance fee of five shillings each visit it is possible to lie on trestle-beds and smoke these cigarettes. More women than men visit these dens'. As if this was not alarming enough, the newspaper claimed that 'in America police figures prove that over 30 per cent of sex crimes are committed by men and women under the influence of marihuana'.[8]

The story may have had a tenuous factual basis as there had been recent experiments with hemp in rural England. A report in 1936 in *The Times* explained that the plant was being grown at Billing in Northamptonshire on a commercial basis. The story was accompanied by photographs of cannabis plants towering 12 foot high over the local workers who were harvesting them with sickles and then carefully laying out the cut stalks for processing.[9] The objective was to see if the plant could be grown for its fibres, and in the photos it was clear that the stems were being arranged on the floor for retting rather than for trampling, which would have been the case if the crop was for narcotic purposes. The man behind the scheme, Lieutenant-Colonel W. B. Bartram, hoped to produce 25,000 tons of hemp annually in order to supply half of that which was usually imported into Britain as fibres.[10]

The article in the *Sunday Referee* was viewed by the authorities as utterly sensationalist to the extent that the Metropolitan Police noted in their files that the story was 'quite unauthorised' and that 'it is not an offence to have it [hemp] in ones garden'. Those compiling the file at the Metropolitan Police scribbled the suggestion that the best course of action to be followed in response to the article was 'to have writer seen, and calmed'.[11] The story certainly had an impact, however. The day after it was printed a Mr Frederick Suckling went to Barking Police Station. He had with him 'a leaf from a plant which he had found growing in his garden, together with a newspaper extract concerning narcotic drugs'. The police in Hounslow were confronted with a similar case as they received a letter from a Mrs Somerville which confessed that 'having read the newspaper cutting enclosed I have in my opinion a plant answering the description growing in my garden'.

Investigations followed and drew in the Barking Park superintendent and experts at Kew Gardens, before police were sent out to deal with the suspect shrubs. Mrs Somerville had acted because she thought that 'I had better inform Police in case my neighbours did so'. Despite the fact that she was told that it was not an offence to have hemp growing in the garden, she destroyed it and was 'sorry to have caused any trouble'. Matters in Barking were more detailed.

> On 19th August I saw Mr Suckling . . . and informed him the plant growing in his garden, the subject of this correspondence, was now known to be Indian Hemp, that the cultivation of this plant was contrary to law, and advised him to destroy it. Mr Suckling thereupon invited me into his garden, and in my presence uprooted the plant, saturated it with paraffin and burned it. The plant was then some 6ft tall and was bearing a flower which resembled small clusters of lilac . . . On leaving Mr Suckling's premises, I saw an identical plant growing in the front garden at 84 D–, Avenue, Barking. I saw Mr William Talbot, occupier, and he too was informed as to the nature of the plant and immediately destroyed same. This plant was about 3ft 6ins in height and bore no flowers. Mr Talbot stated this particular plant grew of its own accord and under the impression it was a species of Fern, had cultivated it as such. Both Mr Suckling and Mr Talbot stated that if they saw similar plants growing in other gardens in this district they would inform Police at this Station.

There is no evidence that either Mr Suckling or Mr Talbot were successful in finding further suspicious ferns. There is plenty of evidence, however, of how the cannabis plants came to be growing in the gardens of Britain. This had little to do with the organized narcotics gangs imagined by the *Sunday Referee*. Mrs Somerville in Hounslow had worked out that 'the plant has grown from waste parrots' food that has blown on to the garden' while the police in Barking reported that 'Mr Suckling is the owner of a Canary and it would appear that the plant has germinated from a bird seed used for feeding the Canary'. The Metropolitan Police agreed that pet birds were likely to be the source of the plant, concluding that 'hemp seed is a common ingredient in bird seed mixtures and can also be bought separately. It is used also as bait in coarse freshwater fishing. Stray seeds dropped in a garden will often grow'. A startling newspaper story of Scotland Yard concern about shadowy syndicates buying up acres in the countryside to grow ganja on England's green and pleasant lands had been exposed as untrue. The more mundane conclusion is that the suburban gardeners of the Home Counties had been unwittingly growing psychoactive plants on their properties because their exotic pets were untidy eaters.

There is only one story in the Home Office files for the entire period between 1925 and 1945 which suggests that effort was expended on domestic production of cannabis to be consumed for psychoactive purposes. In 1935 *The Lancet* carried an article written by E. T. Baker-Bates of the Royal Southern Hospital in Liverpool. It told the story of a young man who had come across the entry on Indian hemp in *The Chemistry of Common Life* by J. F. W. Johnston, an antique text published in Edinburgh in 1855. The book described cannabis as 'an increaser of pleasure, the exciter of desire, the cementer of friendship, the laughter-mover and the causer of the reeling-gait' and the youngster seems to have been impressed by this. As such he decided to remove the hemp seeds from a batch of parrot food and plant them out in June. By September he had a healthy crop, which Dr Baker-Bates reckoned was due to 'the hot summer of 1933', and the young man dried the flowering tops and the leaves and proceeded to smoke them. He experienced 'mild symptoms of cannabis intoxication' to the astonishment of his fiancée, who subsequently decided to join in with the fun. Lighting up at 10.10 in the evening, by 10.30 she had been taken to a doctor and she was subsequently moved by police ambulance to Liverpool Stanley Hospital. There she was treated for shock, as she was suffering from 'loss of power in the legs and inability to stand; dizziness, dryness of mouth, and palpitation'. After nine hours she was sent home, suffering from no more than a sore head. The author of the note in *The Lancet* felt that this episode was important as 'there is a possibility that if the fact that hemp seeds could be grown with ease in England were widely known hemp-smoking might become a national menace'.[12] The story caused something of a stir, as the *Liverpool Echo* and the *Police Journal* both reported the case, and the chief inspector of the Drugs Branch wrote to *The Lancet* to remind readers that it is 'an offence for any person (unless he is licensed or otherwise authorized to do so) to be in possession of, or attempt to obtain possession of, Indian hemp'.[13]

A case from 1938 sheds rather more light on where the cannabis that was illegally in circulation in the UK usually came from. Aly Ahmed Kofheith was a sailor on board the *Star of Suez*, an Egyptian steamship sat in Millwall Dock. He had a quarrel with the ship's cook in the morning, the latter later complaining that

> He started playing music with a big carving fork and a big spoon. I said to him 'Please Aly, take your breakfast and go as I have a lot of work to do for the officers'. Then the defendant swore at me and said my breakfast was too late. Then he caught hold of me by the clothes and shook me and hit me with the fork, and the fork went through my clothes. A man separated us. Then the defendant

took the cover of the hatch and tried to hit me with it . . . the defendant called me
'whore's son' and 'bastard' and said 'I'll murder you', 'I'll kill you'.

Kofheith seems to have been intent on following through with his threat, as
later that evening he lay in wait with an iron bar and when the cook came
into sight he was struck four times before members of the crew arrived to
break up the attack. The victim was taken to hospital while the assailant was
turned over to the police. The seaman ended up at the Isle of Dogs Police
Station where 'whilst being searched the prisoner placed his left hand under
his shirt on his right breast and produced [a] packet (exhibit 2). Inspector
McDonnell asked the prisoner what the package contained. He said "tobacco" . . . he was then told he would be further charged with possessing a
quantity of hashish and again cautioned and he replied "that's all right"'.
The sailor's 'tobacco' was sent to the Government Laboratory where a
chemist declared that it weighed 1 ¾ ounces and 'is the article commonly
known as hashish, a preparation of Indian hemp of which the resins form the
base. The substance comes within the provisions of the Dangerous Drugs
Acts'. Aly Ahmed Kofheith was fined £100 on 5 November for importing
hashish into the UK in contravention of these Acts.[14]

Newspaper reports from throughout the period show that this story was
regularly, if relatively rarely, repeated. Back in 1930 'Mahomed Sakie, a
greaser on board the SS *Machardos* lying in the Royal Albert Docks was
charged with the unlawful possession of 3oz of hashish'. He was fined £5 at
the East Ham Police Court.[15] The following year Norden Hassan was
sentenced at the Thames Police Court for possessing 'ganja' and received
three months with hard labour.[16] In 1933 'Abdulramon Haji, a seaman' was
fined 40s. at the same court for being found with about 8 oz of the drug on
his person.[17] In 1934 Abdul Monaff was similarly convicted for possessing
42 grains of Indian hemp as the police had searched his room on Limehouse
Causeway and had found the cannabis hidden under a floorboard. He
received six months' hard labour.[18] Archibald Bellamy was also found guilty
at the Thames Police Court in 1935:

> It was stated that when arrested Bellamy said that 'when I am hard up I mix
> tobacco with it and smoke it'. He now said that a seaman gave it to him, and
> said it was native tobacco. In reply to the Magistrate (Mr F. O. Langley) a
> police officer said the hemp was made into cigarettes and smoked. It had an
> extremely bad effect on the brain, and was very expensive. There was no
> doubt that Bellamy had been dealing extensively in the drug. The Magistrate
> sentenced him to six months imprisonment with hard labour.[19]

This episode stands out as he was a West Indian, whereas most of the other men who were charged with illegal possession were of Asian or Arabian origin. However, the same picture emerges, of small-scale drugs offences limited to districts of London near the river involving the seamen of the imperial maritime trade, or lascars as they were known, who were passing through British ports.

While most of these stories came from the port areas of London, those from elsewhere in the country retained the link with the docks. At Cardiff Police Court on Christmas Eve 1934 Roakib Ali of Calcutta was fined £10 for possessing opium and hashish, protesting that the latter was 'for his own personal use'. The police had argued that 'Ali was suspected of being engaged in the trafficking in drugs between Rotterdam and the ports of Cardiff and Liverpool'.[20] At Hull, a sentence was appealed in 1937 for hashish possession. Abdulla Jan was a British Indian subject who was listed in the files as 'a confectioner' with a shop on George Street, a couple of minutes' stroll from the docks. He had been sentenced to twelve months' imprisonment because the police had found some cannabis in a cupboard and in a black pipe. Officers told the court that 'when Jan had kept a refreshment house in Mytongate he was cautioned several times about permitting young girls to use the premises, and complaints had also been made about the premises in George St where, it was alleged, several girls had been known to associate with foreign seamen'. However, he had never been convicted of any offence before the drugs charge, and his solicitor added that he could not have been trading in the drug as the amount found was so small. His sentence was reduced to twenty-six days' imprisonment which he had already served, and he was released.[21] The story has interesting echoes of the case of Simon Perrera which was mentioned above, as the latter was a café proprietor at West India Dock Road, Poplar, and a native of Ceylon. When *The Times* covered his story it had noted that the police told the court that 'at one time Pereira [sic] supplied cigarettes which were said to contain Indian hemp, and girls who smoked them left in a dazed condition'.[22] Both stories suggest that the police and the media were tangling drugs, local girls, and foreign men together in a web of anxious surveillance. Concerns about relations between British women and males from abroad were similarly features of the cocaine and opium scares earlier in the century.[23]

Abdulla Jan's appeal against what seems to have been the harshest sentence of the period for possessing cannabis raises the issue of how the magistrates were conducting themselves in terms of punishment. As is evident, sentences could vary widely, from a small fine to a year in prison, and the limited number of cases and scanty details of each make it difficult to pick up a difference in punishments for those simply in possession and those suspected of supplying. Negligible numbers of white British subjects were convicted in this period, mainly because very few of them had any contact with the drug. Where there were rare convictions, however, it is interesting to contrast the sentences of locals with those of Asian, Arabian, or West Indian descent. In 1937 the police went to the flat of Bella Gold in Connaught Mews near Marble Arch. Described as 'a dance hostess' she had in fact been convicted on five separate occasions between 1931 and 1936 of 'soliciting men'. The police had found 'eight grains of cocaine hydrochloride, 12 grains of diamorphine hydrochloride, and 15.2 grains of Indian hemp' and they alleged that 'the defendant's associates were drug addicts, and she was looked upon as a trafficker in drugs'. Officers stated that she was a known associate of Gerald Edward O'Brien, who was convicted of heroin smuggling in July 1937, and who had been a constant thorn in the side of the authorities throughout the 1930s as one of the instigators of a string of illegal drinking dens throughout the West End.[24] He was said by the police to have visited Bella Gold's flat on a number of occasions, and his phone number was scribbled in a book found there.

The legal representatives of the defendant presented a very different picture to the court. They claimed that Bella Gold suffered from bronchitis, which had been aggravated by the late hours, dust, and cigarette smoking of life in a West End nightclub. While on a weekend away in France she met a man who offered her some white powder to treat her condition and 'she sniffed some of the powder and almost instantaneously got complete relief. She at once gave the man some money and he promised to send her further supplies in London, which he agreed to do and he sealed the deal with a gift of some cigarettes containing cannabis'. The solicitor argued that, as a result of this chance encounter,

> the defendant had fallen a victim to drug addiction by casually meeting in Paris one of those pernicious beasts who lived by selling dangerous drugs . . . she had now confessed to her doctor that she had formed the drug habit and there was every hope of a rapid cure.[25]

The cure seems to have been rapid indeed, as the court reconvened a week later to hear medical assessments. The magistrate found that 'a doctor had reported that there was no evidence that she was a drug addict' and as such the police seemed vindicated in the accusation that she was selling the drugs to people at the nightclub and to those visiting her flat. However, her solicitors worked hard to get around this by stating that this made perfect sense as she had 'practically cured herself of the habit' and that she 'now had the opportunity to be cared for by relatives'. Despite the protestations of the police in court that she was a 'trafficker', she was simply placed on probation for two years and fined £25. Intriguingly, her flatmate Freda Roberts, who was also described as a 'dance-hostess', used exactly the same defence a year later. She was arrested for possession of 46½ grains of cannabis, but it was claimed that 'she had been suffering from asthma and was influenced to try Indian hemp and had a small quantity of it. She rolled some into a cigarette, but not liking it, put the rest away where it had remained for two or three months'.[26] The defence worked again, and she only received a fine of £10.

The contrast between sentences for British women and for African or Asian men was most evident in a story from *The Times* of 1933 with the headline 'Prohibited Drug at Limehouse: Indian Sent to Prison':

> At the Thames Police Court on Saturday Darusat Ali, 32, a British Indian, and Rose Darusat Ali, 21, his English wife, were charged on remand . . . with being in possession of a prohibited drug—namely Indian hemp—at the house they occupied in Sussex St, Limehouse . . . Detective-Sergeant Muir said that the man was the owner of the house, which was kept as a boarding house for coloured men. He was strongly suspected of trafficking in the drug and selling it in 1s and 6d packets.
>
> The Magistrate—Indiscriminately to coloured and white people?
>
> The Sergeant—Yes. He added that the woman stated that she had been a dancer, that she came from Stockport, that she had been a maid in the West End, and that Darusat Ali met her while in service.
>
> The Magistrate warned the woman not to get mixed up in the drug traffic again, and bound her over. He told the man he had been guilty of a serious offence and sentenced him to nine months' imprisonment with hard labour.[27]

However, the impression that race was a factor in influencing early sentencing behaviour for cannabis offences in Britain is confused when the case of a rare conviction of a white male, Denis Delattre, is considered. He was a 32-year-old former civil servant when he was arrested by the police. They were put on his trail as he made the mistake of taking a batch of the drug to a chemist for valuation. Delattre had obtained the substance through a friend, apparently because 'he believed in clairvoyance, and he took the drug for that purpose'. His interest in clairvoyance was perhaps prompted by the fact that he had recently lost his wife to a long illness. He had taken the drug to the chemist as he wanted to sell it, because having bought 1½ oz of the stuff he had discovered that it disagreed with him. That he was hard up was likely as he had recently lost his job and been in prison, having been convicted in the wake of his wife's death a year before of possessing moulds for making counterfeit coins. Despite the fact that the police were firmly of the opinion that 'there was no question of his having been engaged in drug trafficking', and despite the rather woeful tone of his life which seemed to have been spiralling downward, he was sentenced to two months' imprisonment with hard labour.[28]

This sentence makes problematic the idea that magistrates were simply handing out harsher penalties to those of African and Asian descent. What it does seem to show is that gender was a factor in sentencing for cannabis offences in the 1930s. While Bella Gold and Freda Roberts had previous convictions, questionable associates, and were thought by the police to be actively engaged in selling drugs, neither was sent to prison for their offences. In contrast, Denis Delattre, Norden Hassan, and Abdulramon Haji found themselves serving custodial sentences with hard labour for simply being caught in possession of the drug. What is certain from these stories is that the picture painted by the Home Office in 1925 of the domestic market for cannabis seemed to hold true into the 1930s and 1940s. The most common users were Asian and African seamen passing through the ports of the Empire. They tended to carry small amounts of their favourite intoxicant which they used for personal consumption or to trade with their colleagues and with those that catered for them in British cities. Indigenous consumers were few and far between and those that do appear in the records rarely seem to have been regular users of the drug.

Control: policing and the drugs branch

The argument could be made that the small numbers of cannabis suppliers and consumers to be brought before the courts is not evidence of a limited domestic market in the period. Rather, it reveals a limited effort on the part of the police to catch them. It is worth addressing such an idea by going back to the shadowy drinks racketeer whose name featured in the story of Bella Gold. Gerald Edward O'Brien was of special interest to the police because he had been convicted in July 1937 of unlawfully possessing and concealing heroin, which he had been found to be carrying at Newhaven Port. O'Brien was 'one of the original instigators of the Bottle Party System'.[29] This was one of the ways in which 1930s London tried to get round licensing laws in order to drink alcohol into the early hours of the morning. O'Brien set up the 'Night Bar' in March 1937. This establishment opened between the hours of 11 p.m. and 6 a.m. (10 p.m. to 6 a.m. on Sundays). It claimed to be a wholesale supplier where each customer ordered 2 gallons of whisky and was given a receipt for this amount. S/he was then served a large whisky, which could be consumed in the comfort of the bar. The scam rested on the idea that the purchaser was sampling what had just become his own wares after a large wholesale order rather than enjoying a crafty double after a retail transaction. J. D. Pollock of the London Police 'C' Division called the scheme 'a daring and impudent ramp, which must be smashed at the earliest possible moment'.[30] The Night Bar was certainly popular, as an eyewitness noted that 'I counted 38 persons (apart from the Staff) seated at tables, and from the attached reports, it will be seen that there were 15 different parties on the premises at the time'.[31] However, with illegal drinking going on and a known drugs dealer involved, the authorities were quickly on the scene. Within a month of the Night Bar opening, a Metropolitan Police officer was able to provide the following account of an evening there.

> In accordance with instructions, at 12.35 am on the 11th April 1937, I accompanied Mr Green and Mr Wilkinson, both officers of H.M. Customs and Excise, into the premises, with other police officers whose names will appear later in this report.
> By pre-arrangement several Customs Officers were already in the Night Bar and purchased drinks without disclosing their identity . . . Inspectors Benton and Forrest of 'C' Division, each in plain clothes, went to the Night Bar and also purchased certain drinks.

In other words, within a matter of weeks of its establishment the enterprise was crammed full of officers from various enforcement agencies who were there to observe what was going on. Needless to say O'Brien was promptly charged and convicted and it was recorded that 'the Night Bar experiment collapsed' during the police proceedings and the premises are still closed'.[32] The story is significant even though it does not mention cannabis. It shows that in the 1930s the police and other agencies were highly sensitized and constantly alert to the issue of intoxication and the law, particularly in

London. The authorities were quick to notice and to challenge all attempts by those who sought to find new ways to defy the law in order to profit from the market for intoxicants.

This seems to have been particularly the case in relation to dangerous drugs. The enforcement demands of the new Dangerous Drugs Acts (DDA) from 1920 onwards meant the development of a new unit dedicated solely to the control of these substances which was given a nationwide remit. What was to become the Drugs Branch of the Home Office had its origins in administrative wrangles in the wake of the 1920 legislation. The bureaucrats at the Home Office worried initially that 'it is difficult to estimate in advance what amount of staff will be required. The work will be partly administrative, partly inspection and there will be a good deal of clerical work'[33] but in the end they settled on the idea of appointing an inspector, an assistant inspector, and a pair of clerks. This was done on the understanding that the fees charged for licences would more than cover the expenses of these new appointments. However, the official at the Treasury who was expected to sign this off was reluctant to do so. He evidently felt that the control of opiates and cocaine under the DDA was not something that should be a significant call on the public purse, stating that 'there is little question I suppose that some of this work will continue, but surely its volume will diminish when the drug craze, or at any rate the public outcry against it, becomes less violent'.[34]

At this point Sir Malcolm Delevingne, the drugs expert at the Home Office who was to play such an important role in establishing both national and international policies on psychoactive substances, personally interceded.[35] The response to the Treasury prevarication was terse:

> I have shown your letter to Sir Malcolm Delevingne and he tells me that it is not anticipated that there will be any falling off of the dangerous drugs work after the beginning. The machinery which has been set up is necessitated owing to the fact that the British Government entered into international obligations when it became a party to the Opium Convention which was approved by the League of Nations . . . It will be necessary to have permanent officers to carry on the work.[36]

The Home Office plan for two inspectors was therefore approved, but it had to make do with just one clerical officer. At the outset the team's main task was simply to inspect, that is to check that licences were in order and that the record-keeping responsibilities imposed by the DDA were being borne. In a short space of time, however, the inspectors assumed additional duties. In 1926 the Home Office noted that they were also advising on the grant of licences, issuing export licences, examining and checking returns for the information of the League of Nations, and negotiating the sale of confiscated drugs. They relied on medical officers of the Ministry of Health to examine the records of doctors who had licences to possess regulated drugs, and on the police to inspect the documentation of retail chemists' shops. The clerical officer also found himself loaded with new jobs, including acting as an assistant to the Under-Secretary of State who represented the UK at the League of Nations Opium Advisory Committee, and fielding enquiries from other departments on the issue of drugs. By the 1930s the inspectors had taken on an educational remit in relations with the nation's police forces. In 1931 alone they worked with officers in places as diverse as Cambridge, Aldershot, Bolton, and Dundee, and the chief inspector was careful to include in his annual report the conclusion that such contact was 'of considerable assistance to the police units concerned, and many officers have expressed appreciation particularly of the practical information gained in the company of Inspectors'.[37] Six years later the Branch was increased in numbers to incorporate four inspectors and five clerks.[38] By the end of the decade it had expanded again, in both size and function, as the staff and responsibility for policing obscene publications was transferred to the Drugs Branch in April 1939.[39]

The significance of this story of the Drugs Branch for understanding cannabis in Britain is twofold. The first is that intelligence captured in its reports seems to confirm how little of the substance was present in the country in this period. In none of the annual reports of the Drugs Branch that have survived for the period to 1945 is cannabis mentioned; it first appears in 1946 when the deputy chief inspector noted at the end of his report that 'a good deal of fresh information concerning the opium traffic in Great Britain, the traffic in Indian Hemp among Negroes, and addiction to Pethidine has been collected'.[40] Elsewhere he argued that 'up to 1939 there was little traffic in cannabis in this country'.[41] There is every reason to accept that assessment as correct. After all, Drugs Branch officers had visited seventy-one of the 250 police forces in the UK in 1939 and fifty-five in 1940, so would have had regular updates on what was being observed across the country.[42]

The story of the Drugs Branch is also significant for understanding the history of cannabis in the UK for another reason. It shows how, long before the arrival of the drug in larger quantities began in Britain after the Second World War, the government had established a well-organized state apparatus to respond to it. The Drugs Branch had evolved out of the demands of the Dangerous Drugs Acts and Opium Conventions of the 1920s and 1930s, set up mainly to control opiates and cocaine. Throughout these decades it developed into a complex organization with a range of functions and relationships that included liaising with and advising international bodies, enforcing regulations at home, tracking transgressors, and stimulating police activity through training and information. As Chapter 4 shows, this meant that once cannabis did begin to arrive in the UK in greater quantities at the end of the 1940s, British enforcement agencies were quick to notice it, and ready to deal with it.

Doctors and scientists

While the police and the Home Office felt that cannabis consumers in the UK were few in number and of minimal concern before 1945, Britain's medical experts in narcotic drug use were similarly little occupied by those indulging in the substance at this time. For example, the *British Medical Journal* (*BMJ*) reported a meeting held by the Section of Psychiatry of the Royal Society of Medicine and the Society for the Study of Inebriety in 1930 which considered 'the prevention and treatment of drug addiction'. Edward Mapother of the Maudesley Psychiatric Hospital pointed out that 'despite the extreme vigilance of the police, the Home Office knew the names of only 250 addicts in England, and probably the real number was not much greater'. The meeting heard reports of 'self-suggestion', 'hypnotism', 'psycho-analysis', 'withdrawal of the drug', and the substance belladonna in the treatment of addicts, who were described by Mapother as 'the "spoilt-child" type, who could not forgo immediate gratification of any impulse. They were the same sort of people who were sexually promiscuous'. Yet nowhere in this meeting was cannabis or any of its products mentioned, and the doctors present only discussed heroin, morphine, opium, and cocaine.[43] A subsequent lecture on the topic in 1934 confirmed the lowly place of cannabis in the British drug addiction experts' set of interests. Sir Malcolm Delevingne gave the Fifteenth Norman Kerr Memorial Lecture of the Society for the Study of Inebriety in October of that year. He argued that morphine, heroin, and cocaine together with the 'newer addiction drugs'

dicodid, eukodol, and dilaudid, were significant as international phenomena. He assured listeners, however, that the opposite was true of 'practices
such as opium-smoking, the use of Indian hemp, coca-leaf chewing and
perhaps opium-eating in India [which] are mainly confined to certain
countries and races, and show no tendency to spread'.[44] For the rest of
the decade cannabis remained no more than a curiosity for medical experts
in the UK working on issues related to drug abuse and addiction.

Among doctors and medical scientists more generally cannabis was similarly little discussed. Evidence from the medical journals suggests that few
regarded it as a useful therapeutic and those that did still refer to it seem to
have belonged to an older generation of scientists and doctors. For example,
David Prain, who as a member of the Botanical Survey of India had done
much to gather accurate information about the plant in the 1890s,[45] continued to publicly allude to it into the 1920s. He gave a lecture in 1925 to
the Pharmaceutical Society of Great Britain, by which time he had retired as
the director of the Royal Botanic Gardens in Kew. The lecture started with
a sketch of the history of the species, and argued that 'it was one of those
plants of waysides and waste places which accompanied man in his migra-
tions' to explain how it came to be found in India despite its native origins
elsewhere. Prain pointed out to the Society that cannabis was among the
'useful plants of India', although he acknowledged that the variation of the
potency of different samples meant that there had developed an 'uncer-
tainty' about it in both pharmacy and medicine. His twin interest in the
lecture was cinchona, from which anti-malarial products were manufac-
tured, and he quickly moved on from cannabis to this topic.[46] A positive
commendation of cannabis as a practical medicine came from another who
admitted that he was 'long retired from practice', a Dr C. E. Matthews of
Kent who wrote in the *BMJ* in 1939. He had recently used a favourite
treatment for shingles on his housemaid.

> A simple method of treating herpes zoster with the extract of cannabis indica is
> not so generally known as it deserves to be. I was a student at St Thomas's
> Hospital attending the clinic of the late Dr J. S. Bristowe when he treated with
> this drug an elderly female patient admitted with severe pains following herpes
> zoster. In two days she was completely cured ... I never forgot this case and
> when in course of time cases of shingles came under my care I used the drug
> with invariable success. The extract was prescribed in pill form, ¼ to ½ grain
> according to age, three times a day ... I offer the suggestion to anyone who is
> interested.[47]

Articles like this, which show that cannabis was still used in practice and which recommended that others try out the drug, were very rare between the wars.

More typical of the tone of the medical press in this period was the *BMJ*'s response to the scare about the drug which had been stoked by the *Sunday Referee* story in 1938. The journal published a short essay on *Cannabis indica* in May of that year, putting the newspaper interest down to 'a great craze for hemp smoking [that] has spread up across the United States from Mexico' and stories about 'hemp-seeds which are sold for feeding birds [that] will sometimes grow in England'. It argued of cannabis that 'in some ways its action is like that of alcohol: it diminishes self-control and gives a feeling of exaltation and increased power' and 'it has a curious action on the sense of time, like that of the New Accelerator of H. G. Wells, though less potent'. It referred to 'a careful investigation of the effects of hemp in the Pretoria Mental Hospital' published in the *South African Medical Journal* in 1938, which found that those intoxicated went from an initial stage of dullness to a temporary emotional instability followed by either irritability or depression relieved in the end by a deep sleep.[48] It concluded that

> Addicts often show moral and mental degeneration, but it is difficult to say whether this is the cause or the effect of addiction. Murders, suicides and sexual assaults have frequently been attributed to hemp, and the word 'assassin' which was first applied to a Muslim sect of the time of Saladin is said to be derived from the fact that this sect was in the habit of committing secret murders under the influence of hemp, which is known as 'hashish' in Arabic.

The only acknowledgement of the plant's medicinal potential came in the brief and dismissive statement that 'it was at one time included in the Pharmacopoeia as a hypnotic, but was found to be too variable in activity'.[49] It is worth noting that this article was not alone in making the link between cannabis and exotic tales from distant societies. This was a recurring theme in the writing on the subject in the medical journals of the 1920s and the 1930s and the association between the drug and the Orientalized 'Others' considered inferior by the Western world was embellished most vigorously in reports from Egypt.[50] While the career of T. W. Russell Pasha of the Central Narcotics Intelligence Bureau (CNB) in Cairo is more fully considered in the next chapter, it is important to note that the reports of this English policeman in Egypt were summarized on an annual basis in the medical press of the 1930s. The *BMJ* of 1930 noted 'the first annual report of the Egyptian Central Narcotics Bureau [which] reveals a condition of affairs regarding drug addiction in that country so bad as to be almost incredible...the drugs used are heroin, hashish, opium, morphine and cocaine'.[51] *The Lancet* carried a similar story with an equally excited tone: 'T. W. Russell Pasha, the Director of the Central Narcotics Intelligence Bureau...startled the League of Nations Opium Committee by describing how Egypt had, in the preceding five years, become a nation of drug addicts. Hashish, cocaine, heroin and morphine had been pouring into the country since 1925'.[52] The following year its readers learned that 'hashish, which has only recently been added to the list of dangerous drugs, nevertheless claims many victims, and it is estimated that there are in Egypt no fewer than 282,000 hashish addicts!'[53] In 1935 it was reported in the *BMJ* that 'hashish has for years been largely used in Egypt, but Russell Pasha is satisfied that it is today a definite menace to the energy and virility of the people. It is often purveyed in the form of manzoul and maagoun, mixed with spices and seeds, retailed at popular prices'.[54] The onset of the Second World War only heightened the tension in stories about cannabis. In 1940 *The Lancet* noted that the reports from Egypt emphasized that 'the war in Europe has already increased the demand for, and loosened the supervision of, narcotic drugs' and reported that the French authorities in Syria had found and destroyed a crop of 1,633 tons of cannabis destined for Egypt.[55] In 1943 a report by Russell Pasha sounded less convinced about the achievements of the French, as he described the Vichy authorities as 'completely hashish-minded'.[56] News in that year of 'Lebanon and Hashish' was reported in *The Lancet*, detailing how Australian and Indian troops had destroyed crops identified by Russell Pasha as destined for Cairo, and noting that he 'expresses the hope that the independent governments of Syria and Lebanon would carry out the law and prevent this flood of poison finding its way into Egypt'.[57] The arrival of Allied troops in the region was not an unalloyed fillip for the CNB, however, and Russell Pasha was quoted in 1945 as complaining that 'drugs are smuggled into Egypt through a hundred mile strip of desert which is constantly crossed by streams of military vehicles whose drivers, of many nationalities, make money by lifting the goods across frontiers. Most of the hashish seized is grown in the Lebanon and Syria'.[58] By the end of the conflict cannabis was being identified as an obstacle to the post-war rebuilding of North Africa: 'the squandering of these vast sums of Egypt's money in smokers' dreams can only be considered a national calamity'.[59] For many reading the medical journals of the 1930s and 1940s, Russell Pasha's reports would have contained the only mention of cannabis that they routinely encountered. These reports represented preparations of the plant as nothing more than dangerous intoxicants traded by criminals who were willing to defy the authority of one of the last policemen of the Empire.

It is worth noting, however, that the Second World War did see a brief revival of scientific interest in the therapeutic potential of cannabis. *The Lancet* announced in 1940 that 'we may find ourselves in the position of having demonstrated that there is a substance that possesses all the virtues of the forbidden fruit and none of its calamitous after-effects'. It referred to studies by Walton and Bromberg, published in the United States, which argued that cannabis was not a habit-forming drug. However, its main purpose was to precis work by chemists in the United States with tetra-hydrocannabinol and the article excitedly concluded that 'pharmacologists have scarcely begun their researches on the active principles already isolated'.[60] The following year the *BMJ* similarly recounted details from two papers recently published in *Nature*. It argued that cannabis 'has never firmly established itself in human therapeutics', which would have surprised many of its consumers in India and Africa who resorted to it for medicinal reasons. It then repeated the claim that this was due to the 'inconstancy and frequent inactivity of the drug'. Nevertheless, it did point to recent breakthroughs in pharmacology that had revealed a number of 'chemical principles' including 'cannin', which affected dogs, and it also alluded to 'synthetic tetrahydro-cannabinols'. The piece went on to argue that one or other of these promised to replace use of the crude substance in medicine, and noted that it was likely to be most useful in the treatment of mental illness, particularly in cases of depression.

> Not even opium gives the same feeling of well-being, both physical and psychical, and opium is also inferior to hemp because of its tendency to addiction, its depressant action on respiration, its tendency to constipate, and the frequency of 'hang-over next day'. Moreover, the power of hemp to revive old memories and recall in detail things long forgotten may be a powerful aid to psychotherapy.[61]

In 1943 *The Lancet* reported 'the chemical researches of Adams and Todd, and the pharmacological work of Loewe and Modell' and looked forward to the identification and synthesis of the active principle itself. Noting that cannabis medicines were 'not even mentioned in the latest edition of the

British Pharmacopoeia' it anticipated a time when the active principle was identified and cannabis was readmitted to medicine as 'the drug possesses several outstanding properties, which might well be valuable in therapeutics, if reliable standardised concentrates could be devised'.[62] A reader wrote a rebuke to this optimism, however, noting how he had 'stagger[ed] about and vomited violently' after a small dose of tincture of cannabis.[63]

Most of these scientific investigations were conducted in the United States: Walter Bromberg was psychiatrist in charge at Bellevue Hospital in New York, Roger Adams was based at the University of Illinois, Loewe and Modell were at Cornell University. Other work not mentioned by the British medical press was also being conducted in the USA, such as that by Haagen-Smit and his collaborators at the California Institute of Technology[64] and Powell, Salmon, and Bembry at Columbia University.[65] However, there was a team working in the UK under the supervision of A. R. Todd at Manchester University. Their research was conducted with samples of cannabis from India in 1939[66] and then, through the Home Office Drugs Branch, with batches from Egypt.[67] They also collaborated with A. D. MacDonald of the Department of Pharmacology at Manchester, who published his summary of developments in the search for the active ingredient in 1941. He argued that 'chemists and pharmacologists have long hunted for a drug with the actions of morphine and none of its disadvantages. A synthetic compound of the tetrahydrocannabinol type may prove, for many patients, to be this eagerly anticipated substitute'.[68] For the chemists and pharmacologists of the period the possibilities of cannabis seemed suddenly exciting and, as Todd concluded in 1940, 'much remains to be done before clarity is achieved; but the rate of progress during the past year has been such that one may expect a speedy solution of the outstanding problems'.[69] By 1945, however, such hopes seemed premature. In an article that year the American pharmacologist S. Loewe wrote that his latest round of experiments had shown simply that 'cannabinol, generally believed to be an inert component of hemp oil, is shown to have marihuana activity'.[70] Cannabis would only begin to yield the secret of its active ingredients in 1964.[71]

The picture from the medical publications of the 1920s and 1930s can be a complex one to interpret. On the one hand these journals may be used to chart contemporary medical interests and practices, and yet on the other hand they served to actively shape these interests and practices by spreading information and ideas. However, the medical journals do provide glimpses of the reasons that cannabis medicines had fallen so far from grace in this period that they were omitted from the British Pharmacopoeia in 1932.[72] In the first place, those that did mention its therapeutic potential in between the wars tended to be members of an older generation of scientists and practitioners who had recollections of the drug from earlier stages in their careers. Their reminiscences may simply have reinforced the idea that cannabis was archaic as a medicine. For example, C. R. Marshall wrote to the *BMJ* in 1938 about the problems of isolating the active ingredient in cannabis.[73] He had been publishing research on cannabis since the 1890s and was keen to use his letter to remind readers of the experiments at the turn of the last century at the Agricultural Chemistry Laboratory at Cambridge which had ended abruptly when one of the research team was killed by an explosion during their work. Medical science and practice had moved on since then and, as an article in *Nature* in 1941 put it, 'with the development of synthetic analgesics and hypnotics, cannabis fell further and further out of favour'.[74] Cannabis medicines appeared outdated and a throwback to the nineteenth century when compared with the new synthetic products of the age. The medical journals also suggest that cannabis had not simply fallen into disuse, it had also fallen into disrepute. Indeed, the medical press may well have been part of the story of how this happened. The drug was most frequently mentioned there in reports from the colonial authorities in Egypt where it was dismissed as a crude and dangerous intoxicant. This would have discouraged practitioners and scientists from considering the therapeutic deployment of the drug, further driving its descent into disuse.

The flurry of interest in cannabis of the 1940s suggests that it had not entirely disappeared from the view of medical scientists even if it had fallen out of favour with practitioners. They may have become interested in it again because of the attention drawn to it by policemen and the media in these years.[75] An article by Walter Bromberg in the *Journal of the American Medical Association* was summarized in *The Lancet* in 1939 in which the reviewer noted that 'he [Bromberg] is sceptical as to whether marihuana really causes its addicts to commit rape, suicide and murder as the popular press in America allege. He even casts doubts on the drug's habit-forming capacity'.[76] On the other hand, mentions of its potential as a painkiller, and as a treatment for depression, suggest that the demands of wartime societies drove much of the renewed curiosity about it in the early 1940s. This was certainly a period when there was expanded investment in pharmaceutical research in general as nations sought medical and chemical solutions to problems caused by the conflict.[77] However, the disappointment by 1945 of those working with cannabis medicines suggests a final reason why they fell from favour in this period. The failure to isolate and extract the active agent in cannabis meant that substances prepared from it remained unreliable and unpredictable to work with.

Conclusion

While cannabis preparations were of little interest to those in government between the wars, they were nevertheless increasingly subjected to the attentions of the state. Consumption of preparations of the drug remained very limited across the nation in these years. Recreational consumers were usually those passing through Britain's ports in the country's maritime trade who brought the habit of consuming cannabis preparations with them from their cultures and communities in Asia and Africa. A limited trade in the drug seems to have existed among those that catered to this transient population in the ports. Where British consumers were caught with cannabis it appears that curiosity had driven them to it. Few had regular contact with it except where small amounts featured in the portfolios of those who dabbled in a wide range of shady activities in order to earn their living. Even enforcement officials seem to have been little concerned about cannabis consumers, but they did come to monitor and prosecute them because the enforcement agencies were increasingly well briefed and organized to deal with drugs offences in general. This is explained by the establishment and rapid development of the Home Office Drugs Branch. Originally set up to implement laws relating to opiates and cocaine in the wake of the 1920 Dangerous Drugs Act, it added cannabis to its caseload after the 1925 Geneva Opium Convention. It also grew an educational function within its remit, enabling it to spread knowledge of drugs around the UK's police forces and Customs officers even where these were rarely troubled by offenders.

A similar picture emerges when medicinal consumption of the drug is considered. Cannabis medicines remained legally available throughout this period and yet were little used. A revival of interest in the early 1940s seems to have been related to wartime needs stimulating research into drugs that had potential as painkillers and psychiatric therapeutics, but this revival only serves to draw attention to the practical obsolescence of cannabis medicines in the 1920s and 1930s. While few used them, many will have been discouraged from even considering them by the brief mentions that circulated in the medical journals. There cannabis medicines were usually associated with old-fashioned practitioners and the difficulties of using the drug, and compared unfavourably with the host of synthetic products that had been coming onto the market in the 1930s. While this chapter has dealt with the issues of recreational consumption and therapeutic application separately, there were points of connection in this period. A media scare stoked by confused policing had provoked the Pharmaceutical Society into declaring cannabis to be a poison in the *Pharmaceutical Journal* in 1924,[78] and for much of the 1930s reports from the British police chief in Egypt dominated references in the medical press to the drug, cementing the notion that it was a suspicious and a questionable substance rather than a viable therapeutic. These points of connection between the therapeutic and the recreational, and indeed between the approaches of enforcers and the ideas of medical scientists and practitioners, were to grow in succeeding decades.

3

'Egypt was taking strong action against the traffic in hashish': 'Loco-weed', the League of Nations, and the British Empire, *c.*1928–*c.*1945

Introduction

This chapter will consider two distinct international contexts in the period before 1945. The first is the League of Nations and the second the British Empire. In doing this it takes up where *Cannabis Britannica* left off. The latter demonstrated that representatives of the British Empire fought hard to keep cannabis out of the regulatory system that was emerging at the League of Nations in the early 1920s. Ironically, at the same time it was information coming from the colonies that provided ammunition for those most keen to include the drug in the Geneva Opium Convention of 1925. This story from the League of Nations pointed to a number of conclusions about the British and cannabis. In the first place, many colonies were cannabis-consuming societies, and long periods of rule by Europeans who had little experience of the drug at home produced a tangled and contradictory set of positions and policies across the Empire as a whole. Despite the tangles and contradictions, these imperial experiences were fundamental to shaping early debates about cannabis at the League of Nations as the international drugs regulatory system was being constructed. Additionally, it showed how experiences and debates abroad resulted in ideas about the drug and approaches to it that impacted back in the UK itself. This chapter returns to both the League of Nations and the Empire to show that, in the twilight years of each, ideas and policies generated by those running British colonies continued to be influential in shaping wider agendas on cannabis. This despite the fact that these ideas and policies remained confused and inconsistent.

The Pasha, Egypt, and the League of Nations

In 1930 Sir Thomas Wentworth Russell Pasha arrived at the thirteenth session of the League of Nations Opium Advisory Committee in Geneva to update it on the efforts of Egypt's police services to enforce the country's drugs laws.[1] He took the meeting by storm with his alarming assertions and some plain-talking:

> Egypt is fighting to save herself, but she cannot do it without your help. If you could see with your eyes, as I do every day, the abject misery and despair of our poor drug victims and their families, you would redouble, retriple your efforts to kill this vile traffic.[2]

The problem that he outlined was one where a population of 14 million people contained 'half a million narcotic victims'. In his account a flow of drugs into the country had grown since the end of the First World War when a Greek chemist in Cairo had introduced the local elite to cocaine and a taste for it had spread among the city's middle classes. By 1928 heroin had largely replaced cocaine and demand for the product had spread to rural areas. It was this that most seemed to perturb the chief of the Central Narcotics Intelligence Bureau (CNB):

> Before the introduction of these European poisons, there was no more healthy, hardworking and cheerful class of peasant in the world: today every village in Egypt has its heroin victims, and they are the youth of the country. The peak age for narcotic addiction, taken from nearly 5000 cases, works out at 26. Can you picture your quiet little villages corrupted and poisoned with dope? You cannot, but I can, as I see it every day in Egypt.[3]

He recounted tales of tracing suppliers across France, Italy, Germany, and Greece back to Switzerland, and asked, 'is it fair that Europe should thus pour its tons of poison into my country?' *The Times* reported that 'in his speech Russell Pasha characteristically dotted i's and crossed t's to an extent that may have disconcerted the representatives of these Governments, but had the desired effect of awakening comatose official consciences and arousing public opinion to the magnitude of the evil against which the Egyptian Government was battling'.[4]

Russell was an improbable figure to be lambasting European governments on behalf of the Egyptian nation. Born in 1879 and a distant relation of Lord John Russell, the Reform Bill prime minister, he was educated at Haileybury College and at Cambridge before joining the Egyptian Civil Service as a sub-inspector in the Ministry of the Interior in 1902. Rising to become the commandant of Cairo City Police in 1917, he served in that office until retirement in 1946. Chief among his duties throughout this period was the maintenance of British colonial influence in Egypt in the teeth of often violent resistance. A report in 1935 from *Time* magazine suggests that he was more than up to the task: 'Russell Pasha, hard-bitten Briton in charge of Cairo police, kept his men at work last week riding down Egyptian students of both sexes with their horses, beating them back with the flats of their sabres, firing into the air'.[5]

He had been drawn to Egypt by the career of a cousin, Percy Machell, who served as adviser to the minister of the interior after service in the colonial Egyptian Army. Russell joined the Ministry and it was while training with the Coastguard that he had his first experiences of 'lying up in the rocks waiting for smugglers to beach their boatfuls of contraband hashish'[6] in pursuit of what he learned was 'the principal job of the Coastguards, which was the prevention of contraband by sea and land, and particularly contraband hashish'.[7] Hashish, or cannabis, was particularly important to the troops for reasons that Russell himself explained:

> The drug was, and still is, the favourite drug of the Egyptian lower classes, and in those days was produced exclusively in Greece, where the particular variety of hemp plant, cannabis indica, was grown in large quantities . . . considerable quantities were smuggled by sailing-boats and ships' crews into Alexandria and Port Said and at points along the north coast, but the biggest consignments were landed in Tripoli outside Egyptian territory and carried by Bedouin caravans across the Libyan desert to the Nile Valley. To intercept these bold and well-armed desert smugglers was the main task of the Camel Corps section of the Coastguards, who had a hard and risky life, mitigated by the good rewards paid on seizures. The Coastguard officers were miserably paid, but they reckoned on adding to their salaries several hundreds of pounds a year by these rewards. Confiscated hashish in these days was sold by the Alexandria Customs at public auction on the written undertaking by the buyer to export the stuff from Egypt, with the inevitable result that it was often merely taken

out to sea and smuggled in again, this time bearing the Government seal. Needless to say, the Coastguard officers raised no protest against this practice.[8]

Russell confessed that as a result of his three months' training with the Coastguard he remained 'just as hashish-minded as any Coastguard officer'.[9] Drugs were to loom large in his career as Egypt's chief policeman. By 1929 he had established the CNB in Egypt with the agreement of the prime minister of Egypt, Muhammad Mahmud Pasha. The new unit was evidently a priority as it was given its own budget, carefully selected staff, and a wide-ranging remit:

1. To trace to their source, in Europe or elsewhere, the imported drugs that were now ruining Egypt,

2. To present the facts to the League of Nations,

3. To pursue and prosecute drug traffickers in Egypt,

4. To put, by every possible means, such difficulties in the way of the traffic that retail prices in Egypt would rise to a height beyond the reach of the fellahin [peasantry].[10]

Russell claimed that he had established the unit to deal with what he called 'the white drug habit', that is the use of cocaine and heroin. However, and despite the fact that he recognized that 'hashish smoking has been a vice in Egypt from time immemorial',[11] cannabis consumption was drawn into the remit of the new CNB. By this time the trade had undergone recent changes. In 1932 the Greeks finally prohibited the cultivation of the *Cannabis sativa* plant and the traditional smuggling route across the Western Desert from Cyrenaican ports died out. Supply was thought to come instead from the Lebanon and Syria across the Sinai Desert in the camel trains of the Bedouin Arabs. Russell equipped his men with a new weapon with which to tackle the cannabis smugglers as motor cars were adapted to desert conditions for the police. In July 1933 the technology had its first triumph:

A report was brought in to a Frontier post that four armed Arabs with camels had been seen entering Egypt near Kosseima ... four of the newly fitted cars raced to the tracks and for the next two days followed them through the maze of wadis ... the old Sudanese sergeant-major had spotted the four smugglers crossing the sand dunes and had driven straight at them ... the capture was a good one, consisting of four well-known smugglers, four modern rifles with 200 cartridges, a field telescope and 156 kilos of hashish worth at that time about £E4000.[12]

While the authorities turned to new technology in their hunt for hashish, the smugglers seem to have exploited the possibilities inherent in rather older methods of crossing the desert. One gang shaved the humps of their camels, glued chunks of the drug to the exposed area, and then stuck the hair back on in order to disguise the cannabis. Another group packed the drug into canisters that the camels then swallowed; one animal had twenty-seven of these containers in his stomach, each 15 cm by 4 cm and made out of the tin of old kerosene drums, in all weighing about 15 kg. To combat this ruse, the CNB consulted radio experts who happened to be in the region creating a mine-sweeping system for the Western Desert. The solution was a metal-detecting device to be aimed by officers at passing camels.[13] The story of this technological triumph was circulated widely, with *The Lancet* reporting that 'great as is the ingenuity of the smuggling gang, it is more than matched by the vigilance and resourcefulness of the Central Narcotics Intelligence Bureau of Cairo'.[14] Russell's greatest triumph in his endeavours to prevent cannabis from entering Egypt was to come during the Second World War. The conflict eventually gave the British direct access to the sources of hashish in the Lebanon and Syria and in 1944 the Allies destroyed 7 million square metres of the crop, estimated to be about 75 per cent of that year's production. However, Russell realized that this was a one-off and argued that even in the 1940s 'Egypt and Palestine . . . succeed in seizing perhaps some 10 per cent of what enters'.[15]

Russell's struggle with drug smugglers would have remained an obscure story of the Empire hidden away in imperial correspondence had it not been for his annual appearances at the League of Nations. These began just after the foundation of the CNB when he got in touch with the Home Office back in London, and he proudly recalled later on that 'by the winter of 1929 our confidential reports to Sir Malcolm Delevingne had been circulated confidentially to all members of the Advisory Committee at Geneva and it was obvious to everybody that the facts they contained were of the utmost importance and must be examined officially by the Committee'.[16] The outcome was his first speech in Geneva in 1930, and the subsequent annual appearances at the League of Nations for the rest of the decade as representative of Egypt at the Advisory Committee.[17]

Throughout these appearances his focus remained on cocaine and heroin. In 1931, for example, he reported that his unit had secured the conviction of 10,000 people for drugs offences and the deportation of 129 foreigners, successes that ensured that 'not an ounce of illicit heroin has come into

Egypt from the factories of Central Europe'.[18] Yet while his greatest ire and energy were reserved for heroin and cocaine, he frequently padded out stories of the CNB's exploits with tales of cannabis. In his speech of 1931 he recounted a tale from the Alexandria branch of the Bureau in which 462 kg of hashish were seized from an employee of the Italian Consulate who had tried to smuggle the goods on falsified diplomatic immunity documents.[19] At the following session in 1932 he reported that 'it is no secret that the hashish traffic in Syria, in general, and the Lebanese Republic in particular, has a number of very powerful local supporters [so that] the Egyptian Government [will] have to continue spending thousands of pounds a year protecting her eastern frontiers from this Syrian contraband'.[20] His reports from Egypt that year carried multiple stories of busted clandestine hashish networks, with colourful flourishes to brighten the bureaucratic documents:

> The coastguards, in plain clothes and in a fishing boat, managed to board the smuggling vessel and arrested the two smugglers. The vessel and the two lots of hashish were also seized. Later on, El Sayed Abu Egaila, a notorious trafficker, committed suicide and it was found that he had done so as a result of having lost all his fortune which he had put into this smuggling venture.[21]

At his appearance in the following session in 1933, he again provided lengthy information on cannabis, and took a more combative approach.

> [He] would like to know whether it was to be taken seriously as a matter of international concern. Egypt was taking strong action against the traffic in hashish, but one country could not cope with it single-handed if it were tolerated in a neighbouring country. Egypt was spending hundreds of thousands of pounds a year on the preventive forces...he thought Egypt was entitled to ask the League to help her over this menace to the Egyptian people. If no such help were forthcoming, Egypt might be forced to adopt some practical form of defence; that might mean some form of legalized toleration and State production, which would completely destroy the profits of the foreign contraband trade.[22]

It is remarkable that, away from Geneva, Russell did not consider cannabis consumption to be such a great problem and his attitude towards its use was often ambivalent. He was utterly convinced of the evil of the 'white drugs' and he was adamant that 'the drug that nearly killed Egypt was heroin'. Yet he stated in 1930 that cannabis was 'the vice of the city slums and did comparatively little harm: in the villages there were a few hashish smokers who were looked upon rather as a joke...in the same way as the village "drunk" is regarded in the English village'.[23] The question therefore remains of why it was that Russell devoted the energies and resources of the CNB to enforcing controls on cannabis. The first response is that it is possible that the use of hashish increased in the Egyptian population in this period and became more visible as a social phenomenon, although it is difficult to verify this. The second is that, as Russell admitted above, he had become accustomed to chasing hashish traffickers at the earliest stage in his career while on patrol with the Coastguard, and as such it is probable that he never saw fit to stop and consider why he was pursuing them.

Finally, the suspicion lingers that cannabis was the bread and butter of his drugs unit, which needed to get results to justify what Russell himself admitted was 'a completely free hand and as much money as I wanted'.[24] It is notable that as soon as his Bureau was formed, 'my first objective was to check the importation of enormous quantities of hashish from Syria... I met with the greatest sympathy and assistance from the Mandatory power...the whole of the new crop [was] completely destroyed by the French authorities'.[25] This impressive show of planning and coordination contrasted with the 'great good luck' that he later admitted had been necessary for the CNB to register its first successes in tackling morphine derivatives. In other words, cannabis hunting provided the opportunity to demonstrate the effectiveness of his unit when seizing 'white drugs' proved to be more difficult. This would have been all the more important if a visible effort to control the flow of illegal narcotics into Egypt acted as a justification for the continuing British presence there.[26]

While Russell's attitude towards cannabis might have been more tolerant than towards other drugs, and while his motivations for pursuing it may have been mixed, the impact of his public stance on the substance at Geneva was clear. His aggressive position on cannabis forced governments into action. For example, his claims in 1932 about 'the hashish traffic in Syria' embarrassed the French administration there into a more vigorous policy so that their representative at Geneva claimed in 1933 that 'armed force had been used in destroying the crops'.[27] Perhaps more significant still was the fact that Russell put cannabis back on the agenda at the League of Nations. It had been a topic of discussion there only sporadically in the 1920s and, while it had flared up as an issue at the 1924/5 Opium Conference and had been forced into the Convention by the Egyptian delegation, it had entirely disappeared from meetings later in that decade.[28] Russell's colourful references to the issue of cannabis in the early 1930s suddenly revived interest in the drug and served to heighten sensitivities to it among the delegates who assembled annually for meetings of the Advisory Committee on Traffic in Opium and Other Dangerous Drugs at the League of Nations. As such, when stories began to come in from elsewhere about rising cannabis traffic few had any point of reference other than that provided by Russell's dark pronouncements.

The first of these stories was from Canada. The Government there had boldly stated in its report to the League of Nations for the year 1931 that 'it may be affirmed with certainty that no quantity of Indian hemp is smuggled into Canada'.[29] Events reported to the League in the following year suggested that such confidence was misplaced. In four separate cases convictions were secured against those importing cannabis from the United States. Two cases occurred in Ottawa and two in Windsor, Ontario, and the source of the drug in all cases was stated to be Detroit in Michigan. At the same time, seizures were reported in Cuba, and 219 g of cannabis were destroyed after being found at a pharmacy which was subsequently closed down.[30] The Mexican representative raised the issue of cannabis at the 1933 meeting, worrying that 'in recent years, the use of hemp, locally known as "loco-weed", had greatly increased in Mexico, the United States and Canada. He asked whether the United States Government had issued any legislation preventing its use'.[31] The American delegate replied that 'this weed grew wild and was therefore difficult to control. The Federal Government had asked the States to introduce uniform legislation preventing cultivation'. There was evidently some further discussion of this matter outside of the formal meetings, as the Committee inserted the following into its report to the League of Nations for that year:

> While a taste for Indian hemp products appears to be prevalent mainly among the Asiatic and African peoples, it is not by any means confined to them. A smuggling trade in cigarettes containing Indian hemp ('marihuana' cigarettes) appears to have sprung up between the United States of America, where it grows as a wild plant freely, and Canada. It may well be that, as the control over the opium and coca derivatives makes it more and more difficult to obtain them, recourse will be increasingly had to Indian hemp for addiction purposes, and it is important that the trade in Indian hemp and the resin derived from it are already, under the Geneva Convention of 1925, subject to the same control as morphine, opium, heroin or cocaine.[32]

Russell's stories from Egypt had primed the Committee to be alert to the dangers of the forgotten drug of the League of Nations, and the fresh crop of stories from the American continent combined with those from North Africa to create the impression of a growing problem that demanded prompt attention. Indeed, further news arrived of a seizure on 14 June 1933 of over 100 marihuana cigarettes at Montreal and those arrested claimed that they had been securing supplies in New York to smuggle into Canada.[33] When the delegates next convened at the League of Nations this was enough to spook them into action:

> At its sixteenth session, the Advisory Committee [AC] drew attention in its report to the concern which it felt at the extension of the smuggling in hashish...several members of the AC have asked the Secretariat on more than one occasion to undertake a study of the legislation regarding hashish in force in the various countries. In order to meet the wish of the AC and to supply it with the necessary material on this question, the Secretariat has already written to a number of countries concerned to ask for all relevant information on the legislative and administrative provisions applicable to hashish in their territory and to extend its enquiry to other countries. As the Secretariat is not yet in possession of all the replies, it proposes to adjourn the discussion of this question to the next meeting.[34]

Subsequent discussion at the next meeting shows just how little Committee members knew about cannabis. The Belgian delegate, Mr Carnoy, sought clarification about cannabis and a member of the Secretariat had to reply that 'there was actually only one species of hemp, *Cannabis sativa L.*, of which *Cannabis indica* was simply a variety, but richer in resin'. He then wondered if 'the use of cannabis indica as permitted in Tunisia, [was] to be regarded as a use of narcotic drugs or merely the use of a stimulant like coca-kola'. Dr Chodzko, the Polish representative, worried that 'Customs nomenclature and statistical documents made no special mention of Indian hemp or the resins which could be extracted therefrom'.[35] This confusion about what the drug was and how the regulations were applied to it meant that the Committee 'decided to adjourn consideration of this matter until a future session. This decision would allow members to study the documentation and obtain further information on this complicated subject'. The largest seizure to date in Canada, of over 1 kg of marihuana smuggled in by a sailor who had bought it in Jamaica, repeated arrests in Egypt, and the discovery of large consignments travelling into Iraq from Syria were the backdrop to these deliberations.[36]

The delegate from the Government of India was Sir John Campbell, who had been attending meetings in Geneva long enough to remember the way in which cannabis had been forced on to the agenda back in 1925. The gathering concern about cannabis at the Advisory Committee obviously reminded him of earlier events, and he wrote to the Government of India to note drily that

> It is already apparent that a determined attempt is likely to be made to secure a Convention covering all hemp drugs, and applying to them the general provisions now in force as regards narcotic drugs. Many of the members of the Committee are not likely to be troubled by considerations of administrative practicability.[37]

He was quite cynical about the motivation of those pressing the cannabis issue, noting that 'the Secretariat, perhaps naturally, wishes to extend its sphere of action; the advanced section of the Committee regards progress as synonymous with the elaboration of further restrictive Conventions, and discussion of the subject will unquestionably show that hemp drugs do give rise to most serious abuses'. A telegram from the Government of India in response to Campbell's letter made it plain that the line to be taken was simply to refer to the 'traditional policy of tolerating the moderate use of raw opium, and of hemp drugs (charas, ganja and bhang), while taking every possible measure to prevent abuse'.[38]

Campbell's predictions about the 1934 meeting proved to be prescient. The Secretariat produced a report for the information of delegates which estimated that there were 200 million users of cannabis products worldwide, and those present heard that in New York there was 'increasing difficulty in combating the abuse of Indian hemp' and were told that in Mexico 'the vice existed in the underworld'. The first and the largest speech came from the Egyptian member, Miralai Baker Bey, who was standing in for Russell. Bey emphasized the 'real moral and physical dangers of hashish' and was sure that 'although hashish has been known and used in Egypt for a long number of years, this fact ought not, I think, to be offered as any excuse for allowing it to continue to poison the youth of the country'. The solution to this was simple and he advocated 'the worldwide outlawing of the cannabis indica plant'.

There were those who were less moved by the hyperbole and who insisted that there seemed to be little hard evidence of what the fuss was all about. The Polish member, Dr Chodzko, 'observed that the material provided very little information on morbid symptoms due to hashish addiction' and specifically wondered if 'the Egyptian Government could give information on the symptoms of hashish addiction'. Moreover, the Government of India representative pointed out that in South Asia 'any interference with the use of hemp drugs by the population would be regarded by consumers as interference with established usage and liberty' and he emphasized that experiments with prohibition there had simply resulted in increased smuggling.[39]

Without a ready consensus on how to regard and approach cannabis the members reached for the solution of any committee which finds itself confronted with a thorny issue: a subcommittee.

> The Committee had a large amount of information before it on this subject and after full discussion, reached the conclusion that the problem of Indian hemp called for a thorough study on its part, in view of the importance of this question to certain countries, such as Egypt, in view too of the new menace which was taking shape in other countries and the apparent inadequacy of the supervision exercised over Indian hemp and its preparations. The Committee accordingly decided to set up a Sub-Committee on Indian hemp, which will be asked to study the whole problem and which may appeal in the course of its investigations for the co-operation of experts. The Committee also requested the Secretariat to collect any further information on this subject to supplement that already furnished to the Committee.[40]

The impression remains that it was the Egyptian delegates that had managed to force cannabis into the spotlight. An internal memo prepared for the Government of India about the meeting in 1934 observed that the drug 'had been included in the agenda at the request of the representative of Egypt, where the smuggling of hashish is a serious problem. The Secretariat has hastily prepared two memoranda on the subject O.C. 1542 and O.C. 1542 (a) from the information at their disposal'.[41] Elsewhere the Egyptians hounded the Health Committee, an entirely separate group to the Advisory Committee on Traffic in Opium and Other Dangerous Drugs, on the subject of 'preparations based on extract or tincture of Indian hemp'. These medicines represented a loophole in the earlier regulations for controlling substances that were an extract of cannabis, but not substances which *contained* extract of cannabis:

> The Egyptian Government proposed (October 27th 1933) that Article 10 should be applied to five specified preparations with a base of extract or tincture of Indian hemp; this letter was subsequently extended (letter of May 28th 1934) to include all preparations based on galenical preparations of hemp . . . as the fact that the Geneva Opium Convention of 1925 has, in the

> Egyptian Government's opinion, permitted of the manufacture of compounds
> containing a large proportion of galenical preparations of Indian hemp, which
> can be used in place of Indian hemp and its galenical preparations.[42]

Relentless though the Egyptian campaign against cannabis had become at
Geneva, it did snag on the recurring concern about sore feet. The Health
Committee adopted the Egyptian proposal and included preparations made
from extract of cannabis in the regulations at its session in 1935. However,
by 1937 protests were being lodged at this decision: 'other governments,
however, were only prepared to accept the recommendation subject to
certain reservations, more particularly in respect of preparations used in the
manufacture of corn cures'.[43] This notwithstanding, it is clear that Russell
and his colleagues from Egypt had driven cannabis back on to the agenda of
the League of Nations by the middle of the 1930s where it had not been a
concern at the start of the decade. They had not convinced everyone to
share their attitudes towards the drug. But they had succeeded in harnessing
many to their anti-cannabis position and had been key players in engineering a subcommittee devoted entirely to the drug.

The Sub-Committee on Cannabis

Egypt, the United States, Canada, and Mexico were among those that
placed representatives on the Sub-Committee, together with delegates
from the British Government and from the imperial administration in
India.[44] Mr Fuller, the American representative who had authored a report
for the Secretariat's OC.1542 document, was elected to chair the group.
The programme of investigations planned at its first meeting in 1935 seems
to bear out the complete ignorance of the subject which had been clouding
discussions of the drug at the League of Nations. The Sub-Committee
proposed a wide-ranging literature survey of published information on the
drug and also an investigation of allegations that the Beam test for cannabinol was unreliable. A call was also issued for all governments to pool
scientific knowledge of the plant and its preparations. The Sub-Committee
also wanted to know what the cause and effect of the abuse of cannabis
might be, and whether the drug was habit-forming. Finally, it sought a term
that was more accurate than 'Indian hemp' for use in discussions and it
resolved to reconsider the existing regulations set out in the 1925 Opium

Convention. In other words, the task was to seek a well-informed and comprehensive position on all scientific, medical, social, and legal aspects of cannabis use.[45]

The Sub-Committee quickly got to work, and by early 1936 had vindicated the Beam test and established that 'from the medical point of view in some countries the use of Indian hemp in its various forms is regarded as in no way indispensable and that it is therefore possible that little objection would be raised to dramatic limitation upon medical, if not veterinary, use of derivatives'.[46] By the following year it had decided that 'the term "cannabis" should, for the purpose of the Committee's study, be regarded as including all parts of the plant cannabis sativa L., whether growing or not...and every compound, manufacture, salt, derivative, mixture, or preparation of such plant'. However, it seemed that rapid progress on other issues was elusive. The medical applications of cannabis, the likelihood of insanity from its consumption, and the relationship between use of its preparations and of other narcotic substances, were all subjects once again deferred to allow time to 'collect all information on these subjects available throughout the world'. Additional experts from as far apart as Ceylon and South Africa were invited to contribute to the work of tackling these tricky issues.[47]

By 1938 the Advisory Committee was still waiting for news of progress, and noted in its report to the Permanent Council that 'the Sub-Committee would have to continue its research work before being able to make precise recommendations'. The research work was certainly ongoing, with sixteen new dossiers arriving at the Sub-Committee that included reports on subjects as diverse as methods of chemical identification of marihuana in Cuba and the state of hemp addiction in Tunisia. Proposals were submitted for further additional expert collaborators including a professor of psychiatry from the University of Algiers and a member of the Faculty of Medicine in Istanbul. With so much activity, and so few conclusions and recommendations, the chair of the group adopted something of a defensive tone:

> The sub-Committee points out that, as a result of the investigations made up to the present time, progress has been made in respect of the chemical identification of cannabis, and information has been collected on other phases of the problem, while, at the same time, certain points still require clarification, especially in connection with the physiological and psychological and psychopathic effects of cannabis and with the relationships between hashish

addiction and insanity and between cannabis addiction and addiction to other drugs especially heroin.[48]

By the following year the chair had gone. The American was replaced by an Englishman, William Walker Nind, who was the representative of the Government of India. On the face of it this was a remarkable change of leadership. Historically the Americans had been among the toughest opponents of cannabis use at the League of Nations. The British in India, on the other hand, had insisted on the continuing right to allow cannabis consumption in their South Asian territories and to enjoy the revenue from taxing it. Indeed, as the next section of this chapter shows, it was also licensing illegal exports of the drug to other parts of the Empire. Given this change of leadership of the Sub-Committee, it is perhaps not surprising that it continued to yield few conclusions or recommendations. Yet another questionnaire was devised to be sent out seeking information,[49] and yet more additional experts were signed up as collaborators, including Dr Stingaris, a Greek specialist in hashish, and 'a new expert whose name will be communicated by the representative of India'.[50] Consensus seemed no nearer and the picture seemed ever more complex as less damning opinions were voiced. For example, the Mexican delegate argued on the basis of recent investigations carried out in his country that

> The most definite conclusion to be drawn from those books was that expressed by Dr Salazar Viniegra who stated that during his fifteen years' work in the general hospital for the insane in Mexico, he had never come across a case of insanity due to marihuana.

Dr J. Bouquet, the Inspector of Pharmacies in Tunis who was present on the Sub-Committee as an expert, weighed in with the statement that 'cannabis addiction could not be said to influence criminality in the Moslem world, and went on to point out that, in North Africa, disturbances of the peace and violence were perhaps caused more by alcohol than by cannabis'.[51]

Finally, the Sub-Committee ground to a halt in 1940 as a result of the outbreak of the Second World War. It had done little to provide a simple or a concise position on cannabis, and had certainly not provided clear conclusions or recommendations for the Advisory Committee to act upon. Its last report was simply a summary of the most recent information and the latest scientific investigations into the plant's active ingredient, together with the news that yet another questionnaire had been issued. If the Sub-Committee had achieved anything, it was to demonstrate that there were great difficulties in trying to establish clear positions on the various scientific, legal, social, and medical aspects of cannabis consumption, and that there was certainly no easy consensus among the experts on matters related to the drug and its consumption.

In acknowledging its failure to coax from the Sub-Committee definitive conclusions and recommendations on cannabis, the Advisory Committee looked to the future in its final communication to the League of Nations on the matter: 'if the research work and investigations are continued during the war and if the material is collected, the Committee will be in a better position at the end of the war to consider, on the basis of the results achieved, an international solution of the cannabis problem'.[52] However, this vision was not shared by all. The Sub-Committee's chairman wrote from London to the chief of the League of Nations Drug Control Service later in 1940 to kill it off. He simply stated that 'correspondence between us is obviously difficult these days . . . such difficulties I suggest make it impossible to contemplate continuing research work in regard to cannabis and I think we must give up the attempt. The India Office people agree with me that it would be better to postpone such work until happier times'.[53]

India and imperial trade in cannabis

There were good reasons for the 'India Office people' to agree with the idea of abandoning further work on cannabis at an international level, related to the fact that the British administration in South Asia continued to permit recreational cannabis consumption rather than to prohibit such use of the drug. Since the nineteenth century the approach adopted by the authorities in India was that laid out by the Indian Hemp Drugs Commission (IHDC) of 1893/4 which stated that 'the policy advocated is one of control and restriction, aimed at suppressing the excessive use and restraining the moderate use within due limits . . . the means to be adopted for the attainment of these objects are adequate taxation, prohibiting cultivation, except under license, and centralizing cultivation, limiting the number of shops, limiting the extent of legal possession'.[54] The questions remain of whether this had been a success in ending excessive consumption and limiting moderate use, and whether the policy was a device that allowed the British administration to appear to be concerned with control while deriving revenue from the trade in the drug. By the 1930s there were those who believed that the system had worked to limit consumption. In 1939 a major study of cannabis consumption in India was published by Lieutenant-Colonel R. N. Chopra, the outcome of a decade's work. It stated that

> We conclude from our investigations in the field that nearly 0.5 to 1 percent of the population of this vast country take hemp drugs habitually at the present time, that the habit is on the whole declining and it is certainly not on the increase anywhere, that there is reason to believe that during the last 15 years the use of hemp drugs has more rapidly declined than in the previous similar period; the cause of this decline appears to be the tightening of control by the Government by reduction of the area under cultivation and the increase in price due to enhancement of excise duty.[55]

Chopra's conclusion 'that the habit is on the whole declining' is not beyond doubt as his arguments do not seem to stack up. In the first place, his view relied on observations of production in Bengal alone, whereas the plant was grown commercially elsewhere in India. It took no account of personal cultivation as those with access to even the smallest parcels of land could nurture a crop for their own use with relative ease. Indeed, the plant grew wild in many parts of India and this could be used to produce a crude intoxicant.

Additionally, Chopra's conclusions failed to recognize productivity gains on the land dedicated to the plant. It is true that throughout the 1930s the area devoted to cannabis cultivation declined sharply. In 1930–1 in Bengal 1,800 bighas were worked and 2,949 cultivators were licensed. On average each bigha produced 1 maund and 38 seers of cannabis. In the following year this had dropped to 1,600 bighas and only 2,822 cultivators. By 1935–6 only 716 bighas were under licensed cultivation and 1,811 cultivators were legally producing the drug. However, it is important to note that the remaining cultivators were now realizing 4 maunds and 8 seers of cannabis per bigha. As such they were producing 3,006 maunds, a relatively small decrease on the figure of 1930 when almost twice the amount of land had produced only 3,431 maunds.[56]

Even if this decrease in production did reflect a drop in consumption, it is not clear that Chopra was right in giving the authorities the credit for this. Nowhere in the excise reports produced by the British administration throughout this period was there any evidence of a concerted attempt by the government to reduce the area involved in production. There is mention, however, of the well-organized Naugaon Ganja Cultivators'

Cooperative Society, and it seems likely that this was responsible for the changes that resulted in reduced acreage and increased yields.[57] If there had really been a drop in consumption then another observer offered a simple explanation. Sir John Campbell attended the meeting in Geneva in 1933 on behalf of the Government of India and discussed cannabis. He 'stressed the fact that the figures for consumption there had shown a constant and rapid decrease for some years past . . . It should, however, be borne in mind that this diminution was not due solely to measures taken by the Government, but was in some measure traceable to the general economic crisis'.[58]

In fact, evidence from elsewhere in the 1930s suggests that administrators in the Government of India were more interested in measures to increase revenue from trade in the drug. A set of correspondence between London, New Delhi, and Rangoon revealed that cannabis from colonial India was being transported to the West Indies and Burma to meet the demand of South Asian workers in these places. The situation in Burma was summarized as follows:

> There is a large illicit traffic in ganja (Indian Hemp) which is consumed solely by Indians. Ganja is smuggled into Burma from Thailand and India but the principal source of supply is small plantations made by hill people in remote densely wooded areas in the Pegu Yomas and in the hills east of the Sittang River. The illicit traffic is financed by Indians. Burmans ordinarily act as carriers of the drug. With a view to combating the illicit traffic, a scheme has been sanctioned during the year for the sale of Ganja to Indians from Government shops.[59]

A subsequent letter from the Government of Burma explained:

> The possibility of obtaining an adequate supply of ganja in Burma was investigated as soon as the licensing scheme was approved but it was found that owing to difficulties in organizing and controlling cultivation a local supply could not be provided. It was therefore decided that for the time being the drug should be imported from India.[60]

In fact the Government of Burma asked the Government of India to sell it 7,480 kg in 1939 and a further 1,791 kg in the following year.[61] British officials often repeated the claim that this was simply a scheme intended as a means of controlling illegal activities within the newly established Protectorate (Burma was separated from the Government of India in 1937). For example, E. G. S. Apedaile, a deputy secretary in the Government of Burma, wrote that 'a system of licensed sale of ganja offered the only practicable method of dealing with the wide illicit traffic'.[62] This does not seem to have been the whole truth though, as a speech by the finance minister in Burma confirmed his reasoning in recommending the changes:

> The proposed measures for the control of the sale of ganja do not involve legislation and we estimate that the yield in licence fees in the coming year will be Rs. 6.81 lakhs against an expenditure of Rs. 81000. I have said before that apart from new sources of revenue there would be a deficit of Rs. 9.05 lakhs in the 1939–1940 budget. The re-imposition of the export duty on rubber will yield Rs. 20000, the table waters excise duty will yield Rs. 4 lakhs net and the control of ganja will yield Rs. 6 lakhs net. Thus, if my proposals are accepted, there will be an additional revenue of Rs. 10.20 lakhs or in other words instead of a deficit of Rs. 9.05 lakhs there will be a small surplus of Rs. 1.15 lakhs.[63]

Officials back in London were well aware that the lure of the income to be had from ending the prohibition on cannabis was uppermost in the Government of Burma's mind. D. T. Monteath at the Burma Office in 1940 declared in a letter to a colleague in the Indian Civil Service that 'it is quite clearly shown that the main object in recommending the legalization of the sale of ganja was to secure a new revenue estimated at about 6 lakhs of rupees . . . it is very evident that the policy on which the Government of Burma have launched out is open to criticism as being no more than an arrangement whereby revenue may be derived from a practice which for long has been regarded as so deleterious that the sale of the narcotic has been forbidden'.[64] Indeed, there was also concern in London that the transactions between Burma and India in order to secure cannabis for the new policy were illegal. Home Office officials acknowledged to one another through internal correspondence that, in this case, 'it seems abundantly clear that the drugs to be imported are not for medical or scientific use and to this extent both countries [Burma and India] are in breach of the [Geneva Opium] Convention'.[65] Remarkably, discussion of the case of Burma's new policy threw light on similarly questionable trading in cannabis elsewhere in the Empire. A Home Office letter in 1939 admitted that

> It is the case that the Government of India is, and has been for some time, allowing exports of Hemp to Trinidad for purposes which are, quite frankly, neither medical nor scientific. They are in fact allowed for the purpose of supplying an Indian population in Trinidad with ganja for smoking. I was responsible for recommending the continuance of this practice on the ground that it was for the purpose of supplying a class of Indians which went to Trinidad many years ago under the indentured labour system.[66]

By the time this letter was written British rule in India was well into its last decade. In its twilight years, and despite its recognition of international regulations, the colonial government found itself embroiled in dubious transactions in psychoactive substances. Trading in such products had certainly declined since the heyday of opium sales to China in the 1890s, but the habit was one that the Raj proved unable to break even in its final days.

Imperial science and the last of the cannabis surveys

By the time that colonial rule in India was coming to an end, the British had been taxing the cannabis trade for over a century.[67] While the history of their dealings with the drug had been marked by the consistent generation of revenue from sales of preparations of the plant, it was also notable that throughout there had been a persistent curiosity and a lingering concern about cannabis. This was most obvious in the regular surveys of the market for these preparations and the reports on the substance that were written during the period of British rule. William O'Shaughnessy, Hem Chunder Kerr, and the IHDC were among those that produced large pieces of work in the nineteenth century. The final word of the colonial period, however, went to Lieutenant-Colonel R. N. Chopra. He rose to become professor of pharmacology at the School of Tropical Medicine and Hygiene in Calcutta and he was an officer of the Indian Medical Service who had graduated from Cambridge University. He spearheaded a 'Drug Addiction Inquiry' which was instigated by the Indian Research Fund Association in 1926 and which produced in the following year its first findings in the report, 'Opium Habit in India [sic]'.[68] Originally published in the *Indian Journal of Medical Science*, this report was reprinted as a separate pamphlet and circulated widely in government departments, with the India Office in London, for example, requesting twenty-five copies in 1929.[69] The work also received considerable press attention in India with *The Statesman* devoting three columns to it in December 1928 and *Capital* carrying extracts from an interview with Chopra in its weekly editions throughout January and February 1929. Back in Britain it was also summarized in *The Lancet*, which noted that 'it is stated that the habit is on the whole decreasing' and that 'one conclusion at which he arrives is that the opium habit is not nearly so common as might be imagined from recent publications'.[70]

The readership for his research quickly grew and by 1934 the League of Nations was referring to Chopra in its investigations and noting that his book, the *Indigenous Drugs of India*, was one of the reference works that it had consulted.[71] By this time he had published reports on cocaine (1931) and 'post'[72] (1930), and he had set in motion the projects that would result in the publication of a study of cannabis in 1939. The paper on cannabis was the largest of the drugs studies, totalling 120 pages. In its opening paragraphs it mirrored the structure of its predecessors in the nineteenth century, particularly the large reports by Hem Chunder Kerr and the IHDC.[73] It dealt with the history of the plant and the processes by which it was cultivated and processed for the Indian market and the reasons that the various preparations of the plant were used. It then catalogued the bewildering array of methods for taking the substance. Broadly speaking it was the case that 'ganja and charas are mostly smoked while bhang is taken by the mouth in the form of a beverage or a confection'.[74] Such a generalization masked a plethora of recipes and delivery systems, however, and authors stressed that 'an important characteristic of the habitual use of hemp drugs, which needs emphasis at this stage, is the tendency of the habitués to mix it with other substances'.[75] The simplest method of taking bhang (the dried leaves and flowering shoots of male and female plants) was to pound it together with a little black pepper and sugar and then to add water. However, the researchers had found that to this basic formula was added ingredients such as 'aniseed, ajowan, cucumber, melon and poppy seeds, rose petals, saffron, cloves, cardamoms, musk and essence of rose' or 'kernels of pistachio nuts and "ceroli" (*Bassia latiafolia*), asafoetida, liquorice, senna leaves and extracts obtained from various other herbs'.[76] Fruit juices could add flavours too, and Chopra noted that all these ingredients were popularly believed to make the concoctions taste nicer and to counteract any harmful effects from regular use of hemp drugs. Ice cream containing hemp leaves was a modern incarnation devised for the wealthy in the cities during the heat of the summer, while the poorest mendicants on the road who could not afford such luxuries simply chewed the leaf. Smoking ganja (dried flowering tops of the cultivated female crop) or charas (resinous matter from the leaves and flowering tops of the plant) was another matter altogether. Most commonly mixed in a chillum with tobacco and inhaled deep into the lungs, it was only in the north-west of the country that both were smoked in a hookah where fumes were allowed to pass through water before inhalation.

Alongside the routine methods of consumption, however, the report provides a glimpse of a market for hemp drugs that often innovated with them, and the tastes of which were subject to change. Chopra noted that

> The addition of alcohol to hemp drugs is not particularly common in these days, although 'lutki', a drink prepared by mixing hemp drugs and alcohol, used to be popular forty or fifty years ago in the Punjab. In certain parts of that province and Baluchistan a drink called 'mudra' containing dhatura, opium, bhang, and alcohol used to be a popular intoxicating drink. In Sholapur district of the Bombay Presidency an alcoholic drink called 'boja' is prepared by fermenting 'jowar' grains to which hemp drugs and seeds of nux vomica are added.[77]

Drinks could contain more imaginative additives still and 'sometimes copper coins are boiled along with bhang or ganja leaves; the decoction thus prepared is believed to possess tonic effects and is said to have purifying effects on the blood'.

While the report compiled information that was readily available, it also conducted two sets of investigations. The first consisted of a series of clinical trials of various preparations of cannabis conducted in laboratories in Calcutta. The second was a number of long term studies of 'addicts' in their social setting. The clinical trials in controlled conditions were designed to provide a clearer picture of the actions of the drug.

> In our experiments monkeys, dogs, cats, rabbits, guinea-pigs and mice were used and the results of the observations were confirmed so far as possible in human beings . . . locally manufactured extracts of Indian hemp or emulsions made from the excise ganja and charas were administered to animals a) through a stomach tube and b) by intramuscular and intraperitoneal injections. Effects of inhalation of ganja and charas fumes were also studied.[78]

Calcutta was once again the centre of bizarre drugs tests, as it had been a century earlier in the 1830s.[79] Cats and dogs were deprived of food for twelve hours before being fed samples of charas and bhang. At first the former became uneasy and the latter excited, and the scientists observed that 'the cats, usually afraid of dogs, lost all sense of fear and repulsion when placed together with dogs who on the other hand became more docile and affectionate and did not attack or even show their usual antipathy to cats'.[80] All the animals became uncoordinated and those who were fed larger doses fell into deep sleeps characterized by slow respiration and low blood pressure.

The clinical trials took to using monkeys as subjects in order to observe the process of addiction to cannabis. Two members of the *Macacus rhesus* species were subjected to ganja smoke for ninety days. It took a while to overcome the initial reluctance of the animals to inhale during which time they tried to resist by blocking the hole through which the smoke passed into their cages. After three weeks this resistance relented, and the team claimed that 'the animals showed some liking for the smoke'.[81] They exhibited the usual signs of intoxication according to the dose administered, and throughout their general health remained robust. However, they developed dysentery after six months, apparently a common problem with caged animals in Calcutta, and died of the condition. The post-mortem simply confirmed that the animals had been in good health until the disease struck. The conclusions drawn from this experiment were tentative, with Chopra reporting that 'some tolerance was developed and the animals showed a certain amount of liking for the drug . . . the desire for repeating a dose and the abstinence symptoms produced were not so intense as is the case with animals to whom opium is repeatedly administered'.[82] The experiments were repeated on cats and albino rats, with similar outcomes and the team drew the broad observations that 'this accounts for the fact that in spite of the widespread use of hemp drugs there are relatively few clinical reports of addiction to these drugs in the same way as there are to opium'.[83]

Having failed to produce animal addicts, the team set out on other trials. Among the results were the conclusion that pharmaceutical preparations of Indian hemp could be used to induce general paralysis in frogs, which passed off within twenty-four hours; that two cats of similar size could have different reactions to the same amount of cannabis; and that rabbits, rats, and guinea pigs were less fun, or as the scientists put it 'these animals practically showed none of the reactions produced by the drug in higher animals'.[84] Among the higher animals involved in the trials were humans, and ten volunteers were subjected to tests, among whom was one of the research team Captain Gurbakhsh Singh Chopra. He had no prior experience of any narcotic and reported the most intense sensations: 'it is not possible to record or recollect correctly the train of symptoms which followed . . . he had a feeling of impending death, mind was flying about everywhere and it was impossible for him to fix his attention on anything'.[85]

The outcome of all this activity was rather more muted than had been the case a century earlier when William O'Shaughnessy had emerged from his Calcutta laboratories to declare cannabis to be a 'wonder-drug':

One of the most striking features about the action of Indian hemp is the extreme variability of results obtained. Equal quantities of the same preparation administered to two similar animals of the same weight and under almost identical conditions may produce depression in one case and stimulation in the other. The effects also vary considerably in different species of animals.[86]

The research team concluded that 'it is difficult to say whether the repeated use of the drug leads to true addiction', that cannabis preparations were unreliable as hypnotics, that it was doubtful that they had any effect on the heart and circulation and that it was true that they had a diuretic action.

The report also contained conclusions from the long-term studies of cannabis 'addicts' in India that the team had conducted. They had worked over eight years with a total of 1,238 'hemp-drug addicts', many of whom had been observed over long periods so that 'careful records of the symptoms and effects produced by habitual indulgence in these drugs were recorded in detail on an index card'.[87] The study concluded that the most common cause of consumption of the drug among the cohort was 'association and examples' which accounted for 24.23 per cent of them, while other reasons for use included religious and emotional factors (19.14 per cent), euphoria and pleasure (16.16 per cent), and relief from fatigue and worry (5.9 per cent). The team found that 'these drugs may be consumed anywhere but mostly they are taken in company, in religious places and akharas and by the people in their homes'.[88] Only 12.12 per cent were consumers of other drugs, and the most common additional substance was alcohol. Socially the 'addicts' fell into the following categories:

> The poorer classes such as day labourers, domestic servants etc. are the principal consumers of ganja and charas; they take them as food accessories. The idlers and persons of below average mental equilibrium who take to the habitual use of these drugs in order to induce a state of oblivion or to overcome feelings of inferiority and the sense of inhibition form the next common group. Also there are idle and rich people who take these drugs for stimulating and euphoric effects. Lastly there are religious mendicants who use them in order to overcome the feeling of hunger and to concentrate on religious and meditational objectives.[89]

Among the cohort the researchers established that users most often started the habit when they were over the age of 20 and that two-thirds of them took between 11 and 90 grains daily.[90] As far as their health was concerned, it was found that in 52.10 per cent of those examined there was no ill effect on general health. About 40 per cent reported that their health had suffered since they took to cannabis, while 10 per cent felt the opposite and could state that it had improved.[91] The greatest impact was in those taking large doses of ganja or charas, so that 'daily repeated dosage of these drugs overburdens the alimentary and excretory systems, the appetite declines and food is not properly assimilated'. The users lost weight rapidly and 'excessive smokers are thin, emaciated persons with a sallow or muddy complexion and dull grey eyes'.[92] Moreover, the team noticed that the incidence of sterile marriages among the cohort worked out to be nearly twice that of the population as a whole, although the fact that those studied were largely drawn from the poor was thought to have influenced this result. Overall, however, it was felt that 'small occasional doses do little harm but larger doses are undoubtedly injurious to the system'.[93] In terms of the mental effects of cannabis on the group of users studied, the report equivocated.

> These can be divided into two stages: a) an initial stage of stimulation and exhilaration and b) a stage of depression when the sedative effects become more marked. The effects during each stage are largely influenced by racial and personal idiosyncrasy and may be entirely modified by the individual temperament. Other important effects observed were perversion of the sense of relativity, slight impairment of the sense of interpreting the relationship of the subject to his environment. The intellectual and emotional character of the individual along with the environmental factors determines the type of symptoms of intoxication to a great extent.[94]

The individual was also thought by the researchers to lie at the heart of the relationship between cannabis preparations and insanity. They concluded that 'the abuse of hemp drugs injures the constitution in the same manner as an excessive indulgence in any other narcotic drug. It does not necessarily produce insanity except in those who have predisposition to it. It may, however, lead to rough manners and apathy and extraordinary behaviour on the part of the individual'.[95] Elsewhere they insisted that 'our experience is that the moderate use of these drugs does not lead to insanity in the majority of individuals, unless some predisposing factor is present'.[96]

In their analysis, society was another, additional variable that could decide the experience and fate of the cannabis consumer. In regions where use of the drug was rare, consumers found themselves ostracized and as such fell into bad company.[97] However, where cannabis consumption was more commonplace users could be 'good citizens, labourers and businessmen who regularly and successfully followed their vocations'.[98] The impact of users on society, however, was negligible:

> We have examined records of murder and crime cases in jails and mental hospitals and found that only in a very few instances (1 to 2 per cent) the temporary or the permanent derangement induced by hemp drugs was directly responsible for a crime. Persons who intend to commit a grave offence may indulge in one of the hemp drugs in order to brace themselves to face the danger . . . in all such cases hemp drugs may not be directly responsible for the crime; they only stimulate bravado.[99]

The conclusions reached by Chopra and his team were adopted as the official position of the Government of India on the topic even before they were published in 1939. The League of Nations sent a questionnaire on cannabis in 1938 and the Government of India turned to Chopra to complete it, which he did by decanting the results of his research into the official response.[100] The outcome of this was that Chopra was appointed as 'the expert selected by the Government of India' for the purpose of dealing with all further requests for information from the League of Nations on matters related to drugs.[101] He was now the spokesman for the largest market in the world for preparations of cannabis.

Perhaps the most striking difference between the report of Chopra's team and that of its nineteenth-century predecessors is the readiness of the former to use the word 'addict' in relation to cannabis consumers. When the research was finally published it had the title 'The present position of hemp drug addiction in India' and the cohort whose use of the drug was studied over the eight years was labelled the '1238 addicts examined in the field'.[102] However, Chopra freely admitted that within his cohort there were individuals who had been using cannabis for less than ten years and also those who had been using it for almost fifty. There were those who used only a few grains from time to time in contrast with others who indulged in up to 360 grains a day. As he also made clear after the clinical trials, 'it is difficult to say whether the repeated use of the drugs leads to true addiction'.[103] In other words, what Chopra's report considered was not addicts at all, but rather the wide range of those that could broadly be considered regular consumers. When he concluded that 'the number of hemp-drug addicts in the whole of British India at the present time works out to be 855,844',[104] he was in fact estimating the total number of users. This should not come as a surprise perhaps, as 'addiction' and the 'addict' had been ill-defined and oft-changing terms since they first came into common usage in the nineteenth century.[105] What it does show, however, is that even the scientist who had the final word on cannabis of the colonial period in India spoke with imprecision when he did so.

Conclusion

The earliest British ideas about, and policies on, cannabis and its consumers originated in Asia and Africa. Circulating from the eighteenth century onwards, these ideas eventually stirred the Victorian imagination to the extent that cannabis was briefly heralded as a wonder drug, and writers waxed lyrical about a 'sister of sleep'. At the same time colonial policies stoked outrage among moralists and missionaries who confused the drug with opium, and troubled Parliament to the extent that the IHDC was ordered as a twin to the Royal Commission on Opium.[106] This chapter has shown that ideas and policies related to the drug from the colonies in Asia and Africa continued to have wider impacts well into the dying days of the Empire in the twentieth century. Nowhere was this more obvious than in the case of Egypt, where the British chief of police used his experience of enforcing a prohibition on cannabis use to drive the drug back onto the agenda at the League of Nations in the 1930s.

However, the stories from the 1930s remind historians that the ideas and policies of the imperial period on cannabis could be complex and inconsistent. At the same time as the British chief of police in colonial Cairo was forcing cannabis prohibition into discussions in Geneva his contemporaries in India were breaking existing controls in order to export the drug to markets elsewhere in the Empire. While research produced there suggested that there was almost a million 'addicts' to the drug, the government continued to generate revenue from the sale of the substance and cultivators made their business ever more efficient by driving up yields. Until its demise the many tentacles of the Empire remained entangled on the issue of cannabis.

It should also be remembered that the ideas and policies that emerged from colonial contexts which were related to cannabis often drew upon a wide range of agendas and were not always based on long and hard thinking about the drug. The British had inherited policies in both Egypt and South Asia and seem to have simply perservered with them rather than given any thought to their effectiveness or wisdom. A change of policy in colonial Burma was based upon a desire to balance the government's budget rather than any fresh attitude towards the drug. The vigorous approach to prohibition in Egypt of the 1930s was down to the creation of a new agency to enforce drugs laws there, and perhaps a need to give the ongoing British presence a veneer of respectability. Even Chopra's exhaustive study of the situation in India seems to bear the shadow of the shifting and unclear nature of scientific discussions about addiction of the period. Indeed, when taken together, much of the writing about cannabis from across the imperial period has the flavour of Orientalist fantasy, where the drug could be either an exotic pleasure or a foreign poison in much the same way as the colonies were often imagined as either tantalizingly unknown or dangerously alien.[107]

With the end of Empire looming into sight throughout much of the period contemplated in this chapter, the contradictions and imprecisions of the colonial experience of cannabis considered here might be dismissed as historical curiosities from a distant past. However, and as the next chapter begins to demonstrate, the decline of the Empire did not bring to an end Britain's connections with the cannabis consumers of Asia, Africa, the West Indies, etc. What did change was the geographical backdrop for these connections, as the cannabis consumers of the Empire began to migrate to live and work in Britain itself.

4

'The prevalence of hashish smoking among the coloured men':[1] Migration, Communism, and Crime, 1945–1962

Introduction

The decade and a half in Britain after 1945 was one of contrasts. The austerity of the final years of the 1940s as the country gathered itself after the war was to begin to evaporate as the 1950s progressed to the point where Harold Macmillan could boast that the country had 'never had it so good' in 1957. The social conservatism of many sections of the population and many parts of the country stood in contrast to the often radical social policies and architectural styles of those in government, and to the new cultural forms and styles of popular music and entertainment. The population that had fought in the war and endured the Blitz settled down to a quieter life of raising the baby-boom generation which was to grow up in a nation shaped by these contrasts and changes. They often found themselves with new neighbours, as the 1948 British Nationality Act had made it possible for those living in the Empire to migrate to the UK without a visa, and by the early 1960s over half a million had acted on the invitation.[2]

The story of cannabis in Britain during this period was caught up in these wider contexts. Of particular significance was the arrival of migrants from the Empire who, as the previous chapter discussed, were often from parts of the world where the recreational consumption of cannabis was common and acceptable. They were to encounter enforcement agencies that had been primed since the 1920s to recognize cannabis use even though this was rare in the UK before the war. They were also to encounter a suspicion of change in certain parts of society at a time when many regarded the unfamiliar as unwelcome after the upheavals of the 1940s. Equally, however, the eagerness of some of the nation's youngsters to embrace the novelties of the period ensured that there were many who were glad to welcome the newcomers and keen to explore their habits. This context explains how, by the end of the period considered in this chapter, there were greater numbers of consumers of cannabis in the UK than ever before, and more widespread concern about them.

Migrants, murder, and the media

Derek Batuma, who was a Ugandan student reading social science at Bristol University, worked at the Family Welfare Association at Bethnal Green in the summer of 1949 in connection with his studies. He took the opportunity of his stay in east London to observe local groups of immigrants. Among them were 'four Indian lads':

> they had come over as ships' cooks. They had come on shore for holiday, so they put it, i.e. they were spending their earnings and when exhausted intended to sign on for another port, or if they could obtain employment, preferred to stay. They were a very happy group and a nice bunch of chaps and seemed to enjoy life immensely, which was divided between attending cinema shows, walking about the streets looking for girls and smoking hashish—Indian hemp.[3]

While this group of 'lascars' fitted the picture of the itinerant seamen who had made up the market for cannabis of preceding decades, Batuma also spent time with the new migrant groups that had been arriving in Britain since the end of the Second World War. Batuma observed that the West Indians 'have their own clubs (mostly dancing; they go in a lot for jazz), they are fond of boxing and generally being the "he-man" which endears them to the women-folk'.[4] In his view they were hard-working and enjoyed a higher standard of living than the other migrant groups in the East End. He discovered that the Africans, mainly from the West of the continent, 'live in some of the worst conditions, and I have reason to suspect that a lot of them actually sleep in bombed out houses. It would appear that they hang about the streets till 1–2 a.m. and then find a reasonably sheltered spot for a night's rest'.[5] Because many of them spoke little English and were often illiterate they struggled to find work and settled for employment as factory cleaners, stokers, porters, etc. He was also of the opinion that they were preyed upon by a particular group of British women whose 'sole intention is to live on the coloured man . . . they will push them on to do the most amazing things for the sake of gain . . . and will instruct them in how to make money in all sort of shady ways'.[6]

Batuma argued that the lack of wholesome recreational opportunities in Stepney and the surrounding area meant that 'there is no properly organised way in which these people could spend their leisure. To break the monotony of their very bad living rooms, there is the street with the cafés, and in the evenings the pubs, or when they have money, the cinema, or to the West End to dance halls'.[7] It was in the context of this poverty and this boredom that Batuma situated cannabis smoking among the migrants:

> The main amusement is sitting in cafés and drinking tea and talking, later, in the evenings, going into pubs for a drink and looking for girls. They are not as a rule heavy drinkers, and in a pub usually ask for half-a-pint, but they indulge in a far greater evil than beer, and this is hashish. This Indian hemp they pay for from very well 'kept' places at the rate of 2/6d for a little that will just about cover a 6d piece. It is rolled into a cigarette and passed round for all to have a puff. This drug is very dangerous and I met one man who had become such an addict to it that he was positively 'funny' in the head. When I pointed out to some of my friends that it was a bad thing to smoke, they said it was something that gave them strength and at the same time they could control themselves, not like drink that made you sway or would not let one stand up.[8]

The author of this report recommended that special agencies be established in the East End to deal with the social and moral welfare of these migrants, as well as to help out with better housing. By doing this, he argued, the migrants would become 'full members of the community', one of the by-products of which would be that they would give up hashish smoking as 'public opinion' was against it.[9] Batuma's report was forwarded to Basil Henriques, a prominent philanthropist and Justice of the Peace in the East End of London. Henriques sent copies to the prime minister, Clement Attlee, who responded personally to express thanks for the report, stating that 'the subject is, as you know, of very close interest to me'.[10]

From this report it is clear that the arrival of the Commonwealth migrants was making the market in Britain for cannabis more complex and less transient. The 'lascars' that had made up this market in previous decades could still be found, but their composition had always regularly changed as individuals came and went with their ships. Many of those arriving from the West Indies and from Africa, however, seemed to be more intent on settling into life as 'members of the community', albeit with habits such as cannabis smoking and jazz playing that would have been unfamiliar to the locals. Greater detail about the lifestyle of these migrants was revealed in the course of the high-profile trial of one of them for murder in 1952. Joseph Aaku was a 25-year-old man of Nigerian origin who was stabbed to death in his flat in Oakley Square in north London on 4 January 1952. He had arrived in the country in 1949 as a stowaway but, as a British citizen by virtue of his birth in the colony of Nigeria, he had been released after paying a fine for his illegal passage and had subsequently worked as a factory labourer and then as a railway carriage oiler at Euston Station. He earned a reasonable wage of up to £8 a week in the latter job and lived with his girlfriend, who had taken to wearing a gold wedding ring to legitimize their relationship. She had been at her parents' house on the night that he was found stabbed to death in the flat. Ironically, she had walked out after an argument about how unsafe she felt when alone at the address while he was working night-shifts.

The police had been called after other tenants in the block were awoken by a heated row in Aaku's room, which had concluded with the hasty exit of the protagonist and cries for help coming from the room. His neighbours found Joseph Aaku alive but repeating over again that 'I am dying, I am dying'. By the time the doctor arrived he had lost consciousness and even though an ambulance managed to get him to hospital, he died soon after. The brutality of the attack was emphasized in the post-mortem:

> The deceased died as a result of a stab wound at the back of the neck which penetrated to the spinal cord between the 1st and 2nd vertebrae. The spinal cord was almost severed and haemorrhage extended to the base of the brain. There were five other stab wounds to the face and side of the head. The left upper second tooth had been knocked out, apparently as a result of a blow from a fist. Dr Teare describes the deceased as a healthy and extremely muscular man, 5'9" in height. So it is evident that he was attacked suddenly and with great violence and, in the opinion of the pathologist, whilst he was running away or cowering from the attacker.[11]

At the scene of the crime 'a small bloodstained packet of hemp was found lying on the carpet' from which the police deduced that 'this packet had been the subject of conversation'. A further search revealed more packets of cannabis in Aaku's jacket. Other clues to what had happened that night included bloodstains on the banister and in the doorway of a nearby working man's club, and a sharpened knife which was found in Oakley Square all covered in blood. It was a distinctive blade as it had the Veer-aswamy's logo on it and had clearly been stolen from the Indian restaurant of that name on Regent Street. Most important of all, one of Aaku's neighbours had seen a man of West Indian or African origin fleeing the scene. The police busied themselves in publicizing the incident in the newspapers in a bid to get information and the *Evening News* carried the story on 5 January 1952 with the headline 'Knife Clue to Stabbed Man' in which it was stated that the police were looking for 'a coloured man with a seriously cut hand'.[12] Eventually Backary Manneh was identified as the suspect, but when he was first questioned about injuries that had occurred to his hand he told officers that he had been assaulted by white youths in a racist attack on the Tottenham Court Road, which he had reported to the police. There was no record of this report, and when detectives found out that he recently peddled a watch that matched the description of one missing from the dead man's wrist, and that he had worked at Veeraswamy's restaurant in 1951, they believed that they had their man. He was arrested on 14 January in the hospital where he was being treated for his wound, and was charged with murder. The police searched the belongings that he had with him there, and found a cigarette which contained cannabis.

The series of interviews conducted with those who knew both the deceased and the accused provide fascinating glimpses of the lives of those who were migrating to London. According to his uncle, who was an accountant at the Board of Trade in London, Joseph Aaku was educated at the Wesleyan Methodist School in Lagos and had served in the Army in Burma in the Second World War. Having returned from the conflict, he headed to the UK rather than wait for a job in Nigeria. Aaku's 'wife', Teresa Maher, revealed that once in London he became a regular customer at The Roebuck on the Tottenham Court Road and she first met him there in 1950. He confessed to her that he made money from selling nylons and cigarettes for American servicemen but once they started a relationship he found himself a job on the railway and they moved in together.[13]

Backary Manneh had also served in the Second World War, spending six years from 1940 in the Royal West African Frontier Force during which time he was wounded in Burma. He married in 1942 and was soon a father, but his family remained in Gambia while he headed abroad to look for work upon leaving the army after the war.[14] He landed as a stowaway at Hull in 1947 and eventually drifted to London. There he struggled to hold down a job, working for no more than a few days at a time with almost twenty companies by 1952. In 1949 Manneh was convicted for possessing Indian hemp, for grievous bodily harm, and for obtaining money by false pretences, for which offences he served two months in prison. He developed a propensity for robbing wristwatches, and was charged with this crime in 1950. He also took to carrying a weapon, and one witness in the murder trial, Momodou Bojang, recalled trouble over a woman in which Manneh had pulled the Veeraswamy knife on him. Another witness, Phyllis Beardmore, was with Manneh on New Year's Eve when he had been racially insulted by a white Liverpudlian and had once again drawn the weapon. Next day he had scolded her for using his Veeraswamy knife to peel the potatoes.[15]

A further witness, Ivan Dias, was sure that he had seen Aaku and Manneh together at The Roebuck on a couple of occasions. The police suspected that cannabis was the link between accused and victim.

> We believe that as both men were hemp smokers, that this was the possible connection between them. It will be remembered that a blood-stained packet of hemp was found at the scene of the crime. Where they met on the night in question is not known, nor is there any evidence other than the finding of this packet of hemp, to suggest why Aaku took the accused to his room. It is assumed therefore that a transaction in hemp was the reason for the meeting and it is significant that the accused denies being a hemp smoker, in spite of the fact that a 'reefer' was found among his possessions at the Hospital.[16]

Teresa Maher was able to provide a glimpse of cannabis consumption among the migrant population in London at the start of the 1950s. She stated that she knew about Indian hemp because she had been friends with migrants in London for a couple of years and they had introduced her to it. She had smoked it on one occasion but it had no effect.

> During the time I knew Joe Aaku I saw him roll reefer cigarettes, taking Indian hemp from a small packet, place it in a cigarette and then twist the end of the cigarette. I have been present when he has smoked these cigarettes and

> I know it was Indian hemp he was smoking owing to the distinctive smell that
> comes from it. It smells like wood burning. He did not smoke a lot in my
> presence but when he has it made him rather happy, just as though he had had
> a few drinks.

She had been present 'on two or three occasions [when] I saw small brown
packages containing hemp and they would all roll themselves cigarettes and
smoke them. I don't think they were buying or selling the hemp but just
meeting there to smoke it. Joe did not seem to be particularly friendly with
any of the men who visited him'.[17] She also revealed that on one occasion
he had tried to conceal a parcel from her which she suspected contained
cannabis. He had gone out with it and returned without it and she had
assumed that he had sold it.

The police believed that cannabis was the reason for the meeting of the
men and that Aaku had taken Manneh home to sell him the drug. The
investigating officers were convinced that the latter had then resorted to
violence in order to rob Aaku of his watch. In other words the drug was not,
in their opinion, in any way connected to the commission of the crime and
it simply explained how the men came to be standing alone together in the
flat. When the case came to trial the prosecution was also convinced that
this was the place of the packet of cannabis in the events that led to the
murder:

> It may be—it is entirely for you to say, and it is not a matter of great moment,
> and I put no great reliance upon it—that there was a link between them of
> hemp, hemp being the product from which is derived a drug sometimes found
> in these days, as you know, in cigarettes as marijuana. On the floor of the
> room where the deceased man had been murdered was found—it is Exhibit
> 16—a packet of Indian hemp which was bloodstained, and had therefore
> come into the struggle or fight or murder which had taken place a few
> moments before.[18]

However, it soon became clear that the legal team for the defendant was
intent on making far more of the packets of the drug. Dr Robert Donald
Teare was called to the stand on the second day of the trial. He had
performed the post-mortem on Joseph Aaku at St Pancras mortuary and
had already reported his findings to the trial. The defence team had recalled
him, not to talk about the post-mortem, but to answer questions as a
medical man about cannabis. This despite his protestation that 'I don't
know a great deal about it'.[19] It was clear that the defence had been doing

some research on the drug and cited, among other sources, a book called *Marijuana in Latin America: The Threat It Constitutes*, written by Pablo Osvaldo Wolff and published in the US by the World Health Organization in 1949.[20] On the basis of their reading, Teare was asked to respond to certain statements put by the defence team on cannabis. For example, did he know that 'Malays . . . have been known to madden themselves with Indian hemp into a homicidal frenzy and run amok'? Teare answered that this was 'a novelty to me'. Did he know that 'a man suffering from this vice feels he is being pursued, imagines the persons around him to be his pursuers and attacks whoever gets in his way'? Clearly irritated, Teare responded that 'my readings have rather led me to believe that was not the effect of hemp, and that it made ordinary things appear delightful, it made bad food taste good and it made boredom more bearable'. He was then read a passage directly from Wolff's book:

> Much more serious, however, are the numerous crimes reported in which the use of marijuana led to a capital crime. Not as infrequently as one might suppose one finds the headline 'Murder committed under the influence of the pernicious weed', or something to that effect. Let the following occurrences serve as examples. A soldier left his home to smoke the malignant weed. When he returned in a furious state he stabbed to death a nephew by marriage with whom he had been on terms of friendship. Near a railway station a man draws a revolver and kills unknown innocent people who have just arrived on the train . . . he committed the criminal act under the influence of the hallucinations produced by the marijuana.

He was then asked if he doubted the authenticity of these reports, and Teare pointedly stated 'yes, there seem on the evidence you have read to me to be many other factors apart from marijuana . . . we have no idea of the mental state of these patients, quite apart from marijuana'. Indeed, he also made it plain that 'I have a personal lack of confidence in some of the material produced on the other side of the Atlantic'.[21] Overall, Teare utterly refused to validate the position that the defence had been trying to establish, namely that cannabis alone could induce murderous behaviour.

Despite his robust performance, the prosecution persisted with its questions about cannabis and simply switched its attention to another witness. Dr Donald McIntosh Johnson was called to the stand on the third day of the trial. His impressive credentials were laid out for the court: he had medical degrees from London and Cambridge, was a Bachelor of Surgery, a barrister-at-law, and a member of Gray's Inn. He was also the author of a 'special study' of cannabis, a book called *Indian Hemp: A Social Menace* which had been published in 1952, and a copy of which was presented to the court as exhibit number 23.[22] Johnson's testimony on cannabis could not have been more of a contrast to that of Teare. The former was sure that 'a few grains will send a person into a state of mania and violence' and that 'in every country in which this vice is known, Indian hemp, or its equivalent marihuana, is associated with sudden outbreaks of violence'.[23] The doctor/surgeon/barrister was firmly of the conviction that 'there is an overwhelming quantity of evidence . . . that marijuana or Indian hemp, as it is called, is a thing which is closely linked with outbreaks of violence of a sudden and unexpected character'.[24]

There was some confusion in the court as a result of this performance. The prosecution declined the opportunity to cross-examine Johnson and the judge questioned why he had been called in the first place. The defence lawyer, Mr Sarch, soon made it clear that Dr Johnson was the expert witness at the heart of the case he was making for Manneh. He argued to the jury that the evidence that they had heard of the victim's recurring possession of the drug 'entitles you to infer that Aaku was a drug addict'.[25] Based on this inference, he turned back to Johnson's statements, and reminded the jury that the latter was 'a most impressive witness'. Given his assessments of the drug, and the idea that the victim was a 'drug addict', the defence lawyer made his pitch to the jury: 'assuming Aaku to have been become heavily under the influence . . . may he not quite well have made a frenzied attack upon his visitor?' In these circumstances, his client's actions would have been committed in self-defence.

It took the jury less than two hours to reject the defence and to find Backary Manneh guilty of murder. Mr Humphreys for the prosecution had pointed out that there was no evidence whatsoever that anyone had smoked the drug on the night of the murder and therefore the defence was a 'fanciful theory'.[26] The judge had also reminded the jury that they had heard much about the deceased's domestic life from Teresa Maher and that 'there is no evidence . . . to suggest that Aaku, during the time she was living in his house, had ever shown any signs of being a drug addict'.[27] When the case went to appeal cannabis was central to the hearing. It was argued that the judge in the original trial had misled the jury in stating that there was no evidence that the victim was a drug addict, as there was evidence 'from which the Jury could infer that the said Joseph Aaku was a drug addict'. A handwritten note on the Notice of Appeal insisted that there was 'No evidence Aaku was a drug addict' and the judges who heard the appeal decided:

> We are now asked to say that because it was shown that Aaku was a man who took drugs and that the prisoner took drugs, that mere fact would justify the jury in finding a verdict of manslaughter, that is to say, the jury would infer from the fact that some Indian hemp was found in the dead man's room the dead man had got into a state of frenzy and had attacked the prisoner and the prisoner acted in self-defence . . . there is abundant evidence here that this man killed the dead man . . . this appeal is dismissed.[28]

The conviction was upheld. Backary Manneh was sentenced to death, and executed on 27 May 1952.

While the prosecution and the presiding judge at the original trial had rejected the defence, they had not challenged the assertions about cannabis made by the expert witness. Mr Humphreys of the prosecution was clear that 'I entirely accept the evidence given by Dr Johnson' and the judge in his summing-up was equally respectful and went so far as to repeat the assertion that 'the taking of this drug is closely linked with outbreaks of violence of an unexpected character'. Dr Teare's more nuanced testimony on the drug went unacknowledged at the end of the trial. As such, cannabis too had been found guilty at the trial of Backary Manneh, of being a dangerous intoxicant which was apt to excite rage and aggression in consumers. Yet closer scrutiny of the expert witness suggests that he was ill-equipped to offer a balanced view of the drug to 1950s Britain. On the face of it Johnson's credentials were even more impressive than made out in court. Alongside his medical and legal qualifications Johnson was a businessman, who owned the Marlborough Arms Hotel in Woodstock and who had started his own publishing firm in 1945. He had also been a Parliamentary candidate before the war, standing for the Liberal Party on four occasions, the last of which was a failed attempt at election in the seat of Chippenham in Wiltshire in 1945. However, closer investigation reveals a more complex picture. Johnson never practised in the legal profession, having passed exams in Roman law, constitutional law, and law of real property on his father's advice to have a back-up in case his medical career failed. He sold his practice as a doctor in the 1930s, partly in response to a run-in with an insurance company over the misuse of a hypodermic needle.[29] His publishing firm faced bankruptcy on a number of occasions.

He was forced to sell off his hotel in 1951 after having been committed to a local psychiatric hospital.

Johnson's interest in cannabis came as the result of this encounter with mental illness. His account of this is grounded in the difficulties that he experienced in running his hotel, during which time the entire staff left to work for a local rival. He found himself 'overwhelmed by the oppressive sense of anxiety' because of these difficulties and both he and his wife felt that 'demonic forces encompassed us inside the building, while, so we thought, gangsters threatened us from without'. Finally, both began to behave oddly, arguing with friends and relatives, screaming at the hotel, and acting in a paranoid manner. A local doctor was called and he quickly involved the police and a magistrate who took Johnson to Warneford Hospital. Johnson admitted that while there he imagined that he was 'a prisoner in the Cold War', and also 'understudy to Sir Gladwyn Jebb as Britain's representative at UNO'. He also formed the impression that he had been 'selected as husband for Princess Margaret'. Finally, after a period of rest at the hospital he took to reading the newspapers again and also to playing bridge. The doctors felt that these were signs enough of a return to sanity and he was released after a six-week stay.[30] Johnson acknowledged that he had been treated for a 'psychotic episode' and that he had been diagnosed as a 'paranoiac'.[31]

It is interesting to note that it was only after a stint in a mental hospital that Johnson finally made it into Parliament, as he was elected in 1955 as the Conservative representative of Carlisle. The period of detention certainly shaped his attitude towards cannabis. Refusing to accept that he had been mentally ill, he took to insisting that he was 'doped' throughout his strange experience and to gathering evidence to support this assertion. He told a local newspaper editor that 'I am the first example of the workings of the Russian truth drug in this country'[32] but this failed to impress the journalist or the various others that he contacted with the theory, including his MP. Finally a friend, a Harley Street doctor, pointed Johnson to the entry in a book on toxicology about cannabis. He immediately identified his symptoms as sensations associated with cannabis consumption and he became convinced that he had been poisoned with the drug.

He was so persuaded that cannabis was at the root of his episode that he set about becoming an expert on the topic:

During the ensuing summer I read about Indian hemp in my suburban train.
I read about it during quiet moments while I was doing Douglas's surgeries.
I read about it in my beach chair by the sea on our summer holidays.[33]

He visited Pont-Saint-Esprit in France, the scene of a mass poisoning in
August 1951 where over 200 people were taken ill as a result of contamin-
ated bread. Many suffered hallucinations and Johnson decided to reject the
accepted conclusion that the outbreak was the result of ergot alkaloids in the
rye used for the loaves. Naturally he attributed the episode to cannabis,
noting that a field of 8,000 square yards of hemp had been found in a village
in the adjacent *département* to that of Pont-Saint-Esprit.[34] Official reports
stuck with the ergot explanation.

   The outcome of all of this research was a decision to produce a book on
cannabis. He wrote hastily and produced *Indian Hemp: A Social Menace* in
1952. It was published by the company that he owned and he was sufficiently confident that it would be of interest to the market that he ordered a
run of 5,000 copies. At this time his firm was in financial trouble so this print
order suggests a confidence that his book was so compelling that it would
inform the public of the menace of the drug while also reviving the fortunes
of his business. His optimism was partly based on the activities of his press
agent who got to work on stimulating coverage in the national newspapers.
They briefly became involved in a bidding war for access to Johnson, who
received calls from the *Daily Telegraph* and the *Daily Mail* before being
warned off any contact with them on the promise of a front page exclusive
with the *Daily Mirror*. 'REEFER MADNESS WAS CAUSE OF BREAD
MADNESS: DOCTOR REPORTS' was the headline on the first edition.
The other papers went with similar reports, the *Daily Mail* leading with a
headline 'DOPE: Warning is given by a Doctor today', *The Star* weighing
in with 'THE MARIHUANA MENACE' and the *News Chronicle* contrib-
uting 'THE GIRL WHO TRIED REEFER SMOKING'.[35]

   Those tempted by these stories to buy the book were greeted with lurid
reports and conjectures. Moving from accounts of cannabis in Asia and
Africa, Johnson surveyed its recent popularity in the USA before considering experiences in England. It reproduced newspaper reports published in
the *Sunday Graphic* by John Ralph on successive Sundays in September 1951
which asserted that

> As the result of my inquiries I share the fears of detectives on the job that there
> is the gravest danger of the reefer craze becoming the greatest social menace

this country has known . . . the other day I sat in a tawdry West End Club . . . I watched the dancing. My contact and I were two of six white men. I counted 28 coloured men and some 30 white girls. None of the girls looked more than 25 . . . 'the day will come', said the dusky Jesse, 'when this country will be all mixtures if we don't watch out. There will be only half-castes'.[36]

Johnson also related what he felt were his own experiences of the drug, albeit in an account of a fictional 'Mr A'. After telling his story he concluded that, because of its effects, cannabis could be used to poison perfectly sane individuals and to render them temporarily unstable to the extent that they could be certified: 'there may be who-knows-how-many of our fellow countrymen living today under the shadow of unexplained mental illness'. Johnson finally ended the book by suggesting that the accused in Russia's show-trials were numbed by cannabis, and by asking 'what more effective weapon could there be for waging the Cold War than by promoting the use and consumption of noxious drugs within the ranks of your enemy that will corrupt his youth; and so rot your foe from inside so that he will crumble of his own accord? For such a purpose the hemp drug would be an admirable medium'.[37]

This volume is an important reminder that writing about cannabis can often be writing about many things other than cannabis. He seized upon the drug as a topic through which he could articulate the Cold War anxieties and racial fears that he shared with many others in the UK in this decade, and also explain away the personal problems that he had with his mental health during a difficult part of his life. The volume also stands as a reminder that claims to expertise should always be scrutinized as they can sometimes serve to falsely elevate opinions on controversial topics above the status of ill-informed prejudice. Johnson's ideas were anything but dispassionate or objective views arrived at through legal reasoning or scientific method. They were in fact the garbled fantasies of a troubled man who sought publicity for a book that he hoped would restore the fortunes of his ailing publishing company. Yet his legal and medical qualifications enabled these garbled fantasies to be passed off as established opinion in a court of law and to spark a round of sensationalist news reporting in the press. Despite this, the epilogue to the story comes in the fact that Johnson's volume failed to sell more than 800 copies within three years of publication.[38] The British public of the period seems not to have been sufficiently alarmed by stories about cannabis to spend their money on books about it.

Policing the new consumers

It is of interest here to refer to a case in Liverpool in December 1945; a Maltese lodging house keeper who was arrested when both hemp and opium were found on the premises kept a pistol in the house, while an Arab, who was present at the time actually tried to draw a loaded revolver. Both men were alleged to be smoking drugged cigarettes when the Police entered the room.[39]

While the story of the policing of cannabis in Britain after the Second World War started in dramatic fashion, it settled into a more mundane pattern for the rest of the 1940s. New Scotland Yard produced an internal report in 1950 that observed that across the whole of the UK in 1947 there were only forty-six 'offences concerning Indian hemp', and that this had risen slightly to fifty-six in 1949.[40] Seizures of the drug tended to be near the docks in London or at ports around the country including Liverpool, Middlesbrough, and Cardiff. Home Office descriptions of the consumers were of 'simple, coloured, seafaring men'.[41] In other words, the lascars remained the chief offenders to be picked up by police for cannabis offences in the years immediately after the war.

Yet by the end of the decade it was becoming clear that the arrival of the migrants from the Commonwealth was providing another source of arrests for the police. A list of those detained in Stepney in 1949 for cannabis offences included the familiar names of Asian sailors, such as the Abdul Rajak of India and Ummer Ali of Pakistan, who seem to have put aside the antagonism between their newly divided countries to get arrested together on Cable Street for possessing cannabis. However, among the others included on the list was Maurice Oliver Forrester, a Jamaican.[42] Indeed, the statistical evidence produced at the time pointed to the increasing significance of those of African or West Indian origin in the cannabis cases dealt with by the authorities. An internal memorandum on the illicit traffic in cannabis produced by the Drugs Branch in 1947 noted that 'of the thirteen persons involved (including two cases in which hemp was seized but no prosecution ensued) two were white men, two Indians, and the remaining nine negroes'.[43] This memo went on to detail that six of the latter had been arrested in the Charing Cross Road area and that a number of them should be considered as 'traffickers'. The report described them as 'rather unsavoury characters [with] several previous convictions for larceny, violence, and drug offences...one was sent to prison for living on the immoral earnings of a white woman'. It concluded that

> The traffic itself is practically confined to the two negro groups in London in the West End centred on the Charing Cross Road and in the East End on the Commercial Road, with its headquarters around Leman Street where the Colonial Club—a hostel for coloured seamen—is to be found. Even within these groups the use of hemp seems to be confined to the more vicious element and not to be widespread. The individuals concerned are loafers, pimps, and petty criminals.

By 1951 the head of the Drugs Branch, F. W. Thornton, had moved to a rather more agitated position on the issue of this new group of consumers.

> I think I should take this opportunity to place on record the fact that unless something can be done, by any of the authorities concerned, to stem the 'invasion' of unemployed coloured men (mostly British subjects) from Africa and the British West Indies, we shall in a very short space of time be faced in this country with a serious hashish smoking problem...they are of little use in our labour market and ultimately drift to the West End of London—Tottenham Court Road area—where they associate with lower class white girls, drink, peddle hashish cigarettes and generally present a problem to the police.[44]

In the following year Thornton produced evidence that seemed to confirm his fears. In 1951 there were 128 convictions for offences relating to cannabis, compared with eighty-six in the previous year and only seventy for the years 1944 to 1947. He pointed out that almost all of those that had been convicted were of African or West Indian origin, and concluded that 'the drug is used to prepare "reefer" cigarettes and normally is distributed among the ever increasing coloured population centred in the larger cities. The sharp incline in convictions from 1947 onwards coincides with the notable increase in immigration from the areas mentioned'.[45]

Few others at the Home Office seemed to share the agitation of Thornton about drugs among the migrants. His superior there, to whom the above reports were submitted, made a point of noting in the correspondence of 1952 that 'we need not be unduly alarmed' because

> the picture is as before, a small drug problem kept within narrow bounds by a rigid system of control...there is still no sign of a widespread, organised traffic, of violent crime arising from the habit, or of the white inhabitants taking to the habit to any degree. Nor is there any indication that hemp

smoking leads to other, and perhaps more deadly, forms of addiction as it does in the USA.[46]

Elsewhere in government others seemed similarly unconcerned about cannabis and migration. 'No special interest in the references to drug trafficking was shown by the Inter-departmental Committee on Colonials' was the handwritten note in a Home Office file of 1950 which suggests that the issue had received wider attention. Indeed, the idea that the 'invasion of unemployed coloured men' was a problem at all was given short shrift by those who were monitoring the impact of the migration and an official at the Colonial Office wrote archly in 1952 that 'it is not, I think, that the migrants behave badly, though naturally they have their black sheep'.[47]

It is likely that Thornton's excitement on the cannabis issue was down to his close involvement in the policing of the drug in the late 1940s and early 1950s. As the story of the Home Office Drugs Branch outlined in Chapter 1 showed, the officers of that unit were primed for the arrival of cannabis long before there was much of the substance to worry about in the UK. Since the 1930s they had been carefully gathering knowledge about the drug and had been out on the road schooling police officers and excise officials in what to look out for. As such, the records show that when cannabis did begin to appear in small amounts among the migrants to the UK of the post-war period, detection was swift and action prompt. As early as February 1947 Thornton boasted that his men had renewed their efforts to get frontline agencies ready for action:

> The attention of preventive officers of HM Customs was drawn to the matter and between 26 August 1946 and the end of the year nine seizures were made at the ports—in comparison with one for the rest of the year. There is little doubt that until these officers were shown samples of the various Dangerous Drugs, including Indian Hemp in its different forms, many of them were unaware of the nature of these innocent-looking dried herbs.[48]

The Drugs Branch maintained its awareness campaign on cannabis among law enforcers, and the annual report for 1951 noted that 'both the Customs and the Police have been well coached by HM Inspectors in their attitude to and knowledge of the users and appearance of the drug through visits to the Branch museum, lectures etc.'. The outcome, according to Thornton who wrote the summary, was that now 'both these services are very much alive to the possibilities in this direction and the number of successful results produces added incentive'.[49]

If the law enforcement agencies were increasingly aware of cannabis they also appear to have had a heightened sensitivity about the migrants. Three drugs raids in London by the Metropolitan Police suggest a process by which the migrants, rather than their drugs, became the focus of police activities in the early 1950s. The first of these occurred early in 1950 in a dance hall in the West End of London, at which 'there were found to be between 200 and 250 persons, male and female, coloured and white . . . these were all searched and ten men (of whom two were coloured) were found to have in their possession small quantities of Indian hemp'. This was followed when

> On the 1st July 1950 the police raided a dance hall in Tottenham Court Road at which there were about 500 persons, the men mainly coloured and the women white. All were searched and eight men, all coloured, were found to have small quantities of Indian hemp in their possession and were subsequently convicted for possessing this drug . . . during the search 20 packets containing Indian hemp were found on the floor of the dance hall.[50]

In the following year the Drugs Branch annual report noted a third raid in the West End:

> The unusual case of a London public house being raided for drugs (believed to be the first occasion this had happened) occurred on the evening of 10th March on a warrant issued under the Dangerous Drugs Act at the 'Roebuck', Tottenham Court Road. The premises were sealed off and all the occupants searched, resulting in the arrest of two men, one being a labourer and the other a corporal in the 509th Bomb Group, US Air Force for illegally possessing Indian Hemp. The men had purchased the drug for their own consumption from another frequenter . . . police had received complaints that drug trafficking was occurring at this licensed house by men of colour and subsequent enquiries showed that 99% of the customers were coloured people who had, in the space of a few months, ousted the local 'regulars' thus reducing the place to a miniature 'Harlem'.[51]

The Roebuck had been the pub where Joseph Aaku and Backary Manneh had convened to trade in cannabis, and was where the former had met his partner, Teresa Maher. When read together, the three raids seem to show an intriguing progression, from searches of nightclubs at which illegal transactions in drugs were suspected to targeting places where men from Africa and the West Indies went in their leisure time. After all, the raid on the first club produced the highest yield of arrests (and prosecutions) for drugs offences of the three events, and it was at a venue where the crowd was made up of a variety of racial groups and where the minority of those committing drugs offences were migrants. Despite this, the focus in the search for narcotics seems to have narrowed to venues where the male customers were mainly drawn from migrant groups. Indeed, the way in which the report of the pub raid is written points to the tensions underlying the police intervention; enquiries subsequent to the tip-off revealed nothing more than the fact that the pub had become the chosen destination for 'coloured people' and that there was a feeling that the former regulars of the place had been 'ousted'. Yet in the account provided by the Drugs Branch this reads as an explanation for the unusual step of raiding a public house to conduct a drugs search. Given the small yield of arrests, it is possible to wonder how far the warrant issued under the Dangerous Drugs Act was any more than an excuse for the police to intervene in a public space that had been contested by locals and migrants and successfully colonized by the latter.

It is important to recall that branches of government were concerned at this time about the racial anxieties being stirred up by the arrival of the migrants. A confidential note sent in 1952 from the Colonial Office to Sir Hugh Foot, the Governor of Jamaica, warned that 'we and other United Kingdom Departments have been worried for some time that the growing influx of coloured migrant workers—and Jamaica provides the majority of those who come—would lead to increased coloured prejudice'. It went on, 'there are naturally people who resent their coming and say that they are getting unfair advantages from the national services to which they have not contributed'.[52] The Home Office had been compiling data on racist attacks[53] and in 1952 amendments to the Defamation Bill were considered that would have made it a criminal offence to utter, publish, or distribute statements calculated to bring any body of persons in the UK distinguishable as such by race, creed, or colour into hatred, ridicule, or contempt.[54] As such, Thornton's agitation at the Home Office Drugs Branch about 'coloured men' and the raids of the Metropolitan Police of pubs and clubs where the immigrants congregated should be viewed in historical context. Racist anxieties were not uncommon, and the habit of using cannabis of many among the migrants, despite its legal position, provided a useful pretext for the authorities to keep an eye on and to interfere with groups considered problematic largely because of the colour of their skin.

Outside of London arrests tended to fit the pattern familiar from previous decades where the policing of ports and sailors led to the detection of offences related to cannabis. For example, in 1954 in Swansea there was a large seizure of almost 5 lb of the drug. A sailor on the SS *Yoma* approached a car mechanic in Liverpool, Herman Silvester McKay, and let him know that he had the drug for sale and that it would be wisest if the latter met his ship in Swansea in order to buy it. This was agreed to, but the police got wind of the transaction and an ambush was arranged for McKay and his accomplice:

> They had walked about fifty yards when I approached them. As I did so I saw packets being thrown into the dock. I could not say which of them threw these packets into the dock. I ran on to Thompson and caught hold of him. He had his hand in the right hand pocket of his raincoat and was in the act of withdrawing something. I caught hold of his hand and took from him the package now produced. I tried to hold him but in trying to secure the package, he struggled and got away.

Officers were able to catch up with the purchasers and their driver, and all were arrested. McKay argued that 'I was not going to sell this gangia [*sic*]. I have been smoking it since I was 14 years of age. It was a family remedy for a bad chest. It grows like a bush in Jamaica. I was going to smoke it myself. I am very sorry about this. I know it was wrong to have this gangia in this country, but in my country we do not consider it in the serious light you look upon it'. He was sentenced to six months in prison.[55]

A similar case from the end of the decade again shows that those involved in the maritime trade were the source of cannabis for the more settled migrant communities. The supplier was a 'West Indian stoker' who lived in Liverpool, and his go-between in London was 'a 38 year old musician, of Leinster Road, Kilburn' and the driver was 'another coloured man, of Bonchurch Road, Notting Hill'. The *Daily Express* reported this story on 13 October 1959 under the headline 'Police Speed Up Anti-Drug Drive', declaring that 'the drive against dope peddlers in this country is being stepped up following recent disclosures of the extent of the drug traffic'. However, there is no evidence from the files that the Home Office or the other agencies concerned with policing the illicit traffic in drugs were stepping up an anti-drug drive. A Customs and Excise file related to the case covered by the *Daily Express* was full of correspondence, but not about the cannabis trade. The trouble caused by the arrest related to the legality of the Customs and Excise authorities seizing a car involved in the case that was in fact the property of a hire purchase company which wanted it back.[56]

A common theme in the reports of the police and the Drugs Branch was the observation that 'there has been [no] indication that the white population, male or female, is in danger of acquiring the habit'.[57] A report in 1947 for the Home Office noted a rare case where locals had been among those arrested for cannabis-related offences:

> The two white men were both of a 'Bohemian' character, one was an author and the other an artist; both dwelt in Chelsea, where there is a well-established coterie of drug-addicts, many of whom have criminal records.[58]

As the 1950s progressed, however, it became clear that members of the local population had grown curious about the habits of the migrants. Teresa Maher, the girlfriend of the murdered Joseph Aaku, confessed in the course of the trial of Backary Manneh that she had encountered cannabis while in the company of migrants and had even tried it once. Another case was of Kathleen Nora Jacobs, a 19-year-old unemployed waitress in Liverpool. She was arrested when she was observed 'behaving in an excited manner' and on a search of her bag she was found to have a small quantity of cannabis, estimated to be enough for three cigarettes. She confessed that she had obtained this 'from a public house frequented by men of colour'.[59]

A third example involved 'two young girls, a typist, and a shop assistant, aged only 17, residing at Northampton [who] made one or two visits to London to visit "modern music" dance clubs'. They evidently made friends at these venues as they exchanged letters with a man called Nwakanama, who they knew as Jimmy Demian.

> In one letter the typist asked Nwakanama to send her some 'doped cigarettes, reefers, marijuana or whatever you call the things', signing the letter in a false name and giving the other girl's address. Nwakanama replied to the letter, enclosing some Indian hemp, but the letter was intercepted by the girl's father, and the police informed. As a result a search warrant was obtained and in the man's flat a small quantity of Indian hemp and two letters from the girl typist were found. Nwakanama was arrested and eventually brought to trial at the Central Criminal Court on the 22nd November 1951. He did not avail himself of the services of counsel and stated in his defence that he did not smoke Indian hemp, alleging that the substance found in his room was put there by the police who made the search.[60]

It is not clear how wise his defence was, as he was sentenced to eighteen months' imprisonment. What is clear, however, is that such cases show that some of those that moved in the same circles as the migrant population were tempted enough to try the cannabis which was the customary indulgence of many of their new friends. While there is no evidence that consumers among the indigenous population were widespread or numerous in this period, such stories do point to an interface at which consumption of the drug was entering the social life of local communities from the migrant population.

There was little concern among the authorities in this period that cannabis was becoming a drug of choice outside of the usual groups of lascars and those of Commonwealth origin. When the issue of cannabis was raised at the Central Conference of Chief Constables which met on 21 November 1957 there seemed to be a calm sense that the matter was contained and under control. The Home Office sent a paper to the meeting in which it pointed to the increasing amount of cannabis seized and worried that there had been 'no corresponding rise in the number of convictions for offences relating to the drug'. The response of the senior officers present was robust:

> Chief Constables did not accept that the increased seizures indicated a grow-ing use of the drug in this country, nor that the decline in the number of prosecutions necessarily meant that police measures were less effective. It was agreed that arrangements should be made to inform Chief Constables of important seizures in their respective police areas and to distribute samples of cannabis for training purposes.[61]

By the time that the drug was next on the agenda at the Central Conference of Chief Constables, their tone had changed dramatically. It was not until late 1962 that senior officers again turned their attention to cannabis, and they met against a backdrop of newspaper headlines in which cannabis was called 'THE DEADLY MENACE IN AN INNOCENT CIGARETTE PACKET'. This time they were forced to admit that

> On the question of cannabis it was agreed that there had been a very consider-able increase in the misuse of this substance and in traffic in it. Whilst this increase was largely due to the increase in the coloured population in London, it was clear that the use of cannabis was spreading to white people, particularly young people. It was agreed that here also there was much more which could be done by the police if they had the men to do it.[62]

Conclusion

Nowhere in the story of cannabis and the British is it clearer than in this account of the period from the late 1940s to the early 1960s that debates about the drug were often about many things other than cannabis itself. Newspaper stories and books talked about cannabis while articulating the acute racial fears and political tensions of a population disrupted by the upheavals of the Second World War and unsettled by the transformations of the 1950s. Yet there were real changes occurring in this period in the control and consumption of cannabis hidden beneath the fanciful accounts of the drug given by the period's scaremongers. Migrants arriving from Britain's former colonies brought with them the habits of using the drug for recreational and therapeutic purposes that had been well documented by imperial administrators for over a century.[63] They encountered Customs officials and police officers who had been primed since the 1920s by the activities of a zealous Drugs Branch at the Home Office to prevent them from indulging these habits in Britain. However, they also encountered a growing interest among local youngsters in what the new arrivals might have to offer.

5

'Considered to be without medical justification': Science, Medicine, and Committees, 1945–1961

Introduction

In 1952 *The Lancet* published the conclusion of the third report of the World Health Organization's Expert Committee on Drugs Liable to Produce Addiction. It stated baldly that 'the use of cannabis preparations is considered to be without medical justification'[1] and was a clear message that *The Lancet* was happy to repeat. This brief statement in a medical journal draws attention to two key aspects of the British scientific and medical approach to cannabis in the immediate post-war period which will be considered in this chapter. The first is a conviction that cannabis had no useful application as a therapeutic substance, a conviction which was embellished by a sense that the drug was at the very least a dangerous intoxicant, at worst a source of addiction. The second is the relationship between the UK and wider international circles when it comes to opinions and information in scientific discussions about cannabis. This chapter will explore domestic medical understandings of preparations of the plant in the 1940s and the 1950s before going on to examine British relations with the emerging international agenda on cannabis in those decades.

British medicine and cannabis

A paper in the *British Medical Journal* (*BMJ*) of 1947 suggested that cannabis was to enjoy a post-war career as a therapeutic in the new form of synthetic tetrahydrocannabinols. G. Tayleur-Stockings was a specialist in psychological medicine and a former major in the Royal Army Medical Corps who served as the Ernest Hart memorial scholar of the British Medical Association after the war. He was intrigued by the potential of 'the new synthetic cannabis-like derivatives of the dibenzopyran class' that had been developed in the USA earlier in the 1940s and had been picked up by the Roche Research Department in the UK.[2] It was his belief that depression was simply a physiological manifestation of thalamic dysfunction and he reasoned that, as with other bodily complaints, an agent might be available that could address the various disease conditions. He was aware that 'during the last century attempts were made to utilize the euphorigenic properties of cannabis in the treatment of depressive states, but these were found to be unsatisfactory for various reasons: chief of these was the difficulty of obtaining reliable and stable preparations of this drug'.[3] As such, the availability of the new synthesized pharmacological product promised the possibility of the euphorigenic properties without the unpredictability of organic hemp resin.

He set up experiments with one of the new compounds, synhexl, on himself and a group of fifty depressive patients. Typical experiences were as follows:

A woman aged 52, with thalamic dysfunction of conversion hysteria type. She had a history of depression for 18 months following evacuation during the flying-bomb raids and an accident to her son. She had also had a previous depressive attack 28 years ago. On examination she was depressed, tense, emotional and anxious. Her main complaints were of insomnia, inability to face up to her household duties, and a persistent neuralgic pain located under the left breast. Physical findings were completely negative. A few weeks previously she received seven applications of ECT [Electro-Convulsive Therapy] with slight improvement but speedy relapse. The response to 30mg of synhexl was immediate; she lost her anxiety and depression, said she felt much brighter, and the thoracic pain became less insistent and distressing.

The author concluded that thirty-six of the fifty patients in the experiment showed improvement, by which he meant 'amelioration of mood, as shown subjectively by clinical evidence of diminution of retardation, anxiety, and inward preoccupation; increased zest for and interest in work and occupation; and increased psychotherapeutic rapport'. He was confident that 'we have in this class of compounds a promising therapeutic agent for the treatment of chronic and intractable depressive states'.[4] The editorial response in the *BMJ* to this article indicated that others were not so sure. It acknowledged that 'the more severe disorders of mood make up a large part of general practice' and as such a convincing therapy would be of great use. On the subject of synhexl it reminded readers that 'it is to be hoped that we shall not forget that it treats only the symptoms and not causes'. It conceded, however, that 'since results with other substances, such as Benzedrine, are usually disappointing synhexl may be worth further study'.[5]

Those who agreed that synthetic cannabinoids were worth further study included Cyril Stansfield Parker and Fred Wrigley who wrote to *The Lancet* in 1947 to report the effects of self-administration of synhexl: 'emotional apathy was pronounced, and in the face of another person's danger there was complete detachment—e.g. a small child running around a room holding a large jagged piece of glass in its mouth did not create a feeling of apprehension'.[6] Parker was a senior assistant medical officer at Whittingham Mental Hospital and Wrigley was the director of clinical research at Roche Products. They continued with their work after this report and published a more detailed paper in the *Journal of Mental Science* in 1950. They dosed patients using synhexl supplied by Roche, and found that 'there is nothing arising from this trial that would justify the claim that Synhexl is a potent substance for the relief of cases of melancholia and endogenous depression'.[7] This echoed a similarly unenthusiastic article of 1948 in which D. A. Pond had reported that 'no evidence that the drug is valuable as a treatment for depression was obtained'.[8] By 1955 a report in *The Lancet* on the treatment of depression using drugs made no mention of cannabis-based substances at all, discussing instead the use of amphetamines, barbiturates, and chlorpromazine.[9]

The story of synhexl sits in the wider context of the period as the post-war years were a time when it was assumed that for every ailment there was likely to be a pharmacological therapy.[10] The antibiotic discoveries of the Second World War had bathed medicine in a glow of success and other events of the period, such as the space race, lent science as a whole the aura of being the key to a better future. Indeed, depression was one of the chief targets of the period and all manner of synthesized chemical products were tried out as therapies for it. Another feature of the period, which is evident in the story of synhexl, is the rise of the pharmaceutical company. These were quickly to become key players in the development of markets for medicinal products and clearly Roche was eager to test the potential of synthetic cannabinoids. It seems that in the wake of the Second World War, an old medicine was caught up in the developments of a new era of scientific experimentation, and briefly featured in the race of the pharmaceutical companies to find treatments for psychological conditions such as depression which became suddenly urgent in this decade.[11]

The evidence from elsewhere in this period points to a clear sense that, apart from this early flurry of interest in synthetic cannabinoids, British medicine in the 1940s and 1950s felt that cannabis was of little significance as a therapeutic substance. On the rare occasions that it was discussed in the medical journals, it was as a dangerous intoxicant. When *The Lancet* briefly alluded to cannabis in 1946 it was to echo the reporting of the medical press of the 1930s which, as Chapter 2 showed, was often content to do no more than summarize events related to the drug at the League of Nations. This had been replaced after 1945 with the United Nations, and its Advisory Committee on Traffic in Opium and other Dangerous Drugs had reported that 'indian hemp, in the form of hashish, was seized in considerable quantities in Egypt, and in the form of marihuana cigarettes in North and South America, while Palestine was not immune to the traffic'.[12] In 1949 *The Lancet* published a report by J. D. Fraser, a Glasgow-trained doctor who was now the deputy-medical superintendent at Whittingham Hospital in Lancashire. He wrote of his experiences as a major in the Royal Army Medical Corps in the Second World War, during which time 'several cases of acute psychosis associated with the withdrawal of cannabis indica from addicts came to my notice'. He had served in Asia and had dealt with Indian troops and altogether he saw nine cases, all of which occurred within four weeks of leaving for a tour of duty.

> A common history was that the man had been on guard duty and had suddenly begun to blaze away with his rifle or Sten gun at an imaginary enemy. This sort of conduct resulted in the man being brought under medical observation; and the strange, and often dangerous fact was that by the time he got back to a medical unit he had become quiet and apparently rational . . . patients have been returned to their units during this quiet phase with disastrous results . . . patients shouted and talked at great length, interfered with other patients, and

were very quarrelsome. They stripped themselves of all clothing and mastur-
bated almost continuously; their habits became filthy, faeces and urine being
passed in the bed or on the floor... at times most of the patients appeared to
be visually and aurally hallucinated and the hallucinations were terrifying.

The upshot of all of this was that the men were sedated after which they
became quiet and co-operative, although weak. They were all sent back to
India. While the author felt that this showed that 'it is clear that some
cannabis-indica addicts cannot manage without the drug', he did feel
compelled to qualify his position: 'it seemed that the proportion of addicts
who developed this illness was comparatively small; certainly there were far
more than nine ganja addicts in Indian units at which I was stationed'.[13]

   The negative representation of cannabis and its users was compounded in
the same edition of the journal by a review of the book by Pablo Wolff that
had featured at the trial for murder of Backary Manneh which was discussed
in Chapter 4. The reviewer cheerfully reproduced the gory stories from the
volume which had reported that 'marihuana parties may be held, sometimes
as religious rites of secret societies in which a convivial exhilaration among
the guests at the start is apt to give place to hallucinatory excitement, uproar,
strife and exhausted sleep'. While one expert witness at the murder trial,
Dr Robert Donald Teare, had been sceptical about Wolff's book, the
reviewer uncritically repeated its claims and endorsed its assessment:

> His concern at the general picture must be generally shared, for this drug
> destroys the addict's relation to society and makes him a member of a special
> class of vicious and delinquent characters. There are more ways of killing a
> man with hemp than hanging him.[14]

More stories from abroad followed. In 1951 *The Lancet* summarized a news
item from the *New York Times* with the headline 'Drug Addiction
in America'. It detailed evidence collected by Nathaniel Goldstein, the
attorney-general in New York, of

> the widespread use of drugs—marihuana, cocaine, heroin, and amphet-
> amine—by boys and girls in the high schools of the city. Some of these
> children acquire the habit at ages as early as 12 or 13, usually beginning by
> smoking marihuana cigarettes—'reefers'—which are sold to them by older
> children in the school.

A sad picture of entrapment followed as 'the inquiry revealed clearly the
stages in which addiction is acquired: a reefer or a "snort" of cocaine is given

free at first, then a moderate charge is made; once the child becomes an addict prices rise'. Comfort was offered by this report in *The Lancet* though, as it included news that a meeting of police officers from thirty-six countries had convened in Lisbon where it was agreed that they would intensify the safeguards against smuggling of narcotics by air.[15] Presumably, the startlingly racist note in a report of the following year was also meant to comfort the British readers of the journal:

> Undesirable as the drug may be, its addicts are apparently drawn only from socially and economically depressed classes who find in it some measure of escape from drab reality or use it to enhance the normal fantasy-weaving of adolescence. In the New York reports, most of the addicts were young Negroes or Puerto Ricans, and it is doubtful whether the drug would have much appeal to a normal well-adjusted person.[16]

There was no mention of the drug in the *BMJ* after the Second World War until the publication of Donald McIntosh Johnson's book in 1952.[17] It was reviewed in July of that year by Ethel Browning, a toxicologist and expert in industrial medicine. She made it clear that she was under the impression that 'marihuana and hashish cannot be regarded in the true medical sense as drugs of addiction, since they do not cause withdrawal symptoms or lead to addiction to other drugs'. However, she did note that 'some investigators have suggested that by their capacity to produce maniacal states they may be a causative factor in major crimes and sexual offences, and that their prolonged use leads to physical and mental degeneracy'. In considering Johnson's book, she lamented that 'the author is not content with factual evidence' and concluded that

> The suggestion that our imports of grain and flour from the Soviet Union may constitute a form of drug warfare, intended to condition our mentality to receptiveness to totalitarian propaganda, is scarcely worthy of inclusion in a publication which claims to be at any rate 'semi-scientific'.[18]

A review of the book in *The Lancet* was similarly unimpressed by Johnson's 'series of imaginative flights'.[19] This was despite the fact that it had just published one of them, a short account of his unusual thesis that a recent outbreak of food poisoning in France was not down to ergot fungi, which was the official explanation, but was instead to be blamed on cannabis.[20]

The rest of the decade continued in a similar vein as cannabis was only ever contemplated in the medical journals in relation to the consumption of intoxicants rather than in discussions of potential medicines. Regular summaries of United Nations reports about drug addiction included brief allusions to cannabis. One author in the *BMJ* had ploughed through the publications of the Permanent Central Opium Board to the Economic and Social Council of the United Nations, but noted simply that 'millions of people consume cannabis (Hashish, bhang, marihuana etc.)' without passing any comment.[21] A digest of the Home Office report to the United Nations in the same journal in 1957 remarked that 'most of the trafficking in cannabis goes on in London. Of the 103 convictions for unlawfully possessing or dealing in the drug, about 60 per cent were for offences in the Metropolitan Police District, and most of the offenders were men of Asiatic, West African, or West Indian origin'.[22]

Even in the rare instances where first-hand experience of the drug informed discussions in the medical press, the focus was on recreational consumers and 'addiction'. A letter in 1959 exclaimed that 'I have just read with great interest Dr Maurice Partridge's excellent article on "Addiction to Drugs"...I was disappointed however to find no mention of cannabis indica'. It went on:

> This drug numbers its addicts today in tens of millions. In certain parts of India, for example, the majority of the people either smoke or eat it, whilst in Africa, South America and the Far East it is scarcely less popular...its use appears to be spreading too amongst Europeans and Americans, not only in their own countries but also in those countries where the plant is indigenous. The present expense and difficulty in obtaining abroad the more traditional alcoholic stimulants may have induced Europeans to adopt this pernicious drug, which can be obtained merely by snatching some leaves as one drives along a country road.[23]

As the author was based in Assam it is difficult to know whether to read this letter as a report of growing cannabis consumption amongst expatriate Westerners in Asia or as a complaint about the price of drink in India.

Further stories at the time suggested that it was not just in South Asia that the British were taking to locally grown ganja. In October 1959 the legal correspondent of the *BMJ* noticed a case that had gone to trial in Cardiff and had resulted in nine months' imprisonment for two offenders. Reuben Ritchie and John Luton of Tiger Bay had managed to harvest 6 lb of cannabis from an unused allotment there that had been sown with budgerigar seed, and the potency of the batch was ascribed to the 'dry warm summer' of that year. The report noted that

It was stated on behalf of each of the accused that they were not members of a 'sinister international drug ring'. One had taken to smoking the hemp medicinally to relieve pain. The other had been given the drug as a very young man and had been unable to break the habit; he grew the drug only for his own use.[24]

This was followed in 1961 by a similar story from Kingston upon Thames. Jonathan Gabriel Phillips was an 18-year-old who was arrested there by police and was found in possession of fifty cigarettes made from Indian hemp. When they searched his home, 'a tumbledown chalet by the river Mole', police found a quantity of the drug and also seed. Phillips claimed that 'he had only grown the hemp for himself'.[25] Such occasional stories and small seizures sat in contrast with the figures of the Permanent Central Opium Board's report of 1961, reproduced in the *BMJ*, which stated that 2,000 kg had been seized in the USA in that year alone.[26]

A trawl through the medical press of the 1940s and 1950s therefore shows that for much of this period there was no interest in cannabis for its therapeutic potential. The occasional mentions of the drug in the medical journals were in connection with its properties as an intoxicant and its potential as a source of 'addiction'. These occasional mentions were as likely to draw on stories or reports from abroad as they were on information from within the UK. However, the question of cannabis 'addiction' did receive a fuller airing in Britain in the closing years of the decade.

Addiction and the Brain Committee

By the 1950s there was an unease growing at both the Home Office and the Ministry of Health about the British approach to the whole question of drug addiction. This was first set out three decades earlier, when the Rolleston Committee on Morphine and Heroin Addiction had reported in 1926. It established the approach of treating addicts as a medical problem rather than a criminal one. The Committee recommended gradual withdrawal of the drug as the preferred treatment, but also condoned the continued administration of morphine or heroin to those who 'while capable of leading a useful and fairly normal life so long as he takes a certain non-progressive quantity, usually small, of the drug of addiction, ceases to be able to do so when the regular allowance is withdrawn'.[27] It did not consider cannabis at any point in its deliberations.

New circumstances in the 1950s had caused some to question the adequacy of the Rolleston Committee's position. T. C. Green of the Home Office wrote in 1956 to a colleague in the Ministry of Health in order to point out that 'we have been taking stock on a number of drugs questions which have been causing us some difficulty over a long period and I think the time has now come to ask for your views on these points'. Among the issues raised was the 'evergrowing list of exotic drugs designated by lengthy polysyllabic names' that was being produced by pharmaceutical companies and the necessity for administrative arrangements to regulate these. Another was the method of treatment of drug addiction which had been advocated back in the 1920s. Significantly, the Home Office had been alarmed by reports from abroad that 'the assumption that it may not be possible with safety to discontinue entirely the use of a drug on account of the severity of the withdrawal symptoms is no longer accepted by doctors in Canada and the United States'.[28] It was agreed that a new expert group should be convened to review the situation.

The Interdepartmental Committee on Drug Addiction first met in June 1958 with Sir Russell Brain in the chair. He was a neurologist who had served as president of the Royal College of Physicians from 1950 until 1957, was an acting consultant at the London Hospital and the Maida Vale Hospital for Nervous Diseases and was an experienced committee man, having served on the Royal Commission on Marriage and Divorce. The new committee's remit included two tasks: 'to review, in the light of more recent developments, the advice given by the Departmental Committee on Morphine and Heroin Addiction in 1926; to consider whether any revised advice should also cover other drugs liable to produce addiction or to be habit-forming'.[29] Unlike previous reports where the term 'addiction' had been used without any attempt to define it, the Committee took care to provide an explanation of what it was talking about. 'Addiction', in the view of its members, was 'a state of periodic or chronic intoxication produced by the repeated consumption of a drug (natural or synthetic)' and its characteristics were 'an overpowering desire or need (compulsion) to continue taking the drug and to obtain it by any means', 'a psychological and physical dependence on the effects of the drug', and 'an effect detrimental to the individual and to society'. It was distinct from 'drug habituation' which resulted in 'a desire (but not a compulsion) to continue taking the drug for the sense of improved well-being which it engenders' and 'some degree of psychological dependence on the effect of the drug, but

absence of physical dependence'.[30] Although cannabis had never been
mentioned in the discussions that led to the establishment of the Committee, it was decided that preparations of the plant ought to be considered.
After all, they were included in the Dangerous Drugs Act, although the
Home Office was aware that 'cannabis is treated differently from Part III
drugs for the purpose of the Act; it is an offence to be in unauthorised
possession of this substance as it is also an offence to be in possession of other
dangerous drugs, but doctors are not allowed to prescribe raw resin'.[31]

Cannabis cropped up rather belatedly in the life of the Brain Committee.
It was not until October 1959, at the third meeting of that year, that the
drug was mentioned in connection with a broader discussion of how addicts
in general were identified in Britain. The answer emerged that there were
two key routes by which they came to the notice of the authorities. The first
was via police inspections of dangerous drugs registers at pharmacists etc.
where large or regular prescriptions pointed to a habitual consumer. The
other was through the courts where the police prosecuted those found
illegally in possession of proscribed substances. It was in connection with
the latter that cannabis came into focus as it was not available at pharmacists.
The Committee noted that 'arising out of this, the question of addiction to
Indian hemp was raised. It has little or no medical use and it is doubtful
whether it leads to addiction in the sense generally understood. The Home
Office representatives will prepare a summary of the information available
about the use and abuse of the substance. A reference will be made to the
question in the final Report'.[32]

This summary finally appeared for the consideration of the Committee
two months later, in the middle of December 1959.[33] The document noted
that 'the improper use of cannabis has not been a serious problem in Great
Britain' although recent increases in seizures suggested that 'quantitively [sic]
the problem may properly be described as the most serious aspect of narcotic
control in Great Britain at the present time'. It argued that this was down to
'coloured persons who have come from the West Indies, Asia or Africa
[who] seem to regard the use of the drug as part of their normal way of life'.
It addressed directly the key question facing the group in stating that, 'as the
Committee will be aware, no medical evidence is available to show that an
addiction to cannabis . . . is aroused in those who smoke reefers'. However,
it pointed to a further matter of potential interest to the Committee in
alerting it to 'reports [that] suggest that heroin addicts also smoke cannabis

and there are some grounds for thinking that the smoking of reefers preceded the resort to heroin'.

The Committee's response to this evidence was a discussion at the next meeting in the following February. They agreed that 'on present evidence addiction to cannabis did not lead to more serious forms of addiction' and that 'the substance had little or no medical use and was not likely to be prescribed'. They also asked if the Commissioner of the Metropolitan Police could get hold of an experienced inspector to give evidence on the subject as members of the Committee felt that they wanted more information to substantiate the claim that the bulk of supplies was used by 'coloured people'.[34] The Commissioner offered an inspector, but argued that he was unlikely to add much to the Home Office memorandum and would only be able to speak of London. The Committee decided not to bother.[35] There was no further discussion of cannabis until the drafting of the report began. The first draft to include any allusion to the drug stated simply that 'we can form no accurate estimate of the extent to which the illicit indulgence in preparations of cannabis indica is being practised in this country. Social implications may arise, but there is no evidence that they constitute a medical problem'.[36] This had been prepared by Dr R. Goulding and Mr W. G. Honnor, the secretaries of the Committee.[37] The section was discussed by members in June, and the minutes of the meeting stated of the cannabis issue that 'although this is not a medical problem it is a matter of much concern socially e.g. to parents. Should the report say more on the subject?' In answering its own question the Committee decided that 'the report should say that cannabis is not a drug of addiction in the strict sense of the word, and explain that the social consequences of its misuse are not within the Committee's terms of reference'.[38] The final report contained a paragraph that was the outcome of this discussion:

> In our view cannabis is not a drug of addiction: it is an intoxicant. Nevertheless it comes within the scope of the Dangerous Drugs Act, 1951. But having virtually no place in therapeutics it is obtained almost solely through illicit channels and there has been some rise in the annual amount seized by the Customs authorities. We have not received evidence that its use constitutes a medical problem. Even if its social consequences should give rise to concern, which we would share with the authorities who are responsible for the suppression of traffic in this drug, we see no indication for further administrative measures within our own terms of reference.[39]

The records do not make it clear which member, or members, of the Committee took the initiative in driving the brief discussion of cannabis during the drafting of the report. It is evident that this initiative was significant, however. After all, the Committee had bandied about the phrase 'addiction to cannabis' in its February meeting and yet had been careful by June to make the precise statement that there was no such thing. The intercession to amend the content of the report on cannabis also suggests a sensitivity to perceived public opinion on the drug. This sensitivity seems to have prompted the Committee to explain that it was not a subject that was within its remit in order to head off accusations that it had ignored or avoided the subject. Because it is not possible to state from the minutes of the Committee exactly who took part in the discussion on cannabis and who was responsible for driving the agreed position, it is difficult to say what considerations shaped the latter. However, it is clear that by the time the report was signed on 30 November 1960, the government's expert committee on addiction was agreed that cannabis was not addictive.

The UN, the WHO, and cannabis to 1955

The Brain Committee was not the only such expert group to be sat in the 1950s considering drugs in general and cannabis in particular. After the Second World War the United Nations (UN) assumed the role of the League of Nations in formulating and operating the international regulatory framework for narcotic drugs. It gathered masses of information from across countries and continents while acting as both a forum and an agent for the emergence of agreed approaches to a heterodox array of substances. Increasingly, it was decisions and pronouncements made in the various committees of the UN and the World Health Organization (WHO) that shaped attitudes towards cannabis in government and scientific circles around the globe.

The Government of the UK positioned itself to play a key role in the emergence of the post-war international drugs regulatory system as the British found a genuine enthusiasm for the rapid re-establishment of such machinery for dealing with drugs in 1945. A note from Philip Noel-Baker, then minister of state at the Foreign Office, admitted that 'the Government of India, and we, ourselves, now desire not to be obstructionist in any way whatever and that we want to make the most rapid progress that is possible' to the extent that 'very radical international solutions' might be considered.[40] The UK was named as one of the ten permanent members of the Commission on Narcotic Drugs, the successor to the Advisory Committee on Traffic in Opium and Other Dangerous Drugs. Major Coles, a veteran of the Drugs Branch of the Home Office, was despatched to serve as the UK representative to the Commission.[41]

The Commission on Narcotic Drugs was appointed at the first meeting of the UN Economic and Social Council in New York in 1946[42] and one of its earliest actions was to broaden its remit: the Paris Protocol of 1948 brought the wide range of new synthetic drugs that had emerged during the 1940s under existing controls on the advice of the WHO. The Commission did not neglect more long-standing interests, however, and quickly attempted to impose a worldwide monopoly on opium.[43] This met with some resistance on the part of the world's opium producers and was eventually watered down in the 1953 Protocol on Opium, which never actually came into force.[44] The chief concern of the Commission throughout the 1950s was to come up with a simplified system to replace the various treaties devised in the 1920s and 1930s and the Single Convention on Narcotic Drugs of 1961 was eventually to satisfy this ambition.

The confusion and curiosity in international policy circles about cannabis in the interwar period was replicated early in the 1950s. As Chapter 3 demonstrated, the Sub-Committee on Cannabis established by the League of Nations in the 1930s had petered out due to the outbreak of hostilities. During its six years of collecting information and opinions the Sub-Committee only managed to conclude that 'certain points still require clarification, especially in connection with the physiological and psychological and psychopathic effects of cannabis and with the relationships between hashish addiction and insanity and between cannabis addiction and addiction to other drugs especially heroin'.[45] Perhaps because so little progress had been made in the 1930s towards a clear and agreed approach to the drug, the issue of cannabis remained largely neglected at the UN in its early years. The Progress Report on the Work of the Division of Narcotic Drugs for the period between May 1949 and March 1950 noted that 'the Division's preoccupations with the many matters with which the present report deals, coupled with the absence of its officials on missions, have made it impossible to give the studies on cannabis as much attention as would have been desirable'. It noted that Professor Bouquet, who had sat on the Sub-Committee on Cannabis in the 1930s, had been contacted by the Division and that it had also been at pains to collect much of the information of the previous decade on the chemical nature of cannabis. It also noted a recent report in *The Lancet* on withdrawal symptoms in cannabis addicts. However, it gave the sense that matters related to the drug were proceeding much as they had in the 1930s, at a leisurely pace in which the collection of information seemed to be the central objective.[46]

The Secretary-General of the Commission quickly changed the pace of action on cannabis with the first draft of the proposed single convention on narcotic drugs which was unveiled in 1950. It had been agreed that his office should prepare this to get the ball rolling on the process of agreeing a single convention.[47] When the Secretariat presented its ideas on 27 February 1950 the proposals for cannabis were radical. Two alternative approaches to the substance were on offer. Both assumed that recreational consumption was bad and ought to be rigorously discouraged. However, the first alternative also worked on the assumption that cannabis had no legitimate medical use that could not be met by other 'less dangerous substances'. It proposed that the production of Indian hemp be entirely prohibited save for those small amounts necessary for scientific experimentation.

The second alternative worked on the assumption that cannabis did have legitimate medical uses. In this case each national state would have to establish a monopoly which had the exclusive right to produce cannabis and trade in it. Each government would be expected to select from a range of measures to ensure that no cannabis leaked out of the system into 'illicit traffic', measures that included starting state-run cannabis farms and the systematic uprooting of wild plants. In countries where there was significant consumption of cannabis products for recreational purposes, it was proposed that 'a reservation' be made that allowed the continued production of cannabis for this market. However, this was on the strict condition that this reservation would 'cease to be effective unless renewed by annual notification made to this effect and accompanied by a description of the progress in the preceding year towards the abolition of such non-medical use and by an explanation of the continued reasons for the temporary retention of such use'.[48] In other words, the starting point for discussions had cut through the patient dithering over voluminous and contradictory evidence which had marked the League of Nations approach and that of the early United Nations. It boldly asserted that all non-medical consumption of cannabis was harmful and proposed that countries where recreational use was common should be obliged to tackle the habit among their people.

Indeed, the possibility that cannabis was entirely useless as a medicine had also been formally recognized in the draft treaty, although only as an option. This draft was considered at the fifth session of the Commission on Narcotic Drugs at New York on Friday, 1 December 1950.

It is not difficult to explain why this firm stance on cannabis was taken as William McAllister has argued that an 'inner circle' of control-advocates was in the ascendant at the UN in the late 1940s and early 1950s and was determined to set a 'radical' agenda on questions related to narcotics.[49] However, the report of the fifth session of the Commission on Narcotic Drugs which discussed the draft convention shows that national delegates did not immediately agree on which of the two options to back: 'many members of the Commission thought that Indian hemp drugs have no medical value and, consequently, expressed themselves in favour of the first alternative . . . other members did not share this view and gave preference to the second alternative'. The records of this meeting show that the representative of the USSR took the initiative to secure the first alternative which was for total prohibition. He was supported by Egypt, Turkey, and Mexico among others but France and the Netherlands were chief among those that resisted. The latter argued that it preferred to leave to its physicians the freedom to choose between medicines, and so therefore favoured control rather than prohibition. The former was also concerned about prohibiting a therapeutic which was currently recommended by the French Academy of Medicine. Iran and India voiced their opinion that 'the question should be thoroughly studied before any decision was taken' and the representative of the USA concurred.[50] The attempt to take decisive action on cannabis by the Secretariat stalled, as the Commission concluded that before agreement was likely, 'it would be necessary to undertake more studies in order to determine whether the control measures proposed in the second version of Section 33 or any other measures would, in practice, prove effective'.[51] Indeed, the misgiving that 'a rigid limitation of the use of drugs under control to exclusively medical and scientific needs does not sufficiently take into consideration long established customs and traditions which persist in particular in territories of the Middle and Far East and which it is impossible to abolish by a simple decree of prohibition' seemed to suggest that even the attempt to impose consensus on recreational, non-medical use was to be challenged.[52]

With the issue of cannabis once again deferred for more information, the Secretary-General of the Commission on Narcotic Drugs wearily reported in 1953 that 'there are a number of major difficulties inherent in the problem of Indian hemp which makes it very hard to decide what measures would be most effective in leading to its solution'.[53] It noted among these the lack of agreement on its medical value, the traditions of recreational and ritual use in parts of the world, the industrial use of the plant, and its ready availability in wild and remote areas. The Secretariat proposed a number of new studies and it is interesting to glimpse the ways in which their call for more information carried within it a presumption about the outcome of this gathering process. The Secretary-General's note was prepared for the consideration of the Commission as follows:

> The Commission may wish to give the Secretariat instructions on the scope of these studies and to formulate more precisely the subject-matter which they should include. It is thought that the studies fall naturally into two categories as follows:
>
> 1. Those that address themselves to the factual situation;
> 2. Those that aim at evaluating and interpreting that situation with a view to adjusting the present control regime for Indian hemp which has become outmoded by changing circumstances to present day condition.

So that everyone was clear that the 'present day condition' was an unhappy one, the Secretariat included in its note a couple of statements. It began with the observation that seizures in 1951 were over ten times those of 1945. The UK was then used as an example of a country that was experiencing 'increased use of Indian hemp as a pleasure drug' and the government's report to the UN was quoted as showing 'there has been a considerable increase in the traffic in Indian hemp in recent years, so that this drug now accounts for more than half the seizures made by H.M. Customs'. This was a particularly selective reading of the cannabis situation in the UK at this time, as it will be recalled from the previous chapter that Home Office officials in 1952 were content that 'the picture is as before, a small drug problem kept within narrow bounds by a rigid system of control . . . there is still no sign of a widespread, organized traffic, of violent crime arising from the habit, or of the white inhabitants taking to the habit to any degree'.[54] Indeed, at the next meeting of the Commission the UK delegate made a point of protesting that 'the smoking of Indian hemp was still a new and relatively minor problem in his country'.[55] Nevertheless, the selective reading of the situation in the UK, when taken together with the tone of the Secretariat's note, leaves the impression that the proposal to seek more information about cannabis was not driven by a sense that the issue was an open one, but rather was based on a feeling that more evidence was needed for the prosecution. The Secretariat's proposed call for information was approved by the Commission at its meeting in 1953, which was particularly keen for data on the 'physical and mental effects of the use of Indian hemp' and which agreed that the term 'cannabis' ought to replace Indian hemp in all future discussions and regulations.[56]

In gathering the research on cannabis the Secretariat decided to target countries where cannabis use was common. The WHO was given the responsibility of tackling the survey of the physical and mental health issues. This recognized the previous efforts of the WHO's Expert Committee on Habit-Forming Drugs to cut through the confusion on cannabis. Established in 1949, this Committee met for only five days in that year and for the same in 1950 and 1952 before declaring that

> It was of opinion that cannabis preparations are practically obsolete. So far as it can see, there is no justification for the medical use of cannabis preparations.[57]

The vice-chair of the 1952 meeting was R. N. Chopra, the expert who had represented British India at the League of Nations meetings before the Second World War and who now represented independent India as the director of the Drug Research Laboratory at Srinigar in Kashmir. Among the other members was the British expert J. R. Nicholls of the Government Laboratory in London and the American N. B. Eddy of the National Institutes of Health in Bethesda. This group had provided a clear and definitive position on the therapeutic use of cannabis, and this was as negative as could be. It was also on the advice of this committee that the term 'cannabis' came to replace 'Indian hemp' in UN discussions and regulations.[58]

The Commission returned to the issue of cannabis on 22 April 1954 as the Secretariat was keen to draw attention to the WHO's 'clear-cut position in the matter [that] there was no justification for the medical use of cannabis preparations'. The representative of the Secretariat did concede that preparations of the plant remained in the pharmacopoeia of a number of countries, but was quick to confirm that it was not mentioned in many others. The WHO representative at the meeting piped up to point out that presence in the pharmacopoeia was not evidence of actual usage.[59] He reiterated that 'from a medical point of view it could be said that cannabis preparations no longer served any useful purpose'. The British representative returned to the issue of corn-plasters that had haunted the country's position on cannabis since the 1920s, before Harry Anslinger[60] of the USA made his nation's position plain: 'stocks held by pharmacies in the United States had been turned over to the public authorities upon enactment of the Cannabis Tax Act. Cannabis was no longer used in the country'. It only remained for Mr Yates of the Secretariat to confirm that

> he agreed with the WHO representative that for all practical purposes cannabis preparations were no longer necessary. The mention in various pharmacopoeia showed, however, that there was still a residual situation to clear up, including the use of cannabis for veterinary purposes.

The chairman, the French representative, proposed that a resolution be drawn up to recognize the emerging consensus at the Commission that cannabis had no legitimate medical use. Those present endorsed the proposal. The Commission now had a clear position on the medical use of cannabis which it had taken straight from the WHO's work in the previous year. It was a position taken by the Commission without any clear sense of what evidence the WHO had used, and without recourse to any scientific data of its own.[61]

South Africa was the first to respond to the Secretariat's earlier call for more information from countries where cannabis use was common. It sent in an extended version of a report it had previously submitted in 1952 to the WHO.[62] The authorities in South Africa had a long history that stretched back into the nineteenth century of concern about cannabis consumption among both the Asian and African communities there. Indeed, it was a report from the Union of South Africa in 1923 that had placed cannabis for the first time on the League of Nations drug control agenda.[63] As such it was not surprising to find that their position was a negative one. Delegates at the meeting who discussed the document were especially struck by reports of cannabis users who were as young as 7, and by the fact that a staggering 229 tons of cannabis had been seized in 1952. Harry Anslinger launched into an attack on the South African Government for being too lenient in its approach, claiming that 'it was regrettable that the police did not pay more attention to drug addiction and illicit traffic and that there was not a special narcotics police division in the Union'. This despite the fact that 18,000 prosecutions for cannabis offences had been made there in 1952. Only the Indian delegate was intrigued by reports of use of preparations of the plant in South Africa's indigenous medical systems and he asked for more information about consumption of the drug there at social and ceremonial occasions.[64]

Cannabis and non-Western medicines

When the Commission met in 1955 it was greeted with new evidence on cannabis from the WHO and others. The Greek representative submitted a statement to the Commission on the question of cannabis that included the following assertions: 'there is a relation between the degree of unemployment and the use of charas, especially in the case of the eastern peoples' and 'apart from the permanent disturbance of their mental faculties, charas users have a propensity to crime and rapidly become dangerous criminals'.[65] He included no evidence to support his statements and provided no references to studies that had formed his position. His document was accompanied by something rather more significant. The WHO submitted its definitive statement on *The Physical and Mental Effects of Cannabis* for consideration. It was authored by Pablo Osvaldo Wolff, a former secretary of the Expert Committee on Addiction-Producing Drugs of the WHO. It was damning in its revelations and in its tone, and drew on over fifty publications and scientific papers to support its argument. He was scarcely interested in its physical effects, referring readers to previous publications by Bouquet that made it clear that 'among cannabis smokers diseases of the respiratory tract are frequent, bilharsiasis and circulatory as well as alimentary diseases become refractory etc.'. It was with its mental effects that he was most concerned. He ranged widely across the work of others and lifted their observations on varied conditions such as 'transitory intoxication', 'mania from hasheesh', 'acute psychosis associated with the withdrawal of cannabis indica from addicts' or 'a certain link between chronic cannabis consumption and the atypical schizophrenic picture'. He made it clear that he had no time for those who would 'minimise the importance of smoking marihuana'. As such he went beyond his remit to outline the social impacts of cannabis use, quoting reports from Greece, South Africa, Puerto Rico, and Mexico which insisted that 'cannabis apparently brings to the surface of the subconscious vices and tendencies which have been submerged by education and environment'.

As these reports were thin on actual examples and instances, Wolff drew on his collection of 'clippings from newspapers from South American countries which suffer particularly from the consequences of marihuana abuse, and which the writer has been collecting for years'. Clearly conscious of how tenuous this looked, he was forced to admit that these were 'somewhat sensational' in character, but he made a point of insisting that the recurrence of such stories, as well as the police statements referred to within them 'show that there must be much truth in them'. Having done this, he did not hesitate to select the most startling of the stories, including a case where the murder of a petrol station attendant by a group of 16-year-olds had been blamed on their cannabis consumption. Despite acknowledging the weakness of such evidence he left colleagues in no doubt about the 'criminogenic influence of the cannabis resin' and he concluded that 'cannabis constitutes a dangerous drug from every point of view, whether physical, mental, social or criminological'.[66]

The document is remarkable in its relentless insistence on that conclusion. Various criticisms have been made of the report and of the author. As stated in a previous chapter, his reliance on data from newspapers was regarded as sufficient to dismiss his views by a British doctor in a court of law who was asked to comment on his conclusions at the trial of Backery Manneh.[67] At least some of the work that he refers to is problematic, not least of all that by Anslinger, and by Warnock.[68] Whatever the shortcomings of Wolff's WHO document, it is important for this study as it shows that by the middle of the 1950s it was opponents of cannabis use who had control of its agenda, however outlandish their statements and dubious their evidence. When the Commission turned to the WHO for a definitive expert position from the medical authorities, it received a statement from one of most firmly established critics of the drug of the period. Mr Yates of the Secretariat commended Wolff's report to the Commission as he felt that it 'embodied not only a statement of the facts, but also a number of critical evaluations'.[69] The chair of the Commission, the French representative Charles Vaille, and Harry Anslinger were careful to publicly record their appreciation of Wolff's efforts. It was agreed that his account should be forwarded with the report of the Commission to its parent body, the UN's Economic and Social Council.[70]

The Commission had endorsed the WHO's position in 1954 that 'from a medical point of view it could be said that cannabis preparations no longer served any useful purpose'. With Wolff's report from the WHO at hand in

1955 the Secretariat was finally able to move the Commission to accept the first alternative of the draft single convention on cannabis that had been presented in 1950. Based on the premise that cannabis had no legitimate medical use that could not be met by other 'less dangerous substances', the Commission approved the proposal that the production of the plant for purposes of manufacturing drugs should be entirely prohibited save for those small amounts necessary for scientific experimentation.[71]

That was not quite the whole story, however, as the agreement included controversial exceptions for India. In 1955 that country's representative had arrived at the meeting to declare that

> his Government was unable at present to comply with [the] Council resolution . . . as cannabis was used in both the unani and ayurvedic systems of indigenous medicine, by which a very large proportion of the Indian population was treated. Unless the possibility of discontinuing the use of cannabis in these systems had been studied by the Indian medical faculties— and there had not been sufficient time for this since the Council issued its recommendation—immediate implementation of the recommendation was not possible. He wondered whether the World Health Organization or any other expert body had given consideration to the question of the utilization of cannabis in indigenous systems of medicine.[72]

The WHO's representative was caught on the hop. He replied that 'he was unable to state the position of his organization with regard to the use of cannabis in indigenous medicine' and contented himself by repeating the doctrine that 'cannabis should be abolished from all legitimate medical practice'. The Indian delegation insisted that the use of cannabis in non-Western systems of medicine should be acknowledged as legitimate and that exceptions would be required to allow for this. This position echoed that of the delegation's British predecessors at the Geneva Opium Conference in 1924/5. Any agreement on cannabis would have to work around South Asia's long experience of using preparations of the plant.[73]

The Indian effort to have practices in South Asia validated by the UN caused consternation. The Yugoslavian representative was worried about the effect of entering reservations, and the Mexican delegate insisted that 'his delegation in principle favoured total prohibition' as he was anxious that 'the danger that production permitted in exceptional cases might be exported to other countries must be avoided'. The representative of the USA was adamant that Asian therapeutic traditions should be dismissed as 'quasi-medical uses'. This provoked a fierce rebuke from the chief delegate of the Government of India:

> Indigenous systems of medicine such as the Ayurvedic and Unani systems which had been in existence in India on an organized basis for hundreds of years, and on which large sections of the population continue to depend for medical treatment, were just as much entitled to be called medical, and not quasi-medical, as the allopathic and homeopathic systems were. They did not become quasi-medical merely because they were not Western systems.[74]

Eventually the Government of India succeeded in forcing the UN to recognize as legitimate the production of cannabis for non-Western medical systems. In 1957 'the Commission adopted a compromise proposal whereby the abolition of the medical use of these substances, except in three indigenous medical systems—the Ayurvedic, Unani and Tibbi systems—was recommended to Governments'.[75] This was a significant achievement. The Indian delegates had frustrated the efforts of the Secretariat and the WHO to declare that cannabis was of no medical value whatsoever. They had also challenged the hegemonic assumptions of the Western-trained doctors of the WHO about the legitimacy of south Asian medical systems. It should be emphasized, however, that it was the interests of 'large firms which produced indigenous medicines'[76] that were being protected in India rather than those of the humble bazaar herbalist.

By 1957 the Commission had also moved on to consider the surveys of the cannabis situation that had been commissioned by the WHO back in 1953 and which had focused on the most important centres of consumption such as South Africa, India, Brazil, and Morocco.[77] Each of these reports conformed to a set format, so that data was collected from different contexts in order to be readily compared. The first set of questions related to the plant itself, the second to the industrial outputs from the plant. The third looked at the legal uses to which psychoactive preparations were put, the fourth to any international trade in cannabis plants, the fifth to medicinal use which was followed by details of non-medical use. The rest of the questionnaire focused on matters relating to illegal traffic, including surveillance and police measures. The surveys were designed to give a sense of what the existing legitimate interests were in the plant, and of the difficulties that were being experienced in controlling its illegitimate use.

As such most of the reports simply repeated the common mantra that possession and consumption of cannabis were illegal, that the police worked hard to arrest consumers and peddlers, and that traffic in the drug was troublesome. For example, the report from Brazil noted that 'cultivation of the cannabis plant is most prevalent in the northern and northeastern parts of the country' and that the traffic flowed from 'the backlander who cultivates the cannabis plant through the middleman to the ultimate users . . . Braganca, a city in Northern Brazil . . . is one of the largest centres of the cannabis traffic in that part of the country'. It assured readers that 'as the State and Federal authorities are fully aware of the existence of the illicit traffic in and use of cannabis in Brazil and as they know the places where these mainly occur, their concerted drive against the spread of the traffic in and use of the drug has not slackened'. However, the report was forced to admit that such was the extent of consumption that it was 'not possible to give even a rough estimate of the number of maconha smokers in Brazil'.[78] The report from Southern Rhodesia similarly intoned that 'police patrol all native areas regularly, and any cannabis plants are destroyed and the grower prosecuted'[79] and at the opposite end of the continent, the authorities lamented that 'at one time packets of kif were found in family parcels sent to Moroccan soldiers serving in Europe by their families'.[80] These glimpses of obstinate consumers and persistent markets suggest that there was on-going resistance to, or ignorance of, attempts to prohibit use of a favourite intoxicant in many parts of the world:

> Group smoking is general . . . the pleasure seems to lie not only in the use of the drug but also in the collective euphoria it produces. This they smoke in cafés, sometimes in a private house, very often on a small shopkeeper's premises. This small shopkeeper is very often a barber or tailor. The master craftsman smokes with his staff or forms groups with his customers, to whom, it is said, he gives the drug and equipment free of charge solely for the pleasure of smoking in company . . . kif addicts only incur the half-hearted disapproval of the healthy members of the population. The fact that the use of kif is so widespread and taken for granted most certainly influences their views: a practice as common and as widely tolerated as this could not be regarded as a very serious offence or the drug a very harmful product.[81]

While the above report from French Morocco pointed to the place of cannabis consumption in the routine social life of the region, the survey of Brazil identified the role of the substance in the country's cultural practices:

> In Alagoas the drug is used during sambas and batuques, dances introduced by Negroes: it is also consumed by those who porfiam na colcheia i.e. contend with semi-breves, which among country folk is a rhymed and sung dialogue in

which each reply (usually in quatrains) begins with the challenger's cue or last words. It is claimed that the cannabis gives contestants great inspiration and facility in rhyming and leads them to issue the challenges for the desafio or poetic duel.[82]

This contrasted somewhat with the picture in Southern Rhodesia where 'it was used before going into battle, and more recently before hunting expeditions and sporting events'.[83] Similar applications were encountered in India where it 'is still sometimes used by contestants in wrestling contests and other athletic sports as well as in games requiring great effort and endurance'. In that country it was reported 'that to meet a man carrying bhang was regarded as an omen of success; similarly to think of the cannabis plant in a dream was considered lucky'. This was because the cannabis plant was represented in Hindu holy texts as sacred.[84] Such glimpses add to the sense that the picture presented in these reports was of a police problem rather than a social problem. In other words, the regulations on cannabis since the 1920s had imposed a new set of obligations on the authorities rather than it being the case that the behaviour of cannabis consumers had forced officials to act. Poetry contests, folk dances, sporting events, and afternoon gatherings at the local shop hardly look like the stuff of social mayhem given the wider history of the 1950s. Needless to say, none of these glimpses of routine cannabis consumption were singled out for discussion by the Commission. Delegates had reports from eighteen countries in front of them and lingered for little more than an hour and a half in chewing them over. Much of this limited deliberation was taken up by the Indian delegate's report on a meeting in his country of that year and some excitement about mixtures of hashish and chocolate available in Arab countries.

That the glimpses of routine users of cannabis engaged in harmless activities were not discussed and were disregarded as evidence may well be down to another of the documents that accompanied the national surveys for consideration in 1957. The Secretariat presented its summary of where the Commission had reached on cannabis as it entered the final phase of redrafting the Single Convention. It quoted Wolff's conclusion that cannabis drugs were dangerous from 'every point of view' and added its own assertion that 'they are used for euphoric purposes in many parts of the world where their consumption constitutes a traditional and widespread habit and often a serious social evil'.[85] The same report was forced to admit that

> While cannabis drugs are addiction producing within the meaning of this term
> as defined by the WHO, it is agreed that they do not cause physical depend-
> ence in the same way as morphine, i.e. that there are no physical abstinence
> symptoms equivalent to those which occur in the case of withdrawal of
> morphine

The issue of addiction was yet to be discussed by the Commission and as
such it recommended that further attention be paid to the 'special character
of addiction to cannabis drugs'. The only reference to this point in the
Commission's thoughts on their report was the observation by Harry
Anslinger that 'medical officials of the United States Air Force had held
that, contrary to the assertion . . . cannabis caused physical dependence'. He
had to acknowledge, however, that 'their theory had been challenged'.[86]

Cannabis and the Single Convention

The uneasy consensus on the medical obsolescence of cannabis that the
WHO and colleagues in the UN had worked so hard to establish in the
1950s faced a final challenge late in the decade, this time from the microbial
world. British delegates, together with those from the US, Canada, and
France, tabled a draft resolution in April 1959 which pointed to recent
reports of the antibiotic properties of certain extracts of the cannabis plant.
They were mindful of the fact that these antibiotic properties could undermine the WHO's insistence that cannabis was no longer a useful source of
medicine and therefore requested the organization to prepare an account of
antibiotic properties in cannabis as a matter of urgency.[87] The French
delegate acted as a spokesman for the group that had introduced the
resolution and he asserted that new techniques, such as ionizing radiation,
meant that cannabis might now be used to produce useful drugs. He pointed
to reports of experiments in Hungary which suggested that cannabis was the
source of substances that were effective against *Staphylococcus aureus* and
various gram-positive bacilli. The American delegate was insistent that
'the door should not be closed to further research on any natural material
which might be of use to the medical profession' and in a rare show of unity
the USSR and China supported the draft resolution of the US, the UK,
Canada, and France, as did others including India and Iran.

As governments such as the US and the USSR had been entirely
convinced that the plant had no legitimate medical uses throughout the

1950s it is striking that the mention of antibiotics had rapidly caused them to reconsider. This was because, since the development of mass production techniques for penicillin in the 1940s, such products had been widely regarded as the wonder drugs of their generation which were capable of controlling an array of infectious diseases for the first time. The economic and political power that such control could confer was highly attractive to national governments and the development of new and improved pharma-ceutical products, particularly antibiotics, was high on the scientific agendas of many modern states in this period.[88] This context explains the readiness of so many nations to back the draft resolution asking the WHO to investi-gate reports of antibiotic properties in cannabis more closely.

The WHO reaction to this sudden show of unity on the part of the Commission's members reads as one of piqued professional pride. Dr Halbach, the representative of the organization at the Commission, blustered that 'he was convinced that the Expert Committee's statement on the obsoleteness [sic] of cannabis as a therapeutic agent would remain unchanged' and pointedly asserted that 'it was not easy to imagine, in the present state of knowledge, the reintroduction of cannabis as a means of rational therapy based on modern conditions'. His reluctance comes across in the minutes, as he conceded that 'he felt that the WHO would have to carry out the study desired by the Commission'.[89] Halbach was the chief medical officer of the addiction-producing drugs section of the WHO and evidently did not take kindly to diplomats challenging statements on medi-cines that were designed by his fellow scientists to be final and authoritative.

The WHO response finally appeared late in 1960 as a paper with the title *The Merits of Antibiotic Substances Obtainable from Cannabis Sativa*. The report noted that results published between 1957 and 1959 from experiments with extracts of cannabis had indeed suggested antibacterial activity. These results supported the theory that such extracts inhibited the growth of staphylo-cocci, streptococci, and other gram-positive organisms and actively des-troyed the tubercle bacillus. However, the WHO paper went out of its way to problematize these results. It questioned the validity of the experiments and argued that 'none of the available reports on clinical use appears to refer to a properly conducted trial with adequate controls'. It pointed out that 'no experiments are reported on its effects on isolated mammalian cells'. It noted that 'it would appear that these studies, which have been going on for several years, have not carried enough conviction to induce a material production of this substance on a commercial scale'. Finally it speculated that,

> Even if the clinical reports in the publications under survey are to be fully credited, it still remains to be decided whether they illustrate a curative action not obtainable by other and more orthodox means...it would be very surprising if a direct comparison between them [neomycin and bacitracin] and the cannabis substances in question did not show that their action, especially if they were used together, was superior.

The report reads as a hatchet job as it questioned the legitimacy of the science behind the positive reports with no good reason, inferred that lack of a corporate backer was evidence of ineffectiveness on the part of a substance, and speculated on the likely results of an imaginary trial of cannabis antibiotics against those already available to conclude that the latter were superior to the former. Any chance that the imaginary trial would take place was denied by the report's assertion that 'the case has not been proved in favour of making cannabis available for the extraction of therapeutic substances, particularly with antibiotic properties equal or superior to those obtainable otherwise'. It finished by referring the reader back to the report of the WHO Expert Committee of 1952 and confirming that 'cannabis preparations are practically obsolete and there is no justification for their medical use'.[90]

At the same time as the WHO was producing this report the Secretariat authored a final survey of the cannabis issue designed to inform delegates as they began to work on the agreement that would become the 1961 Single Convention. This was largely a compilation of observations from the country surveys on the subject conducted since 1952. It is instructive to read the summary against the originals, as the selective nature of the document seems obvious. Consumers from across the continents were lumped together in the following brief description:

> Apart from unemployed persons who generally figure prominently among consumers, there are also mentioned traffickers who also consume the drug, labourers, odd-jobbers, vagrants, criminals, seamen and a few students and cabaret artists.

Nowhere was there mention of the shopkeepers and craftsmen who smoked in the Moroccan afternoon, of the Brazilian country festivals where cannabis was inhaled to encourage dancing and poetry, or of the Indian and African sports for which contestants prepared with a dose of the drug.[91]

Instead, the Secretariat's survey carried details of an ambitious new development that neatly summarizes the position of the UN on cannabis by this time. As part of its Mediterranean Development Project scheme $703,000 had been provided to 'assist the Government of Morocco with two concurrent phases of its plans to develop the Rif region ... which includes a large part of the lands traditionally cultivated for kif (the chopped up parts of the flowering or fruiting tops of the cannabis plant)'.[92] For the first time the organization was involving itself in a hands-on programme of eradicating cannabis production, through replacing it with 'forest and fruit-tree planting, livestock raising, and field crops'.

Finally, a Plenipotentiary Conference was convened at which delegates were expected to thrash out the details of the Single Convention. The WHO and the Secretariat of the UN had made their positions on cannabis clear. The 1950 proposal to entirely prohibit the production of cannabis save for the small amounts necessary for scientific experimentation was presented as article 39.[93] At this stage a number of governments acted to prevent this position being adopted in the final draft, and one of these was the UK. The British position was not taken out of any great concern about cannabis and the preparations of the plant, but rather was driven by suspicion of the political implications of the proposals. It was not alone, as a number of governments were outraged at the suggestion that the UN had the power to determine the domestic affairs of national states, or as the UK's delegate pointed out:

> It is, in Her Majesty's Government's view, wrong in principle, in a matter which affects the treatment of the sick, to require governments, if they wish to adhere to the Convention, to consent to the prohibition of whatever drugs a majority at a plenipotentiaries' conference may decide to include ... a mandatory prohibition of internal manufacture and use such as is contained in paragraph 1 of Article 2 seems to Her Majesty's Government to be quite unjustifiable.[94]

The British position was that, unless modifications were made which gave the final decision on the scientific and medical use of any drug to individual national governments, the UK would not agree to the Convention.

The proposals on cannabis were also a sticking point for the Government of India for the simple reason that they entirely ignored the earlier discussions about Asian medicines. The Indian delegates there opposed article 39, insisting again that 'cannabis drugs are used in indigenous systems of medicine in India and it has not yet been proved that these drugs are as dangerous as the other drugs listed in the Schedule or total prohibition of these drugs is absolutely necessary'.[95] Iran backed this position and submitted an amendment to the cannabis section of the treaty that read 'the parties shall prohibit the production of cannabis and cannabis resin, except for purposes of their use in indigenous medicine or of scientific research'.[96] Harry Anslinger of the US Government even contributed on the side of cannabis, stating that 'a product derived from the cannabis plant was thought to have possibilities for the treatment of certain mental diseases'.[97] On the other hand many nations held an unblinking view of the drug and the representative of Egypt 'urged countries in which the cannabis plant was cultivated to assume the obligations set forth in article 39' while the Brazilian made it clear that 'his delegation was...in full agreement with article 39 as it stood'.[98] The Commission's response to this divided position on the issue of cannabis was to send it to an ad hoc committee which included representatives from India, Pakistan, the US, the UK, and Canada.[99]

In advance of the meeting of this committee the British and Canadian delegates drafted a much simplified version of the article on cannabis. Their intention was to place preparations of the plant alongside opium in the Convention as a substance that could be prohibited in domestic medicine by national governments if they so wished. Most were satisfied with this but the Government of India insisted that the leaves of the cannabis plant should be excepted from any provisions on cannabis whatsoever, stating once again that they were 'far less harmful than alcohol and...used by the poorer people of India to make a mildly intoxicating drink or as a substitute for analgesics and tranquillizers'.[100] Once this was accepted by everyone it was agreed that 'cannabis leaves should be subject to a less rigid regime than the fruiting or flowering tops or the resin of the cannabis plant...it was proposed to this end [that] the leaves may be omitted from the definition of cannabis and that a separate provision may provide for their control'.[101] The British had seen off the ambition of the UN to dictate policies to national governments on medicines, and the Indians had ensured that cannabis leaves would be treated differently from other parts of the plant. The Conference finally agreed on cannabis in the afternoon of 20 March 1961.[102]

The Single Convention on Narcotic Drugs 1961 remains the basis of international laws on cannabis to this day and its key intention was to 'limit exclusively to medical and scientific purposes the production, manufacture, export, import, distribution of, trade in, use and possession of drugs'. Specific measures included prohibiting in the name of public health the cultivation of cannabis plants for anything but scientific and medical use, annual reporting on the area of cultivation of cannabis for these purposes, and establishing national agencies to control the cultivation of crops for medicinal and scientific purposes. Modern medicines that contained cannabis were in Schedule I of the Convention and their prohibition was not recommended. Cannabis and cannabis resin, however, were included in Schedule IV of the Convention, which meant that the prohibition of their medical use was recommended. Significantly, the definition for the sake of the treaty was as follows:

> 'Cannabis' means the flowering or fruiting tops of the cannabis plant (excluding the seeds and leaves when not accompanied by the tops) from which the resin has not been extracted, by whatever name they may be designated.

This was the section that meant that India's reservations about cannabis leaves had been respected and that the only stipulation regarding these was the vague assertion that 'The Parties shall adopt such measures as may be necessary to prevent the misuse of, and illicit traffic in, the leaves of the cannabis plant'.

Conclusion

The story of the place of cannabis in the 1961 Single Convention is an important one in the wider context of this book and its consideration of the control and consumption of the drug in the UK. In the first place it serves as a reminder that the British position does not exist in isolation from events and agendas abroad. The previous chapter showed how international migration served to establish a whole new set of consumers of cannabis in the UK in the 1950s. This chapter has shown that at much the same time ideas about cannabis from abroad were circulating in British medical and scientific circles, and that it was in the international context of the United Nations that the UK's controls on cannabis were being formulated. Crucially, however, the chapter has also shown that Britain was not a passive recipient of international decisions. On the one hand the UK's experts could arrive at their own positions regardless of the international hubbub about cannabis, and the Brain Committee's clear conclusion that cannabis was not addictive stood in contrast to the contention voiced by the UN's Secretariat that 'cannabis drugs are addiction producing'.[103] On the other hand British actors could act decisively to shape international decisions on cannabis that would affect the UK. The ambition of the WHO and the UN to impose a total prohibition on the use of cannabis in medicine was thwarted by the UK, even if this had less to do with any great belief in the drug's therapeutic potential, and more to do with a concern about the political implications of transnational bodies like the WHO and the UN seeking to control domestic arrangements in countries where national governments had their own bodies and advisory groups to drive policy.

A final conclusion from this chapter is that it is important to look in detail at what the international context consists of in order to fully understand how the cannabis agenda was shaped. Different governments held various positions on cannabis throughout the 1950s, and the actions of the Indian delegation show how a specific national interest could shape the final version of the 1961 Single Convention. However, the Indian intervention draws attention to a further feature of the international context in this period, one that was more pronounced in the 1950s than previously. This was the place of transnational bodies such as the UN and the WHO in driving the agenda on drugs, and in particular on cannabis. Bodies such as the Expert Committee on Habit-Forming Drugs at the WHO and the Secretariat at the United Nations were determined to assert the darkest picture possible of cannabis in this period and to force through the strictest possible control mechanisms.

The reasons that the UN and the WHO took such a dim view of cannabis are various. In the first place, the position of control advocates in key roles and on important committees in these organizations ensured that negative views of a whole range of substances were the starting position for international discussions throughout the 1940s and 1950s. Moreover, both the UN and the WHO were nascent bodies that were engaged in carving out positions for themselves in the post-war world. Their interest in cannabis can be seen as just one instance of a wider project of empire-building and territory-claiming by the staff of ambitious organizations at a time when a growing remit for these bodies ensured their significance and survival. In the 1920s cannabis had first been caught up in the international regulatory system because of the competing interests of national and colonial governments such as the UK, the US, Egypt, and India. In the 1950s cannabis was located closer to the heart of the international drugs agenda than ever before, and it was put there not by national governments, but by the UN and the WHO, transnational bodies seeking to widen their spheres of interest by finding new problems that they claimed it was their responsibility to fix.[104]

6

'Cannabis was spreading to white people': New Consumers, New Controls, 1962–1971

Introduction

Historians have been distracted by some of the more colourful events of the 1960s when considering cannabis in the UK in the period. For example, Martin Booth's *Cannabis: A History* includes an excited account of the decade in Britain, making breathless statements such as '1967 was termed the Summer of Love in America, in Britain it could have been renamed the Summer of Action', while reaching broad conclusions such as 'the Government ignored the [Wootton] report' and 'one man in particular, Detective Sergeant Norman "Nobby" Pilcher came to epitomize the police anti-drug stance'.[1] The colourful events of the decade come thick and fast in his account and Booth was particularly interested in the arrest and conviction of Keith Richards of The Rolling Stones in 1967. This episode was certainly controversial as the *News of the World* newspaper stood accused of orchestrating the police raid, the officers involved were later convicted of corruption, and within a month of Richards starting his sentence *The Times* had published a pro-cannabis advertisement placed by the hastily assembled SOMA (the Society of Mental Awareness) and a demonstration had taken place in Hyde Park against existing laws on cannabis. According to *The Times* the latter was attended by 'several hundred so-called "flower-children"' although later accounts have inflated this number into the thousands.[2]

This chapter will seek to place such stories in the broader context of the decade and to find answers to the questions that they raise but which have often been missed by historians. The first of these relates to the 'flower-children' of Hyde Park and the extent to which they were representative of the changing market in Britain for cannabis products in this decade. The second relates to the methods employed by police to tackle matters related to cannabis and how far officers in London were typical of forces across the country. Linked to this is a third set of questions about the nature of the law and the ways in which the government sought to renew it in the face of a changing market and the diversity of responses to it. A final issue touched upon is the place of the media in the events of the period.

'Flower-children' and other consumers

Continuities in the market for cannabis in the UK were obvious to observers from the outset of the 1960s, one Metropolitan Police report of 1961 noting simply that 'there is still a demand by the coloured population of London for Cannabis Sativa'.[3] However, even at this early stage of the decade changes were being noticed, and the same report stated that 'information has been received from various sources of the increased use of these drugs amongst teenagers. It is not now confined to the so called "beatnik" types but also amongst students, particularly where foreign students are found'.[4] Indeed, a more detailed report on the cannabis situation in London prepared in that year was able to provide a fuller picture of the new cannabis consumer:

> Of the white users of the drug they are mainly in their late teens or early twenties and are of the type frequenting the jazz clubs and coffee bars of the West End where this activity is mainly confined. There are signs, however, of it spreading to whites of similar tendencies in Brixton, Kensington, Chelsea, Paddington and the Notting Hill area...the most dangerous trend is the interest shown by irresponsible young white people of both sexes in this drug. Two cases in point are the separate instances of Godfrey Peter Manley Glubb, age 20, the son of Major General Glubb (Glubb Pasha) who on 23 April 1960 at West London Magistrates Court was convicted of possessing Indian Hemp and Terrance Keith Sullivan who at the age of 15 was convicted at South Western Juvenile Court of a similar offence and admitted smoking hemp on several occasions.[5]

Here then are early glimpses of the white, middle-class, cannabis-smoking teenager familiar from the many writings left by such people from the period.[6] Glubb is an interesting example, as his father was the noted British military officer Sir John Bagot Glubb, who had been wounded in the First World War and had been commander of the Arab Legion during the Second World War. Godfrey evidently rebelled against his Establishment father as he ran away from Wellington School and ended up at the School of Oriental and African Studies as a student in the 1960s. Despite his youthful brushes with the law, his Arabic qualifications and his origins in the region (he had been born in Jerusalem while his father was on duty) meant that he went on to enjoy a career with the Popular Front for the Liberation of Oman and the Arabian Gulf and as a journalist.[7]

Many similar stories can be found from the 1960s, of middle-class white youths attracted by the possibilities of the loose set of ideas that can be grouped under the term 'counter-culture'. Their politics were self-consciously radical and consisted of various challenges to what they perceived as the established order by seeking to 'exist within a world whose only limits were of their own definition'.[8] Consumption of unfamiliar intoxicants was a feature of the 'counter-culture' as it was a means of challenging the norms of the period in a variety of ways. In the first place, use of substances such as cannabis could be a physiological method of escaping the existing order on an individual basis as a successful smoke would intoxicate the consumer to the extent that he or she would experience an alternative form of consciousness. However, cannabis also came loaded with symbolic meaning which ensured that consuming it could be interpreted as a gesture of defying social norms and political traditions. The intoxicants of the British had traditionally been tobacco and alcohol. Cannabis was a drug associated more with the Africans and the Asians that had been the subjects of the British Empire, an association that had been cemented in the 1950s as migrants from across the Commonwealth arrived in the UK and brought it with them. In this hierarchy of meanings, cannabis was therefore the drug of the 'colonized' rather than the 'colonizer'. At a time when the Empire was in rapid decline and the politics of imperialism were being rejected, to smoke cannabis and to refuse alcohol meant to identify with the oppressed of Britain's past and to dismiss the cultural and political relations of the old order. In this context consuming the drug became a political act to be staged publicly, not simply a matter of taste that shaped private habits.

It was certainly the case that the newspapers made much of such young-sters, 'dressed in brilliant colours, some with their faces painted in vivid hues [who] preached the hippy philosophy of absolute love, gentleness and kindness [and] who believe in the mind-expanding powers of drugs, which means they are in a state of constant, peaceful war with the "fuzz" or police'.[9] The significance of this new type of consumer for the history of cannabis in Britain lies in the way in which they publicly questioned legal and penal approaches to its consumption in the UK and succeeded in establishing a voice for the consumer in British politics for the first time. The examples of Caroline Coon and the Release organization and Steve Abrams and SOMA serve to illustrate how this happened.

Caroline Coon was from a well-to-do background and spent her child-hood between boarding schools and her family's estate. As her parents refused to support her education after school she defied them and headed to London to study art.[10] Her fashionable contacts ensured that she social-ized with the likes of Dirk Bogarde and Kenneth Tynan in the evenings, while her impecunious life as a student meant that she worked as a waitress and as a nude model, and lived in bedsits in the seedier parts of the capital. As such she observed the sheer variety of cannabis users in London by the middle of the 1960s, with liberal members of the political and cultural elites smoking it at dinner parties while West Indian migrant workers shared it on the way home after an evening in the nightclubs. As a non-smoker who did not drink, she paid little attention to cannabis until her Jamaican boyfriend was arrested for possession of the drug. She attended the Old Bailey on the day he went for trial and was outraged that he received three and a half years in prison for the possession of 3 g of cannabis, especially when he was sentenced to only nine months for having a gun. She was also surprised at the response of his friends, one of whom told her to think of his term of imprisonment as a 'holiday' for him. Another, a co-defendant, played on his Rastafarian appearance, refusing to swear on the Bible and appearing to go into a trance when questioned in the dock. He was declared to be mentally ill and sent to a hospital, from which he was released after only three months of confinement.

These responses on the part of the Caribbean community to prosecution for cannabis offences suggest an acceptance that this was something to be wearily tolerated or mitigated by resorting to sly strategies. No doubt this reflected the insecure place of the various groups that made up the migrant community in a society that was often racist and suspicious of newcomers.

However, Caroline Coon's response to this was that of a member of British society who had enjoyed greater access to its privileges. She recalls that her sense of disappointment at the harsh sentences drew on the fact that she had always been brought up to believe in the quality of British justice. Her response to this disappointment was that of someone from a family that had always turned to a good lawyer when trouble arose. She met the co-founder of Release, Rufus Harris, while on a demonstration against the *News of the World* and its perceived role in the case against The Rolling Stones. Their shared sense of the need for those in trouble with the police for drugs offences to have better access to effective legal services led them to set up a twenty-four-hour emergency phone service. The organization, which they christened Release, was quickly adopted by those that identified with the 'counter-culture' and musicians like George Harrison provided funds.[11] It rapidly grew so that it was soon handling over 400 new enquiries a month on a variety of social issues rather than those related just to drugs.[12] By the end of the decade it had taken to lobbying on a range of these issues, using the tactic of producing surveys and publishing reports such as *The Release Report on Drug Offenders and the Law* in order to influence political processes.[13] Significantly, however, Coon recalls that the organization was rarely used by the members of the migrant community that she had first set out to help.[14]

At about the same time SOMA was founded by Steve Abrams. He was an American who had arrived in the UK as a student at Oxford to write a thesis on extrasensory perception, and it was in the university newspaper that the idea for the organization first appeared in 1967. Its moment of greatest notoriety was achieved a few months after its foundation when Abrams organized the famous advertisement in *The Times* newspaper which called for reform of the laws relating to cannabis and included such signatories as Francis Crick and David Dimbleby. Paid for by Paul McCartney, the advertisement provoked a sympathetic editorial in *The Times* and debate in Parliament, although the idea that it was inspired by the treatment of members of The Rolling Stones was a myth as it was first mooted as a response to the arrest of John Hopkins, a friend of Abrams, for cannabis offences.[15] While Release was most concerned about drug users, SOMA was to focus on the drug itself. It became the SOMA Research Association Ltd with Abrams and Crick among the directors, and was licensed by the Home Office to handle tetrahydrocannabinol (THC) for research purposes until it was wound up in 1970.[16]

Release and SOMA may have had different interests but they had much in common. Each was established by well-educated, liberal youngsters who were irked by their perception of reactionary attitudes among the governing elites. Both served to establish the presence of a pro-cannabis lobby in British politics and culture for the first time. Both had emerged from the same social circles, in which another member, Paul McCartney, felt 'we were sort of cocooned . . . it was the London set and it was a crowd that accepted certain standards'.[17] This observation raises the question of how far the new consumers, for all the noise that they made and the impact that they had in articulating a case for cannabis consumption, were anything more than a phenomenon of liberal London.

Part of the answer lies in a set of documents compiled by police authorities across the country early in 1968. In some places where cannabis use was reported, the picture seemed little changed from that of the 1950s. In Northamptonshire, for example, the author of the police report contented himself with the observation that 'there is a large coloured community living in this county, particularly in the Northampton and Wellingborough districts and to them the smoking of cannabis is an accepted way of life'.[18] In Derby it appeared that 'there is evidence that the drug cannabis is being used by the coloured community . . . there is no evidence to show that the trade is increasing and it is thought that the smoking community has not grown to any degree'.[19]

Elsewhere, it seems that even in the latter stages of the decade there were parts of the UK that had little experience of cannabis use at all. In 1968 in Swansea it was reported that 'illicit use of soft drugs exists only on a very small scale'[20] and in Southend-on-Sea the police could confidently state that 'cannabis is not a serious problem in this borough'.[21] In Coventry it was felt that 'it will be seen from the figures that the use of drugs can hardly be termed a problem in this city' as the police had only taken twenty cases to court all year, and just three of these involved cannabis.[22] This was despite setting up a joint drugs squad with Warwickshire forces in that year. On the other side of the Midlands West Mercia Police could happily conclude that 'considering the relatively good communications between Birmingham, Liverpool, Bristol, and this Force area, the drug situation is remarkably quiet'.[23] In Lincoln the police could report that 'it is known through informants that some cannabis is occasionally offered for sale but there is very little of this and only one prosecution, without conviction, occurred during 1967'.[24] In the north similar statements were common. In Wakefield the author of the report was clear that 'the drug problem in this force area does not appear to be of serious proportions' and he noted that there had been no prosecutions for drugs offences in 1967.[25] A neighbouring chief constable was adamant that 'there is nothing to suggest that there has been any problem relating to the supply or use of drugs in Warrington, to any degree'.[26]

Where drug use among the local youth was reported by the police it often seemed to be on a very small scale. In Newcastle-upon-Tyne,

> At present it is estimated that there is a nucleus of approximately fifteen persons between the ages of 19 years and 25 years using cannabis and LSD in this City. From time to time this number is enlarged by a group of about ten beatnik types who wander the country and occasionally visit this City. The regularity of their use depends on the availability of supplies. Our information is that these supplies invariably come from London and are usually brought to this City by one of the group with money, who then distributes the drugs amongst his associates.[27]

Even in locations where alternative types and students could be found in sizeable numbers, active consumption often appears to have been limited. In 1962, for example, the authorities in London noted that 'in the last quarter certain publicity was given to a police raid at the Café Des Artistes, 266 Fulham Road, S.W.10, carried out by officers from Chelsea Police Station in conjunction with this Office. Only six persons out of a total of 435 frequenters were found to be in possession of Indian Hemp and the quantities were small'.[28] A similar story was told by the chief constable of Brighton in 1967. He complained that the press had misrepresented the town as a den of drug-taking owing to the presence there of a large, floating population of youthful visitors. To make his case he produced the following account:

> My officers have recently arrested a man in possession of cannabis. Our information is that this man . . . obtained in London a total of about 500 grains of the drug. In three weeks of circulating among beatniks and students in their haunts, he managed to sell only half of this, sufficient for about 50 'reefers'.[29]

It seems that even in a town popularly associated with drugs consumption and where those thought to use cannabis congregated, it was difficult to sell more than two or three cannabis smokes in a day.

While cannabis use was limited or little known in many parts of the UK late in the 1960s, there were places where the new consumers of the drug had been observed. In Cardiff, for example, the police reported that 'it is believed that some teenagers were introduced to the use of drugs as a result of their association with "beatniks" types connected with the Committee of 100 and the C.N.D. Groups'.[30] Such explicit reference to politics in accounting for cannabis consumption was rare, however, one officer noting rather vaguely that 'it is noticeable in a number of large towns and cities throughout Hampshire that there is a continuance of the movement to legalise cannabis, whilst just as strong on the other hand is the feeling to oppose any such action'.[31] Just how hazy were the ideas of those that expressed political motivations for taking the drug comes through in a note from York:

> Conversations between the students and the Police informants indicate that the reasons for their using drugs are two-fold: 1. They feel that a person should be allowed freedom of thought in connection with drugs and that the law is too prohibitive. 2. They feel that they need some stimulation to enable them to cope with their rather full and hectic academic and social life.[32]

If police officers rarely ascribed cannabis consumption among the young to politics in 1968, more common was the sense from Surrey that 'the usual reason given by the majority when asked why they had started to use drugs was "curiosity"'.[33] Officers in Preston had reached a similar conclusion, reporting that 'we have long held the view that soft drug taking is an adolescent aberration which most of them will grow out of'.[34]

Indeed, the police tended to link the new consumers to the old consumers rather than to radical politics or counter-cultures. In Cardiff officers sketched the history of the cannabis market as follows:

> Following the influx of Commonwealth coloured immigrants around 1950, it became evident that they were obtaining supplies of cannabis for their own use. During the 1960s it appears that a small volume of trafficking amongst the younger elements of the community started, based upon the association of the coloured youths in cafés and dance halls with other teenagers resident throughout the City.[35]

This interface between migrant communities and their local counterparts was also noticed in other cities, so that in Birmingham it was observed that 'illicit drinking clubs, mainly frequented by the immigrant population, do exist and drugs are there peddled to other members of the immigrant population and the lower-class type of white person'.[36] In Gwent it appeared that 'young persons of a lower social group tend to graduate towards the coloured element, and so in the main adopt a coloured person's way of life and use cannabis more frequently than their counterparts of the higher social group, which indicates that their type of drug taking activities are motivated by their particular environment'.[37] The idea that cannabis consumption among young white users was not always a middle-class political phenomenon was borne out by further details provided for Cardiff. The police report from there includes a list of the fifty-five cases brought to court for drugs offences in 1967 together with brief details on race, occupation, etc. Forty-four of these involved cannabis. What is striking is the working-class nature of many of the local consumers as the majority were from local rather than migrant communities and had occupations such as 'labourer', 'carpenter', 'jobbing builder', 'metal burner', or 'shop assistant'. Only four of the cannabis offenders were classified as students.

Other forces shared the interest of the Cardiff police in the class status of consumers. In Hampshire the authorities were convinced that

> by far the majority of people coming to the notice of Drug Squad officers in the Hampshire Constabulary are in the under 23 age group. A number are so-called students but in reality are no more than members of the Beatnik fraternity, whilst another portion are [sic] made up of the young unemployed labourer type. The favourite drug continues to be cannabis.[38]

Bristol police argued that cannabis consumers there could be divided roughly into the following categories; Immigrants and prostitutes; Working class teenagers; Students; Beatniks; Intellectuals.[39] In Essex a distinction was made between the 'Beatnik-lay-about fraternity' as opposed to the 'Intellectual Beatnik type'.[40] In Sheffield the message was simpler: 'cannabis is used mainly by working class youths and young women'.[41]

A curious episode from 1966, however, is a reminder that the youth of the period in Britain were not uniformly committed to a taste for new intoxicants. Lawrence Abel was a doctor and member of the second Brain Committee who gave a speech to the British Medical Association in that year. His intention was to provide something that would 'appeal to members of the Press who were present. He felt that the subsequent publicity might "jolt" the authorities into taking some action on the recommendations of the Brain Committee which had been put forward almost a year ago'.[42] The 'something' was a proposal to set up a group known as the 'Young Vigilantes' or 'Harley Street Irregulars'. Abel was reported in the *Evening Standard* as saying:

I am certain that there are enough high-minded, decent-living teenagers in London today who would be willing to go around clubs and coffee bars, get hold of these drugs and report to such a committee—or to the police.[43]

A policeman was despatched to point out to Abel that he should not be establishing vigilante groups and should refrain from asking teenagers to buy cannabis, even if the intention was to hand it over to the police in order to encourage them to arrest the suppliers. The officer reported that Abel proudly showed him 'a large number of letters which he had received from young people in response to this article in the *Evening Standard*, all of whom offered their services should a "Young Vigilantes" movement be formed'. Some members of Britain's youth in the 1960s could be as enthused by the idea of opposing the consumption of cannabis as others were about advocating it.

Supplying demand

The picture that emerges of the market for cannabis in the 1960s is therefore one of increasing complexity. It was certainly the case that this market had diversified beyond members of the migrant communities who had been the most regular consumers of cannabis in the 1940s and into the 1950s. The drug was adopted as a symbol by those among Britain's youth that had an overtly, if ill-defined, political agenda that drew on the 'counter-culture' aspiration to challenge the existing order. However, the information from a nationwide survey of consumption filed by the police suggests that for all the excitement generated about the drug by those associated with the 'counter-culture', cannabis use remained patchy among the youth of the UK. Where it was consumed, new users were more likely to have tried the drug through association with migrant groups than with radical politics, and were as commonly workers or labourers as they were students or the offspring of the well-to-do.

As the market for cannabis developed, suppliers stepped in to make sure that demand was met. Birmingham City Police noted in 1968 that 'a great deal of information has been amassed with regard to the activities of Pakistani drug smugglers and it is anticipated that positive action will be taken in this connection in the near future'.[44] The author of the report from nearby West Midlands Constabulary also stated that 'my specialist officers in

this field believe that a certain amount of large scale smuggling and importation of cannabis is undertaken by certain successful businessmen of Indian
extraction, resident in the West Midlands area'.[45] Evidence for this included
the arrest of a Sikh from Tipton at Dover as he came off the car ferry with
£30,000 of cannabis. In Buckinghamshire it was reported that

> With regard to the smuggling of drugs there has been only one instance during
> 1967 which is of note and this was a Pakistani who came into the country at
> London Airport. He was arrested by Metropolitan Police Officers in Slough
> shortly after his arrival and was found in possession of a large quantity of
> cannabis resin.[46]

A similar account was presented from Northallerton where the chief
constable reported a number of arrests of Pakistani seamen and their
accomplices and argued that 'these arrests disclosed a well-organized
ring for smuggling this type of drug for use by coloured people living
away from the seaports'.[47] By 1969 a national conference of drugs squad
officers heard that 'both Customs and the police have ample evidence that
the main organizers of large scale traffic in cannabis are members of the
Indian and Pakistani communities in Birmingham, Bradford and Southall
(Middlesex) between which there was very considerable communication
and movement'. Evidence for this included 1 ton of cannabis that had
been seized in shipments from Pakistan and the recent interdiction of
3 tons of the drug at Karachi that was bound for the UK.[48] Speculation
on the country's market for cannabis by groups that had ready links in
South Asia is hardly surprising given the history of the region as a source
of the drug. It is worth recalling that as recently as the 1930s the British
authorities in India had themselves been illegally exporting preparations of
the plant during the last days of the Raj.[49]

Evidence from elsewhere suggests that others sought to benefit from the
cannabis market in the UK, albeit on a smaller scale than that noted above.
For example, in Suffolk the police reported that 'an American serviceman
serving on an airbase in the district was found to be in possession of
cannabis, which he admitted having imported into the country through
Mildenhall air base when he was posted to the United Kingdom for a tour of
service. This was purely a profit-making venture on his part for he sold the
drug that he had obtained cheaply in the United States at inflated prices in
this district and in Norwich'.[50] Foreign servicemen were not alone in taking
advantage of the travel associated with military duties in order to smuggle

drugs, and Hampshire police noted in 1968 that '3 naval ratings were recently dealt with for offences involving cannabis'.[51]

Students were also implicated in bringing supplies from abroad. In Newhaven it was suspected that 'small-scale smuggling of cannabis takes place at this port, the offenders being mainly students on return from holiday'.[52] A similar picture emerged elsewhere, the Mid-Anglia Constabulary pointing to 'small-scale smuggling of cannabis by Cambridge undergraduates after spending holidays on the Continent and in other foreign countries'.[53] Oxfordshire Constabulary reported a story in a related vein:

> Comment should be made about the seven persons cautioned, who were pupils at a local boarding school. One of the pupils—a 15 year old girl—when returning from holiday in Africa brought with her some cannabis given to her by an African. At the school she and six colleagues experimented with the drug, by smoking it. With the knowledge of the parents, the pupils were disciplined by the school and, as it was considered that the whole matter had merely been juvenile curiosity, it was decided to caution them as to their future behaviour.[54]

It was also evident that once inside the country cannabis could be moved around to reach markets. In Bristol it was reported that 'the immigrant population of the St Paul's area of Bristol is largely responsible for the illicit supplies of cannabis which are used in the City most of which is imported into Bristol from other immigrant centres such as London, Birmingham and, to some extent, South Wales; 75 per cent of all arrests made in this City in connection with drug offences, involve coloured immigrants, consisting mainly of West Indians'.[55] A similar case was presented in the East Midlands where it was thought that 'cannabis and cannabis resin is transported into Leicester in motor vehicles by coloured immigrants, mainly of West Indian origin, from Manchester, Liverpool, London and Birmingham'.[56] Of course it was only a minority of these migrant communities that were involved in these activities and reports such as that from Lincolnshire emphasized that 'although Scunthorpe has a high proportion of drug trafficking there is no evidence that the coloured immigrant population is involved at all'.[57]

In Bournemouth it was not migrants but 'beatniks' who were thought to be couriers for the drug: 'it is known that supplies of heroin, cannabis and other soft drugs have been obtained from London, Reading, Birmingham, Southampton, Portsmouth and brought into this area to be disposed of...a block of cannabis will represent to a beatnik his bank balance, and by hiding this substance often in a public place such as a public gardens a beatnik can live in an area, selling his wares to young people and thus avoid visiting the Ministry of Social Security for monetary assistance'.[58] The view from Hampshire was darker and it was feared that 'perhaps a more significant factor is that some local criminals are now believed to be entering the field of drug trafficking, undoubtedly with an eye for the vast scope for swindling drug purchasers, with small fear that their activities will ever be reported to the Police'.[59] Norfolk Joint Police [*sic*] had also noticed that 'one disturbing factor which has become evident during the past year, however, is that professional criminals who previously centred their unlawful activities against property have entered the drug sphere as illicit traffickers, obviously because this has become so lucrative'.[60] The opposite was felt to be true in Hertfordshire, however, as 'there is no evidence that professional drug peddling, merely for financial gain, is taking place in this county'.[61]

While it is difficult to reconstruct the business of meeting demand for cannabis in Britain in the 1960s given its illegal and clandestine nature, the police records do suggest that, like any other speculators, those seeking to profit could sometimes struggle to do so. The story of the peddler who failed to sell all of his wares in Brighton, mentioned above, is an instance of an investor who seems to have overestimated demand. A note by the Metropolitan Police report in 1965 pointed to one of the reasons for this, namely the rapidly changing nature of the marketplace:

> it is known that students who used to smoke 'pot' (cannabis) for 'kicks' now prefer amphetamines. Illicit prices of cannabis have also fallen and £5 an ounce is now asked whereas two or three years ago the price was double. This, therefore, indicates that there is not the demand for cannabis rather than a failure to detect importations.[62]

While cannabis could fall out of fashion in some parts of the country, it could become the taste of the moment in others, so that in 1967 in Oxford, for example, it was reported that 'the young people are turning their attentions to smoking cannabis and taking LSD which at the present time seems to be the "in thing" in Oxford, and by doing so they are considered to be much more intellectual and sophisticated than they would be by taking "pep-pills"'.[63] The limited market for illegal intoxicants in the UK by the middle of the 1960s seems to have been a localized and a volatile one, where the experience of Cambridge was probably not unusual: 'a considerable number of teenagers and young people . . . felt that they must conform to the current trend . . . many of them have since lost interest and have discontinued the practice'.[64] If seizures of cannabis are anything to go by, imports of the drug into the UK in the 1960s may well have been increasing. But they could be speculative gambles rather than guaranteed profit-makers. In this light the report from Leicester of car-loads of cannabis arriving from as far afield as Manchester and Liverpool suggests not a well-planned system of distribution, but a risky search for a market.

The police and the law

If police reports only contain glimpses of markets and suppliers, they do provide a more detailed view of the attitudes and approaches of the law enforcement agencies to drugs in general and to cannabis in particular in the 1960s. What they reveal is a rather more diverse picture than is often supposed. Heavy-handed policing was one of the accusations made in the period by those representing cannabis consumers, with Caroline Coon of Release arguing that 'by 1969 the arrest and imprisonment of young people accused of violating the Dangerous Drugs Act of 1965 was one of Britain's most urgent social problems' which she recalled was the prompt for the report that the organization published that year which was 'an analysis of the detailed records of all our cases since 1967 with emphasis on corrupt police procedure'.[65] Historians like Martin Booth have been happy to parrot this, arguing that aggressively interventionist and corrupt officers 'came to epitomize the police anti-drug stance'. The question remains then of how far the police across the UK singled out drugs users for particular attention in the 1960s.

The situation in London seems to have been particularly complex. The Metropolitan Police had established its own drugs squad in 1954 and its officers had subsequently worked closely with the inspectors of the Home Office Drugs Branch.[66] By the end of the decade both shared the anxiety that they were understaffed and had ambitions to expand their numbers. As early as 1959 officials at the Drugs Branch of the Home Office had worried about the quality and quantity of inspections of retail and wholesale chemists in London as they felt that the resources of both its own inspectors and of colleagues in the police were stretched. Their proposal to address this was that the Metropolitan Police should find the resources to create eight new posts to deal with drugs inspections.[67] Officers within the Drugs Squad of the Metropolitan Police itself were making similar noises at their end. A memo prepared early in 1961 by members that was ostensibly about cannabis moaned that 'if this grave problem is to be tackled seriously the strength of the Drugs Branch must be augmented to ensure we are in a position to deal with this rapidly growing menace before it becomes uncontrollable'.[68] Appeals for additional resources, even those that attempted to induce a sense of looming crisis, were ostentatiously ignored by senior officers. Indeed, the chief superintendent at the Metropolitan Police cheerfully argued after reading the 1961 memo that 'there is no room for complacency, but considering the staff available we don't do too badly'.[69] This lack of interest frustrated those within drugs enforcement circles and a note by a Home Office official in April 1962 complained that they had still 'heard nothing' by way of a response to a proposal for more resources to be provided by the Metropolitan Police.

It is clear that in 1962 Drugs Squad officers took the decision to adopt a new approach to the drug. A report on cannabis from July of that year revealed that 'divisional officers have been encouraged to detect persons in possession of this drug rather than merely referring information to this Office'.[70] It seems that CID officers had been in the habit of passing on cases involving cannabis to members of the Drugs Squad to follow up, but had been requested to take a more immediate and interventionist course in 1962. It was subsequently concluded that 'figures prove these efforts to have been valuable' as numbers of arrests soared.[71] Against this backdrop of a sudden jump in arrest figures for cannabis offences one of the Drugs Squad officers, Detective Sergeant Ernest Cooke, was despatched to the fifth symposium of the Forensic Science Society held at the University of Birmingham in April 1962. He revealed that 102 arrests had been made for cannabis offences in the first four months of 1962 alone compared with 152 for all of 1960. He stated that 'if these rises are alarming, you will also realise, and no doubt agree, that it shows that we in the Metropolitan Police are doing something about it'. He was careful to pointedly lament that the Drugs Branch had 'such a small staff'.[72]

Cooke's report to the conference was published in the *Journal of the Forensic Science Society* in September and immediately caused a storm in the wider national press. *The Times* carried an article and an editorial with the headlines 'Big Increase in Marihuana Smoking' and 'Drug Addiction'. Both were prompted by Cooke's article and he was quoted as saying,

There is evidence that teenagers are being infected, he added, and a danger that those intoxicated by marihuana may try the 'hard' drugs—notably heroin and cocaine—which may lead to further addiction.[73]

The *Evening Standard* gave the story the most sustained attention with a series of scandalized reports into London's drug scene. Starting on 1 October and under a dark banner headline that ran 'The Dope Takers, by Frank Entwisle', daily reports followed for the rest of the week, each on page 8 of the paper and accompanied by drawings of drug-smoking girls, queues of addicts, and police and Customs officers in action. Ernest Cooke's 'evidence that many London teenagers are smoking reefers' was produced once again, and was accompanied by stories from the courts:[74]

> Last week a 20 year old English girl and two American students were jailed for a total of 11 years for possessing Indian hemp. In their flat in Sloane Gardens they had enough to make 3000 doped cigarettes. The Recorder, Sir Anthony Hawke, said he was satisfied they were peddling it. And the court was told how they had used London University notepaper to lend respectability to their letters to suppliers in North Africa. All three were from good families.[75]

The author of the series, Frank Entwisle, produced what he claimed was an interview with a 'dopetaker' in the second of his reports. Described as a '25 year old London secretary', she was reported to have tried her first 'reefer' in a flat in Earl's Court while listening to jazz records. She found her appreciation of art was enhanced, that the drug smelt like thyme, and that she became very relaxed:

> I thought, well, all the problems of man—political problems, the bomb and that kind of thing—weren't really problems at all. They were just little annoyances which I'd be able to solve in the morning...there would be no more poverty or wars or hunger, or people hating each other any longer.

Despite the fact that the interview presented an overwhelmingly positive experience, the reporter was careful to conclude that 'in one respect she is fortunate—so far she has been able to avoid the sexual and criminal degradation that is often the eventual penalty of taking that first puff'.[76] In the last of his reports on Friday, 5 October, Entwisle was quick to point the finger of blame at those in authority. He concluded that 'the official mind is misled and complacent', and outlined recommendations to address this which included the proposals that the Metropolitan Police Drugs Squad should be expanded and that the Home Office Drugs Branch be similarly reinforced.[77] While it is difficult to say for sure that the paper and the police directly colluded, it is certainly the case that Detective Sergeant Cooke and his colleagues in drugs enforcement had sparked a media storm that called for exactly the resources that they felt they had been denied since the end of the 1950s.

The response to this storm in the press was remarkable and swift, as before the month was out the Home Secretary was demanding that 'present arrangements for dealing with drugs matters should be reviewed'.[78] He made it clear that the urgency was due to his concern about the 'good deal of Press comment on the alleged increase in the use of cannabis' and in particular about the reports of Cooke and Entwisle.[79] This was a new Home Secretary, Henry Brooke, who had only been in the job since July. The replacement in the post for the long-serving Rab Butler, Brooke was explicit that it was his job to prove to the country that the Conservatives could compel 'the young of our country to grow up straight'.[80] Two sets of meetings were immediately organized to address the Home Secretary's concerns. The first was ordered on 25 October and convened on 19 November 1962 at the Home Office and considered the drugs situation in London. Present were representatives of the Metropolitan Police, the Home Office, and the Home Office Drugs Branch. An internal police memo prepared for this meeting noted 'the Secretary of State's personal interest in this matter'[81] and the chief Home Office official made it plain that the discussion was to focus on the matter of 'the staffing of the Dangerous Drugs Department at Scotland Yard'.[82] The second meeting considered the wider issue of drugs on a nationwide scale and met three days later on 22 November 1962. Present were those at the first meeting and also representatives of the Customs and Excise Service and senior police officers from thirty-four of the largest police forces from across the country and including those from such places as Glasgow, Liverpool, Manchester, and Cardiff. The Home Office acknowledged that this meeting would be the first time that it had brought the subject of cannabis to the attention of chief constables since 1957.[83]

Cooke's colleagues from the Metropolitan Police Drugs Squad stuck to the line that cannabis was the key problem:

> During 1962 every effort has been made by the officers of the Drugs Squad to prevent supplies imported into this country from reaching the distributors. Parcels have been intercepted ranging from a few ounces to 16 pounds in

weight where drugs (Indian Hemp) have been sent enclosed in newspaper, parcels of clothing and food, ships' life-belts, bars of soap, coconut shells etc. Every possible means are being tried to get the drugs into this country . . . the present staff of the Dangerous Drugs Squad are doing an excellent job and are working to their extreme limits, but it is quite clear that they are merely scratching at the surface of the dangerous drugs problem.[84]

The solution that they presented to the problem of just 'scratching at the surface' was an ambitious plan to swell the ranks of the Drugs Squad by tripling its establishment from five staff to fourteen. Their audacity paid off. The Home Office piled pressure on those in charge at the Metropolitan Police and the Commissioner made a point of noting 'recent discussions at the Home Office between his officers and Mr R. J. Guppy regarding the drugs position in London and the staffing of the Dangerous Drugs Squad'[85] in declaring on 18 April 1963 that it would receive all the reinforcements requested. Action was hurriedly taken to getting the new force ready as the Home Office approved funding on 8 May, three offices were organized by 8 June, and training was completed by the end of that month so that 1 July was the start date.[86] In the first report of the newly expanded Squad in November 1963 Detective Inspector Stubbings noted that 'attention should be drawn particularly to the increasing trafficking in Indian Hemp, enough work could be found for all the officers in this field alone'.[87] Obviously eager to justify the new appointments the Drugs Squad busied themselves in London and by the end of the year the same officer could report for cannabis offences that 'the overall figure for the twelve months ending 31st December 1963 is 577 as against 514 for 1962'.[88]

Officials at the Home Office clearly suspected that it had been man-oeuvred into putting fresh resources into drugs enforcement as they were careful to seek assurances from colleagues at Scotland Yard that 'there was no danger of similar articles by Metropolitan Police officers appearing in the future'.[89] Nevertheless, the Home Secretary remained agitated about drugs and was responsible for the Drugs (Prevention of Misuse) Act and the Dangerous Drugs Act of 1964 (which was incorporated into a further Dangerous Drugs Act in 1965). While the former was largely concerned with amphetamines, the latter introduced new offences related to cannabis. The cultivation of cannabis was now an offence and the legislation also targeted people who permitted cannabis to be consumed on their premises.[90] The latter was a radical piece of legislation for reasons that were soon apparent. An article in *The Times* in February 1966 reported the conviction of a man in Cambridge for managing a house in the city where cannabis had been smoked, despite the fact that he claimed he had no knowledge of what the tenants were consuming. The implications of this conviction were immediately voiced with anxiety by the educational authorities in the city. The principal of the Bell School of Languages declared that 'the Act means that if any of my students—or undergraduates in any college—takes drugs secretly and they are discovered, then, if I am prosecuted, I am automatically convicted'. The master of Magdalene College at Cambridge University railed 'how Parliament could let this through I cannot imagine. It is not only an unjust law, it is terribly unwise'.[91]

Keith Richards was the highest profile victim of this law as he was charged after a police raid with the offence of permitting cannabis to be consumed at his house in Redlands Road in 1967. This was the raid that resulted in the general furore about the treatment of The Rolling Stones of that year. However, it was a rather less famous figure who took the law on and ultimately defeated it. Stephanie Sweet was a 24-year-old schoolteacher who sublet a farmhouse in Oxfordshire to tenants while she lived in Oxford itself. The police found cannabis during a search there and Miss Sweet was charged and convicted under Henry Brooke's law, despite the fact that it was accepted by the court that she did not know that the drug was being used on the premises.[92] Public and political concern about this was quick to surface. Russell Kerr, Labour MP for Feltham, pointed out that landlords could not be prosecuted for being involved in the management of premises where other offences (such as buggery or incest) were committed.[93] A reader wrote to The Times to complain that 'it is truly terrible that a person can be convicted of a criminal offence who has no knowledge of such offence and no intention of committing it'.[94] When Sweet's application to take an appeal to the House of Lords was refused, The Times published an editorial which insisted that 'in order to establish criminal liability under the common law guilty conduct must be shown to be accompanied by a guilty mind. Without mens rea there is no offence . . . if the law is severe without being just, if it disregards common standards of fairness, it will become too vulnerable to serve its purpose'.[95] A group of MPs which included the future Labour leader Michael Foot set up a meeting with the Lord Chancellor and finally Sweet was allowed to take her case to the House of Lords. On 24 January 1969 it quashed her conviction. The House of Lords decided that whenever a law was silent on the issue of mens rea, the court must assume that it was a fundamental principle behind that law. With regards to Brooke's law, Lord Pearce on the panel admitted that their judgement 'would rob the section of much of its force'[96] and Lord Reid called the case 'a public scandal'.[97] Miss Sweet's reaction to the good news was to declare that 'I do not think I shall ever want to be a landlord again'. When asked about cannabis she stated, sweetly, that 'smoking it is an unpleasant habit, and an unfortunate thing; but in many parts of the world where people are very poor it does help to keep their mind off things'.[98]

Brooke was long gone by this point but the Drugs Squad of the Metropolitan Police which he had done so much to bolster was very much in evidence. Caroline Coon remembers that by 1967 policemen such as Vic Kelaher were familiar characters in the West End of London and their sharp suits and shades meant that they were very much part of the period.[99] However, the enthusiasm for policing cannabis that had seen the expansion of the Drugs Squad in London was also to be the source of its undoing as by the early 1970s a number of its members had been accused or convicted of corruption. This emerged after the Metropolitan Police Drugs Squad seemed to foil a cannabis smuggling ring that was operated by the Salah family, who were of Pakistani origins. At the trial of two members of the family the jury accepted that they had been securing cannabis in Kabul and smuggling it into Bulgaria but wavered about whether it was in fact destined for the UK and as such whether an offence had been committed under British law. Crucial evidence was provided by the police officers who had been observing and phone-tapping the family and it was this which persuaded the jury to find the defendants guilty. However, it emerged at the trial that there were considerable discrepancies between diary entries and evidence given in court and when police operations were investigated it seemed that the officers involved had lied up to sixteen times in order to produce a stronger case against the Salahs.[100] Finally a case was brought against Victor Kelaher, the head of the Drugs Squad, and five other members of his unit who were variously charged with perjury and conspiracy to pervert the course of justice.

One of the detectives, Norman Pilcher, had to be extradited from Australia where he had retired. He is of particular interest as he was one of the most experienced members of the Drugs Squad and had been involved in some of the high profile arrests of the period, including those of Brian Jones of The Rolling Stones and John Lennon. Caroline Coon recalls that Pilcher was often accused of taking bribes and of attempting to plant drugs on suspects, and had the nickname 'Groupie' at Release for the amount of time he spent hanging around with pop stars trying to incriminate them.[101] That he was found guilty of perjury and sentenced to four years' imprisonment throws an interesting light on the allegation of John Lennon, for example, that cannabis had been planted by the police at his house.[102] Two of Pilcher's colleagues at the trial were also found guilty and received sentences of eighteen months. The judge chided those convicted:

> You poisoned the wells of criminal justice and set about it deliberately. What is equally bad is that you have betrayed your comrades in the Metropolitan Police force, which enjoys the respect of the civilized world, and not the least grave aspect of what you have done is to provide material for the crooks, cranks and do-gooders who unite to attack the police whenever opportunity offers.[103]

Officials at the office of the Director of Public Prosecutions privately acknowledged that this was not the first time that the Drugs Squad had operated outside of the law in order to try to secure cannabis convictions. An internal memo in the run-up to the court case noted that 'as you may be aware, between May 1971 and May 1972 we were considering proceedings against Kelaher for conspiring with others to import and possess drugs and there is little doubt that we would have prosecuted him if we had been able to adduce evidence of certain telephone intercepts'.[104]

The Drugs Squad of the Metropolitan Police force in London was not alone in this period in harbouring officers who were prepared to operate outside of the law to secure convictions for drugs offences and accusations that police officers had framed innocent citizens by planting cannabis on them were not uncommon in the 1960s. An early example where the case was proven and a police officer was convicted was in Leeds in 1963. Police Constable John Mosey had worked together with a private detective called Howell to incriminate a West Indian migrant worker called John Hawley. Howell had broken into Hawley's flat and planted cannabis in a suitcase on a wardrobe. He had then arranged for Mosey and a colleague to search the premises:

> Mosey then opened the topmost of the three suitcases and took out a small packet which he threw to Mr Hawley saying: 'What's this? Is this Indian

hemp?' Mr Hawley did not catch the packet and avoided putting his finger-
prints on it. He protested that he knew nothing about the . . . packet.

Hawley was the victim of this set-up as the private detective had been
employed by the father of a white girl who had been dating the West
Indian. The father objected to the couple's plans to marry and wanted the
young man out of the way. In convicting the policeman for his part in the
plot the judge made it clear that 'it is a dreadful duty to have to deal with a
young man like you who had commited these truly terrible offences. The
police and policemen hold an exceptional position of trust which you have
deliberately betrayed'.[105]

Instances where police officers were found guilty of planting cannabis
were rare in this period but accusations were far more common. Common
too in these accusations were the elements of the story above, where the
drug was caught up in the racial tensions of the period. One example from
the end of the decade resulted in a complaint from the High Commission
for Jamaica to New Scotland Yard about 'the harassment by police officers
of coloured youths in the Croydon area'. It was alleged that 'the police have
been heard to say that they intend to get a few more [arrests of coloured
youngsters] within the next three weeks' and that on the evening of
12 September they acted. After a racial fight between white and coloured
youths outside The Gun Tavern in Croydon, the police had arrested a
number of the latter. One, O'Caul Gladstone Edwards, complained that he
had been leaving the pub in his car when he had been pulled over by a plain
clothes officer. When the car was searched, Edwards alleged, the police
officer had tried to place a package wrapped in silver foil in the boot but had
then withdrawn this after Edwards asked him what he was doing. However,
he left his car keys with the officer while he was taken to the police station
and when the wallet with the car keys in appeared next it contained a silver
foil packet of cannabis. Edwards maintained that he had no knowledge of
where this had come from and when in court stuck to his story: 'these
serious allegations were well aired at the trial and, in fact, formed the basis
of the complainant's defence'.[106] However, he was found guilty and after
the Director of Public Prosecutions investigated, it was decided that there
was no 'evidence to justify any criminal proceedings against the officers
concerned'.[107]

A prosecution was brought in Nottingham at about the same time however. Two detective constables and a detective sergeant there were put on trial for a range of offences and it was

> Alleged that the officers brought pressure to bear on a selected number of immigrants to get them to plant cannabis on people they knew. Then the police carried out raids, found the cannabis and caused false charges to be made. Victims of the plot were prosecuted and in most cases, convicted on false evidence.[108]

One witness was Vincent Robinson who ran a shebeen, or illegal drinking den. He alleged that he did this with the connivance of the police for whom he performed a 'little job' in return; he was an informant and also planted cannabis supplied by the detectives on members of the immigrant community. However, the case ended suddenly when another witness disappeared and the police officers were acquitted.[109]

As was argued with the 1950s in Chapter 4, the habit of many among the migrant communities of using cannabis despite its legal position, provided a useful pretext for some police officers to interfere with groups considered problematic largely because of the colour of their skin. That some police officers took this further still and sought to use planted cannabis to persecute migrant communities is consistent with accounts of the period that highlight the racism of many in authority. The records of Release show, however, that it was not only members of the migrant communities that were victims of these police tactics. Rufus Harris and Caroline Coon were certain that 'young people with long hair may be stopped and searched for really no other reason than they are perceived as being of a suspect generation'. Indeed, some officers seem to have been willing to go further and to plant drugs in order to make arrests. For example John, a 19-year-old trainee psychiatric worker, was stopped and searched by the police in Hendon in 1967. When they found nothing on him they produced a cigarette containing cannabis that they claimed to have found nearby. Despite denying any knowledge of it, he was charged with possession of cannabis but because Release provided a lawyer to contest the case in court the charges were hastily dropped. Despite such examples, Rufus Harris and Caroline Coon admitted that 'we had thought that a large percentage of the people contacting us would claim to have been "planted". We were mistaken, as only a very small number of our cases made this allegation'.[110]

This is an important reminder that any assessment of police approaches and attitudes towards cannabis in this period needs to be a balanced one where shocking stories of corruption and illegal practices should be acknowledged but carefully placed into context. Many police forces across the country were relatively unconcerned about cannabis consumption and about drug use in general. The clearest statement of this position came from the chief constable in Preston:

> To put the subject in perspective . . . it should also be appreciated that more than 72000 persons were prosecuted for various offences in Lancashire in 1967 and that only 80 of those offences related to drugs. Similarly, the 46 attacks upon chemist's shops represent only 1% of the total number of shopbreakings which came to police notice in this Constabulary area in 1967. We have long held the view that soft drug taking is an adolescent aberration which most of them will grow out of. We have no evidence of progression to 'hard' drugs although we are conscious of the possibility. We firmly believe that the undue publicity accorded to the subject in the press and on television has led to a good deal of imitative behaviour . . . In any event, we regard the misuse of drugs as a medical subject rather than one for the police to advise upon.[111]

Arrest figures from parts of the country tend to justify such circumspection. In Middlesbrough no one was arrested for cannabis offences in 1965, one man was arrested in 1966 for possessing cannabis and in 1967 the police only managed to find three in possession and four trying to supply.[112] In Wigan there were no arrests in 1965 for any drugs offences and by 1967 this figure had jumped to five.[113] In Surrey in 1967 there were twelve prosecutions for cannabis offences and in Essex there were twenty-three.[114] In Birmingham it was stated that 'during the past three years there has been a marked increase in the use of this drug [cannabis] and there is evidence to show that its use is widespread amongst the immigrant population and an ever increasing number of white teenagers'. However, the police there reported only seventy-two cannabis offences in 1967, an increase of six on the previous year.[115] With few forces generating more than a couple of cannabis offenders per week the impression remains that police across the country saw enforcing laws on the drug as only a minor concern that jostled for attention with their many other duties.

In fact the Home Office grew increasingly frustrated with police inaction as the decade wore on. As early as 1962 and as a response to Henry Brooke's concerns, senior police officers from across the country and representatives of the Customs and Excise were gathered together by Home Office officials. They gave those assembled the clear message that the government expected them 'to pool information about the extent of the traffic in cannabis and the methods employed by the traffickers, and to consider possible means of more effective co-ordination of the work of the enforcement agencies'.[116] However, in April 1967 they were once again brought together as the Home Office Police Department had observed that 'there appears to be considerable differences between forces in the organization, the rank and number of officers who are concerned [with drugs offences]' and 'it appears that there is little or no formal training of police officers in drugs work'.[117] At this meeting with senior officers, the Drugs Branch of the Home Office carefully laid out its recommendations:

> The Chairman said that a stage had been reached when a full time drugs squad in each force appeared to be justified . . . it was also agreed that in each force there should be one drugs liaison officer with whom Mr Jeffery could communicate on matters of detail. This would usually be the officer in charge of the drugs squad.[118]

Quite how the senior officers responded at the time is not recorded but evidence from across the country the following year suggests that the Home Office call for a nationwide network of drugs squads had not been met with enthusiastically. In February 1968 the police in Northampton, for example, reported that 'the Force has no established Drug Squad . . . this has not been established owing to shortage of manpower and that there would not appear to be a particular drug problem in the area'.[119] In Kent at the same time it was revealed that 'a central drugs squad does not exist in this Force'[120] and colleagues in Berkshire were in a similar position as they reported that 'this Force does not have an established Drugs Squad'.[121] In Wakefield the call had been similarly ignored as 'there is no established Drugs Squad in this force and all drug enquiries are confined to certain members of the Criminal Investigation Department, namely one Detective Inspector and two Detective Sergeants'.[122] Indeed, even where such agencies had been established it was sometimes on a piecemeal basis, so that in Halifax it was stated that 'A Drug Squad, consisting of a Detective Sergeant and two Detective Constables, was formed in the latter half of the year. This Squad is centralised and operates on a "part time" basis, combining enquiries into drugs with routine C.I.D. work'.[123] This diversion of the time and resources of drugs squads was not simply a feature of small, local forces. In 1970 it was reported that 'one of the problems of the Metropolitan Drugs Squad is that the senior officers spend most of their time on murder and complaints investigations to the detriment of work on drugs'.[124] By 1970 the Association of Chief Police Officers was asked by the Home Office to look into the problem of enforcing drugs legislation and it rather lamely repeated the recommendation of three years previous that 'each force should have appointed a drug squad whose sole responsibility will be to deal with this problem'.[125] After a decade of unprecedented law-breaking related to narcotic drugs the Home Office was forced to admit in a private memo that 'the scope for improvement in the present operational, training and intelligence arrangements at force level is so great that it is worthwhile to see whether the police service can put its house in order'.[126] It may have been the case that officials at the Home Office were keen to turn the police into vigorous upholders of drugs laws, but forces around the country often seem to have been less inclined to take the issue too seriously.

Government and science

The perils of ill-thought-out legislation formed against a backdrop of agitated media reporting had resulted in Henry Brooke's unworkable law on allowing cannabis to be consumed on one's premises and it appears that his successors decided to seek a more informed approach. As such, when the Interdepartmental Committee on Drug Addiction (Brain Committee) recommended in 1965 that a standing committee on drug dependence be established to monitor the situation and provide expert guidance on emerging issues the proposal was accepted. The establishment of the Committee was announced on 31 October 1966. Lord Brain accepted the invitation to act as its first chair but died before its inaugural meeting, and was replaced by Sir Edward Wayne, Regius Professor of Medicine at Glasgow University. Its members included experts from a range of fields: Roger Bannister, the athlete and physician, William Deedes the MP, and Nicholas Malleson of the Research Unit for Student Problems at the University of London were selected alongside psychiatrists, doctors and pharmacists, a magistrate, a policeman, and a prison governor.[127] With such a variety of professional and personal backgrounds the Home Office guaranteed that all manner of voices were represented and the proceedings could sometimes reflect this, one memo noting diplomatically that 'the

Committee's activities have been disturbed from time to time by an unexpected show of disharmony'.[128]

The LSD and Cannabis Sub-Committee of the Advisory Committee on Drug Dependence was established at the third meeting on 7 April 1967. Lady Wootton was appointed to the chair[129] and its remit was outlined as follows:

> The sub-committee was charged with reviewing evidence on LSD and Cannabis with reference to pharmacological, clinico-pathological, social and legal aspects. Its object after such a review was i. to express an informed opinion about medical and dependence dangers of LSD and cannabis ii. to suggest accordingly the type of control which should be established to limit such dangers.[130]

As with many of the committees that had preceded it, the initial task confronting the group was that of mastering the existing research. The first gathering on 11 May met having perused papers as diverse as a report on cannabis use in Nigeria, an interview with Timothy Leary in *Playboy* and an editorial from the *Journal of the American Medical Association*. Perhaps reflecting this eclectic homework, the Committee reached a tentative feeling that 'the social dangers from its use were too uncertain for decontrol to be a practical proposition'.[131]

Still the information kept on coming however, and members of the Sub-Committee began to show that they were not prepared to accept at face value all the information that was presented. An extract on cannabis from 'Drug Addiction with special reference to India', published by the Chopras in 1965, was criticized as 'somewhat out of date' and it was reported that 'members did not agree with certain statements contained in this paper'. More crucially, the Sub-Committee demonstrated that it was prepared to critically engage with the positions suggested by the Home Office civil servants who were working with it.[132] For example, the first draft of its report had been prepared by the Secretariat and was presented at the second meeting of the Sub-Committee. This draft stated that 'in industrial countries cannabis users often have a psychopathic personality and consumption of the drug was considered by the Commission on Narcotic Drugs (1963) to frequently be the first step towards later addiction to heroin and morphine'. Once the Sub-Committee had finished with it, however, the draft read as follows:

Cannabis consumption assumes a different character in some industrially developed countries from the one assumed in countries in which its use is a traditionally accepted practice. In UK consumption appears to be confined to young people...in UK the desire to take the drug is basically an anti-authoritarian protest by young people.[133]

If a more extreme position had been rejected in favour of a moderate one in this instance, the Sub-Committee was to show itself capable of amelioration at other times too. Sir Harry Greenfield, president of the Permanent Central Narcotics Board at the United Nations, reported to the Committee at its third meeting. He made it clear that 'the stringent controls of cannabis were instituted because of the international view that the use of Cannabis was associated with progression to hard drugs' although he did point out that 'respective countries are at liberty to exercise some discretion regarding appropriate penalties in specific cases'.[134] Yet the Sub-Committee was to include the following statement in its next draft of the report:

It is widely believed that consumption of cannabis leads to the use of 'hard' drugs. No reliable evidence of such escalation has been produced...in the UK the desire to take the drug may be an anti-authoritarian protest by some young people or an attempt to deal with personal problems on the part of others...there are many analogies to the taking of alcohol and tobacco though it may produce less craving than either of these substances. It should not be equated in its harmful effects to heroin and cocaine.[135]

The Sub-Committee's critical engagement could work the other way too. Having declined an opportunity to interview The Beatles on the grounds that 'nothing useful was likely to be achieved by interviewing these gentlemen' the Sub-Committee opted to talk to representatives of *International Times*, *Oz* magazine, and SOMA. Lady Wootton listened for a while to Mr Sharpe of *Oz* magazine explaining what the 'underground scene' was and where drugs fitted in before snapping that 'it sounds a little as though you were creating a religion without any dogma, since much of what you say is almost religious in tone' and reminding him that 'one is not always a good judge of one's own abilities'. More interest was shown in the testimony of R. D. Laing who was a member of a group that called itself the Research Committee on Cannabis at SOMA and which was made up of 'psychiatrists, economists and socialists' of British and American training. Early in 1967 this group had distributed 1,600 questionnaires in places that they thought likely to be frequented by cannabis users in London and had received 526 replies, some from as far away as Scotland. Their findings were provisional when they reported to the Sub-Committee in January 1968 and their recommendations far from extreme. Laing answered on the therapeutic properties of cannabis that

> It seems to be a symptomatic relief to some people in states of depression. I am not sure however whether it does not sometimes set up a vicious circle, whereby a depressed person takes this, feels his depression ameliorated, but has not thereby come to be in a better position for overcoming the conditions which are generating the depression in the first place.

When questioned about the law, he similarly prevaricated, 'I think the main feeling that I have is that I do not feel it should be regarded as such a serious offence as the law judges it to be by the penalties which are laid down'.[136] When prompted on the possibility of changing the law, he stated that 'the British compromise is sometimes the best way, not to get so worked up about it and let public opinion come round to the point, then the law can be changed'. Laing was sure that 'supposing as things are at the moment, without changing the law at all, the law was not enforced so energetically, then I think that would improve the situation'.[137]

While the Sub-Committee was to become attached to the notion of this 'British compromise' it continued to reject extreme positions. Indeed, one of its own members, Michael Schofield, produced a paper for the fifth meeting of the Sub-Committee advocating radical proposals. He had written this over the summer of 1967 and when he sent it to Lady Wootton he complained 'that certain important points have been left out' of the drafts produced to date and argued that his paper should act as 'an alternative report' to be sent to the main committee.[138] He advocated making legal possession of small amounts of cannabis, treating cannabis in the same way as alcohol in law, encouraging scientific experiments, and adopting a new international stance on the drug.[139] Wootton agreed that the paper should be considered at the Sub-Committee where 'after careful consideration it was decided that this was a minority report with which the other members of the Sub-Committee were not in any way associated'.[140] Disappointed, Schofield still sought to use his document to influence the debate by publishing it, albeit anonymously, through the National Council for Civil Liberties.[141]

The two key documents that were to shape the Sub-Committee's final positions did not appear for their consideration until 1968. The first of these was compiled by a member, Sir Aubrey Lewis. He had been a professor of psychiatry at the Institute of Psychiatry in London until retirement in 1966 and he had not joined the Sub-Committee until its fourth meeting in 1967. The task that had been presented to him was to conduct a thorough review of the literature in order to establish a clear position on the facts as they related to cannabis and its consumption. He examined 1,750 pieces of work and his report was a masterpiece of scholarly criticism and balance: 'there are diverse opinions about the effectiveness of penal legislation'; 'even on such straightforward matters as tolerance and the development of physiological dependence, there are contradictory statements'; 'benefits have been claimed from cannabis, but trustworthy reports have been few and vague'; 'there is no unequivocal evidence that cannabis can be the major or sufficient cause of any form of psychosis'; 'published statements regarding the association between crime and cannabis illustrate the confused and contradictory standpoint taken up by experts'; 'whether or how far particular features of personality conduce to the establishment of the cannabis habit is a highly contentious question'; and so on.[142] In other words he carefully demonstrated that there was no clear evidence to support the darkest assessments of cannabis, while on the other hand there was no clear evidence to support the more optimistic. He went on to note that 'total prohibition of all indulgence in cannabis was firmly rejected by the IHDC in 1894' but added that it had reached the conclusion that 'a regulating influence is necessary and should, in future, be exercised by the Government of India'.[143] On the matter of control he concluded:

> It seems, reading the contrasting statements on this matter, that most persons with relevant experience would like to have legislation applicable to the excessive user and the trafficker, but they object to blanket legislation which permits, and even encourages, the imposition of long terms of imprisonment or other stringent punitive measures. It is generally acknowledged that it is not so much law as the way it is acted on by police, customs officers and magistrates that determines its efficacy (which is, in any case, limited).[144]

Lewis had reached the same conclusion that had been presented earlier by R. D. Laing, that a British compromise was the way forwards where the law remained much the same in theory but where in practice those enforcing it did so with less vigour. The civil servants clearly took this message away as the brief notes scribbled on the file read: 'more research needed', 'not justified in lessening control but discretion', 'status quo if handled with discretion'.[145] All were to end up as features of the final report of the Wootton Committee. Indeed, it was the presentation and discussion of the Lewis document at the eighth meeting of the Sub-Committee in February 1968 that prompted Lady Wootton to drive the group in a new direction, from information-gathering to conclusion-reaching. As soon as Lewis finished speaking about his paper she 'invited each member to submit a short statement before the next meeting, setting out his view on the present law relating to LSD and cannabis, and how this might be amended'.[146] Such was the confidence placed in the Lewis document that the 'first draft outline for report on cannabis' prepared by Lady Wootton shows that large swathes of it were to be included in the Sub-Committee's final statements.[147]

Members reported back on their positions at the next meeting in March. The London magistrate, K. J. P. Barraclough argued that

> The evidence produced before the subcommittee, and in particular the detailed survey produced by Sir Aubrey Lewis, leads me to the conclusions that the harm to the individual, and hence to Society, occasioned by recourse to cannabis simplicities is very much less than that occasioned by heroin and the other drugs ... there is evidence that cannabis is smoked by a fairly large number of otherwise intelligent and law abiding citizens in a social environment which appears to be harmless as far as the individuals engaged therein are concerned ... the possession of cannabis could be separated and the penalty for this offence be reduced.

He recommended that all drugs legislation be revised into a single Act. Indeed, all agreed that new legislation was necessary, although Philip Connell and J. D. P. Graham were more interested in issues relating to the manufacture of substances than in talking about cannabis in detail. Aubrey Lewis was prepared to treat both cannabis and LSD in the same way, declaring that 'possession or consumption of cannabis or LSD should not in itself be an offence' and that 'no penal or other legal action should be taken which would tend to throw cannabis or LSD users into the company of narcotic addicts'. Peter Brodie, Assistant Commissioner of the Metropolitan Police, was concerned that those in law enforcement had made it known to him that 'any relaxation with regard to the sale of cannabis being made legal would be a retrograde step'. T. H. Bewley was sure that 'the main problems of cannabis are those which occur with the socially acceptable drugs, in that when taken by a large number of people over a long period of time, they may lead to serious public health problems', but he was aware that simple prohibition had never worked for either alcohol or tobacco. As such he was content that, 'if there are to be any changes in the law regarding cannabis, there should be a diminution of the penalties'. Timothy Raison, the editor of *New Society* magazine, was not in favour of legal change 'because of sheer social caution or cowardice' and as such 'would leave it to the courts to use their discretion as they do at present'.

Michael Schofield and Nicholas Malleson took rather more radical positions. The former wanted a two-phase legislative process, the first taking cannabis out of the Dangerous Drugs Act of 1965 and aimed at controlling only smoking in public places, and the activities of suppliers. The second phase, which would come into effect within three years, would focus on the behaviour of users rather than on the fact of their use so that only those 'drugged and disorderly' would be subject to penalties. Malleson was convinced that 'the drug should be freed from legislative control' and that notice should be given to the United Nations that unless clear evidence of the harmfulness of cannabis was forthcoming in the next five years the UK would go ahead and legislate on the assumption that it was not so.

Lady Wootton's approach was to articulate the British compromise:

> In the light of these observations my present (highly provisional) opinion is that the penalties for possession of cannabis ought to be drastically scaled down. I should be content with penalties substantially less even than those imposed by the Drugs (Prevention of Misuse) Act of 1964. One would hope that this would be a sufficient hint to the police and the courts as to how to deal with the youngster who is experimenting with the odd reefer: or the West Indian, whom I saw in court the other day, who 'went out and had a reefer' after a row with his wife.[148]

Her intention was not to radically overhaul the legislative apparatus but rather to influence 'the holders of high judicial office [who] are not all aware that there is a body of responsible (including medical) opinion that regards cannabis as certainly no more, and possibly less dangerous than alcohol'. These diverse views were discussed at the ninth meeting of the Sub-Committee where it was agreed that LSD was a more harmful drug than cannabis, that legislation should differentiate between cannabis and other drugs in the Dangerous Drugs Acts, that penalties for all kinds of cannabis offences should be 'considerably reduced', that fines ought to be made appropriate to the gravity of the offences committed, that possession should not be regarded as an absolute offence, and that the UN Single Convention's inflexible system might be considered for revision.[149] As work progressed on putting these agreed positions into a draft paper, a second document appeared that was to shape the Sub-Committee's recommendations. Its significance was such that the production of the final report was delayed in order to consider it, Lady Wootton reporting to the full Committee on 28 June that 'the subcommittee would also need to review their findings in the light of a report on marijuana which was being published by the American Medical Association'.[150] This was a paper called 'Marihuana and Society' and it appeared in the *Journal of the American Medical Association* on 24 June 1968. This was the outcome of a 'careful appraisal of available information' by the Council on Mental Health and the Committee on Alcoholism and Drug Dependence of the American Medical Association and the Committee on Problems of Drug Dependence of the National Research Council, National Academy of Sciences. Its conclusions were:

1. Cannabis is a dangerous drug and as such is a public health concern;

2. Legalization of marihuana would create a serious abuse problem in the United States;

3. Penalties for violations of the marihuana laws are often harsh and unrealistic;

4. Additional research on marihuana should be encouraged;

5. Educational programmes with respect to marihuana should be directed to all segments of the population.

The American conclusions were broadly similar to those that the Sub-Committee had been working towards. While the records of the meetings of the Sub-Committee after June 1968 are missing, it is clear from reading their final recommendations that the American paper had confirmed the group in its position that there was a great need for further research given the gaps in existing knowledge and that rigorous enforcement of tough laws was not necessarily the most effective approach to cannabis use in contemporary Western countries. Indeed, in its emphasis on education the American report echoed the position taken by the Sub-Committee since September 1967 when it had first noted that 'much could be done by the spread of information and advice' and advocated the establishment of advisory centres.[151]

The Sub-Committee's final report was endorsed by its parent body the Advisory Committee on Drug Dependence and Sir Edward Wayne submitted it to the Home Office on 1 November 1968. It took a sympathetic view of recent developments, arguing that 'an increasing number of people, mainly young, in all classes of society are experimenting with this drug, and substantial numbers use it regularly for social pleasure' and being careful to assert that 'there is no evidence that this activity is causing violent crime or aggression, anti-social behaviour, or is producing in otherwise normal people conditions of dependence or psychosis, requiring medical treatment'. Nevertheless, it felt that cannabis was a 'dangerous drug' and was sure to point out that 'we conclude . . . that in the interests of public health it is necessary to maintain restrictions on the availability and use of this drug. For the purpose of enforcing these restrictions there is no alternative to the criminal law and its penalties'. Legalization was ruled out in the 'near future' and was only to be considered when further research had satisfactorily provided data to tackle the 'difficult and complex problems most of which have not been given much thought even by those who favour legalisation'. Both social and scientific research ought to be encouraged for this reason and the Committee felt it important to 'most strongly urge that every encouragement, both academic and financial, be given to suitable projects'. On the topic of criminal law and its penalties there was some detailed argument which came down to ways in which British laws could be formulated and exercised in such a way as 'to bring about a situation in which it is extremely unlikely that anyone will go to prison for an offence involving only possession for personal use or for supply on a very limited scale'. This was because

> We believe that the association of cannabis in legislation with heroin and the other opiates is entirely inappropriate and that new and quite separate legislation to deal specially and separately with cannabis and its synthetic derivatives should be introduced as soon as possible. We are also convinced that the present penalties for possession and supply are altogether too high.

Anticipating the outcome of the Sweet appeal, the Committee also felt that 'we are convinced that there is no sufficient justification, in the harmfulness of cannabis, for placing occupiers and landlords of private premises under any special obligation to prevent cannabis-smoking'. On the issue of the policing of the drug, the Committee decided that 'we recommend that as a matter of urgency the Advisory Committee should begin a general review of police powers of arrest and search in relation to all drug offences... particularly as regards cannabis'. Finally, the recommendations found that 'The law alone cannot dispose of the problem of cannabis. However wise the law and whatever it says there will be those who will use cannabis and some who will suffer by it. Education too has a part to play'.

The difficult reception that these recommendations would receive in certain quarters was hinted at even before it was published. Elspeth Hobkirk, governor of Greenock Prison, and a member of the Advisory Committee on Drug Dependence, tendered her resignation from it to the Secretary of State for Scotland. She disagreed with the Report on Cannabis and the proposal that the Advisory Committee should review police powers of arrest and search for drug offences, but withdrew her resignation after discussion with Scottish officials.[152] The final report also contained two sets of reservations, one by Peter Brodie which advocated more severe penalties for large-scale trafficking and one by Michael Schofield that was a rather rambling call for more mechanistic legislation that limited the discretion of the magistracy and the police.

The report of Wootton's Sub-Committee was to suffer further criticism once it was in the public domain. Perhaps most damaging was the reception it was given in the House of Commons in a debate on 27 January 1969. James Callaghan, the Home Secretary, rejected the recommendation that penalties for cannabis offences be reduced and accused the Wootton Sub-Committee of having been 'over-influenced' by what he called the 'lobby in favour of legalising cannabis'. Quintin Hogg of the Conservatives theatrically listed the supposed effects of the drug including euphoria, excitement, 'disturbed associations', illusions, and hallucinations; 'This is what we are invited to legalise,' he concluded. Tom Iremonger, Conservative member for Ilford North, condemned 'the sophisticated academic drivel in this Report' and another Tory, Patrick McNair-Wilson, stood up and declared that it 'is really a most important day for the House of Commons when both Front Benches, on a matter of such importance, can show to the people of the country that we at least march together'. Characters as questionable as Pablo Osvaldo Wolff and Russell Pasha were cited as authorities in the Commons debate, as were the World Health Organization and the United Nations whose agendas have similarly been explored in this book.[153] Few were prepared to speak in defence of the report, and when Labour MPs David Kerr and Hugh Gray tried to draw attention to the merits of the Sub-Committee's work, they were met with the statement of their fellow Labour MP and Under-Secretary at the Home Office, Elystan Morgan who made it clear that 'it is the absolute duty of the Government to proceed with circumspection and care, and with the full support of the public, in refashioning the law'. This after explicitly noting newspaper headlines that had labelled the Wootton report a 'Charter for Junkies'.

However, a closer reading of the debate shows that much of it was not about the report at all. Hogg's point was absurd given that the Sub-Committee had made it clear that there was no case for legalization. Callaghan picked a fight with the pro-cannabis lobby, declaring that 'it is another aspect of the so-called permissive society and I am glad if my decision has enabled the House to call a halt in the advancing tide of so-called permissiveness'. This chimed well with members of the House, one noting that 'that was the first time I have heard a Minister of the present Government take his stand to stem the tide of the so-called permissive society instead of swimming with it' and another, Douglas Glover, a Tory former colonel, declaring that

> We should resist the modern vogue that anything goes, that a person who ruins himself or herself does not have a great effect on other people and that that has nothing to do with society as a whole. This House should stand firm tonight and say that we want to produce a responsible society and, therefore, we reject the recommendations of the Wootton Report.

When viewed in this light, it is clear that little of this debate was about cannabis itself or even about the work of the Sub-Committee. Coming at the end of a turbulent decade, and with little more than a year to go until the next general election, most of it was reactionary hot-air, or playing to the gallery, on the idea of the counter-culture for which cannabis was being taken as a symbol.

Indeed, some in the House of Commons that day acknowledged that Parliamentary disapproval of the Sub-Committee's recommendations on maximum penalties did not necessarily mean frustration for its key objective of making it unlikely that anyone would go to prison for an offence of simple possession. Tom Iremonger pointed out that

> Sentencing is a question for the Court, and the setting of the maximum penalty is a question for the House. I should not like to see the House usurp the function of the Court.

This point was echoed by others, the Labour MP David Weitzman stating for example that 'there is ample power for a court in appropriate circumstances to impose a lesser penalty than imprisonment'.[154] Parliament was not the only branch of government that had it in its power to implement the Sub-Committee's recommendations as it was the judiciary and the magistracy which actually decided what sentences were meted out for cannabis offences. Wootton had herself recognized this in stating that the Sub-Committee's findings should come to act as 'a sufficient hint to the police and the courts'. As the next chapter shows, the recommendations were to enjoy considerable success in this direction, but as early as 1970 Baroness Wootton was able to voice satisfaction that 'the Minister of State for the Home Office had commented, in regard to Recommendation 5 of the Report on Cannabis, that he thought that the sentences passed since 1967 for possession of small amounts of cannabis partly reflected the fact that the courts had had regard to the recommendation that possession of small amounts of cannabis should not normally be regarded as a serious crime to be punished by imprisonment'.[155]

Of course, in time the Wootton report was to enjoy success in the House of Commons too, as most of it was incorporated into the 1971 Misuse of Drugs Act, something which was acknowledged while the latter was passing through Parliament in 1970 when Norman St-John Stevas noted that 'these proposals for reclassification are based on those put forward by Lady Wootton [who] has been proved right and a tribute should be paid to her'.[156] As such, historians like Martin Booth are wrong to conclude that the government ignored the Sub-Committee, as within a year of its submission it was influencing legislators as well as magistrates and judges in both the framing and the practice of drugs laws. Indeed, it is telling to look at the behind-the-scenes work that had to be done at the Home Office in the immediate aftermath of the Home Secretary's intemperate initial response to the Sub-Committee's findings. At the very next meeting after the savaging in the Commons, officials worked hard to smooth ruffled feathers.

> Mr Beedle said that it was understandable that the Committee should feel disappointment over the Government's rejection of certain of their recommendations on cannabis. He wished, however, to give the Chairman and the Committee full assurance that the Home Secretary valued the work they were doing and wanted them to continue. As regards the proposal for new drugs legislation the Home Secretary was looking to the Committee for the fullest

advice and confirmation of this was to be seen in the reply to a Parliamentary
Question put down by Mr Blenkinsop for Written Answer that day.

It was agreed that a press statement should be issued noting that the
Advisory Committee 'unanimously expressed its full confidence in the
Chairman and in the Chairman of the sub-Committee on Cannabis' and
that it 'noted with satisfaction the Home Secretary's recent statement of
intent to recast the drug laws in a more comprehensive and flexible
form'.[157] At the next meeting the chairman reported that he had met
with the Home Secretary who 'reaffirmed his confidence in the Advisory
Committee'.[158] The Advisory Committee on Drug Dependence emerged
stronger than ever from the controversies surrounding the Wootton report.
It was constituted as a permanent statutory body in the 1971 Misuse of
Drugs Act.

Conclusion

It is clear that cannabis became caught up in the politics of the 1960s. The
small numbers of British youth that sought to challenge the traditional order
with notions of the counter-culture took to the drug as a means of achieving
alternative mental states. They also saw in its association with the colonized
of Britain's empire a symbol of opposition to the politics of the past. Their
readiness to appropriate cannabis as an emblem of their position meant that
the media seized upon the drug in sensationalist reporting and that reactionary politicians identified it as a target for their ire. A Conservative Government's desire to tackle what they perceived to be the indolent among the
nation's young prompted hasty legislation on the drug and increased powers
for the police. That is only part of the story however, as the origins of this
legislation also lie in the more prosaic ambitions of drugs enforcement
agencies for enhanced resources and their willingness to take the case into
the public arena and the media when they found that their superiors were
reluctant to support them. It is clear that the fresh resources and impetus
provided to the police to tackle cannabis supply and consumption more
vigorously were often directed into the racial and generational clashes of the
period. At the extreme end of this, cases where cannabis was actively
planted on those that had none show that the drug itself was not the chief
concern but rather it was the person who was framed that was the target of

police activity. Cannabis laws could be used as a tool with which to deal with white youth or black migrants who were thought to be threats to British society. However, this must not be overemphasized. Throughout the decade it is clear that there remained significant differences among the agencies responsible for enforcing drugs laws about the effort that should be devoted to it. While the Home Office in London was keen to impose a rigorous approach, many police forces resisted this and the evidence suggests that few dealt with more than a couple of dozen cannabis offenders in any one year.

While in practice both the consumption and the control of cannabis could often be very limited in the 1960s in the UK, in policy circles the decade was marked by an ever expanding debate. The cannabis user was represented in this for the first time, albeit on a limited and a partial basis. Organizations like SOMA and Release were invited to express their ideas and opinions while policy was being formulated, but they were not invited onto the committees that actually made the decisions. Indeed, organizations like SOMA and Release never claimed to speak for all cannabis users and certainly did not do so, and those from migrant communities remained particularly divorced from policy discussions and processes. Besides consumers, experts also found their voice within policy circles. At key moments such groups had been important in the past, for example in 1924 when the Pharmaceutical Society had been unnerved by media reports about the drug and had rushed to include cannabis on the poisons schedule. However, the sheer diversity of professional backgrounds included on the Wootton Committee and the amount of attention it devoted to cannabis were unprecedented. So too was the decision to make the Advisory Council on the Misuse of Drugs a permanent feature of the policy process.[159] Along with Parliamentarians, the police, the magistrates, and the judges, the experts were now formally incorporated into the process of formulating Britain's drugs policies. Indeed, by 1971 they had played a decisive role in this, as it was their decision to back 'the British compromise on cannabis', of leaving the law much as it stood but of advising the police and the courts to apply it less stringently, that was to shape approaches to consumers for the next quarter of a century.

7

'The British Compromise': Devolved Power and the Domestic Consumer, 1971–1997

Introduction

Lord Hailsham urged magistrates not to 'dive off the deep end' when confronted with cases of possession of cannabis. Parliament had drawn a distinction between possessors and traffickers, and magistrates should treat users of soft drugs with 'becoming moderation' and take great care over ascertaining the background ... 'Do not lose your heads as judges because the offence is new to your experience or has a sinister ring. Look at the objective facts. Probe the background of the offence. Do not be misled by specious or purely sentimental pleas in mitigation, but equally do not let your prejudice, if you have one, against the offence lead you to deal unduly harshly with the offender'.[1]

The above summary of an address by the Lord Chancellor to the annual conference of the Magistrates' Association in London in 1973 shows just how influential the Wootton Sub-Committee's recommendations became in the years immediately following their publication. The Lord Chancellor by that point was none other than Quintin Hogg, who had enthusiastically joined the attack on the Sub-Committee's findings in the House of Commons in 1968. His party came to power after the 1970 general election and it quickly passed the Misuse of Drugs Act which incorporated such Wootton Sub-Committee recommendations as reduced maximum sentences for cannabis offences, and which addressed such concerns of the Sub-Committee as the legal differentiation between possession for personal use and possession in order to supply. In the wake of the Act receiving Royal Assent in 1973 Hogg, as Lord Hailsham, found himself advising magistrates to adopt moderation in sentencing those found guilty of simple possession, in what amounted to a very large version of the 'hint' to be lenient advocated by Baroness Wootton herself.

Wootton had suggested too that such a hint be put the way of the police, and there is evidence that this had been also been given in the early 1970s. Glimpses of new approaches at that level can be difficult to find, but the impression of one London magistrate in 1975 was that 'the police are more tolerant in enforcement'[2] and members of the Advisory Council on the Misuse of Drugs (ACMD) also concluded that officers sought 'a more "social" role than previously' and that there was 'a growing tendency for the police to focus their attention away from the ordinary drug-user onto the trafficker'.[3] It appears that the 'British compromise' was implemented early in the 1970s, where possession of cannabis remained illegal, but maximum sentences for offences related to the drug were reduced and a less than severe application of these laws by those who enforced them was openly advocated. This chapter argues that this 'British compromise' was to continue to shape approaches to cannabis in the UK for more than a quarter of a century after the 1971 Misuse of Drugs Act.

Policy and practice, 1971–1982

'The British compromise' would only work if those charged with enforcing laws took the advice to do so with 'becoming moderation'. The evidence suggests that over the course of the 1970s they did so. The report of the Wootton Sub-Committee had observed that in 1967 over two-thirds of cannabis offenders did not have a record of non-drug offences and that 90 per cent of all cannabis offences were for possessing less than 30 g. About a quarter of those convicted received a custodial sentence, about 13 per cent were made subject to a probation order, and about 17 per cent of first offenders were sent to prison. By 1975 the ACMD analysed sentencing and found that only 6 per cent of those punished for cannabis offences received custodial sentences. Most found guilty of such crimes were fined less than £50 and a handful were let off with a caution.[4] On the whole those found guilty were male and in possession of small quantities of the substance and half of them had previous criminal convictions for offences unconnected with drugs. Less than 3 per cent of the sample was reconvicted within two years.[5] By 1979 just over 14,000 people were found guilty of, or cautioned for, drugs offences. Throughout the decade this total had been steadily increasing by around 5 per cent per annum and by 1979 87 per cent of these offences were related to cannabis with the majority of these for simple possession. However, there were significant increases in those found guilty of, or cautioned for, unlawful import or export of cannabis, and this number had grown by an average of 19 per cent per annum in the previous five years. When it came to custodial sentences three-quarters of the 772 people in prison for drugs offences on 30 June 1979 had been found guilty of trafficking. Less than eighty of those prisoners were there simply for possession. It was noted that over the period 1973 to 1979 only about one in five of those convicted for drugs offences received a custodial sentence.[6] When further investigation into figures for cannabis was made it was discovered that 'there was at most one first offender... awarded an immediate custodial sentence in 1979 for a single offence of possession of cannabis' and that this sentence had been appealed.[7] This brief statistical overview suggests two conclusions. The first is that the process of educating magistrates not to send offenders to prison for simple possession first advocated by the Wootton Committee and then adopted by governments early in the 1970s had been a success and that trafficking became the offence most likely to result in a period of custody by the end of the decade. What it also suggests is that the police were more zealous than ever in enforcing drugs laws and that increasing numbers of cannabis consumers were finding themselves with criminal records simply for using the drug, even if they were avoiding prison.

The police were not just more zealous in enforcing drugs laws, they were more enthusiastic than ever before in using the powers that the legislation conferred upon them. Officers had been given the right to search persons and vehicles on suspicion of possessing illegal drugs under the Dangerous Drugs Act of 1967. The Wootton Sub-Committee's report had flagged this up as a source of controversy and the ACMD had set up another subcommittee to look into the issue with the MP Bill Deedes as its chair. It did not recommend radical change and as such officers retained the right to stop-and-search on suspicion of drugs offences. Home Office statistics show that the police remained keen to exercise it. For example, of the 10,754 individuals stopped and searched in 1973 by the police about a third were found to be in illegal possession of controlled drugs.[8] In other words the officers concerned had used their stop-and-search powers on twice as many occasions where their suspicions were unfounded as where they had been right to use them. By 1977 Release wrote a report which claimed that by then 'over 3/4 of all recorded "drugs searches" are wrongful in the sense that police suspicions were groundless'.[9] Some were convinced that the police were using these powers to justify more general interventions in the activities of those that they considered suspicious or difficult, or as one member of the ACMD noted in 1975 'he was still concerned about the possible harassment of teenagers; in Brixton in particular the situation was becoming explosive'.[10] However, the picture was not necessarily a simple one, as there seemed to be marked regional differences in the use of the stop and search powers. In 1975 a document from the Cannabis Working Group of the ACMD noted the 'wide variation between forces both in the number of persons stopped and the number found to be in illegal possession of drugs'.[11] It was clear that outside of London the use of stop-and-search powers was rather more limited and could vary considerably. For example, in Leicester only seventy-three people had been approached by the police using these powers, while in Liverpool this number was 120, in Manchester it was 322, and in Northumberland 498.[12]

Stop-and-search powers joined maximum sentences in the range of targets for those that remained convinced that the country's cannabis laws and policies were an affront to British civil liberties. A Criminal Law Bill in 1977 gave reformers the opportunity to thrust cannabis legislation and policy back into the political limelight. Lord Anthony Gifford was a noted civil rights lawyer who would go on to be involved in such high profile cases as the Birmingham Six appeals and the Bloody Sunday Inquiry. In a debate in the House of Lords in 1977 he moved an amendment to the Bill that would have removed the possibility of imprisonment in a magistrate's court for the simple possession of cannabis. His suggestion was not that possession be made legal, but rather that it should be punished by a fine of up to £500. He added that cannabis should be the only Class B drug to be treated in this way, and that possession of others in that category should remain subject to terms of imprisonment.[13]

Gifford had been prompted to take up the issue by Rufus Harris, one of the founders of Release. Both were lawyers with interests in cases that had civil liberties implications and Gifford remembers that discussions with Harris led him to devise and offer the amendment. He freely admits that he had no particular interest in the drug itself, but rather was concerned about the heavy-handed approach of the police and the illogical position of cannabis in relation to other drugs.[14] In the House of Lords he made it clear that he was part of a 'body of opinion' that remained convinced that cannabis 'used in moderate quantities does not cause anyone any harm' and that as such imprisonment for possession was a 'barbarity'.[15] Lady Wootton was there to speak up in support, along with various other peers including the magistrate Baroness MacLeod of Borve who pointed out that in her court those in possession were usually fined and put on probation rather than imprisoned.

Opposition to the amendment came from the government spokesman Lord Harris, who pointed to the British compromise in stating that after the Wootton report there had been 'a substantial reduction in the use of custodial sentences ... and that judicial processes now emphasized the desirability of alternatives to custodial sentences wherever possible'. Moreover he pointed out that the government's Bill itself proposed a step in a more liberal direction as it planned to reduce the maximum term of imprisonment from six months to three months. The intention was to reinforce the message to the courts that simple possession of cannabis was seen as among the less serious drugs offences. However, he pointed out that there was still considerable confusion about the long-term impacts of cannabis use and that as such any decision to entirely remove the prospect of imprisonment for the offence of simply possessing cannabis ought to be deferred until the Cannabis Working Group of the ACMD came to a definitive conclusion.[16] Supporters of the amendment were not put off easily and accused the government of prevarication: 'I would say to your Lordships that a time comes when inquiries have to cease and politicians have to take decisions,' argued Lord Avebury.[17] He would have been surprised to learn that at this stage it seemed as if the government had taken a decision and that it was to go along with the amendment proposed by Gifford. The government spokesman, Lord Harris, had been perturbed to see that 'representatives of all three parties, including Baroness Wootton, spoke in favour of the amendment [and] there was no support for the Government'.[18] In a confidential note prepared by Home Office officials for a meeting of the Cannabis Working Group of the ACMD it was admitted that 'the Minister received no support for his defence of the status quo [and] is satisfied that the substance of amendment (a) will have to be conceded'.[19] Elsewhere it was acknowledged that 'he feels strongly that there should ... be a government amendment to the Bill removing imprisonment on summary conviction for possession of cannabis or cannabis resin, and he has asked for this to be considered as a matter of some urgency'.[20] At this stage, it looked as if the government was about to give in to the pressure to remove imprisonment as the ultimate sanction for simple possession of the drug.

The lack of consensus at the ACMD served to thwart this. Its Cannabis Working Group convened for an emergency meeting about the Gifford Amendment and entirely rejected it. Instead, it recommended that imprisonment be removed for a first offence involving any Class C drug and that in time cannabis and cannabis resin should be reclassified as Class C substances.[21] Any brief clarity that this provided was quickly shattered as Griffith Edwards, a member of the Cannabis Working Group who had missed the emergency meeting, announced that he was opposed to these recommendations, arguing that 'the impact of present laws on individuals had not been shown to be so damaging as to justify a retreat from the health concern'.[22] So determined was his opposition that two of the Working Group's other members changed their minds and chose to dissent from the position that they had agreed at the emergency meeting. Indeed, the ACMD's Legal and Administrative Working Group made it clear that it also disagreed with the Cannabis Working Group recommendations on reclassification.

This division within the ACMD seems to have caused Lord Harris to reconsider his inclination to yield to the Gifford Amendment. As such when it came up for a full debate in the House of Lords on 24 March 1977 his determination to oppose change was renewed. He pointed out that the amendment would only confuse the classifications established by the Misuse of Drugs Act as it would render cannabis neither a Class B nor a Class C drug. He also referred to a recent series of court cases that had brought to light a legal anomaly whereby cannabis leaves were not illegal whereas the cannabinol within them was. He claimed that until the law was clarified on this issue no amendments ought to be made that might further confuse the matter.[23]

Quintin Hogg, as Lord Hailsham, then piped up to make it clear that he suspected those supporting the amendment to have ulterior motives. Hailsham's chief concern was that 'every argument that has been adduced . . . for reducing the penalty of imprisonment is equally applicable to the abolition of the offence altogether'.[24] In other words he employed the same tactic in this debate as he had used almost a decade earlier in that about the Wootton report in which he muddied the waters with mention of legalization. He then produced a lengthy argument against the wisdom of legalizing cannabis which largely drew on the logic that it was unwise to encourage a third intoxicant alongside alcohol and tobacco. The response of Lord Gifford made it clear that he was really concerned with imprisonment rather than cannabis. As a civil rights lawyer his anxiety was that

> As a matter of social policy it is not healthy to retain as an imprisonable offence an activity which, for better or worse, many thousands of people commit every day and in committing it think they are doing no wrong. That does not mean that one legalizes the substance; but it does give pause to consider whether in fact it is wise to imprison people for having it.[25]

When a vote was taken the result was close, but with seventy-seven for and eighty-three against, the amendment was not approved by the House of Lords.

A similar tactic was adopted in the House of Commons whereby those seeking alterations to cannabis laws attempted to use the Criminal Law Bill as a vehicle for change. Robin Corbett's Amendment number 126 was debated on 13 July 1977. This was part of a larger proposed alteration to the Criminal Law Bill which addressed a range of issues related to cannabis. Those that spoke for the Corbett Amendment that day were convinced that 'it produces fewer ill effects than tobacco' and indeed that it was 'totally harmless'. The main discussion in the Commons, however, was of stop-and-search powers. It was pointed out that in no other context were the police given such sweeping licence to arbitrarily halt individuals and insist on searching them 'on suspicion'. Indeed, such powers had recently been denied the police in another context during a debate about the Prevention of Terrorism (Temporary Provisions) Act 1976. Corbett pointed out that the police tended to employ the powers only in relation to young people with long hair and unconventional dress and that as such 'this single power has proved to be one of the most damaging to the police–public relations, particularly to relations between the police and young people'. His thrust was clear: 'it is an abuse of civil liberties which cannot be justified by the results and which cannot be tolerated in a country which holds dear its civil liberties'.[26]

In a later interview Corbett admitted that he had been prompted to raise the issue of cannabis by Rufus Harris of Release, and that he had been happy to do so because he had been aware of complaints about police use of stop-and-search powers related to drugs in his own constituency of Hemel Hempstead.[27] However, Corbett was persuaded to withdraw this motion by the Minister of State, Brynmor John. Like his colleague in the Lords back in March when the Gifford Amendment had been presented, John was able to use the position of the ACMD to justify deferring action on legislative change on cannabis. To this end he referred to a letter from the Advisory Council to the Home Secretary of 17 June 1977. This was the outcome of a series of meetings hastily organized between the ACMD's Legal and Administrative Working Group and its Cannabis Working Group after the former had rejected the latter's alternative to the Gifford Amendment. When a vote was taken on the question of whether the law should be amended so that it would no longer be possible to receive a custodial sentence for a first offence of simple possession of cannabis the meeting was split with six members in favour of the change and five against it.[28] However, all were agreed that 'the Council should... be informed of the present disarray of the law on cannabis and the view of the meeting that this should be rectified'.[29] A meeting of the full ACMD to address this disarray resulted in the letter to the Home Secretary. It stated that the full Council endorsed the position that it should no longer be possible to receive a custodial sentence for a first offence of simple possession but it specifically stated that the ACMD did not consider the Criminal Law Bill to be an appropriate vehicle for reform of law relating to cannabis. Furthermore it provided the government with the ideal tool for a delaying tactic on the issue of cannabis as it offered 'as a matter of urgency, a comprehensive review of the classification of drugs and of the penalties under the Misuse of Drugs Act'.[30] As the letter was discussed in the House of Commons, and as Corbett had himself referred to it approvingly in his own speech, there was little option but for him to accept it and to withdraw his proposed amendment.[31] The outcome of all of this was that the government successfully followed its own course on cannabis tariffs, and the 1977 Criminal Justice Act reduced the maximum possible sentence for possession of cannabis on summary conviction to three months' imprisonment. It is worth noting that this was one month less than the maximum proposed by the Wootton Sub-Committee in 1968.

It is worth dwelling on these attempts in both the Lords and the Commons to use the Criminal Law Bill to reform legislation on cannabis in 1977. They shared common features that show how far the dynamics of the position on cannabis had changed since the Wootton report. The place of

Rufus Harris and Release in the origins of each amendment shows that those who had sympathies with cannabis consumers had continued to organize themselves into an effective lobby. While Caroline Coon had been unafraid to knock on the doors of Home Office bureaucrats and senior police officers in the 1960s,[32] Harris had clearly taken this one step further in the following decade by seeking not just to influence policy but to initiate it. Both Gifford and Corbett were happy to give Harris the credit for seeking them out and persuading them of the need for action. However, it is also worth noting that neither was an advocate of cannabis consumption, and indeed Harris does not seem to have been particularly energetic in recommending use of the drug. Rather, his concerns were with the rights of others to consume it without fear of arrest, imprisonment, or a criminal record. It was these rights that Gifford and Corbett were similarly keen to defend, and as such the efforts to reform laws on cannabis of 1977 must be seen in the wider history of activism on issues related to civil liberties in the period. That these efforts on the part of legislators were scuppered was down to the new-found place of the experts in the process of establishing policy on drugs in general, and on cannabis in particular, of the period after the Wootton report. The ACMD had been invoked by the government in order to oppose both the Gifford and the Corbett amendments as division among the experts had bolstered the government's commitment to the status quo. If anything then, the impetus to change provided by the organization of a lobby sympathetic to cannabis consumers was balanced by the complicating factor of the establishment of a permanent presence for expert advisers to government.

This was the case as the ACMD was a broad church, which included professionals and experts from a wide range of backgrounds and with diverse personal and political beliefs. As such, further research was often pursued rather than the more difficult business of seeking agreed positions. For example, when the committee came to deliver its first interim report in December 1973 it was unable to do more than point out all of the areas in which more information was required, and it could not even guess how many people in the UK had used cannabis. Its proposal to conduct a house to house survey to resolve this was quickly resisted by the Office of Population Censuses and Surveys which pointed out that any meaningful result was likely to require a survey of at least 50,000 households which would cost over £200,000.[33]

It was only in 1977 with the Gifford and Corbett Amendments that a sense of urgency was injected into the ACMD's deliberations on cannabis. This urgency simply served to expose the divisions there between those that saw cannabis as a civil liberties issue and those that were more concerned to see it from the 'Public Health view'.[34] M. J. Power made a forceful early statement of the civil liberties case in September 1977:

> Universal education and increased standards of living had led to higher expectations and the desire of individuals to exert more control over their own destinies. At the same time a collective social conscience had developed . . . It could be in line with trends in Government social policy in recent years that the number of controlled drugs should be kept to a minimum . . . the regulation of individual freedoms should be handled with a light touch.[35]

For the other side Griffith Edwards articulated the case from the public health point of view soon after, arguing that 'he was strongly opposed to the opinion that enough was known about cannabis in terms of population use to recommend liberalisation'[36] and reminding colleagues at a later date that 'he considered the implications for public health of increased use of cannabis to be crucial'.[37] The chair of the ACMD's Cannabis Working Group, J. D. P. Graham, however, was careful to voice his opinion that the public health position was no less a political one than the civil liberties argument, stating that 'if one took the paternalistic view, which he did not, then one felt justified in trying to prevent people harming themselves'.[38]

At each stage when key decisions had to be made these divisions surfaced. By 1979 the full Advisory Committee was ready to consider recommendations produced by a subcommittee charged with the 'comprehensive review' promised in 1977. When it came to voting on each recommendation unanimity was scarce: fourteen voted against the recommendation that possession of a Class C drug should remain an arrestable offence while thirteen voted for it; sixteen voted for the recommendation that the maximum penalty on summary conviction of unlawful possession should be a fine of £200 while eleven voted against it; twenty-one members voted for the key recommendation that cannabis and cannabis resin be moved from Class B to Class C in the drugs schedules while six voted against it.[39] The chairman summarized the divisions on the ACMD as follows:

> Some members' appraisal of all the available scientific evidence so far leads them to conclude that some alleviation of the penalties for unlawful possession could be contemplated at the present time without undue concern about its

encouraging increased use and possible risk to public health. Others, having regard to reports of current, although inconclusive, scientific investigations are not satisfied that enough is known to recommend action which would be widely regarded as implying that the risks of using cannabis and cannabis resin are less serious than was believed; and which would encourage increased use.[40]

The key recommendations endorsed by the ACMD, though not agreed unanimously, were that cannabis and cannabis resin should be transferred to Class C and that the maximum sentence on summary trial for Class C drugs should be reduced to £200, and on indictment two years and/or a fine.[41] On the face of it this was a victory for the civil liberties side of the argument whose advocates had been able to force through lighter penalties in the face of those that wished to maintain the status quo.

The report was finally presented to Parliament on 15 January 1979 and made public on 22 June, despite the fact that the Advisory Council had voted against publication.[42] Officials seem to have decided to go ahead anyway, one writing that 'this subject has been in travail too long and for the time being we must reach, if not the end of the road, at least a compulsory stop line'.[43] The publication of the report was done in such a way as to emphasize to readers the division over the recommendations within the Advisory Council. The published version contained as its first item a letter by the chairman to the Home Secretary in which he made it clear that key decisions had been the matter of controversy and that many members had voted against some of the recommendations.[44] The press release that accompanied the publication of the report couched the key recommendation, that cannabis be reclassified, as follows:

> On the question of cannabis and cannabis resin the Advisory Council unanimously concluded that the use of these drugs should not be legalised or decriminalised. The recommendation that the drugs should be transferred from Class B to Class C was passed by a majority (21 to 6) of the Council. The Report recommends that the UK Government should continue to pursue with the utmost vigour the aims of the UN Single Convention on Narcotic Drugs (i.e. to limit the use of certain drugs, including cannabis and cannabis resin, to legitimate medical and research purposes).[45]

In other words, some effort was taken to represent the proposed change as anything but radical and to portray it as nothing more than tinkering with an existing system that remained very much intact. Indeed, by publicly drawing attention to the division within the ACMD over the recommendations it could be argued that care was taken to undermine confidence in them.

Responses to the ACMD recommendations were divided. Apathy seemed to be the general approach, as it was noted by one official that 'the proposals in the report, which were given some coverage in the press in January when they were announced to Parliament, did not arouse significant public interest at that time'.[46] Pro–cannabis campaigners were rather more agitated, however, and the recently founded Legalise Cannabis Campaign (LCC) published a response in September. In it the LCC portrayed the recommendations as 'the ultimate political compromise: they will give the Government an opportunity to be seen to be cautiously responding to the call for cannabis law reform without having to make any meaningful changes'. The key complaint was that civil liberties issues had not been adequately dealt with as 'the most important single omission of the Report is any discussion of the damage caused by the criminalization of cannabis. The hypothetical harmful effects on public health caused by drug use must be balanced with the damage done to the individual and society by prohibiting it'. The response specifically tackled the health argument by insisting that 'no clear evidence has emerged that cannabis use presents any significant risk to health, unlike almost all other recreational drugs (including alcohol, tobacco and caffeine)... the demand that further research is necessary before any reform can take place is now meaningless'. Moreover, the LCC argued that 'the Council has not consulted a great deal of the available relevant material ... The Report also contains actual mistakes of fact, as well as omissions, and the lack of advice on matters of law is apparent'.[47] The civil liberties advocates at the ACMD may have won the day there but outside of its confines campaigners for change in cannabis laws felt that too little had been achieved. By contrast, the response in government was muted. While officials may have been keen to press 'this tedious problem of cannabis'[48] back into the public eye at the end of 1978 the brakes seem to have been quickly applied by the end of May 1979. Within three weeks of the new Conservative Government coming to power a memo in the Department of Health and Social Security (DHSS) decided that 'there are certain arguments for delaying a decision on the substance of the report' which included leaving time to gauge public responses to it and the opportunity to consult with ministers of the European Drugs Cooperation Group in November.[49] As it transpired, a decision was delayed by almost three years until March 1982.

Perhaps the most significant outcome of the civil liberties case coming out on top in the 1979 recommendations was the fightback launched by those on the ACMD who advocated a public health approach to cannabis laws. Griffith Edwards had trained as a doctor and had served as the director of the Medical Research Council-funded Addiction Research Unit since 1968. He was not keen on having non-scientists offer opinions on scientific papers, and as early as 1977 had worried that 'members of the Council who are not specially technically qualified . . . assume that there is a consensus on safety where none exists'[50] and had advocated a 'small technical group' to review the scientific evidence.[51] He was also unconvinced by the quality of the scientific information that had been produced on cannabis by the ACMD to date, pointing out at one stage that 'I had considerable misgivings in relation to the evidence which the Technical Committee put before us at the time when the recent report was being prepared which gave the appearance of being superficial'.[52] He seized upon a volume published in 1979 that contained scientific papers from an academic conference to argue that it 'casts doubt on the validity of the report from the Scientific and Technical Group which was fed into the recent cannabis report' and that he was now 'anxious about the possibility of our misleading ministers'.[53] He kept up the pressure on the Home Office, a month later writing that 'the time has come for calling on some additional expertise' as 'if, at this juncture, we failed to make a major investment in serious and unbiased reading of the available evidence, we will lay ourselves open to deserved criticism'.[54] Rattled by this prospect, and perhaps stung by the Legalise Cannabis Campaign barb that it had not 'consulted a great deal of the material available', the ACMD agreed at its meeting of 17 January 1980 that the chairman needed to act. The outcome was the establishment of the Expert Group on the Effects of Cannabis Use, the remit of which was 'to assist the Council in its consideration of the implications for future policy on the use of cannabis and cannabis resin of the current scientific evidence on the effects of such use'.[55] In other words this group was designed to separate out the health issues from those related to civil liberties and to focus solely on the former. The membership of the Expert Group reflected this as the social scientists and legal experts on the ACMD were excluded and only scientists and medical men were included, with three pharmacologists, two professors of medicine, one psychiatrist, one pharmacist, one neuropatholo- gist, and two doctors making up the group. Leading it was the ACMD's chair, J. D. P. Graham, who was himself a professor of pharmacology at Cardiff University. Edwards was another of its members.

It is important to note that when Edwards referred in 1979 to scientific papers from a recent conference in persuading the Home Office that more was needed by way of expertise, it was in fact a volume edited by William Paton and his long-term collaborator Gabriel Nahas from a meeting that they had organized in Rheims in 1978. Nahas and Paton were high-profile opponents of cannabis consumption and collaborated regularly throughout the 1970s on the issue.[56] For example, Nahas wrote to Paton in 1977 to excitedly report that in the USA 'the fight against marihuana is really heating up' as the decriminalization campaign had enjoyed some successes, of which Nahas concluded that 'it is pretty hard to stop a roller coaster, but we are still trying'.[57] Paton reported from the UK that he had 'spent yesterday afternoon recording material for a programme on our national radio (BBC 4) on cannabis: refreshing that the producer actually wanted somebody willing to voice a cautionary attitude'.[58] As such their assertions in the 1979 volume that cannabis use could result in 'long-term damage to lungs, reproductive function, and the immune system' and that 'cannabis satisfies the usual criteria for an addictive drug' were not uncontroversial.[59] Indeed, a World Health Organization meeting held in 1981, which was chaired by Paton, actually resisted endorsing such conclusions.[60] This was not the first time that their thoughts on cannabis had been challenged, and as early as 1973 the *Journal of the American Medical Association* had published a review of a book by Nahas in which a critic had argued that his work on cannabis was 'essentially moralistic' and guilty of 'biased selection and interpretation of studies and omissions of facts'.[61]

Edwards had used the controversial and contested work of these authors to maximum effect, as he had been particularly concerned to draw attention in his letter to the Home Office to the 'possibilities of brain damage' reported by Nahas.[62] More pertinently still, he then personally intervened to ensure that William Paton was appointed to the Expert Group. The chair had initially decided that Paton should only feature as a witness, as he was aware of the latter's 'strong opinions about cannabis'. Edwards took to the phone to press the case for including Paton as a working member of the group, and Graham relented during the call.[63] One newspaper saw this as a 'new setback for [the] "legal pot" campaign' and *The Observer* reported Paton's statement that 'if you test cannabis on the stiff tests that are available, it seems to be at least as bad as cigarette smoke'.[64] Paton's family background might explain his unforgiving approach to cannabis as he was the son of evangelical Scottish Presbyterians who had been influential missionaries in India and had authored critical reports on the opium trade in the 1920s.[65]

Whether Edwards believed that he was loading the Expert Group to find against cannabis or was simply ensuring that it was better balanced by including representatives with negative views is unclear. Paton certainly became influential, as when the Group finally reported it made a point of thanking 'William Paton and the staff of the Department of Pharmacology, University of Oxford' for the assistance given in helping to identify 'from the multitude of research papers on cannabis those which were of potential relevance to members of the Group'. This report appeared in November 1981 and it covered various topics related to cannabis including pharmaco-kinetics, respiratory effects, psychiatric outcomes, and impacts on reproduction and immunology. Having scoured the scientific and medical literature selected for it by Paton's team, and consulted a range of reports from various other bodies, the Expert Group came to the position that 'there is insufficient evidence to enable us to reach any incontestable conclusions as to the effects on the human body of the use of cannabis'. It did offer the tentative observation that much of the research had failed to prove that cannabis was harmful, but it balanced this with the statement that studies did exist that suggested harm in certain circumstances. The report also made it plain that members were persuaded that cannabis substances had therapeutic potential.[66]

While there was nothing particularly surprising about these observations, the lack of 'incontestable conclusions' about the effects of cannabis on the human body was enough for those who advocated a cautious approach to change in laws related to the drug on grounds of fears about public health. Indeed, the Expert Group's report provided the government with the justification to finally reject the ACMD's 1978 recommendations to reclassify cannabis and to reorganize sentences for offenders. That the government was prompted to do so when to all appearances it seemed content to ignore the recommendations was down to its Criminal Justice Bill. A centrepiece of the Conservative administration's legislative programme, its progress through Parliament presented an opportunity for campaigners to force the ACMD's recommendations back on to the political agenda. Robert Kilroy-Silk, then Labour MP for Ormskirk, tabled an amendment that would have removed the option of imprisonment following summary conviction of unlawful possession of cannabis.[67] An official at the Criminal Policy Department noted the government's approach as follows:

> Now that Ministers have decided the line to be taken in dealing with the amendment to the Criminal Justice Bill put down by Mr Kilroy-Silk ... it seems desirable to make the [Expert Group] report available as part of the background material for the Standing Committee's debate, well before the amendment is reached. We propose to arrange publication on 5 March.[68]

Bearing in mind that the report had been submitted to government in November of the previous year, it is interesting to note that this memo was sent on 23 February 1982. In other words, it seems that only once the political worth of the document became apparent did any urgency lend itself to the process of making the Expert Group report public.

Its political worth was quickly realized as the report became a central feature of government statements on the issue. In the House of Lords, for example, the minister announced that 'a group of eminent scientists [was asked] to assess the evidence of the effects of cannabis use. The group's report ... states after very careful assessment that there is insufficient evidence to reach any incontestable conclusion ... we do not intend to introduce or support legislation to alter the existing law concerning cannabis'.[69] In a letter to the ACMD the link between the government's position and the Expert Group's conclusions was also made explicit:

> The decision that the Home Secretary did not favour any change was announced on 11 March in the House of Commons by Mr Patrick Mayhew, Minister of State, Home Office, during the Committee stage of the Criminal Justice Bill. Mr Mayhew explained that the decision was taken both on grounds of principle and on practical grounds. The Home Secretary considers that any relaxation in control could be taken to mean that the health risks from using cannabis had been exaggerated, thus encouraging its use, especially by young people. He took very much into account the report of the Council's expert group and concluded that the Government should not seek or support a change in the law as long as the dangers of using cannabis are not adequately known.[70]

The civil liberties advocates may have had their way in 1979 when the ACMD had recommended less severe maximum penalties in law for cannabis offences. However, the public health advocates who took a more cautious line based on their fears about the unknown impacts of cannabis on humans worked hard between then and 1981 to ensure that it was their anxieties that resulted in the rejection by the government of the earlier position.

It is important to bear in mind the change of administration between 1977 and 1982 in seeking to understand how this had happened. As already stated, the division on the ACMD was between those who felt that the civil liberties costs of existing laws outweighed the possible health risks and those who held the reverse position, that evidence of detrimental impacts on health demanded government action even though this might serve to limit personal liberties. In essence this was a fundamental split between two visions of modern government in Britain: the first believed that behaviour which only affected the individual was no business of the state and the second took a more paternalistic view that involved the state protecting its citizens from harm. Changes in British law were most likely in 1977 as Labour politicians leaned towards the former position in a period when, as one member of the ACMD observed, 'Government had been tending to withdraw from responsibility for protecting people from the consequences of their own actions'.[71] As such it was Labour MPs and peers that had introduced amendments to legislation in order to try to force through change and had come close to succeeding when their own ministers found themselves embarrassed to be opposing them.

On the other hand changes in British law were firmly ruled out in 1982 as Conservative ministers came from a tradition that leaned towards the more paternalistic vision. When the Tory Home Secretary, William Whitelaw, had spoken to the ACMD in 1981 he had explicitly used the language of paternalistic government. He accused those that thought of drug use as a 'self-induced, so-called victimless crime' of being 'callous, inaccurate and dangerous'. He underlined his government's conviction that 'we must contain the growth of drug abuse if we are to maintain a sound foundation of our society and to keep it healthy and vigorous'. As such he did 'not think it is entirely fanciful to talk of a battle against drug abuse'.[72] With the rise to power of a Tory administration the vision dominating government had changed and the language of the drugs debate switched from one of civil liberties to one of paternalistic control. As if to gird the ACMD for this 'battle' change was imposed on it as the Home Office appointed a new Secretary to oversee its functioning. His name and track record seemed portentous, as out went Mr Turner and in came Mr Hardwick, with his experience of counter-terrorist contingency planning and firearms legislation.[73]

Cannabis and the 'battle against drug abuse', 1982–1997

By 1982 more cannabis consumers than ever before found themselves in trouble with the police, even if fewer ended up in prison than had been the case a decade earlier. Part of the reason for this was that there were greater numbers of consumers to arrest. Evidence of just who these consumers were and why they used cannabis products is difficult to come by, but throughout the 1970s glimpses show that the market for the drug continued to diversify. A set of arrests in Luton in 1972 suggests that the drug was being used by young members of the working class as part of their routine recreational habits. The police raided a house on the evening of 28 January in Victoria Street and arrested four youths. Three were residents at the property and one was formally the tenant. They were caught in the act of smoking cannabis and once the police had searched the premises they found sixteen cigarette ends and an ashtray that contained traces of cannabis. When the case came to court probation officers prepared reports on each which give an insight into the social backgrounds of the accused. The tenant of the property was 20 at the time of his arrest and working in Luton as a labourer at a local building company. As a youngster in Middlesbrough he had been in trouble with the police for housebreaking, but he chose to leave his home town in 1967 to avoid further contact with his peer group and thereafter had enjoyed continual employment. He had been in his labouring job for about a year when arrested, and before this had worked around the Midlands in such places as the Vauxhall car plant at Luton and the Boots factory in Nottingham. When contacted former employers confirmed that he had been a 'satisfactory' worker. The first of his flatmates was the son of a Polish father and English mother who had been born near Carlisle and had passed his teenage years in the care of the county council as his mother had abandoned the family. At the time of arrest he was 17 and he had been in trouble with the police for theft. He had worked on the construction of the M1 as a junior engineer for two years and had only arrived in Luton in the month of his arrest. A second flatmate was a 24-year-old Irishman and the son of a furniture retailer who had left school at the age of 15. He had lived in London since 1967 and been employed as a labourer, before moving to Luton and working at the Granada Motorway Services on the M1 and then at the Luton car plant. A third flatmate was a 20-year-old Londoner who had been a baker until late in 1971 when he had resigned in order to travel.

The probation officer dealing with these cases said of the tenant that his 'strong point is his willingness and ability to work hard and whilst employed he has looked after his mother very well indeed. He is confident that he can find work quickly once his trial is complete and provided he gets the chance ... the home has been completely refurbished through [his] hard work'.[74] His Irish flatmate had also previously been in trouble, and had served a month in prison for carrying an offensive weapon in a pub. Now, however, he was a father by his regular girlfriend and the probation officer described him as 'an able young man who is confident and competent of working out his own future'.[75] When questioned about their drug taking both seemed to have well-thought-out positions. The flatmate 'attempts to follow his own brand of philosophy and outlook on life which includes the hope that the smoking of cannabis will be legalised ... he personally feels that he has in no way offended against his own moral code by smoking cannabis'. The tenant, 'having studied and read extensively about drug taking, believed himself something of an expert and does not appreciate that it is illegal to participate in this form of drug-taking ... of quite good intelligence, insists that he is not addicted to the soft drugs and has never partaken of the hard drugs and insists that he never will, knowing full well the consequences'. The probation officer who spoke to the latter was convinced that 'he is the type of youth who feels that the Law, rather than himself, is wrong on the matter of drug-taking'.

The overall impression from these reports is of ordinary working-class lads who had managed their fair share of scrapes while teenagers, but who were subsequently taking their place as members of the working population. They had travelled and changed jobs when it suited them, and as they matured had taken on responsibilities such as children and senior relatives. Not that all of the examples that fitted this picture were male. For example, a young mother was arrested while sitting with friends in the Lawns Park in Swindon. The police confiscated a cigarette which contained cannabis and she was charged for illegally being in possession of the drug. The 22-year-old had qualified in graphic design at Swindon Technical College, had worked as a shop assistant and a clerk, and was expecting her second child.[76]

While such glimpses of consumers are difficult to come by, it is clear that numbers of them were increasing nationwide by the turn of the decade.

North of the border, for example, it was stated at the end of the 1970s that 'the only drug whose increasing misuse was reported from most parts of Scotland was cannabis...a few described its misuse as experimental or sporadic'.[77] A survey conducted in Lothian at about the same time provides greater insight into consumption among the young in Scotland. In 1979 around 1,000 young adults aged 15 and 16 were interviewed and it was found that about 7 per cent had used cannabis, the single most popular of the substances taken within the cohort. By 1983, when they were 19 or 20 years of age, about a third of them claimed to have tried the drug, which was still the most popular choice within the group. The study found that those who were regularly using alcohol when 15 or 16 were most likely to have tried drugs by the time they were 20, and that levels of drug use were highest among those who were unemployed. An NOP Market Research Limited survey published in 1982 showed that 21 per cent of those interviewed in Scotland had used cannabis while 28 per cent of those in London had experience of the drug. In the North of England, the Midlands, East Anglia, and Wales, and the South of England excluding London, these figures were lower at around 15 per cent. In each case cannabis was the substance that had been most used amongst drug takers. Similarly small studies in Cheltenham and South Hampshire showed that of those that admitted drug use, almost all had tried cannabis.[78] The drug was certainly something recalled by members of some of the country's most successful bands of the period. Groups like UB40, The Specials, and Musical Youth grew out of the Midlands of the 1970s. Their music and style evolved from experimentation with the wide range of cultures that had arrived in cities like Coventry and Birmingham with the waves of migrants that had settled in the UK after the Second World War. Cannabis consumption was also a feature of this hybridizing cultural context and while musicians like Robin Campbell of UB40 recall using it as a teenager when it was passed around the clubs he visited, Musical Youth went a step further and took the song 'Pass the Dutchie' to the top of the charts for three weeks in 1982. It was a cover version of the song 'Pass the Kouchie' by The Mighty Diamonds, Kouchie being a West Indian word for a cannabis pipe.[79]

While consumers were increasing in number, suppliers were ensuring that the market was catered for. A jaunty Home Office survey reported that 'Cannabis too seems to be ever increasing in popularity and the total quantity seized in 1980 was 28,131 kilos, a rise of 16,000 kilos on 1979'.[80] The most substantial increase occurred in the amount of herbal cannabis detected, 20,660 kg compared with 6,403 kg in 1979, and included the largest seizure so far made in the UK of some 11,000 kg, the source of which was believed to be Colombia. This seizure resulted from the discovery in May of about 1,000 kg which had been washed ashore on the Isle of Mull in Scotland. Further enquiries revealed that the entire consignment had come to the UK in a single vessel sometime towards the end of 1979 and subsequent seizures were made at three separate locations. A number of persons were charged with unlawful importation, the majority of them British subjects.[81]

While this was a particularly noteworthy story it also seemed to be an unusual one as a Customs officer reported to a drugs intelligence meeting between his agency, the police, and the Home Office in 1981 that Africa and the West Indies continued to be the main sources of cannabis.[82] However, the Mull load bore out the anxiety that cannabis smuggling was increasingly well organized. In 1979 'the statistics on seizures of drugs indicated that there had been large scale activity relating to cannabis ... the police had evidence of involvement by professional criminals and this was causing concern'.[83] Indeed, cannabis was only part of a wider picture where the police identified 'the increasing involvement of "top class" criminals in drug dealing and the difficulties posed in combating this trend'.[84] Seizures hovered at a similar level throughout the early 1980s, with almost 20,000 kg seized in 1983 and just under 21,000 kg seized in 1985. By the end of the decade this had grown, however, with 44,000 kg and over 50,000 kg seized in 1988 and 1989 respectively,[85] although these figures dropped back to between 20,000 and 25,000 kg in the early 1990s.[86]

In part these seizures reflected a policy turn towards dealing with traffickers. The Home Secretary, William Whitelaw, stated in his speech to the ACMD in 1980 that 'we must continue to look for means of further concentrating resources in these areas on pushers and on the organisers of this illicit traffic'.[87] He was true to his word as he locked horns with the Treasury about resources for officers to tackle traffickers early in the 1980s. Whitelaw wrote to the Chancellor of the Exchequer in 1982 to ask him to 'look again at the adequacy of the manpower resources that are devoted by HM Customs and Excise to enforcing the prohibition on drug smuggling', pointing out that 'even a small reinforcement of the manpower active in this area, if it were possible, would be likely to have much more public impact than anything we can do on the treatment side'.[88] The response from Geoffrey Howe suggests that the 'battle against drug abuse' was to be fought on the cheap: 'I am afraid that there can be no question of relieving Customs of the need to reduce their manpower resources in line with our policy of reducing the size of the Civil Service'.[89] While the Treasury may have lacked enthusiasm for dealing with traffickers at this time, the courts did not. For example, in 1981 over half of the 600 people convicted for the unlawful import or export of cannabis were immediately jailed for nine months or more, and only fifty received short sentences of less than three months.[90] It also seems that police forces around the country embraced the emphasis on traffickers. A glance at the annual report of the chief constable of Strathclyde in the late 1970s, for example, shows regular weary observations along the lines of 'the number of persons arrested, mostly in the 15–25 year old age group, rose by 15.5 per cent...once again the most abused drug was cannabis'.[91] By the early 1980s the tone was rather different, and it was stated in 1982 that 'my officers continued to concentrate on the dealers in death who supply illicit drugs for huge profit'[92] and in 1983 that

> I have said consistently in my annual reports that the emphasis will be to strike at dealers to proscribe scope for the permeation of this world wide affliction in Strathclyde. During the year 343 persons were charged with dealing in drugs, an increase of 217 compared with 1982 ... I wish to affirm my declaration that this type of crime will be pursued relentlessly in Strathclyde to bring to justice those who seek easy profits in this sad exploitation which destroys so many young lives.[93]

As the 1980s was a period in which there were more cannabis consumers than ever before in the UK and increases in supplies by better organized traffickers to meet the demand, it may seem surprising that the drug almost entirely slipped from political view in that decade. In 1985 Leon Brittan, the Home Secretary, simply endorsed his predecessor's position on the drug by stating that 'it is my firm policy that there should be no change in the law relating to cannabis'. This met with little comment from MPs.[94] Between 1986 and 1989 there was no mention of the substance in the House of Commons at all. At the end of that year a debate in the chamber lasted over four hours on the issue of drugs misuse and heroin, cocaine, and crack cocaine were considered in detail, while even alcohol and tobacco smoking were discussed. Cannabis was mentioned by name just once.[95] A de facto cross-party consensus seems to have emerged on cannabis in the 1980s, as all seemed to agree that it was not a matter worthy of the attention of legislators.

One reason that cannabis fell down the list of matters to be addressed by government can be found at the ACMD. David Hardwick took over as secretary in 1980 and wrote to a colleague in the DHSS that 'we need, I suggest, to try to give a new impetus to the Council's work, and to ensure that they devote their energies to problems on which there is some hope of progress. For example, I think we need to avoid for the time being any further broad-ranging studies... Sir Robert Bradlaw has already indicated that he too would prefer to have smaller working groups working on specific studies within a shorter timescale'.[96] As cannabis consumption had proven in the 1970s to be one of those problems that demanded broad-ranging studies, and which had often offered little hope of progress, it was not an issue that sat easily alongside the ambition of bureaucrats to reinvigorate the ACMD.

The Home Office did not need to look far in order to find new matters for the ACMD to occupy itself with. Another reason that cannabis slipped from the view of politicians and experts was the urgent concern in the 1980s with other substances and new phenomena in the drugs sphere. As early as 1980 the ACMD noted that 'during the past year addiction to heroin had increased and the pattern of heroin traffic had changed. Previously the UK had been a trans-shipment point but now much of the heroin was being imported for the domestic market'.[97] By 1982 the police were reporting that 'illicit heroin could now be found throughout the United Kingdom and that its market price was approximately half that of last year'[98] and by the end of 1983 the chief inspector of the Drugs Branch reported 'the vast increase in the smoking of heroin' that had followed the market for the injected product.[99] By 1985 heroin consumption in Britain was perceived by politicians and the press as 'a crisis, an epidemic and a plague'.[100]

If the emergence of urgent concerns about drugs other than cannabis explains why the latter suddenly seemed less pressing to politicians, officials, and drugs experts, it also partly accounts for the changes in the policing of cannabis in the 1980s. If one of the key elements of the story of cannabis in Britain of the 1970s had been the turn away from custodial sentences for offences of simple possession by the courts, it is changes in police approaches to dealing with cannabis offenders that is the most striking feature of the following decade. Sir Kenneth Newman's *The Principles of Policing and Guidance for Professional Behaviour* was issued in 1985 in order to provide a contemporary outline of the considerations that should guide the conduct of London's police officers and to update the last attempt to do this in writing, Richard Mayne's *Primary Objects of the Police* published in 1829. It included an extensive discussion of the reasons for exercising discretion and as an example he sketched a hypothetical situation involving cannabis. Although lengthy, it is worth considering in full:

> For a second example we can take a subject on which there is a variety of views among many responsible members of society, which is reflected I daresay in the views of police officers: the smoking of cannabis: What should I do if you see that people at a party are smoking a substance which you think may be cannabis? This is a very difficult decision for anyone to make. It is much easier to advise what you should *not* do; you should not attempt to arrest as many cannabis users as you can see. Indeed, prudence may tell you that you should not take any action at all at the party, because you will not be able to take *effective* action.
>
> Your decision—in this, as in all things, on or off duty—should be made with a sharp eye to what is feasible and likely to achieve your purpose, as well as to what is strictly legal or morally correct.
>
> Depending on how flagrant the smoking has been, whether there was encouragement given to others to smoke, or whether there was any attempt to sell cannabis, you may leave the party and go to the local police station to report the facts so that they can take such immediate action as they consider appropriate. You may decide to stay and attempt to identify any person who might have been supplying cannabis so that action can be taken against him later, if that is appropriate. On the other hand, if it was clear that the smoking was not widespread and took place merely for the personal satisfaction of a few, and you were, in any case, not sure that the substance was a controlled drug, you may decide to do nothing except perhaps, leave a note for a collator or a drugs squad officer, outlining what you have seen or suspect.
>
> You would also not want to neglect your obligation to your host in all this. Your decision about how, if at all, to approach him, would of course be influenced by the extent to which you knew him, how sure you could be of his good reputation and intentions, and what evidence there was of fore-knowledge on his part. Certainly, if you were to have taken some action thoughtlessly about his party without telling him of it, he would be bound, on discovering that, and if he was free of guilt himself, to question your purpose. He would regard you as uncivilised to say the least—and this would be so, particularly if the party had taken place at his home and had comprised principally his close friends or family.
>
> It is only if there was some clear ground for suspecting complicity by your host that you should, in such circumstances, justify taking action behind his back. Much the best course, if the situation allows it, would be to tell him what you have seen and explain carefully what action you propose to take. His

reaction to that can be an important factor for you when deciding how to handle things.

As is nearly always the case with the exercise of police powers, none of the above courses of action could be judged wholly wrong or wholly right in the circumstances described. It is quite possible that another person, who was present or who learned afterwards of your action or inaction, could take a different view from yours.

But if challenged about what you did or did not do, you would be able to say with some justice that you had assessed the issue as sensibly as you could, that you had considered as a priority what was practicable and would serve the public interest, and had given no more weight than was reasonable to your personal view of the culpability of the offenders and the seriousness of the offence.[101]

If Baroness Wootton had spoken in 1968 of 'hints' to the authorities to enforce laws on cannabis with discretion, this was the most powerful yet to appear in print by a senior policeman to his officers. The booklet specifically stated that 'to do nothing' could be legitimate and Newman's publication listed cannabis smoking as an offence for which discretion could be exercised as opposed to an offence 'so appalling and seemingly so indefensible that only the interests of the victim and of public justice need trouble you at the time you take your initial action' such as 'serious assaults, robberies and other violent thefts'.[102] The statement on cannabis insisted that police officers weigh up a series of complex issues when confronted by cannabis offences which included the context and extent of the consumption, the practicality of intervention, the 'public interest', and the presence of suppliers. It was a powerful licence to prevaricate.

Yet it is important not to take this statement on cannabis out of its context. *The Principles of Policing and Guidance for Professional Behaviour* was Newman's statement on police practices in general rather than on cannabis in particular, and was part of his drive to reform policing in London. The Home Secretary had committed the authorities to 'securing good relations between all parts of the community in this country'[103] after the low points of the 1970s and early 1980s which included the death of Blair Peach in police custody and the riots in Brixton, Handsworth, and elsewhere. Newman had been appointed because of his promise to 'make the police more responsive to the needs and feelings of local communities'.[104] His approach to cannabis should be seen as serving not just the drugs policy of the government but also the wider demands of policing in British cities in the 1980s. At a time when young, black men in London reported that they regarded the smoking of ganja as 'normal, natural and even...respect-able'[105] despite the fact that it was illegal, it was consistent with the wider political and social agendas of the government and the police to make the enforcement of laws on the drug more flexible.

Newman had arrived with a further objective in mind in reforming the police in London, and this was the more efficient deployment of resources. An early sense of one way of doing this appeared in a letter he wrote to the Home Secretary in which he advocated 'variations/extensions of cautioning procedures in relation to...juveniles [and] drunks with a view to manpower savings'.[106] It seems that he was not alone in seeing greater use of a wider array of police powers as a means of deploying resources more efficiently, as by July 1984 it was reported that the police forces in Merseyside and South Yorkshire were not prosecuting those in possession of small amounts of cannabis and were simply cautioning them. The explanation given for this when it was reported in the House of Commons was that they planned to 'concentrate their resources on those involved in hard drugs'.[107]

The caution was an alternative to prosecution where the police were in a position to pursue the latter and where the offender admitted committing the crime and agreed to being cautioned. As early as 1981 the Royal Commission on Criminal Procedure had noted the disparities between UK police forces in the rates at which they were issuing cautions. The Home Office and the Crime Committee took up the issue of cautions and by early 1985 had agreed to recommend an extension of the use of caution-ing for juvenile and adult offences.[108] The idea was that where offences were considered to be 'not particularly serious' the offender would be formally cautioned at a police station rather than prosecuted in a court. The caution would remain on the offender's criminal record for three years and could be considered if the offender once again found him/herself in trouble. In this way it was felt that the authorities were doing what they could to keep minor offenders from troubling the courts and to prevent juveniles and minor offenders from becoming more embroiled in the criminal justice system than was necessary. The types of offence considered to be ineligible for cautions were 'homicide, rape, arson, endangering life, serious public disorder' but the police had it at their discretion to proceed with all other offences through a caution. It was recommended in par-ticular for juveniles and young adults (aged 17–20) and 'minor victimless offences or offences where only a small amount of property is involved'.[109]

A subsequent Police Order of 1985 seems to have been the first to go a step further and specifically name 'drugs' as among the 'cases where it is likely that an alternative to prosecution may be invoked'.[110] Newman's 1985 recommendation of discretion on cannabis should therefore be seen in another context. It was part of a wider drive by the authorities to use the caution more often for a range of crimes in order to free up police resources and time in courts for offences considered more serious, and also to keep younger offenders from getting dragged through the full criminal justice system for misdemeanours associated with the rash or insolent impulses of youth.

It was not only police forces that had come to view small-scale cannabis offences as only a minor problem to be dealt with swiftly and with as little fuss as possible. In 1982 a Parliamentary question revealed that the 'Commissioners of Customs and Excise propose to institute experimentally at London airport compounding of proceedings for some customs offences involving 10 grammes or less of cannabis'.[111] This meant that where an individual was caught with a small amount of the drug and had admitted to its possession, a spot fine would be issued upon payment of which the offender was free to go without fear of further punishment. By 1984 this had been extended to other ports and airports.[112] These moves did not go unnoticed however and were not unopposed. Peter Bruinvels MP asked the Home Secretary in the House of Commons if 'he will meet with the Commissioner of Police of the Metropolis to discuss the Metropolitan police force's policy towards cases involving the possession of cannabis'. The reply was clear:

> No. Chief officers of police, including the Commissioner of Police of the Metropolis, are already aware of my right hon. and learned Friend's views about drug misuse. They have available to them in exercising their responsibility in this matter the Attorney-General's guidelines on criteria and my right hon. and learned Friend's advice to them on the appropriate use of cautioning. It is also open to them in any case of doubt or difficulty to seek the advice of the Director of Public Prosecutions.[113]

By the end of the decade 75 per cent of cannabis offenders were being cautioned in the UK, with some 11,715 people being dealt with in this way for offences of possession of cannabis in 1989. However, this disguised considerable regional variation between different police forces, with the

Metropolitan Police force issuing cautions in 88 per cent of cases whereas Avon and Somerset used cautions in only 20 per cent.[114]

While it is clear that enforcement agencies in the 1980s came to view simple possession of cannabis as a relatively minor offence that did not merit a trip to court, let alone imprisonment, this does not mean that cannabis consumers were less likely to encounter enforcers. Indeed, what was noticeable by the end of the decade was the large number of drugs offences that were being dealt with by the police, and the significant increases in cases that involved cannabis. One reason for this has already been mentioned, that is the growth of the number of consumers of the drug. Another clue as to why more and more people were being caught in possession of cannabis comes late in the decade. David Mellor, a Minister of State at the Home Office, revealed in 1989 that in the last decade the number of Customs officers had trebled and that in the previous five years alone an additional 854 posts had been created.[115] A couple of years later it was confirmed that in England and Wales 1,400 police officers were now wholly engaged in policing drug-related crime, and in Scotland 120 officers were so devoted. The Secretary of State for the Home Departments confirmed that it cost £147 million a year to his office to enforce the Misuse of Drugs Act.[116] It seems that while the government early in the 1980s had been eager to 'reduce . . . manpower resources' in the enforcement apparatus, there had been a change in policy from the middle of the decade. From this time there had been a significant growth in this apparatus which was increasingly well organized through new agencies such as the National Drugs Intelligence Unit and new legislation such as the 1986 Drug Trafficking Offences Act. This enhanced apparatus brought with it greater activity: in 1979 there were 600 seizures of heroin and 348 of cocaine, whereas in 1992 these figures had risen to 2,968 and 2,365. In the same period cannabis seizures went from 14,116 to 57,663.[117]

This increase in officers and resources in the latter half of the 1980s was not driven by cannabis, but rather by anxieties in government about heroin and later crack cocaine and other substances such as Ecstasy. Nevertheless, as cannabis remained far and away the most popular of the illegal substances throughout the period its users ended up snared in a net designed for other groups. It is also likely that for enforcement agencies that needed to justify new and generous resources, a ready supply of cannabis users provided a source of activity through which officers could demonstrate effectiveness. Between 1989 and 1992 the number of cannabis offenders shot up from

15,620 to 34,705. While the majority was issued with a caution rather than taken to court, it was still the case that by 1992 cannabis offenders made up almost two-thirds of those found guilty under the Misuse of Drugs Act.[118]

This left the UK in a position where the tacit assumption on the part of the authorities was that possession of small amounts of cannabis for personal use was a minor matter that should take up as little police time as possible and should certainly not trouble the courts. Yet it was one of the most common offences committed, and gave criminal records to thousands of people who would otherwise never trouble the authorities. It is this situation that ensured that cannabis resurfaced on the political agenda again in the early 1990s. A full decade after Kilroy-Silk had last sought change to laws on cannabis there, the House of Commons heard Tony Banks, Labour MP for Newham North-West, ask in 1992, 'is it not time to consider the possibility of legalising soft drugs, especially cannabis? After all, cannabis does much less harm to a person's health than nicotine, and yet cigarettes are legal. It is the criminal activity surrounding the supply of illegal drugs that we should really worry about. If we were to legalize soft drugs that would no longer be a problem'. His question came in the middle of a bruising session where the government was attacked on its economic policies, and its spokesman seemed less interested in the question and more concerned to seize the opportunity to strike back at Opposition MPs: 'would it be the policy of the Labour party to legalise those drugs?' No response was forthcoming and the discussion lurched back to the topic of unemployment.[119] Nevertheless, the question from the Conservatives was to prove to be a thorny one. As the next chapter shows, the issue of what the Labour Party would do about cannabis was to trouble it repeatedly after it came to power in 1997.

Conclusion

The significance of the quarter-century or so after the 1971 Misuse of Drugs Act lies first in the broadening and the indigenization of the market for cannabis in the UK. While it is often difficult to get a sight of the ways in which this happened, it is clear that the number of consumers grew and that in this period they were as likely to be people born and raised in the UK as they were migrants to the country. As the stories above show, by the early 1970s the drug had been incorporated into the recreational habits of working-class lads after a hard day's graft or of young mothers enjoying a day in the park. By the 1980s members of Britain's multicultural cities had integrated cannabis into their lifestyles and their creative endeavours, and by the 1990s their numbers were so great that more than 30,000 consumers a year were in trouble with the police thanks to their taste for the drug.

It seems that much of the approach of the legislators and the experts to cannabis consumers in this period was devised in isolation from them. Almost none were invited to address the relevant ministers or committees and instead experts were expected to talk about them or for them. As the 1960s faded further into memory, government approaches to cannabis and cannabis consumption became increasingly shaped by laws and policies directed at other issues and problems. This was not the case at the outset. In the 1970s many hours and much effort were devoted to the issue of cannabis legislation and policy. The outcome of this was the gradual implementation of the recommendations published in 1968 by the Sub-Committee chaired by Baroness Wootton. Penalties for cannabis offences were reduced, magistrates took the advice not to send those guilty of simple possession to prison, and eventually even the police found ways of dealing with consumers which meant that few received permanent criminal records, let alone custodial sentences. This had been achieved not because those in power had been persuaded that smoking cannabis was harmless, but because the habit had become something of a *cause célèbre* among those that felt that civil liberties were under threat in Britain in this period and who therefore sought to protect these by seeking less oppression of consumers. However, experts could not agree unanimously that using cannabis was sufficiently harmless to justify more radical action on cannabis laws, and the public health view enabled the Conservative Government's rejection of calls to reclassify cannabis.

Yet it was under the Conservative regime that the greatest change of the period occurred, as lower proportions of cannabis offenders found themselves in court than ever before and more found themselves simply cautioned for their offences. This was certainly not evidence of a forgiving attitude towards the drug by the government and was more to do with its wider political and social agendas. Cannabis consumers were a matter of little concern to an administration that had larger and more urgent social policy objectives, such as reforming the police, settling race relations in inner cities, addressing the public health AIDS emergency, and controlling the impact of cheap heroin and crack cocaine. As such punishments became less draconian as new mechanisms were devised for dealing with cannabis users that freed up time and resources for more pressing issues. But the British compromise, of not changing laws but of changing the way that they were implemented, came to have perverse outcomes. By delegating power over the application of cannabis laws to the discretion of those in enforcement, legislators and the government ensured that the often complex agendas of police officers on the ground came to be the single most important factor shaping the experience of the cannabis consumer. This resulted in greater numbers of cannabis consumers than ever before finding themselves in trouble with the police, albeit in ways that resulted in less severe punishments than previously. As the next chapter shows, when these perverse outcomes were finally acknowledged by legislators and the government in the 1990s it proved difficult to wrest the power back from enforcers in order to do something about it.

8

'I have decided to reclassify cannabis, subject to Parliamentary approval': Legislators, Law-Enforcers, Campaigns, and Classification, 1997–2008

Introduction

The first statement on cannabis of the New Labour Government that came to power in 1997 was made in the House of Commons in June of that year. It revealed that the last set of official figures (for 1995) showed that 41,155 people had been cautioned for possession of cannabis and that a further 32,393 had ended up in magistrates' courts because of the drug.[1] As the previous chapter explained, record numbers of consumers came to find themselves with criminal records for their habit because the swollen ranks of the drugs enforcement agencies encountered the swollen ranks of cannabis users in the early 1990s. As more and more people found themselves in trouble with the police for minor cannabis offences than ever before, the civil liberties anxieties of the 1970s began to resurface to drive cannabis back into the concerns of government. The decade after 1997 was to be one in which the uneasy order of the preceding twenty-five years, where legislators, politicians, and experts had ceded control of policy on cannabis consumers to the courts and then to the police, was to be robustly challenged and roundly criticized only to be reassembled and reaffirmed.

Consumers, experts, and politicians

One of the key features of the drugs debate in the 1990s that was to shape the period after 1997 was the re-emergence of a consumers' lobby. Yet consumers certainly did not speak with one voice and a number of organizations took it upon themselves to articulate matters related to cannabis use. Release had broadened its remit since the 1960s and dealt with the full range of drugs used by young people and also with a number of other civil liberties and human rights issues; its publications during the 1990s included *Sex Workers and the Law* in 1997 and *Safer Clubbing*.[2] It continued to contribute to discussions of cannabis but had plenty else to concern itself with. The Legalise Cannabis Campaign (LCC) had also endured. A well-organized critic of cannabis policies in the 1970s, by the 1990s it did little more than produce the occasional copy of its journal, *The Hookah*. New organizations also emerged which reflected the changed nature of consumers since the 1960s and the challenges of the political and enforcement context of the 1990s. The Alliance for Cannabis Therapeutics in Britain founded by Clare Hodges became an important voice for those that consumed cannabis for medical purposes, and is discussed in more detail below. The Legalise Cannabis Alliance was more concerned to articulate the position of recreational users, and was founded in Norwich in 1992 as the Campaign to Legalise Cannabis International. Its members were moved to act as they felt 'dissatisfied with the legalise cannabis campaign at the time and felt that more action was needed' in the wake of a police campaign against cannabis users in Norfolk. It came to national prominence in 1997 when Howard Marks, the celebrity cannabis smuggler, represented the group as a Parliamentary candidate in Norwich North, Norwich South, Southampton West, and Neath constituencies, campaigning on the single issue of legalizing cannabis.[3] While the Legalise Cannabis Alliance chose the electoral route to attract attention to the cannabis issue, others adopted different strategies. Free Rob Cannabis (formerly Rob Christopher) was a civil engineering graduate of Loughborough University and a member of the generation of cannabis users who had first tried the drug in the 1980s and 1990s. His interest in the issues related to the substance led him to the Legalise Cannabis Campaign early in the 1990s but he had found that 'I could not work with the high level of fear and paranoia that I felt existed within the LCC'.[4] Rejecting this organization he founded the Cannabis Hemp Information Club in 1995 aged 27 and the Cannabis in Avalon (CIA) organization in 1999, and used an online presence to organize rallies and a campaign of civil disobedience. On 28 September 1996 Howard Marks and Free Rob Cannabis claimed to have distributed free cannabis from Speakers' Corner at Hyde Park before offering themselves for arrest at the local police station and they repeated the stunt on the same day of the following year. They were unable to provoke the police into arresting them on either occasion, and a spokesman for Marylebone Police Station was reported in 1997 as saying that 'there was no evidence against the man apart from his own claims . . . officers continually exercise their discretion on how to proceed on a whole host of incidents and allegations and this occasion was no different'. Press reports noted that there were about 300 demonstrators there in support of the activists.[5] Free Rob Cannabis was to enjoy greater success in his civil disobedience campaign over subsequent years, going to prison for the first time in 1998 for non-payment of fines and appearing in court on five occasions for cannabis-related offences. This culminated in a month at Belmarsh Prison in 2002 which included a week on hunger strike.[6]

Perhaps the most significant impact of the campaigning by Free Rob Cannabis was in the inspiration that it provided to the *Independent on Sunday* to start its campaign for the decriminalization of cannabis in 1997. It was launched to coincide with the second event organized by Free Rob Cannabis to distribute cannabis at Speakers' Corner on 28 September 1997, and featured an editorial by Rosie Boycott with the title 'Why We Believe It Is Time to Decriminalise Cannabis'. This statement was rather light on evidence for its arguments, simply asserting that 'the truth is that most people I know have smoked at some time or other in their lives. They hold down jobs, bring up their families, run major companies, govern our country, and yet, 30 years after my day out in Hyde Park, cannabis is still officially regarded as a dangerous drug'. The statement was full of references to earlier political positions on cannabis:

> I rolled my first joint on a hot June day in Hyde Park. Summer of '68. Just 17. Desperate to be grown-up . . . When Mick Jagger was heavily fined thousands of pounds after a punitive trial for possession of cannabis, the conservative and middle-aged thought he deserved it. But William Rees-Mogg, then the editor of the *Times*, was unhappy . . . Here was establishment-speak for the common cries of 'Mick's been made a scapegoat', or, less stridently, 'Cannabis is a

harmless component of contemporary relaxation'. The pro-cannabis campaigners backed their demands with weighty medical evidence. No one
took any notice.[7]

The *Independent on Sunday* campaign took this nostalgic link with the
cannabis campaigns of the past even further and organized a second cannabis
march in Hyde Park on 28 March 1998 which the paper claimed had
attracted 16,000 supporters. Its coverage explicitly made the link with events
of previous decades: 'there was a sense of deja-vu as the marchers gathered
in Hyde Park, the scene of the first cannabis rally in July 1967. Some people
remembered seeing Lennon and McCartney there, others, now respectable
businessmen, recalled being arrested for raining flowers on police'.[8] No
doubt the *Independent on Sunday* wished to make the link with the 1960s in
order to lay claims to the civil liberties high ground that had been at issue
back then, and indeed Rosie Boycott was clear that this was her concern in
the speech that she gave to the meeting in Trafalgar Square in 1997 when
she declared that 'the campaign is now much bigger than any of us ... It [is]
a much bigger movement that [is] to do with Civil Liberty, that [is] to do
with changing the law'.[9] However, the link established with the past was
not without its drawbacks as it allowed Alastair Campbell, New Labour's
most powerful spin doctor, to dismiss those campaigning for change in
cannabis laws and policies as 'just a bunch of middle-class, middle-aged
hippies wanting to smoke dope'.[10]

Quite why Rosie Boycott chose to use the *Independent on Sunday* to
champion the cause of change in cannabis policies is open to question.
She quickly left the newspaper after initiating the cannabis campaign early in
1998 and took up the editor's post at the rather less liberal *Daily Express*. She
showed no inclination to replicate her commitment to the cause of cannabis
decriminalization during her short stint there. Indeed, it is worth bearing in
mind that her own account of the episode suggests that she had pragmatic
motives for the campaign at the *Independent on Sunday* that were narrowly
focused on the exigencies of the newspaper business:

> The editor of the 'Independent on Sunday', Rosie Boycott, is on a high, but
> not for the reason some of her critics might suspect. Her campaign to
> decriminalise cannabis has struck a strong public chord — and is pushing up
> circulation ... The fact is the IoS is now selling comfortably over 300,000
> copies per week for the first time in a long time. At least part of our growing
> popularity must be a result of our cannabis campaign. A lot of people who had

never heard about the 'Sindy' before or gave it only a passing glance on the news-stands have suddenly been eagerly seeking us out.[11]

If consumers found their voice in the 1990s it was to prove more difficult to turn this into a sustained or a coherent presence in policy circles. The *Independent on Sunday* campaign fizzled out once Rosie Boycott had departed. The Legalise Cannabis Alliance fielded thirteen candidates in the 2001 general election and twenty-one contenders in the following one, while also fielding candidates in a variety of local polls. Its greatest electoral success was to secure 7 per cent of the vote in a local election in Halton, and in 2006 it deregistered as a political party to revert to a role as a pressure group.[12] Despite his commitment and efforts at martyrdom, Free Rob Cannabis was to complain that he received little support in maintaining his organization, lamenting in 2005 that 'though I have had much support over the years, the truth of the matter is that for almost eight years I have been working at CIA [Cannabis in Avalon] HQ almost single handedly'.[13] This situation provides an interesting contrast with the 1960s and 1970s, as those prepared to campaign on behalf of reform in cannabis policies and laws in the 1990s were advocates of consumption of the drug rather than simply those interested in the civil liberties of consumers. This may well explain their inability to mobilize sustained support. It certainly accounts for the greater success of Rufus Harris in lobbying at Westminster in the 1970s, as he focused on wider issues rather than on the perceived benefits of cannabis consumption. The impression from the 1990s is that cannabis smoking may have been a feature of many people's lives but that it was not an urgent political issue for the vast majority of the nation's cannabis smokers.

The success of the *Independent on Sunday* campaign and of organizations such as Cannabis in Avalon and the Legalise Cannabis Alliance therefore did not lie in electoral achievements or the establishment of a mass base from which political pressure for legislative change could be applied. Rather, it can be found in the impact they had in forcing the issue to once again become a matter of urgent public and political concern. The Conservative Government of the period 1979 to 1997 had been little exercised by cannabis, particularly in the 1980s when it had the more pressing concerns of heroin and crack cocaine to deal with. When its attention did turn to the drug in the 1990s there was some confusion in the ranks. In 1994 Ian Lang, as Secretary of State for Scotland, proposed relaxing the approach to personal possession of the drug there by introducing fixed penalties for small amounts which would have meant no criminal record for those caught.[14] His colleague the Home Secretary responded by increasing the maximum fines in England and Wales from £500 to £2,500 and the prime minister, John Major, was reported as stating that 'I know some people make a case for legalising some soft drugs but frankly I don't agree with it'.[15] The New Labour Government swept to power in May 1997 and a number of its prominent members had previously spoken out on cannabis. For example, Tony Banks, who had revived the issue in the House of Commons in the 1990s, found himself a minister in the Department of Culture, Media and Sport and Clare Short was appointed as Secretary of State for International Development. While a member of the Shadow Cabinet she had suggested that cannabis be sold legally and taxed.[16] At the time she had been dismissed by her colleague, the future Home Secretary Jack Straw, who told BBC Radio's *The World This Weekend* that 'Labour's position on drugs is very clear. We are against the legalisation of cannabis and other soft drugs'.[17] When the new government took power it confirmed that it would be 'tackling the problem with renewed vigour', and revealed that 'the Government will be appointing a "drug tsar" to co-ordinate action against drugs . . . one of his or her first tasks will be to review the existing drugs strategy'.[18] As such it provided a fresh focus for cannabis campaigners in this new 'drug tsar' and his review. Indeed, the *Independent on Sunday* admitted that this was a factor in the decision to take its stance, noting in its opening statement on the issue that 'the campaign comes as the Government prepares to appoint its first US-style "drugs tsar" to co-ordinate the anti-drugs efforts of the police, customs, intelligence services and social services'.[19]

The New Labour administration inherited a situation on cannabis that was assuming ever greater proportions. In 1998 figures for convictions and cautions of those caught in possession of cannabis peaked at 84,310, the highest number before or since.[20] As early as October 1997 the Lord Chief Justice recommended an inquiry into cannabis laws, stating that 'it is a subject that deserves, in my judgement, detached, objective, independent consideration'.[21] A range of expert bodies launched their own investigations into various aspects of the cannabis issue. The British Medical Association published its report on the medical potential of the drug in November 1997; the Advisory Council on the Misuse of Drugs requested the Department of Health to conduct three literature reviews which were produced in May

1998; the House of Lords Select Committee on Science and Technology decided to look at cannabis in February 1998, which prompted the Royal Society and the Academy of Medical Sciences to investigate the matter and publish a report in June of that year.[22] The Institute for the Study of Drug Dependence, an independent centre of expertise on drugs, also published its summary of the cannabis issue in 1998.[23] The House of Lords Select Committee report was published later that year, and was followed in 2000 by the Independent Inquiry into the Misuse of Drugs Act of the Police Foundation (a think tank in part funded by the Prince's Trust). Its inquiry was led by Viscountess Runciman, a former chair of the UK Mental Health Act Commission.[24]

The media attention followed by the flurry of activity by various expert groups ensured that cannabis became an issue on which the major political parties felt obliged to take a position, particularly in the months leading up to the general election of June 2001. In October 2000 the prime minister reiterated the New Labour position, stating that 'there is a debate about whether you decriminalise cannabis or legalise it and I am against it'.[25] In part he was forced to do this as his administration's official line on cannabis had been increasingly undermined by Mo Mowlam, the Cabinet Office minister at the time who was charged with the government's anti-drugs campaign. She had attracted a lot of media coverage back in January 2000 when she had confessed to trying cannabis as a student in the 1960s.[26] She was reported later that year as hinting that the government was not committed on principle to keeping cannabis illegal, and was prepared to consider relaxation of the law if scientific evidence showed it was not harmful and did not lead to harder drugs.[27] This provoked a clear and unequivocal response from the Shadow Home Secretary, Ann Widdecombe, who advocated

> zero tolerance of possession. No more getting away with just a caution, no more hoping that a blind eye will be turned. If someone possesses drugs, the minimum for a first offence will be a fixed penalty of £100. But not for a second offence. Then it's into court.[28]

Almost immediately this stance was undermined from within Widdecombe's own party. She spoke on 4 October and by 8 October British newspapers carried the story that seven members of the Shadow Cabinet had confessed to smoking cannabis while students in the 1970s, including Shadow Foreign Secretary Francis Maude who stated that 'like many of my generation, it was quite hard to go through Cambridge in the 1970s without doing it a few times'.[29] Widdecombe's stance was quickly dropped by the Conservative Party.

A closer look at these tangled efforts to establish public positions on cannabis by the main political parties draws attention to the possibility that much of this discussion of the drug was not about cannabis at all. In the Conservative Party of the period there was an ongoing controversy about the nature of its ideology in Opposition. Those that were gathered around the Shadow Chancellor, Michael Portillo, were sure that the party needed to reject aspects of its right-wing, reactionary tradition and to present itself as adapted to the perceived moral geographies of modern Britain. Portillo made a speech at the party conference in 2000 in which he focused on the issues of sexuality and race to emphasize his contemporary credentials, as he urged the Conservatives to adopt a more liberal agenda so that they could claim to speak for 'people whatever their sexual orientation' and 'for all Britons: black Britons, British Asians, white Britons'.[30] Meanwhile Widdecombe sought to represent those that felt that the party must stay true to its traditional principles and chose drugs as an issue through which to articulate this; by clearly aligning herself with the right-wing position of 'zero tolerance' she badged herself as on the side of tradition and distant from the liberal camp. The response of the 'Portillistas' shows how far the language of the cannabis issue was in fact an idiom in which a different controversy was being expressed. By rushing to claim that they had smoked cannabis they were in fact simply hastening to demonstrate how far they were situated politically from the traditional positions of the Conservative Party and how much they had embraced the mores of what they perceived to be important voter groups in the UK. The spat about cannabis among the Conservatives in 2000 was hardly about the drug at all, but was instead about the future of the party, as the ready-made positions for and against cannabis provided quick and easy ways of expressing alignment with differing political standpoints.[31]

While Conservative discussions of cannabis at this time can be related back to ideological debates within the party rather than to any intrinsic interest in the consumers of the drug and their legal position, New Labour pronouncements on the substance seem to have been driven more by the argy-bargy of political manoeuvring between individuals in the governing elite. Veteran Labour backbencher Tam Dalyell has noted that Mo Mowlam's time in the Cabinet Office was 'unhappy'[32] and that she felt overlooked for a more important job in the Foreign Office. A number of other commentators drew a similar picture, of a woman who was very disappointed at her position between 1999 and 2001: 'she was disillusioned with New Labour and all its works and angry in the extreme with the way in which she felt she had been sidelined' was the assessment of one of her friends, Julia Langdon.[33] In this light her statements on cannabis during her time at the Cabinet Office can be read as attempts to make life difficult for a prime minister who she felt had demoted her.

There may be more to it than that though. As Tony Blair's position on cannabis had been made clear since the 1990s and was maintained during his period in office, discussion of the drug provided a safe means for some in the Labour Party to express distance from him. After all, it was a topic on which lines were clearly drawn and as such if a political opponent was on a particular side of the line it was easy to publicly demonstrate distance from, or opposition to, him/her simply by locating oneself on the other side of the line. At the same time the topic was not so significant that disagreeing on it signalled an irreconcilable political division. In other words, differing with Tony Blair on cannabis could be a public gesture of distance or defiance which at the same time carried the message that there was no greater disagreement, say on economic or social policy. Such a message could serve twin purposes. On the one hand it allowed the critic to demonstrate to observers that s/he was no lackey. On the other hand it signalled to the leadership that there was no difference between the prime minister and the critic on any of the fundamental questions of the day. This alerted the leadership to the option of drawing the dissident closer by promotion. Tony Banks, Clare Short, and Mo Mowlam were among those in New Labour that confessed to smoking cannabis and who publicly discussed the possibility of changes in the law, and who subsequently found themselves in government posts.

There is also the suggestion that discussion of the legal status of cannabis could serve similar purposes for the smaller political parties. In the period before the start of the Iraq War in 2003 there was often little that these parties could do to establish themselves as distinctive from the New Labour administration. After all, the government was at pains to claim the middle ground of British politics and had been careful to adopt policies and positions from a number of ideological backgrounds. As such it was difficult to appear distinctive from the government and at the same time to appear electable, particularly as New Labour's policies resulted in a second landslide victory in June 2001. Promises to look into the cannabis issue when elected therefore provided political parties with a quick and easy means of distinguishing themselves from the government. For example, within a week of being appointed leader of the Liberal Democrats in August 1999 Charles Kennedy had declared that 'our position is that there should be a Royal Commission and that it should be not just directed at the legislation of cannabis but the whole drugs issue'.[34] This had the desired effect of distancing his party from the government which insisted that 'Tony Blair is against decriminalisation of cannabis and sees no value in a Royal Commission'.[35] In September of that year the Green Party took a public position on the substance by declaring that their policy was to allow the public to grow cannabis for both recreational and medicinal purposes.[36] By 2001 Plaid Cymru had followed, by promising to approve the use of cannabis for recreational consumption.[37]

In the lifetime of the first New Labour Parliament cannabis was re-established as an issue that recurred in media, political, and policy debates. Consumers and those that claimed to represent them, the media, various expert bodies, and the full range of political parties, had all contributed to this, although for reasons that were often little connected to the practical problems of cannabis consumption and the legal and penal approaches to this. The reshuffle of the Cabinet following the 2001 general election was to bring the issue to a head. It ushered in a period of intense activity where legislators and politicians attempted to assert themselves over the British compromise that had evolved since the 1960s where cannabis policy had been devolved to the hands of the courts and the police.

Legislators, experts, and enforcers

Although pressure had been growing on the government since it first came to power in 1997 to take a softer position on cannabis, the Home Secretary at the time, Jack Straw, had remained committed to the status quo. Keith Hellawell, the government-appointed drugs tsar, recalled Straw asking 'if I was seriously suggesting that he should be the first Home Secretary for a decade to preside over a fall in drug-arrest figures' when the former had suggested a more relaxed approach to policing cannabis.[38] However, Straw moved on to become Foreign Secretary after New Labour's victory in the election of June 2001. In October his successor, David Blunkett, suddenly declared that he was willing to look into the possibility that cannabis should be reclassified as a Class C drug.

It seems that Blunkett was keen to use the cannabis issue to assert his authority in his new office, or, as Keith Hellawell was told when he protested about Blunkett's position, the Home Secretary's 'change of mind' was 'political'.[39] In the first place a quick and sudden reversal of the previous position on cannabis served to distance Blunkett from his predecessor's time in the post. One civil servant noted that this had been a period in which 'neither Jack Straw nor Richard Wilson [the previous Permanent Secretary, who then became Cabinet Secretary] did anything', so swift and decisive action by Blunkett would clearly signal a change of management.[40] The move also seemed to chime with the new Home Secretary's desire to stamp his authority on his department, which he later admitted was a body that he thought was characterized by

> incompetence and inefficiency . . . there were my policies and there was what officials called 'Home Office policy' and that was what they worked to. I had to say to them over and over again, 'There is only one policy and it's what we say it is'.[41]

In this context Blunkett preferred to arrive at his own position rather than take advice from the Home Office: 'you've got to go for it rather than be dissuaded' was his summary of this approach during his tenure there.[42] The government position on cannabis was one that had been worked out under the auspices of the Home Office since the 1971 Misuse of Drugs Act as the 'very British compromise' of magistrates and policemen exercising their own discretion and judgement in interpreting the law. As such, it presented an ideal issue on which he could make a swift change to signal to his department that he was a 'very robust and very tough Home Secretary . . . able to do things that others have not done'.[43]

While the decision to reclassify cannabis suited Blunkett's personal agenda, he was careful to ensure that there was support for it from various key organizations. He spoke to the chair of the Home Affairs Select Committee and the chair of the Advisory Council on the Misuse of Drugs (ACMD). With them in line he made his announcement to the former that he would 'be putting to the Advisory Council on Drug Misuse a proposal that we should re-categorise cannabis to C rather than B, thereby allowing the police to concentrate their resources on Class A drugs'.[44] The chair of the Home Affairs Select Committee helpfully noted that 'on the re-classification of cannabis you are in fact accepting the recommendation that Dame Ruth Runciman made in her Police Foundation report' and Blunkett was careful to make it clear to the Home Affairs Select Committee that 'those who are more versed in these matters than I am will go back to 1981 when the Advisory Council at that time did, not unanimously but by a majority, publish a report recommending re-categorisation, so there is nothing new about this debate'.[45]

All of this mutual recognition and consensus-making was effective as it ensured that Blunkett could proceed with the support of key legislators and experts. Sir Michael Rawlins reported back in March 2002 from the ACMD that 'the Council recommends the reclassification of all cannabis preparations to Class C'. He made it clear that it was doing so as it thought that the drug's status as a Class B drug was disproportionate in relation to its toxicity and to other drugs, although it was convinced that cannabis remained 'unquestionably harmful'. It was careful to note that 'the Report itself is based on a detailed scrutiny of the relevant scientific literature including four reviews commissioned by the Department of Health in 1998 as well as an update commissioned by the Home Office and completed in November 2001'.[46] The Home Affairs Select Committee followed suit in May and concluded that while 'cannabis can be harmful and . . . its use should be discouraged . . . we do not believe there is anything to be gained by exaggerating its harmfulness . . . We support, therefore, the Home Secretary's proposal to reclassify cannabis from Class B to Class C'. It too was keen to point to the evidence base that it drew upon, which included 'oral evidence from 45 witnesses over a total of 11 evidence sessions [and] more than 200 people and organisations who provided written submissions'.[47] Drawing on the reports of various organizations such as the Police Foundation and the British Medical Association in the 1990s, and prodded by the Home Secretary, a political consensus among experts and politicians had been established by 2002. In July of that year, having taken the reports of the ACMD and the Home Affairs Select Committee into account, and having received a review of the Lambeth cannabis warning pilot scheme (see below) from the Metropolitan Police,[48] Blunkett announced that cannabis would be reclassified within a year.

The police were to have the final word in the matter. The consensus achieved among the experts and legislators contrasted with the position among the police, which was far more complex and which ultimately undermined Blunkett's ambitions. The older discussion of the 1970s that

pitched concerns about civil liberties against anxieties about public health
had faded in government as the conversation became dominated by a more
pragmatic concern with police resources. Brian Paddick, a commander of
the Metropolitan Police in charge of Lambeth, had decided by January 2001
that

> it was clear that arresting people for cannabis in Lambeth was using up a lot of
> police time and public money for only minor penalties at court [and that] this
> time, effort and money would be better spent focusing on reducing the high
> levels of burglary and street robbery, crack cocaine and heroin dealing,
> particularly when I was so short of officers.[49]

He embarked in July 2001 on a policy of instructing officers in his area not
to arrest people for possession of small amounts of cannabis intended for
personal consumption, leaving it to his officers to decide what a small
amount consisted of. David Blunkett, who met Paddick in June 2001
shortly after taking over as Home Secretary, found that this approach was
consistent with his desire to 'nail' traffickers and pushers and to concentrate
on Class A drugs and violent crime.[50] As such, the government swiftly
adopted the rhetoric of resources, and one of the Home Secretary's arguments to the Select Committee on Home Affairs in 2001 was that the
proposed changes were in part aimed at 'trying to . . . direct police resources
a little more towards Class A drugs where the most damage was being
done'.[51]

   The desire to concentrate resources on Class A drugs was nothing new of
course as this had been attempted by governments in the UK since the
1980s. Indeed, advice to caution those found in possession of small amounts
of cannabis had been given to the police then too. As such Paddick's
initiative and Blunkett's reclassification should certainly not be seen as
driven by liberal impulses or by concerns about civil liberties, and the
former has pointed out that while in charge of other stations where his
resources were less stretched he was content to fully enforce the law on
cannabis.[52] Their actions should be seen more as attempts to impose central
control over the behaviour of officers on the ground than as efforts to
radically depart from previous policies.[53] Paddick admitted that in Lambeth
he faced a challenge in '"encouraging" officers to engage with the new
policy' as it was 'difficult to control what the officers did on the street' and
his solution was to tackle 'custody sergeants, who were tied to the station,
were within easy reach and so had no choice but to follow orders. I gave

them instructions to refuse to deal with anyone who had been arrested for a small amount of cannabis which was obviously for personal use'.[54] The reluctance of many of the police to adopt a relaxed position on minor cannabis offences, despite being encouraged to do so by senior officers and those in government since the 1980s, was explained as follows by Keith Hellawell, the former drugs tsar and chief constable:

> These measures have not been as successful as I had hoped, partly because of lack of conviction within the police, who had gained comfort from increasing the number of arrests of drug offenders—largely cannabis users—year on year. I am struck by the duplicity of some of my former colleagues, who argue they would save police time if the law on cannabis was softened; they would have achieved this aim within the existing law if they had adhered to the strategy.[55]

While this suggests that police officers ignored guidelines as they found it useful to swell numbers of arrests for drugs offences by dealing with cannabis consumers, a report commissioned by the Joseph Rowntree Foundation in 2000 argued that the situation was more complicated still. It examined police behaviour towards cannabis offenders and found that it was complex and varied. Small numbers of officers were responsible for large numbers of the arrests, 3 per cent of the former accounting for over 20 per cent of the latter in their study. Those who were in the first years of service, who worked in rural areas, or who rarely encountered the drug were most likely to make an arrest. Those arresting could do so for reasons entirely unrelated to the drug, as detaining someone for possession of small quantities could be designed as a 'door opener' to more serious offences, as an excuse to impede persistent serious offenders who the police suspected of being on the way to commit crimes such as burglary or street violence, or to give probationary officers 'real-time' experience in the techniques of arrest. On the other hand, many officers interviewed claimed that 'they had effectively decrim-inalised cannabis in their everyday working practices'.[56] This was largely a decision reached by individual officers based on their own experience. The study also confirmed that while guidance on dealing with cannabis had been issued by the Association of Chief Police Officers of England, Wales, and Northern Ireland (ACPO) before 2001, 'senior managers were aware of this [but there] was little evidence that the guidance had penetrated to front-line officers'.[57]

In other words, at every level, from front-line officers to senior managers, there was division among the law enforcers as to how cannabis should be policed. Significantly, just before Blunkett announced his reclassification senior police officers intervened to resist his ambitions to impose a position from the Home Office so that they could maintain for themselves the right of deciding where and how the law should be enforced. The whole point of reclassifying cannabis as a Class C drug was that possession of substances in that category was not an arrestable offence. On hearing of the Home Secretary's plans 'at the last minute, Mike Fuller, then a DAC in the Met with responsibility for drug policy, and Ian Blair, then deputy commissioner, went and saw Blunkett and convinced him to retain the power of arrest'.[58] They succeeded, and while cannabis was eventually reclassified as a Class C drug the meaning of the Class C category was itself redefined. This meant that possession of drugs in that category could now be an arrestable offence and the maximum possible sentence for supplying them was increased. It appears that while the police could not decide among themselves how best to deal with cannabis offenders, they did not welcome the efforts of the Home Secretary to decide for them.[59]

Having resisted the Home Secretary's attempts to seize the power to impose on the police a consistent policy on cannabis offenders, senior officers themselves sought to introduce a more coherent approach. ACPO issued guidance to its members in September 2003 that was intended to draw their attention to the spirit of the new classification. It stated that 'the presumption should be against using this power [of arrest] for simple possession offences' and it recommended that street warnings should replace formal cautions or arrests in these circumstances. The 'street warning' involved the offence of possession being recorded against the individual but this did not constitute a criminal record against them.[60] However, it did note a number of exceptions where arrest was advisable, which included situations where those using cannabis were in public view or were repeatedly caught offending.[61] A report by the Institute of Criminal Policy Research at King's College London found in the wake of this advice that 'the eventual outcome of being found in possession of cannabis was not predictable and depended on factors such as the views of the officer, the amount of cannabis found, the attitude of the offender and local policy'. In other words, officers on the beat were continuing to ignore the guidance of senior officers when it suited them. The Institute's report also found that use of street warnings varied significantly across the four case studies conducted, and they were issued to 22 per cent of those caught in possession of cannabis in one police district but to 42 per cent of them in another.[62]

The reclassification and advice from ACPO has failed to impose a standard-ized approach on police officers to those caught in possession of cannabis.

If power over cannabis offenders remained in the hands of the police on the street, and if the evidence shows that they continued to exercise it unevenly and inconsistently, the overall picture suggests that the advice of ACPO was heeded. In 2003 the number of offenders formally cautioned or convicted in a magistrates' court was almost 77,500, but in 2004 and under the new classification, this number had dropped to 45,490. In addition to this the police issued 27,520 'street warnings' as advised by ACPO in its guidelines of the previous year. In other words the police in England and Wales were dealing with similar numbers of cannabis offenders but now chose 'street warnings' for a large proportion of them.

Medical cannabis in the 1990s

As outlined in Chapter 4, the medical use of cannabis in modern medicine had faded by the 1950s and was entirely dismissed by the World Health Organization in 1952 as 'without medical justification', a position which found its way into the 1961 Single Convention on Narcotic Drugs. Since then there had been major advances in the understanding of cannabis as in 1964 the active ingredient tetrahydrocannabinol (THC) was isolated and in 1988 cannabinoid receptors were discovered. However, research into its applications as a modern medicine remained patchy although growing recreational use of the drug had resulted in an awareness among consumers of its therapeutic potential, and it can be argued that in the late 1980s and early 1990s cannabis became a folk medicine in Britain as people recom-mended it for pain relief to those suffering from such ailments as multiple sclerosis and cancer. This phenomenon surfaced in the press in the early 1990s as Anne Biezanek, a 65-year-old doctor, was charged with supplying drugs to her daughter. She sent parcels of cannabis to her daughter's GP along with instructions about how to administer the substance. The GP alerted the police who arrested Dr Biezanek. When the case came to trial the defendant pointed out that the drug had been supplied to relieve the symptoms of her daughter's serious illness and the jury at Liverpool Crown Court cleared her of the charges of supplying cannabis and possessing it with an intent to supply.[63]

Dr Biezanek had an interesting history as an activist on health issues as she had courted controversy in the early 1960s as Britain's first Catholic doctor to operate a birth-control clinic and to advocate the use of oral contraceptives.[64] It was Clare Hodges however that became the leading proponent of medical cannabis use in the 1990s. An Oxford graduate and journalist, she had suffered with multiple sclerosis since 1983 and began to use cannabis in 1992 after reading a medical report from the US. She found it useful in relaxing muscle spasms and relieving pain and bladder problems and became an advocate of the medical application of cannabis. Eventually she established a UK branch of the Alliance for Cannabis Therapeutics with the assistance of the American organization of the same name that had been founded in 1982.[65]

Hodges was successful in presenting herself as 'a middle-class mother with two young children' who 'hated being branded a criminal' simply for being one of the many 'poorly people trying to get relief from our symptoms'.[66] In opening an office of the Alliance for Cannabis Therapeutics in Britain she was careful to sign up to an agenda that sought to 'reform the laws which prohibit medical access to marijuana'[67] as opposed to seeking wider changes to legislation on cannabis that would make recreational consumption easier too. Hodges kept her activities focused on the narrower issue of medical use of the drug through interviews and press stories and with an advertising campaign aimed at the newspapers.[68] The outcome of this was that she became established as the respectable face of the medical cannabis consumer and succeeded in organizing two meetings with the Department of Health and the Home Office. She contributed to the shape of the British Medical Association's 1999 report, *The Therapeutic Use of Cannabis*, was interviewed by the House of Lords Select Committee of 1998, and appeared as an expert witness when medical cannabis cases came to court.[69]

At the meeting with the Home Office she advocated the licensing of medical experiments with cannabis by Geoffrey Guy. He made a substantial fortune from opium painkillers in the 1980s and 1990s and turned his attention to cannabis products after contact with various other scientists that had been looking at the drug over the previous decade. These scientists recalled that their work had been gently encouraged throughout the mid-1990s by the Home Office which had licensed use of cannabis in scientific work with greater enthusiasm than in previous decades. As such it was no surprise when Geoffrey Guy was given permission in November 1997 to press ahead with his work.[70] The timing of this was ironic though; just as a private company was being licensed to develop a medicine from cannabis by the Home Office, the Home Secretary blurted out that

> it does not follow that because there are no deaths from a drug, it is therefore not harmful. There was a drug which was quite good for its original purpose in the 1960s, called Thalidomide but it turned out to have terrible side-effects. It is said that the continual use of cannabis can cause personality disorder and many other serious side effects.[71]

It seems that the civil servants were not at pains to keep their elected boss clearly informed of their strategy or direction. Scientists such as Roger Pertwee and John Notcutt who had been working with cannabis since the 1980s recall that this sudden receptiveness of the Home Office to licensing experiments with cannabis medicines was quite deliberate. Officials such as Alan MacFarlane at the Home Office were increasingly troubled by the medical consumers' lobby and the sympathetic headlines that they generated, not least of all because the legalize cannabis campaigners showed signs of trying to co-opt them for their more general purposes. As such, the bureaucrats could see the merit of encouraging controlled scientific trials with the drug as by demonstrating that they were committed to establishing the efficacy and safety of cannabis medicines they hoped to clearly mark out the medical potential of the drug as a separate issue from those related to recreational consumption.

As such, Geoffrey Guy and GW Pharmaceuticals came along at the perfect time for the Home Office as their project was not simply to look into the potential of cannabis medicines but to develop modern pharmaceutical products from them. This raised the prospect of standardized and homogenized medicines available through modern modes of delivery coming on to the market for those in need of them. Such products would mean that those suffering with multiple sclerosis, cancer, arthritis, etc. would not have to rely on smoking or eating unpredictable lumps of organic cannabis. This prospect perfectly suited the Home Office agenda of separating out the medical from the recreational uses of cannabis as in this scenario the cultures of consumption would be entirely divorced from one another; the tablet or spray would be distinct from the joint or hash-chocolate.[72] Such was the enthusiasm for this development at the Home Office that the latter put GW Pharmaceuticals in touch with HortaPharm, a company that they were aware of in Holland that had been developing cloned THC-rich cannabis plants there since the 1970s.[73]

In time GW Pharmaceuticals were to develop these products and became the first legitimate company in the UK to have a direct commercial interest in cannabis products since the corn-plaster retailers of the 1920s. Their products include Sativex and THCV, with the former being delivered by an oromucosal spray and having received approval for prescription in Canada in 2005. It is currently undergoing late stage clinical development in the UK. It is worth noting, however, that it was consumer demand and activism that created this situation. As those with multiple sclerosis, cancer, arthritis, etc. became dissatisfied with the array of drugs that they were provided with by modern pharmaceutical companies in the 1990s they experimented with cannabis and become unafraid to champion its virtues when they found it useful despite the medical orthodoxies that they en-countered.[74]

Skunk and the u-turn

Almost as soon as Blunkett's decision to reclassify cannabis came into law in 2004 the move was called into question. At the heart of the challenge was the issue of 'skunk'. This was defined by the ACMD as a form of 'sinse-milla'; they described it as 'a higher potency preparation' derived from 'the flowering tops from unfertilised, female *Cannabis sativa* plants and . . . most commonly produced by intensive indoor cultivation methods'.[75] Alarming accounts of the widespread availability and unknown dangers of this al-legedly super-strength cannabis began to surface in 2004 and 2005. News-paper reports carried stories about users such as 'Ryan, 19' who was said to have stated that 'I think if I smoked hash it wouldn't be so bad, but I smoke skunk and that really knocks you out' before pointing out that 'in January cannabis was downgraded from a Class B to a Class C drug . . . many are concerned this gives young people the impression it is a safe drug and encourages them to experiment'.[76] All this under the headline 'ALARM AT RISING CANNABIS ADDICTION'. By March 2005 the *Daily Express* had progressed onto headlines like 'THE CANNABIS DISASTER THAT IS DESTROYING OUR CHILDREN'S MINDS' and claims that 'skunk is a super-powerful hybrid, which contains 20 per cent of THC (the hallucinogenic ingredient that gets people stoned) as opposed to 3 per cent in the stuff that was smoked in the old days'.[77] Experts began to join the chorus, with Dr Clare Gerada, the head of the drugs unit of the Royal

College of General Practitioners, reported early in January 2005 as stating that 'with cannabis now more popular among young people than cigarettes and higher potencies more widely available than ever before, it is time we looked again at the health risks'.[78] Finally, on 18 March the new Home Secretary, Charles Clarke, declared that he would ask the Advisory Council on the Misuse of Drugs to assess how far its position was changed by recent reports from New Zealand and Holland of the impact of cannabis use on mental health. He would also 'welcome advice on claims of increased prevalence of cannabis with high levels of Tetrahydrocannabinol . . . known as "skunk"'.[79]

Quite how far this was prompted by a concern about cannabis, and quite how far the decision was taken for more political reasons, is a question that draws attention to the fact that 2005 was the year of a general election. It was certainly the case that the Conservatives had decided to attack the government on cannabis in the run-up to the May ballot, and to raise the spectre of 'skunk' in these forays. As early as 18 January 2005 David Davis, the Shadow Home Secretary, announced in the House of Commons that 'Cannabis is not a harmless drug. Super-potent varieties have emerged in the past 20 years, and scientific evidence continues to show a heightened risk of mental illness for those who use cannabis regularly'. This was part of his attack on the 2005 Drugs (Sentencing and Commission of Inquiry) Bill in which he criticized the government for not reclassifying cannabis.[80] The campaign was maintained in the newspapers, with Davis rarely missing the chance to be quoted on a cannabis story with the observation that 'Downgrading cannabis was a mistake, which has sent mixed messages to the young and the vulnerable about the dangers of drugs' and a pledge to reverse reclassification.[81] Whether Clarke's decision to ask for a review of the cannabis evidence was driven by a desire to take the issue out of the hands of the Opposition ahead of the May general election is unclear, but it was certainly the case that he acted suddenly on the matter. Within six weeks of Davis launching his first attacks on the subject Clarke suddenly requested the review, despite showing no previous interest in the subject of cannabis during his three months in the post of Home Secretary.

The outcome of the review was to endorse the status quo. When the ACMD reported back (after the May general election) in December 2005 it was clear that 'the Council does not advise the reclassification of cannabis products to Class B'. On the issue of 'skunk' it was less than convinced that high potency cannabis was the great threat to public health that had been alleged in the newspapers and by the Conservatives. The ACMD report noted that

> the extent to which the potency of cannabis products, as used by consumers, has increased over the past few years is unclear . . . while the potencies of cannabis resin and 'traditional' imported herbal cannabis have remained unchanged over the past 10 years, the average potencies of sinsemilla seizures have increased more than two-fold.

It went on to point out though that sinsemilla was not the most common product on the market. The response to this report was to change the political landscape of the way in which drugs policy was driven in the UK. The Home Secretary accepted the recommendations of the ACMD that cannabis remain a Class C drug, and that an education programme should be used to reinforce the message that cannabis was harmful and illegal. However, he did so in a way that established a distance between himself and the ACMD. When revealing his conclusions in the House of Commons Clarke was keen to state that 'on cannabis, I have considered very carefully the advice that I have received from many sources'[82] and to note that the ACMD gave only 'a scientific assessment' and that he did 'not think that medical harm is the only consideration; there is also harm to society and a range of other questions'.[83] Such statements served to marginalize the ACMD, by representing it as only one of the sources of information that he was considering. His statements also portrayed the ACMD as a rather limited scientific body responsible simply for monitoring medical data. The ACMD was of course rather more than this, having been established as a statutory body by the Misuse of Drugs Act 'to keep under review the situation in the United Kingdom with respect to drugs which are being . . . misused and of which the misuse is having or appears to them capable of having harmful effects sufficient to constitute a social problem'.[84]

This marginalization of the ACMD was not simply a feature of Charles Clarke's approach as it seems that politicians across the parties were increasingly keen to publicly dismiss its evidence and conclusions. In April 2007 the Conservatives introduced a Drugs (Reclassification and Roadside Testing) Bill which sought to return cannabis to the Class B schedule. To justify this it was asserted that 'we already know that 10 per cent of all those with schizophrenia in the United Kingdom would not have developed the illness if they had not smoked cannabis—that is 25,000 individuals whose lives have been ruined by cannabis, not to mention their families, friends and loved ones'.[85] Such an assertion ignored the ACMD's 2005 conclusion that 'the current evidence suggests, at worst, that using cannabis increases the lifetime risk of developing schizophrenia by 1 per cent' and was subsequently dismissed in its 2008 report. This made it clear that such definitive assertions about mental health were unlikely to be scientific as 'there are very considerable difficulties in establishing a 'cause and effect' relationship between the use of cannabis and the subsequent development of a psychotic illness'.[86] It was not only Conservative politicians who were unwilling to take any notice of the expert evidence provided by the ACMD in airing their opinions. For example, Lindsay Hoyle, Labour MP for Chorley, insisted in a House of Commons debate in 2007 that 'people start off with cannabis and go on to harder drugs. I do not care what people say—there is a definite link between soft drugs and hard drugs. We must be tough and reclassify cannabis'.[87] This despite the ACMD's conclusion in 2002 that 'the majority of cannabis users never move on to Class A drugs'.[88]

It was one of Charles Clarke's successors, Jacqui Smith, who was to take the marginalization and diminution of the experts of the ACMD to its extreme conclusion. Having taken over as prime minister in June 2007, Gordon Brown sought to take control of the cannabis issue by announcing in the following month that 'the Home Secretary will consult on whether it is right that cannabis should be moved from class C to class B'.[89] Smith immediately requested the ACMD to once again return to the issue of cannabis in order to review its classification 'in the light of real public concern about the potential mental health effects of cannabis use and, in particular, the use of stronger strains of the drug'.[90] There then began a period of niggly exchanges between the government and the ACMD about the way to decide drugs policy. In the same month that the ACMD was requested to report again on the cannabis issue the Home Office issued its consultation document on building a new drugs strategy called 'Drugs: Our Community, Your Say'. The ACMD dismissed this document as 'self-congratulatory and generally disappointing' and was particularly concerned that

> the evidence presented, and the interpretation given, are not based on rigorous scrutiny. It is not acknowledged that in many cases the information is uncertain and sometimes of poor quality. It is disappointing that the consultation paper makes no mention of needing to improve the evidence base of drug misuse and treatments nor makes use of international evidence, for informing and guiding policy.[91]

Clearly there was real anxiety at the ACMD that it was not just MPs and ministers that were ignoring its evidence, but that the Home Office was also now conjuring up policy from convictions rather than from consideration. The government responded by letting it be known through press leaks that it would be dismissing the ACMD advice on cannabis even before that advice had been offered. In January 2008, four months before the ACMD report was due, *The Times* published an article which was co-written by its chief political correspondent, which claimed that

> Cannabis is to be reclassified as a Class B drug after an official review this spring, *The Times* has learnt. Gordon Brown and Jacqui Smith are determined to reverse the decision to downgrade the drug when the Advisory Council on the Misuse of Drugs completes its report in the next few months. While its recommendations are not yet known, ministers are already making plain that the Home Secretary is prepared to overrule the expert body if necessary.[92]

Other newspapers carried similar stories on the same day, with the political correspondent of *The Telegraph* stating that 'Brown will move to reclassify cannabis'[93] and the *Daily Express* claiming that 'A senior Whitehall figure said yesterday: "The sentiment from Number 10 and the Home Office is very much towards reclassification"'.[94] That the stories appeared on the same day and under the byline of senior journalists on the nation's broadsheets suggests that officials had been careful to orchestrate the coverage.

The stories were certainly prescient. The report of the ACMD was published on 7 May 2008. David Nutt, the chair of the ACMD, was careful to point out in presenting its report that it was the outcome of 'a most careful scrutiny of the totality of the available evidence' and he stated clearly that 'the majority of the Council's members consider—based on its harmfulness to individuals and society—that cannabis should remain a Class C substance'. In other words the ACMD was not denying that the drug was harmful, but rather that its dangers were most similar to the other drugs in the Class C schedule rather than those in Class B.[95] This recommendation was rejected by the Home Secretary, who declared in the House of Commons that 'I have decided to reclassify cannabis, subject to parliamentary approval, as a class B drug'.[96]

In order to justify this decision Jacqui Smith revealed to MPs that 'my decision takes into account issues such as public perception and the needs and consequences for policing priorities'.[97] Yet the ACMD had explicitly addressed both of these issues in its report. The Committee had commissioned its own opinion poll in order to get a clear sense of what public perceptions actually were. They found that there was 'some inconsistency in the responses with respect to the classification system . . . a majority of respondents wished for cannabis to be reclassified as a Class A or B substance [but] there seems little desire for the penalties for possession to increase'.[98] The Committee had also made a point of looking at policing concerns and had acknowledged that ACPO did want reclassification to Class B. It noted that its reasons for this were the perceptions that the 2004 change in classification had stimulated a greater illegal market, that the potential for cannabis users to suffer associated mental health problems had increased, and that policing cannabis as a Class C substance had not enjoyed public confidence.[99]

While the ACMD did not offer opinions on the case made by ACPO, it is worth analysis as it was evidently weighed above that of the ACMD by the Home Secretary. In the first place it could be said that it was hardly the responsibility of the police to concern themselves with the 'the potential for cannabis users to suffer associated mental health problems'. This issue was something that was more squarely within the remit of the ACMD, which as noted above, had declared repeatedly since 1997 that this was a complex issue with no easy answers. Secondly, it could be argued that many of the problems of public confidence in the policing of cannabis had been caused by the law enforcers themselves rather than by the legislators or their expert advisers. After all, it had been police officers that had persuaded David Blunkett to dilute his original proposals and to make offences involving Class C drugs arrestable. Additionally, inconsistent policing since then had further contributed to public confusion.

Even the argument by ACPO that the 2004 change in classification had stimulated the market seems to be unconvincing. The ACMD pointed out that by 2007 the number of users seemed to have been decreasing for the best part of a decade, with the most significant decreases coming since reclassification in 2004. The market had been shrinking, not growing. What appeared to have been growing was the supply side of the relationship. Stories had regularly featured in the media since reclassification of criminal gangs using illegal immigrants to staff suburban drugs factories that were dedicated to producing high-THC cannabis both for the UK market and for export.[100] Indeed, in discussing Jacqui Smith's decision to reclassify cannabis in 2008 the ACPO spokesman had proudly pointed to the 'police raids on over 2000 cannabis farms in the last 12 months' and the fact that the police 'want those criminals who are investing extensively in cannabis factories to realise that the UK is not a soft touch—a message backed by police raids on over 2000 cannabis farms in the last 12 months'.[101] This all seems confused, however, as reclassification did not deal at all with suppliers and traffickers of the drug who faced the same maximum sentence of fourteen years under Smith's classification of 2008 as they did under the Blunkett classification of 2004. It seems that the government decided to act on the basis of confused public opinion and on the questionable assertions of the police rather than on the advice of the ACMD whose task it was to review all of the evidence available from a variety of perspectives.

The Home Secretary was also keen to point out that she was using reclassification 'to send the clear and unambiguous message that the use of cannabis is dangerous and harmful to health, and should not happen'.[102] This echoed the prime minister's statement, to GMTV, shortly after receiving the report of the ACMD, that 'I have always been very strongly of the view that cannabis is unacceptable and we have got to send a message'.[103] Some mocked the idea that announcements in the House of Commons were effective mechanisms for communicating with young consumers:

> After listening to Jacqui Smith MP talking about skunk cannabis in Parliament today millions of young people have decided to quit using cannabis and drink 3 litre bottles of white-lightning cider instead. Across the housing estates of Britain vulnerable young people, more used to the daily truant ritual of a skunk fuelled psychotic axe-rampage, could be witnessed huddled around radios hanging on Home Secretary Smith's every word. Interviewed afterwards many were of the opinion that now they faced a super-stern warning from the police for cannabis possession, instead of a mere moderately-stern warning like in the old days, the risk was simply too great. It was time to quit weed and hit the cider big time.[104]

Others wondered whether the message intended by the government was aimed at cannabis consumers at all, with an article in *The Independent* claiming that 'This is a political row fuelled by the Prime Minister's anxiety to pacify Middle England'.[105] It was certainly the case that the decision to reclassify cannabis in 2004 had provided opponents with political ammunition. The Conservative response in the House of Commons to the Home Secretary's announcement demonstrates how potent a weapon this had become. The Shadow Home Secretary even managed to use the government's reversal of its reclassification as an opportunity to attack the administration:

may I say that I fully support the Government's decision to upgrade the classification of cannabis to class B, even if their decision to do so has come rather late? The Government's historically lax approach to drugs has been a hallmark of our broken society under Labour. The UK has the worst level of overall drug abuse in Europe. Drug crimes have increased by almost a half under this Government, and Britain has the highest rate of teenage cannabis abuse in the European Union. We all hope that today's statement means that the Government now recognise that cannabis is a very dangerous drug—that it wrecks lives, is a gateway to harder drug abuse and fuels crime.[106]

This statement suggests that discussion of cannabis had become about more than the drug itself. Reclassification had provided the Opposition with a springboard from which to attack the government's entire social policy, its record as an administration and its impact on Britain. This explains why the relationship between the legislators and the experts broke down in 2008. The latter had been speaking with a voice that was far more united than it had been back in the 1970s and the 1980s, when divisions within their ranks had enabled a government to disregard its recommendations. Despite this, the New Labour administration felt that it had to ignore the advice of the experts because it feared that a failure to reclassify cannabis to Class B, no matter how logically inconsistent or constitutionally questionable this was, carried with it too great a political cost.

The question remains of exactly who it was that the government claimed to be sending a message to. Perhaps the most difficult part of the recent story to tell is that of the consumers. A number of tentative statements can be made about the nature of the market in Britain and its historical development. In the first decade of the twenty-first century the market for cannabis was complex, differentiated, and changing. Statistics produced by the ACMD showed that 2.6 million people claimed to have used the drug at some point in 2006/7 in England and Wales, a little over 8 per cent of the population. This figure was about 11 per cent in Scotland. Consumption was most prevalent amongst the young, with almost half of 20–24-year-olds claiming to have tried cannabis at some time in their lives and a third of 16–19-year-olds reporting the same. Only around 12 per cent of each age group claimed to have used the drug in the last month, which suggests that in the majority of cases cannabis had not become a regular feature in the lives of those who tried it. Indeed, a third of 35–44-year-olds claimed to have tried cannabis while under 5 per cent of that age group admitted to using the drug in the last year. The ACMD noted that 'The data are also compatible with the suggestion that, at least in the past, most young cannabis users had stopped by their mid-thirties' although it noted the difficulty of making more definitive statements as there was a lack of 'reliable longitudinal data'. The ACMD was forced to rely on a study from Holland to explore the habits of those beyond the age of 24, and was keen to emphasize that even this relied on evidence from customers in cannabis coffee shops there. It found that regular customers were divided into three groups, the first of which was young males (mean age 22.7 years) who sought high levels of intoxication, the second of which were older people (mean age 27.7 years) of both sexes who sought moderate intoxication, and a third group that consisted of mature cannabis smokers (mean age 37.5 years) whose consumption was consistently high and whose pattern of use was little affected by the strength of the product. However, the ACMD was forced to admit that this glimpse of older users and their habits was difficult to translate to the British context as 'we do not yet know if the use of cannabis in the UK shows similar profiles of consumption; nor whether there are changes in the pattern of use over time'.[107]

Evidence of behaviour among younger consumers gathered by the ACMD suggested that fewer members of the 16–24-year-old age group were using cannabis regularly than had been the case a decade earlier. For example, in 1996 a quarter of those in that age group claimed to have used cannabis in the previous year, while only a fifth of that group reported the same in 2006–7. The ACMD also noted that 'use appears to have declined by around 20 per cent to 25 per cent over the past five years in all age groups', and the date showed that the years when reporting of consumption retreated from the highest levels were 2001 to 2003 after which there was a steady decline. The ACMD did not make a link between the decline from this period and the reclassification of cannabis to a Class C drug that was announced in the middle of 2002. While it is tempting to speculate that this coincidence is significant, it is important to remember that the behaviour of consumers of intoxicants is complex and that cannabis is only one of a number of products in the market. Part of the story of declining cannabis use in the first decade of the twenty-first century is alcohol. It has been argued that during the 1980s and 1990s the alcohol industry faced competition from a range of illegal substances including cannabis for the disposable income of those under the age of 24 looking for intoxication. Rave and club culture of the 1990s was associated with water-drinking drug takers eager to remain hydrated during long dance sessions rather than with alcohol consumers.

However, by the end of the 1990s the industry responded with new products such as 'alco-pops' and new advertisements using imagery that co-opted that of the drug and dance experience and presented alcoholic drinks as consistent with the latter. The alcoholic drinks industry repositioned itself to compete for the young adult's recreational pounds and the decline in cannabis use may be a measure of its success.[108] A 2009 report on ecstasy by the ACMD confirms that any simple conclusions about cannabis and its consumers are difficult as trends and tastes are constantly changing when it comes to intoxication. It found that cocaine seemed to be back in fashion and that it was 'the preferred drug of young clubbers' but that 'cannabis, ketamine or benzodiazepines may be used . . . to prolong the socialising by attending post-club "chill-out" parties and . . . to reduce the negative effects of the stimulant drug "comedown" phase'.[109]

Further evidence of young consumers of cannabis in this period was produced in a Rowntree Foundation report published in 2008. It found that young people tended to use cannabis for the purpose of being sociable, and that it was a practice that was important in contexts of friendship and networking where acts of sharing were significant. There was some sense given that cannabis use was not a constant or consistent feature of the lives of these consumers. Almost a third of the sample reported that they had reduced their intake over time and that they had done so for a variety of reasons that included concerns about the health implications of using the substance, the cost of consumption, and the impact on wider life choices and prospects: 'the school I'm attending is a sports academy. It [cannabis] was affecting my health, I was running out of breath', reported one respondent.[110] This was consistent with another Rowntree investigation published in 2007 which found that about 40 per cent of the teenagers interviewed had reduced or given up cannabis use within four months of first being questioned. This was put down to 'positive changes to the young person's social situation and/or maturation' in the intervening period.[111] The Rowntree research also emphasized that the market for cannabis was further complicated by geographical considerations. It took respondents from London and those from rural towns in south-west England and found distinct differences in the ways in which the two groups interacted with cannabis products. For example, those in London were more likely to purchase cannabis to use on their own and were more likely to report that they used it to help them sleep than were their counterparts in the rural

South-West. They were more likely to consume cannabis in groups for purposes of social interaction.[112]

The image provided in these reports, of young consumers who smoked cannabis for purposes of sociability and who often gave up using it as they matured, contrasted sharply with much of the media coverage of the period. 'Cannabis caused a 14-year-old to kill' was the headline in the *Daily Mail* in 2005 when Luke Mitchell was convicted of killing Jodi Jones in Dalkeith. It had been alleged at his trial that Mitchell was both a cannabis consumer and supplier who was also a devotee of Marilyn Manson and influenced by Satanism. Lord Nimmo Smith, the judge at the trial, had explicitly stated that his cannabis use may 'well have contributed to your being unable to make the distinction between fantasy and reality, which is essential for normal moral judgments'. The *Daily Mail*'s article, written by Melanie Phillips, ended by worrying 'How many more Luke Mitchells will it take before our society wakes up from its lethal, drug-stupefied trance?'[113] The emergence of the idea of the 'feral youth' in the media in this decade was dependent on the notion of the cannabis-smoking teenager crazed by intoxication: 'They are not hard to find. Every few days brings a fresh tale of feral youths meting out random acts of violence with unfathomable intensity. Apart from the shocking brutality, the speed with which a seemingly trivial argument or confrontation can assume murderous proportions, the stories have a common theme: the perpetrators of the violence, often in their very young teens, were high on "skunk" at the time', alleged *The Observer* in 2008.[114]

If the politicians were content to ignore the experts then it appears that the newspapers were prepared to do likewise. There was something of a paradox here. Since 1997 cannabis and its consumers in the UK had been researched to an unprecedented level, by organizations as diverse as the British Medical Association, the Police Foundation, and the House of Lords. A decade of investigations had culminated in reports by the ACMD and the Rowntree Foundation which produced evidence of young consumers who experimented with cannabis in sociable circumstances and who moderated their consumption if it interfered too much with the rest of their lives. Yet at a time when more research than ever before was available on the drug and its consumers, the newspapers preferred to reproduce images of cannabis users as violent and criminal that echoed myths that stretched back to the nineteenth century and journalistic traditions that were over 100 years old.[115]

Conclusion

Research published by the Joseph Rowntree Foundation suggests that little had been achieved by the tinkering of officials, legislators, and experts throughout the decade after 1997. Published just before Jacqui Smith's decision as Home Secretary to reclassify cannabis as a Class B drug, a 2008 Rowntree publication argued that 'on the strength of the findings of this study, we very much doubt that a change would have any impact whatsoever on young people'.[116] No wonder, as the media and political furore of the previous decade had resulted in very little change in the position of cannabis users in relation to the law and to the police. Possession of cannabis remained an arrestable offence and the police continued to be the key power-brokers in matters related to the drug throughout the period. They had successfully seen off attempts by legislators, experts, and consumers to wrest from the police control of state approaches to the drug and it could be argued they had actually been able to increase their powers in this area. In 2008, as in 1998 or indeed 1968, it was the police that made the policy: at each stage it was the police officer who was empowered to decide who was stopped, who was warned, who was cautioned, who was sent to court, and even how much cannabis constituted a serious offence. As this book goes to press in 2012, it is the opinions, beliefs, and mood of the police officer that stops the individual in possession of cannabis that decide what will happen to that individual, not the will of Parliament, the conclusions of the scientists, or the interests of the user.

9

Conclusion

Cannabis and British history

The history of the relationship between the British and cannabis stretches back over two centuries. This chapter returns to the themes of the book, control and consumption, and argues that current positions on cannabis in the UK can only be understood clearly when they are placed back into that history. The events and processes of the last 200 years reveal how those current positions were arrived at, and how well founded they are.

The nineteenth-century history of cannabis and the British shows how contradictory positions were quickly voiced and established. Within the Empire the Government of India sought to generate revenues by taxing local trade in the substance and yet at the same time colonial administrators in Egypt attempted to enforce a prohibition on the consumption of cannabis preparations. Pioneering medical men argued that potions containing the plant were among the wonder drugs of the age, and set about incorporating them into innovative treatments, and yet by the end of the century MPs were declaring cannabis to be the 'most horrible intoxicant the world has yet produced' and demanding an official inquiry into its sale within the Empire. In 1893 the government was forced to order the Indian Hemp Drugs Commission in response to these demands and while its conclusions were sympathetic to both medical and recreational consumption they were equivocal and rejected by some of the members of the Commission itself. At least these conclusions were based on extensive research, as it is clear that many of the positions adopted on cannabis in this period were founded on little or no accurate information about the plant and its preparations, and instead reflected the moral, political, and economic positions of the age. Colonial officials endorsed the drug as it was a valuable source of revenue, or condemned it in the name of the civilizing mission. MPs with anti-imperial agendas found in it another stick with which to beat the government on the issue of the iniquities of Empire. Doctors and scientists lauded it as they sought to promote their own careers and reputations or disapproved of it when consumers offended their prejudices.

It was international events related to the Empire rather than domestic concerns that first shunted cannabis into the early drugs control regime in Britain. The 1924/5 Second Geneva Opium Conference was convened to consider tighter controls on cocaine and opium. Cannabis was suddenly thrust onto the agenda by the Egyptian delegation. In part it did this to embarrass the country's former colonial masters, the British, who had failed to effectively enforce a prohibition on cannabis products while in charge there and who also allowed a free trade in cannabis substances in the South Asian part of the Empire. Indeed, the British representatives of the Government of India were chief among the opponents of the effort to include the drug in discussions at Geneva. The Egyptians relied on the force of their rhetoric rather than any clear technical evidence to condemn cannabis. Although few delegations there had any experience or knowledge of the plant, and in spite of a lack of medical or scientific data, the Conference ignored British efforts to strike cannabis from the agenda and ended up by including preparations of the drug in the controls agreed there early in 1925.

This meant that as a signatory to League of Nations treaties, the UK was forced to ratify controls on cannabis that British representatives at the Conference had opposed. These controls were eventually put into force in 1928 through the mechanism of the Dangerous Drugs Act. This legislation had been passed in 1920 after wartime concerns about the consumption of opium substances and cocaine in Britain. Cannabis was not originally included in the Act, and was only declared to be a poison in 1924 when some confused policing of opium and a media scare prompted the Pharmaceutical Society to place the drug in the Poisons Schedule.[1] Once cannabis was included in the Dangerous Drugs Act in 1928 it fell to the recently formed Home Office Drugs Branch to see that controls were enforced. Though the formal requirements of the Dangerous Drugs Act were simply that inspectors from the Home Office visit the premises of wholesale pharmacists to check their registers, ambitious and entrepreneurial staff there set about expanding their remit. Before long they were travelling around the country briefing the police on illegal drugs, even where these were rarely found, and circulating an annual report to keep colleagues in government up to date with nationwide narcotics news. In this way enforcement mechanisms across the UK were primed to deal with drugs offences even where officers infrequently encountered them. This was particularly the case with cannabis which was little used in the period and limited mainly to the itinerant Asian and African sailors who passed through the ports.

There was one crucial difference, however, between cannabis and the other drugs in the history of the period. The work of the Rolleston Committee (the Departmental Committee on Morphine and Heroin Addiction) in 1924 and its subsequent impact on the revised Dangerous Drugs Act of 1926 fixed notions of drug users. It established that regular consumers of substances like morphine and heroin were to be viewed as ill and therefore subjects for medical treatment rather than as criminals who should be prosecuted for breaking the law on drugs for their personal gratification. It has been argued that this liberal view reflected understandings of the habitual users of the period, who had usually taken to the substances through medical treatment and who were from respectable backgrounds, which meant that they were not perceived to constitute a social 'problem'.[2] Cannabis users enjoyed no such status. Where they did come to the attention of the authorities consumers were from the country's colonies whose peoples were considered at the time to be inferior races. They either featured in exotic stories as enemies of the order imposed by the colonial authorities, or as disruptive itinerants who had troubled the peace maintained by the police in the nation's dockside cities. As such, cannabis consumption and consumers were firmly rooted within the remit of law enforcers at a time when more lenient approaches were adopted for those using other drugs. The decline of therapeutic applications of preparations of the plant by the 1930s would have sealed the sense that they were no concern of the medical profession.

When looked at this way it is clear that from the outset the regime in the UK to be applied to cannabis was not designed to deal with a domestic market for the drug. Control came before consumption in Britain. The regime had its origins in British concerns about the wartime use of opiates and cocaine, and in colonial disputes and anxieties about cannabis consumers of African and Asian origin. The mechanisms for enforcing this regime were enthusiastically put in place by officials in the government's Home Office Drugs Branch, not because of their fears about cannabis, but because of the zeal with which they sought to establish their new department. With minimal discussion about the substance, its properties, or its consumers, cannabis was lodged within the duties of Britain's law enforcement agencies by 1945.

The next set of key events to shape the control and consumption of cannabis in the UK came in the late 1940s and 1950s. The arrival of the Windrush generation of migrants from across the nation's former colonies was to transform the market for the drug in the UK. Before the end of the Second World War this had been limited to the sailors of Asian and African origin who passed through the country's ports on their way across the Empire's trading networks, and to the few members of the local community tempted to experiment with exotic substances. Once workers from the West Indies, Africa, and Asia began to settle in the UK many brought their favourite intoxicant with them and established a permanent domestic market for cannabis in the country for the first time. When the migrants were befriended by the curious among the local population the latter began to try what the newcomers had to offer and the domestic market put down deeper roots still. Because the country's law enforcement agencies had been primed to detect cannabis offences since the 1930s it is no surprise that they quickly began to apprehend more and more of the increasing numbers of consumers. Little wonder too that no one paused to ponder what approach ought to be taken to cannabis or to think about whose responsibility the new market should be. As control had come before consumption it was already well established as a matter for law enforcement. This would have seemed more appropriate than ever in a decade when the reputation of the drug hit an all-time low following the decision by the World Health Organization (WHO) to condemn cannabis medicines as 'obsolete'.

The 1960s was a decade when many of the processes behind the control and consumption of cannabis of the last half-century or so combined to create a sense of crisis about the drug. The rise in cannabis arrests in the 1950s, and the fact that those apprehended tended to be migrants who were arriving from the Empire, gave rise to an association between the drug and that group. For those who resented or feared their arrival cannabis therefore became connected with racial anxiety and criminality. For those who saw in their arrival a welcome injection of new energy into British society, their drug, and the perception that they were persecuted for using it, became *causes célèbres*. The more politically-minded of the nation's youth incorporated use of the substance into the wider challenges that they sought to make to the UK's traditions. They did this partly because the plant and its preparations were so readily associated with those from Africa and Asia, places that were thought to possess ways of life that offered alternatives to those of the West. This association also meant that those who took to the drug were identifying with peoples that had been oppressed by the imperialism that protestors sought to condemn and distance themselves from. Some might even have seen in the drug's psychoactive properties a mechanism for achieving a sort of personal liberation. Once adopted by the self-consciously radical, cannabis consumption, and the controls on the drug and its users, were reframed within the political tensions of the period. For some the right to smoke cannabis became an emblem of a wider civil liberties debate about personal freedom and nonconformity; they asked why consumers of what they perceived to be a harmless substance should face long prison sentences for their habit. For those offended by this position cannabis consumption became symptomatic of a wider rejection of cherished norms and of paternalist authority, and using the drug constituted not an idle indulgence but a threat to the social order. The former group saw the enforcement of laws on cannabis as a campaign by 'the establishment' against migrants and against politicized members of Britain's youth, while those fearful of these groups advocated ever stricter enforcement as a means of checking sedition. The politicization of cannabis consumption and control in the 1960s was inextricably linked to the meanings that they assumed in the inter-generational squabbles of the decade.

This politicization of the consumption and control of cannabis in the 1960s had a lasting impact. Cannabis consumers found for the first time a voice, or rather voices, that some of them were keen to use in policy and legal processes. None could claim to be representative of all users however. Additionally, there was a rush by those in government to seek to use legislation to bolster the control regime in order to tackle what they saw as a damaging growth in the consumption of cannabis. This rush produced hastily prepared and ill-considered laws which had to be quickly and convincingly rethought. The Home Office drew in experts from a range of professions to help it to do this, partly because this was a model much used in this period in a range of government activities, and partly because the involvement of experts would enable the administration to claim back some credibility in drugs policy after the failures of the early 1960s. The upshot was a permanent place thereafter for experts of various hues in the process of shaping government approaches to drugs.

Most important of all, the experts drawn into the policy process by the Home Office in the second half of the 1960s came up with 'the British compromise' which has shaped the UK position on cannabis since. Advocated by members of Baroness Wootton's Committee, it was designed specifically with the political tensions over the drug in mind. The idea was to keep the country's more traditional elements content by retaining laws that made the recreational consumption of cannabis illegal. At the same time ground could be conceded to those that felt strongly about the civil liberties position of cannabis consumers as advice would be given by the Government to those applying the laws on the streets and in the courts to enforce them in a sensitive and liberal manner. It was hoped that this would act to ease the tensions over the topic so that at some point in the future the law might be reconsidered in a calmer atmosphere. The politicians of the period readily accepted this, despite some public bluster, as it enabled them to back off from a tricky issue while appearing to have done something about it. 'The British compromise' that was to shape the control regime on cannabis for the next four decades was set in place as a temporary measure that was designed with at least one eye on the need to deflate a difficult and fraught political situation rather than a clear focus on establishing a logical or consistent policy on cannabis consumption.

Yet for all their significance in terms of the control regime, the 1960s are less important in terms of understanding the market for cannabis. Some may have been tempted to experiment with the drug because of the hype around it among the London elites of Britain's youth, but it seems that regular users remained limited to those from migrant groups and their associates in local communities. Established in the 1950s, this link between migrants and locals was the basis for the expansion of the market in the 1970s. In this decade a new generation of consumers grew up in the inner cities where newcomers and their neighbours had been gradually sharing ideas, habits, and interests for over two decades. Those born into these contexts found that the musical styles, dress, food, and intoxicants brought to the UK by migrant communities were not exotic temptations from faraway places but familiar features of local life. This explains why demand grew in the 1970s for cannabis alongside the growth of the market for ska and reggae music, or for biryanis and kebabs. The wider history of the emergence of multicultural centres in Britain lies behind the establishment of a growing consumer base for the drug from the 1970s onwards.

This was also the decade in which the implications of the 'British compromise', of retaining prohibitive laws but not enforcing them in a draconian spirit, began to shape the practical mechanisms of the control regime. After the 1971 Misuse of Drugs Act policy decisions were increasingly in the hands of the courts and of the police. They were expected to work out issues that the politicians and the experts could not settle back in the 1960s, matters like the amount of cannabis that is clearly for personal consumption, the amount that suggests that supply is the intention, and how minor offenders should be dealt with. Solutions included careful sentencing in magistrates' courts to reflect advice from the Lord Chancellor and police improvization with their powers of caution. This improvization continued in subsequent decades, with Customs and Excise officers choosing to compound proceedings for offences involving small amounts of cannabis in the 1980s and the 'street warning' devised by the police in the 1990s.

What also became apparent is that approaches to cannabis consumers and consumption, particularly those used by the police, were often arrived at for reasons largely unrelated to the drug and its users. For example, the police of the 1970s were accused of using their stop-and-search powers in relation to cannabis in order to harass or conduct surveillance on groups that they considered to be social problems, like youths or migrants. The increase of the use of cautions for cannabis offences in the 1980s was directly influenced by the then government's concern to reform police practices and to deploy policing resources more effectively and to other ends. The Lambeth experiment in the late 1990s was similarly driven by a concern to redirect police energies rather than a decision that cannabis was less harmful. The adoption of 'the British compromise' in the late 1960s and early 1970s explains how key policy decisions about how to treat cannabis consumption and users of the drug have come to be taken by the police and magistrates. It also explains how it is that these decisions are often taken with little regard for the drug or its consumers. The licence afforded by the police to stop and search people on the pretext of looking for cannabis, and to arrest them even where offences detected are minor, has provided officers with discretionary powers that enable them to pursue all manner of agendas and strategies. Cannabis laws have not always been deployed, and indeed may rarely have been deployed, to stop people using the drug.

In the 1980s and 1990s cannabis continued to be alluring because earlier associations, particularly with African and West Indian cultures and with the radical postures of the 1960s, ensured that consumption of the drug remained superficially 'alternative' and 'cool'. This explains why it is mainly teenagers and those in their early twenties who consume the substance even today, and why most of them seem to grow out of regular and excessive use as their lives become more complex and stimulating and 'cool' becomes less important. The exception to this is those who take preparations of cannabis for therapeutic purposes. Patient-activism has grown in Western societies since the 1960s. A disaffection with prescribed drugs and official medical advice has ensured that consumers of medicines have often become more assertive about their right to reject standard therapeutic substances and to explore a wide range of self-medication options. This is the context for understanding the appearance of organizations like the Alliance for Cannabis Therapeutics (ACT) in the 1990s. Members were people who found themselves ill enough to consider breaking the law and who were driven to consume cannabis solely because of their condition. They draw attention to the changing and diversifying nature of the market for cannabis in the UK since it was first established in the 1950s.

Over the course of the 1980s and the 1990s the growing market for cannabis, and the less draconian but nonetheless vigorous policing of consumers, combined to create the context for the controversies of the initial decade of the twenty-first century. The increased body of users came into contact with the expanded numbers of enforcement officials that had grown in the 1980s to deal with heroin and other 'hard' drugs. The outcome was more arrests than ever before for offences connected to cannabis at a time when they were not considered to be a priority by the police and were not high on the agenda as a social problem for politicians. Most of these offenders were not in trouble with the police for any other reason than their consumption of cannabis so the civil liberties aspect once again became pressing. When the question had been raised in the 1970s as to why consumers should fall foul of the country's law enforcement apparatus for using a product that only constituted a threat to their own health, the public health response had been that the extent of this threat remained unknown. As such government was required to prevent consumers taking the substance and recommending it to others for their own good, and this was a position that the Conservative Government had been happy to adopt as it was consistent with a paternalistic streak in their philosophy. However, subsequent experiences gradually undermined this position. As 'the British compromise' was worked out in practice it seemed to suggest that there was a tacit assumption among the authorities that consumption of cannabis was not so grave a threat to the public health that it required a vigorous enforcement of the law to address it. This was particularly the case in the 1980s when the sudden crisis of dealing with regular users of heroin and other 'hard drugs' drew a contrast with cannabis consumers. By the late 1990s the balance had swung back in the direction of the civil liberties argument because the numbers of consumers in trouble with the police had hit an all-time high and because reviews by various expert bodies of the evidence of health impacts confirmed that no unequivocal position could be established. A new generation of consumers articulated their various arguments for the freedom to access the drug and made clear their dissatisfaction with 'the British compromise' which had entangled so many of them with the law. A canny newspaper editor eager to boost the circulation of her traditionally liberal newspaper took up the issue and by the end of the decade it was once again an urgent matter in the media, for politicians, and for expert bodies. Once back in the limelight the question of controls on cannabis was one that took on various meanings that were often unconnected with the drug itself and its consumers, not least of all because discussions of the topic became an idiom in which the political differences within and between the main political parties were expressed. An ambitious new Home Secretary casting about for a means of stamping his authority on the Home Office saw in 'the British compromise' an ideal target, as by decisive action he would bring clarity to an apparently confused position that had become ossified through customary use.

David Blunkett's efforts failed because discussions of cannabis control and consumption were once again obscured by interests that were only indirectly related to them. The police resisted his plans, not because of some great concern over cannabis consumers, but because they wished to retain the powers of arrest granted to them by laws on the drug that gave them licence to pursue wider policing agendas. The Conservative Party simply breathed new life into the vague old associations between cannabis consumption and social problems in order to claim that New Labour's policies lay behind what the Tories came to call 'Broken Britain'. Serving up a political hostage of this nature to the Opposition ensured that Blunkett's reclassification, however ineffective it may have been in the wake of police intervention to retain the power of arrest over cannabis offences, would be undone by his own party. For political rather than policy reasons Jacqui Smith ignored the conclusion of the Advisory Council on the Misuse of Drugs (ACMD) that it was logically consistent for the substance to remain in Class C.[3] She saw the cannabis issue less as a question of balancing the civil liberties and health risks of consumers and more as a matter of denying political opponents easy pickings.

The foundations of British positions on cannabis

Does this brief overview of the ways in which current positions in the control and consumption of cannabis have been arrived at answer the question of how well founded those current positions are? The answer lies in the fact that at few moments in the past has detailed knowledge of the plant and the effects of products prepared from it influenced decisions. The question of evidence and policy is of course a complex one. The story of Donald McIntosh Johnson in the 1950s is an example which serves as a reminder that what appears to be sound evidence from a reliable expert may in fact be carefully selected material that simply reflects individual preju- dices. Other episodes show that the gathering of evidence on cannabis could sometimes hinder, rather than help, as information became an end in itself. This certainly seemed to be the case at the League of Nations in the 1930s, for example, where the Sub-Committee on Cannabis found that the ques- tions which needed to be answered about cannabis, and the number of those willing to provide answers, expanded uncontrollably for over five years. However, it seems clear that even where detailed knowledge was gathered and recommendations based on it have been made, these have often been ignored in the decision-making process. The Indian Hemp Drugs Com- mission of 1893/4 remains the most detailed survey of a cannabis-using society produced to date and yet it was forgotten within a generation when the drug was first thrust, on the flimsiest of evidence, into the international regulatory system designed for opium in 1925. The material gathered before the ACMD made its recommendations in 1978 took the best part of a decade to collect and yet it was firmly ignored when the government finally made a decision in 1982. The same body was at pains to assemble evidence that directly addressed the concerns that had prompted the Home Secretary to order in 2007 a third review of the classification of cannabis for the New Labour administration. She made it clear that this material was not valued when it failed to point to conclusions that suited her purposes. Subsequently, she chose to pursue a policy that was in fact confounded by the evidence.[4]

On the subject of evidence and policy it might also be noted that the nature of cannabis itself has made straightforward conclusions difficult. It is a complex substance that interacts in many ways with human bodies, and the impacts of which can be affected by such variables as the content of a particular sample, the mode of consumption, and the age, condition, and mood of the individual using it. For this reason the search for simple answers in scientific research or sociological surveys to the various policy dilemmas posed by the drug may prove to be as frustrating in the future as it has been in the past.[5] In short, definitive statements that point the way such as 'cannabis is harmful' or 'cannabis is not harmful' are likely to continue to be elusive.

The factors that shaped the key decisions about the control mechanisms that were developed to deal with cannabis have most often been related to wider contexts and interests rather than to detailed knowledge of the drug or of its effects on consumers. The long-forgotten politics of the Empire, the racial anxieties of a half-century ago, the now-dated medical assumptions of the antibiotic era and the ill-thought-out claims of those that dreamed up the counter-culture all encrusted the issues of cannabis consumption and control with layers of meaning up to the end of the 1960s. Ambitious bureaucrats and police officers, scandalizing journalists, pompous pop stars, and grandstanding politicians were among those that made gestures or took actions on the drug and its users that usually reflected their own prejudices or personal agendas but which served to incrementally limit the options for debate and policy about cannabis and its consumers. Since the 1960s 'the British compromise' has remained in place because cannabis became caught up in the contest between various professions and disciplines to shape the newly formed ACMD in the 1970s, because it was a convenient issue through which to discuss wider visions of British government which centred on debates about civil liberties and public health, because it dropped down the list of priorities when heroin and cocaine arrived in the 1980s and because enforcement agencies found in the powers bequeathed to them by 'the British compromise' a convenient device for dealing with all sorts of situations. Canny senior police officers, bullish Home Secretaries, fragmented consumer groups, shrewd newspaper editors, and calculating politicians have all brought their ambitions and anxieties to bear on the debates about cannabis control over the last forty years. The result has been that 'the British compromise' has survived for four decades despite its imprecisions and imperfections as this multiplicity of ambitions and agendas has made it difficult to see its shortcomings and impossible to initiate inclusive discussions about alternatives.

If this begins to answer the question of what history reveals about the foundations of current control mechanisms, then how far is it possible to answer the same question about the market for cannabis? It is tempting to link the post-war growth of the market for cannabis in Britain to wider sociological trends. For example, Nikolas Rose argued recently that over the last two decades or so members of modern societies have become 'neurochemical selves'. He concluded that we have come to understand ourselves, our desires, moods, and discontents, as outcomes of brain functions rather than as the results of more mysterious psychological or spiritual processes. As such, efforts to maximize our potential and to increase our happiness or contentment have become focused on strategies to modulate our physiology, particularly through the use of pharmaceutical products to alter our neurological responses to the world.[6] While the work of Rose has focused on allopathic medicines and systems it is tempting to see the use of psychoactive substances alongside these and to relate the rise of the cannabis market to the processes that he describes. It is similarly instructive to link the increased numbers of consumers of the last half-century or so to other grand accounts of society, such as that by Avner Offer who has explored changing notions of self-control and wellbeing in modern societies. Arguing that post-war capitalist democracies have consistently delivered affluence to their citizens through a 'flow of novelty and innovation' he concludes that in turn this has 'undermine[d] existing conventions, habits, and institutions of commitment [and] reinforce[d] a bias for the short term'.[7] Extremes of behaviour have emerged as individuals find it difficult to defer gratification and are constantly encouraged to seek new pleasures and to indulge established ones. The growth of the market from the 1950s onwards for what were then considered exotic intoxicants certainly fits such a picture.

The challenge to making such connections is the difficulty of speaking with any certainty about cannabis consumers in the UK. Those that do openly talk about their use of the drug rarely seem representative of other users and the tribulations of Free Love Cannabis and the Legalise Cannabis Campaign over the last two decades have demonstrated that there are few who feel strongly enough to share their commitment to sustained campaigning on the issue. Those working with the contemporary situation insist that it is not easy to speak with any clarity about those who use the drug.[8] Those observing cannabis consumers over previous decades have also been at pains to stress that its use was rarely something easy to isolate or to summarize. It is as difficult to generalize about 'the British cannabis consumer' of the last eighty years as it is to describe such a character at any particular point in that period. It is therefore more difficult still to know what has typically been behind the decision to take cannabis at any one time. From the glimpses of consumers found in these pages it seems that only in the case of the chronically ill does the use of preparations of the plant seem to be based on an effort to grasp the information available about them. For most recreational users, the fashions and tastes of the period, the ideas and beliefs in circulation at the time, the company kept, the age of the consumer, and the other intoxicants available seem to have been among the many variables that have influenced the decision to consume cannabis. The market for the drug in the UK has been shaped and reshaped by the complex interactions of personal predilections and the forces of British history.

What use are these conclusions and to whom? For historians they offer a number of insights and reminders. The first is that it is important to trace domestic histories of drugs markets and control regimes. Virginia Berridge was right to remind colleagues a decade ago that international dimensions of narcotics issues must not be neglected.[9] Indeed, this book has been keen to acknowledge the importance of events in the Empire, at the UN, and at the WHO. Equally, it has argued that the British have been able to play key roles at significant moments in the evolution abroad of agendas and policies on cannabis. However, this book seeks to balance a view of the international with a call for attention to the details of the national.[10] Particular features of British history, from the fuss about drugs caused by the anxieties of the First World War, to the twisted inconsistencies of the imperial experience, through to the impact of the arrival of migrants in the 1950s, and the development of extra-governmental expert groups to tackle thorny social issues in the 1960s and 1970s, have all shaped the story of cannabis in Britain. It is not possible to understand the latter without taking into account the peculiarities of the country's past.

The second is the observation that there may be a danger in over-theorizing the processes that drive current positions on cannabis. While there is little space here to dwell on the wealth of literature that tackles network theories of political science it is worth reflecting briefly on the implications of the history of cannabis in Britain for such ideas. The story has certainly shown the dynamic tension between policy communities, interest groups, and the networks in which both have been embedded. It also suggests, however, that there can be a danger in imposing labels like 'policy community' or 'interest group' on what are often loose aggregations of actors with divergent opinions, agendas, and beliefs. It seems clear that the story of cannabis in the UK makes little sense without taking into account the impact of entrepreneurial bureaucrats like F. W. Thornton, driven scientists like William Paton, enthusiastic consumers like Free Love Cannabis, and committed campaigners like Rufus Harris. The energy and commitment of these individuals was often decisive in shaping events and outcomes and it is important that the key role of such actors in policy processes is not lost in technical discussions about 'communities', 'groups', and 'networks'.[11]

If over-theorizing when writing about drugs policy is a risk then this book also raises the issue of over-generalization. In writing an account of cannabis in the UK it has become clear that it is important to separate out individual substances when writing histories of drugs. Preparations of can-nabis are very different from opiates and cocaine, and indeed from more recent compounds such as amphetamines or ecstasy. Much of the story that has been told in this book and in *Cannabis Britannica* has been of the difficulties in dealing with cannabis and its consumers that have arisen from them becoming tangled up in the politics of opium and other drugs. Historians who write histories of drugs in general rather than providing accounts of particular substances risk perpetuating these tangles.[12]

For Philip Emafo, whose quote kicked off this volume, and for others who are directly involved in formulating policies and shaping contemporary discussions, the book seems to offer important perspectives. The most use that a historian can be in this context is to clearly trace how the present system came to be established and to unearth the reasons why it has assumed its current shape. What this book has shown is that the present system is not the outcome of clear-eyed and well-informed assessments of cannabis and its consumers at some point in the past. Rather, current arrangements have their foundations in a time when the patchy information available about the drug was shaped by the politics and cultural relations of Empire, and long before there were many consumers in the UK itself. Since then these arrangements have been buffeted by shifting forces within British society and the system's shape reflects the convictions and agendas of the politicians, policemen, campaigners, and experts of the past. Most of these are now long gone, and if those that have replaced them want to address cannabis and its consumption in the UK in a fresh way then the lesson from the past is to reject it. Put aside the status quo as something that has been twisted by the tergiversations of previous generations rather than formed by their wisdom, and start with a blank sheet of paper and an honest declaration of interests. Even if that which emerges from such a process resembles what is in place today, at least it will have been arrived at through a fully informed and transparent process, rather than warped by the ebbs and flows of British history.[13]

Endnotes

CHAPTER I

1. 'Cannabis law sends "wrong signal"' http://news.bbc.co.uk/1/hi/uk_politics/2798285.stm, posted 26 February 2003, accessed 24 January 2011.
2. Examples include House of Lords (HL), *Select Committee on Science and Technology Second Report 1998–99, Cannabis: Government Response* (London: The Stationery Office, 1999); HL, *Select Committee on Science and Technology, Second Report 2000–01, Therapeutic Uses of Cannabis* (London: The Stationery Office, 2001); British Medical Association, *Therapeutic Uses of Cannabis* (Amsterdam: Harwood Academic Publishers, 1997); Academy of Medical Sciences, *The Use of Cannabis and Its Derivatives for Medical and Recreational Purposes* (London: The Royal Society, 1998); G. Hayes and H. Shapiro, *Drug Notes: Cannabis* (London: Institute for the Study of Drug Dependence, 1998). For the review see J. Mills, *Cannabis Britannica: Empire, Trade and Prohibition, 1800–1928* (Oxford: Oxford University Press, 2003), 8–16.
3. W. McAllister, *Drug Diplomacy in the Twentieth Century* (London: Routledge, 2000); W. McAllister, '"Wolf by the Ears": The Dilemmas of Imperial Opium Policymaking in the 20th Century', in J. H. Mills and P. Barton (eds.), *Drugs and Empires: Essays in Imperialism and Intoxication, c.1500–1930* (Basingstoke: Palgrave, 2007); W. Walker, *Opium and Foreign Policy: The Anglo-American Search for Order in Asia, 1912–1954* (Chapel Hill: University of North Carolina Press, 1991); C. Trocki, *Opium, Empire, and the Global Political Economy: A Study of the Asian Opium Trade, 1750–1950* (London: Routledge, 1999).
4. D. Courtwright, *Forces of Habit: Drugs and the Making of the Modern World* (London: Harvard University Press, 2001); R. Rudgeley, *The Alchemy of Culture: Intoxicants in Society* (London: British Museum Press, 1993).
5. F. Dikötter, L. Laamann, and Z. Xun, *Narcotic Culture: A History of Drugs in China* (London: Hurst, 2004); Y. Zheng, *The Social Life of Opium in China* (Cambridge: Cambridge University Press, 2005).
6. A. Mold, *Heroin: The Treatment of Addiction in Twentieth-Century Britain* (Champaign: Northern Illinois University Press, 2008); V. Berridge, *Opium and the People* (London: Free Association Books, 1999); V. Berridge, *Marketing Health: Smoking and the Discourse of Public Health in Britain, 1945–2000* (Oxford: Oxford University Press, 2007).

7. M. Booth, *Cannabis: A History* (London: Doubleday, 2003), 333.

8. S. Walton, *Out of It: A Cultural History of Intoxication* (London: Hamish Hamilton, 2001); P. Matthews, *Cannabis Culture: A Journey through Disputed Territory* (London: Bloomsbury, 1999); S. Blackman, *Chilling Out: The Cultural Politics of Substance Consumption, Youth and Drug Policy* (Maidenhead: Open University Press, 2004).

9. The control and consumption of cannabis in the USA have received more attention. Books that concern themselves with cannabis in the UK have tended to focus more on cultural history and meanings. See L. Sloman, *The History of Marijuana in America* (New York: Bobbs Merrill, 1979); L. Grinspoon, *Marihuana: The Forbidden Medicine* (London: Yale University Press, 1993); A. Mack and J. Joy, *Marijuana as Medicine?* (Washington: National Academy Press, 2001); R. Bonnie and C. Whitebread, *The Marihuana Conviction: A History of Marihuana Prohibition in the United States* (Charlottesville: Virginia University Press, 1974); V. Rubin, *Cannabis and Culture* (Paris: Mouton, 1975).

10. The chief exponent of the conspiracy theory is Jack Herer, *The Emperor Wears No Clothes: Hemp and the Marijuana Conspiracy* (Van Nuys, Calif.: Queen of Clubs Publishing, 1992), 24–7.

11. Sloman, *The History of Marijuana in America*, 31–83; L. Grinspoon, *Marihuana*, 10–11; A. Mack and J. Joy, *Marijuana as Medicine*, 158.

12. W. Walker, *Drugs in the Western Hemisphere* (Wilmington: Scholarly Resources, 1996), p. xvi.

13. R. Bonnie and C. Whitebread, *The Marihuana Conviction*, 152–3; see also K. Grivas (trans. D. Whitehouse), *Cannabis, Marihuana, Hashish* (London: Minerva Press, 1977), 45–58.

14. R. Bonnie and C. Whitebread, *The Marihuana Conviction*, 154.

15. Ibid. 174.

16. I. Campos, *Home Grown: Marijuana and the Origins of Mexico's War on Drugs* (Chapel Hill: University of North Carolina Press, 2012), 278.

17. M. Martel, *Not This Time: Canadians, Public Policy and the Marijuana Question* (Toronto: University of Toronto Press, 2006).

18. J. Jiggens, 'Marijuana Australiana: Cannabis Use, Popular Culture and the Americanisation of Drugs Policy in Australia, 1938–1988' (PhD thesis, Queensland University of Technology, 2004).

CHAPTER 2

1. National Archives (NA), HO 144/6073 (57), Draft Memorandum by Kirwan: The traffic in Indian hemp in Great Britain and Northern Ireland.

2. For a detailed account of the origins of the actions on cannabis of the Pharmaceutical Society and the League of Nations during the 1920s, and of the response of the UK's corn-plaster industry, see J. Mills, *Cannabis Britannica: Empire, Trade and Prohibition, 1800–1928* (Oxford: Oxford University Press, 2003), 152–207.

3. Taken from NA, HO 144/6073 (57), The traffic in Indian hemp in Great Britain and Northern Ireland.

4. NA, HO 45/14213 (13), Home Consumption Returns.

5. Clipping included in NA, MEPO 3/1051, Max Fisher and Simon Perera.

6. Interestingly, Perera had used the same argument when accused of supplying opium back in 1933. The argument was rejected then and he was sentenced to three months in prison and a fine of £50. See *The Times*, 19 Dec. 1955, 4.

7. This account is taken from the correspondence contained in NA, MEPO 3/1051.

8. *Sunday Referee*, 14 August 1938, in NA, MEPO 3/1059, Indian hemp growing in a Barking garden subject of a newspaper article.

9. *The Times*, 17 September 1936, 16.

10. Ibid. 8.

11. Handwritten file notes in NA, MEPO 3/1059.

12. 'A Case of Cannabis Intoxication', *The Lancet*, 1 (1935), 811.

13. W. H. Coles, 'Cannabis Indica', *The Lancet*, 1 (1935), 904 and 'A Case of Cannabis Indica Intoxication', *The Lancet*, 1 (1935), 1301.

14. The account is taken from correspondence in NA, CRIM 1/1055, Kofheith, Aly Ahmed.

15. *The Times*, 1 August 1930, 8.

16. *The Times*, 28 September 1931, 9.

17. *The Times*, 13 April 1933, 11.

18. *The Times*, 21 August 1934, 20.

19. *The Times*, 25 October 1935, 9.

20. *The Times*, 24 December 1934, 7.

21. *The Times*, 4 February 1937, 4.

22. *The Times*, 19 December 1933, 4.

23. M. Kohn, *Dope Girls: The Birth of the British Drug Underground* (London: Granta, 1992).

24. For details of O'Brien's career see NA, MEPO2/4487, Illegal sales of liquor at West End night bar. Imprisonment for defendant already serving sentence for drugs offence.

25. *The Times*, 11 October 1937, 9.

26. *The Times*, 13 October 1938, 4.

27. *The Times*, 5 June 1933, 7.

28. *The Times*, 28 October 1935, 21; 4 November 1935, 8.

29. NA, MEPO2/4487, Request for SD Insp Pollock (C Division) to attend Lewes Police Court on 7/7/37.

30. NA, MEPO2/4487, Report of J. D. Pollock, 19 April 1937.

31. Ibid.

32. NA, MEPO2/4487, Report of J. D. Pollock, 23 October 1937.

33. NA, HO45/24761, Letter of 7 January 1921.

34. NA, HO45/24761, Letter of 28 June 1921.

35. For more on Delevingne and his approach to cannabis see Mills, *Cannabis Britannica*, 161–87.
36. NA, HO45/24761, Letter of 1 July 1921.
37. NA, HO45/24761, Report of the Inspector under the Dangerous Drugs Acts for the Year 1931.
38. NA, HO45/24761, file 31.
39. NA, HO45/24761, file 32.
40. NA, HO45/24948, file 10.
41. NA, HO344/32, The illicit traffic in Indian hemp in Great Britain since the war, 4 February 1947.
42. NA, HO45/24948, files 7 and 8.
43. 'Prevention and Treatment of Drug Addiction', *British Medical Journal* (*BMJ*), 1 (1931), 495.
44. 'Problems of Drug Addiction', *BMJ* 2 (1934), 690.
45. D. Prain, *Report on the Cultivation and Use of Ganja* (Calcutta: Thacker and Spink, 1893).
46. 'Useful Plants in India', *BMJ* 2 (1925), 963.
47. 'Cannabis Indica for Herpes Zoster', *BMJ* 2 (1939), 431.
48. Quite how careful the investigation at Pretoria Mental Hospital was is difficult to determine. Asylum statistics from other African and Asian contexts which had been influential in establishing a link between cannabis consumption and mental health problems in the nineteenth century were, in fact, highly prob-lematic. See Mills, *Cannabis Britannica*, 82–92, 183–7.
49. 'Cannabis Indica', *BMJ* 1 (1938), 1058.
50. These terms refer to the concepts developed by Edward Said in *Orientalism* (London: Vintage Books, 1978). He argued that the inferiority of non-Westerners was a cultural construct assembled in various forms in order to justify imperialism and colonialism. It certainly makes some sense in terms of discourses on drugs in this period, where a fondness for intoxication among Africans, Asians, etc. was seen as evidence of their 'natural' weaknesses. At the same time, drugs such as opium and cannabis came to be viewed with suspicion by Westerners who associated their consumption with the weaknesses of 'inferior' races. For recent research that reaches these conclusions see L. Kozma, 'The League of Nations and the Debate over Cannabis Prohib-ition', *History Compass*, 9/1 (2011), 61–70.
51. 'The International Traffic in Dangerous Drugs', *BMJ* 1 (1930), 560.
52. 'Drug Addiction in Egypt', *The Lancet*, 1 (1931), 713.
53. 'Dangerous Drug Traffic in Egypt', *The Lancet*, 1 (1932), 1372.
54. 'The Campaign against Dangerous Drugs in Egypt', *BMJ* 1 (1935), 1274.
55. 'The Drug Traffic in Egypt', *BMJ* 2 (1940), 21. A summary of the same report was also carried in *The Lancet*, 2 (1940), 18.
56. 'Control of Narcotics', *BMJ* 2 (1943), 718.
57. 'Lebanon and Hashish', *The Lancet*, 2 (1943), 745.

58. Reports from elsewhere suggest that sailors were also involved in smuggling hashish into Egypt during WWII. Dawood El Assi, an able seaman on HMS *Nile*, and Abdel Hadi Omar Zaben, an ordinary seaman on HMS *Stag*, were court-martialled in 1945 and 1944 respectively, as they were caught in possession of contraband cannabis. See NA, ADM 156/262, Court Martials of Able Seaman Dawood El Assi of HMS *Nile* and Abdel Hadi Omar Zaben of HMS *Stag*.

59. 'The Anti-Narcotic Campaign in Egypt', *BMJ* 2 (1945), 612.

60. 'More Light on Marihuana', *The Lancet*, 2 (1940), 370.

61. 'Indian Hemp', *BMJ* 1 (1941), 676.

62. 'Cannabis Indica', *The Lancet*, 2 (1943), 296.

63. Ibid. 368.

64. A. Haagen-Smit et al., 'A Physiologically Active Principle from Cannabis Sativa (Marihuana)', *Science*, 91 (1940), 602.

65. G. Powell et al., 'The Active Principle of Marihuana', *Science*, 93 (1941), 522.

66. *Biochemical Journal*, 33 (1939), 123.

67. A. Jacob and A. Todd, 'Cannabidiol and Cannabol: Constituents of Cannabis Indica Resin', *Nature*, 145 (1940), 350.

68. A. MacDonald, 'The Actions and Uses of Hemp Drugs', *Nature*, 147 (1941), 168.

69. A. Todd, 'Chemistry of the Hemp Drugs', *Nature*, 146 (1940), 830.

70. S. Loewe, 'Marihuana Activity of Cannabinol', *Science*, 102 (1945), 615.

71. Y. Gaoni and R. Mechoulam, 'Isolation, Structure and Partial Synthesis of an Active Constituent of Hashish', *Journal of the American Chemical Society*, 86/8 (1964), 1646–7.

72. A. MacDonald, 'The Actions and Uses of Hemp Drugs', *Nature*, 147 (1941), 167.

73. 'The Active Principle of Cannabis Indica', *BMJ* 2, (1938), 40.

74. A. MacDonald, 'The Actions and Uses of Hemp Drugs', *Nature*, 147 (1941), 167.

75. Cannabis earned the name 'marijuana' in the USA and had been subjected to the attention of Harry Anslinger and his Federal Bureau of Narcotics in the 1930s. It had quickly been demonized in American popular culture, with films such as *Marihuana* (1936) and *Assassin of Youth* (1937) stoking anxieties about consumption. See R. Bonnie and C. Whitebread, *The Marihuana Conviction: A History of Marihuana Prohibition in the United States* (Charlottesville: Virginia University Press, 1974), 154–74.

76. 'Marihuana', *The Lancet*, 2 (1939), 567.

77. R. Bud, *Penicillin: Triumph and Tragedy* (Oxford: Oxford University Press, 2007); M. Harrison, *Medicine and Victory: British Military Medicine in the Second World War* (Oxford: Oxford University Press, 2004).

78. For details of this story see Mills, *Cannabis Britannica*, 204–7.

CHAPTER 3

1. For a wider sense of the politics of drugs at the League of Nations in this period see William B. McAllister, *Drug Diplomacy in the Twentieth Century: An International History* (London: Palgrave, 2000). An interesting discussion of the League of Nations in general can be found in S. Pedersen, 'Back to the League of Nations', *American Historical Review*, 112/4 (2007), 1,091–117. A useful account of developments in a field parallel to that of drugs at the League of Nations is provided by I. Borowy, *Coming to Terms With World Health: The League of Nations Health Organisation 1921–1946* (Frankfurt: Peter Lang, 2009).

2. British Library (BL), League of Nations Documents and Microfilm Collection (LN), SPR Mic. B. 23/12, C.123.M.42.1931.XI. Egyptian Government, Central Narcotics Intelligence Bureau, *Annual Report for the Year 1930* (Cairo: Government Press, 1931), 88.

3. Ibid.

4. *The Times*, 27 January 1931, 13.

5. 'Egypt: Appeal Without Standing', *Time*, 2 December 1935.

6. Thomas Russell Pasha, *Egyptian Service 1902–1946* (London: Murray, 1949), 16.

7. Ibid. 18.

8. Ibid.

9. Ibid. 19.

10. Ibid. 226.

11. Ibid. 231.

12. Ibid. 274; the currency is given in Egyptian pounds.

13. Ibid. 279.

14. 'A New Way of Smuggling Narcotics', *The Lancet*, 1 (1940), 464.

15. Russell Pasha, *Egyptian Service*, 282.

16. Ibid. 238.

17. A useful account of the contrast between Russell's approach at the League of Nations and that of his counterparts from French North Africa can be found in L. Kozma, 'The League of Nations and the Debate over Cannabis Prohibition', *History Compass*, 9/1 (2011), 61–70.

18. BL, LN, SPR Mic. B. 23/12, C.88.M.34.1931. XI. 'Drug Situation in Egypt' in minutes of the fourteenth session of the Advisory Committee on Traffic in Opium and other Dangerous Drugs (AC) 1931, 142.

19. Russell's story to the League of Nations about the Italian legation was reported in *The Times*, 19 February 1931, 11.

20. BL, LN, SPR Mic B. 32/12, C.575.M.282.1932.XI. AC, minutes of the fifteenth session, held at Geneva from 15 April to 4 May 1932, 32.

21. BL, LN, SPR Mic B. 32/12, C.124.M.52.1933.XI. AC, summary of illicit transactions and seizures reported to the secretariat of the League of Nations between 1 October and 1 December 1932.

22. BL, LN, SPR Mic B. 23/12, C.480.M.244.1933.XI. AC, minutes of the sixteenth session, held at Geneva from 15 to 31 May 1933, 31.

23. BL, LN, SPR Mic. B. 23/12, C.123.M.42.1931.XI. Egyptian Government, *Central Narcotics Intelligence Bureau, Annual Report for the Year 1930* (Cairo: Government Press, 1931), 85.

24. Ibid. 86.

25. Ibid.

26. Britain governed Egypt directly between 1882 and 1922 at which time a measure of independence was granted, the British retaining control over imperial communications, the defence of Egypt, the protection of foreign interests and minorities, and the administration of the Sudan. See M. Daly, 'The British Occupation, 1882–1922', in M. Daly (ed.), *The Cambridge History of Egypt: Modern Egypt, from 1517 to the End of the Twentieth Century* (Cambridge: Cambridge University Press, 1998).

27. BL, LN, SPR Mic. B. 23/12, C.480.M.244.1933.XI. AC, minutes of the sixteenth session, held at Geneva from 15 to 31 May 1933, 33.

28. See J. Mills, *Cannabis Britannica: Empire, Trade and Prohibition, 1800–1928* (Oxford: Oxford University Press, 2003), 152–87.

29. BL, LN, SPR Mic. B. 23/12, C.236.M.123.1933.XI. AC, summary of annual reports of governments on the traffic in opium and other dangerous drugs for the year 1931, 14.

30. BL, LN, SPR Mic. B. 23/12, C.246.M.128.1933.XI). AC, summary of illicit transactions and seizures reported to the secretariat of the League of Nations between 1 January and 31 March 1933, 29–32.

31. BL, LN, SPR Mic. B. 23/12, C.480.M.244.1933.XI. AC, minutes of the sixteenth session, held at Geneva from 15 to 31 May 1933, 18.

32. BL, LN, SPR Mic. B. 23/12, C.345.M.193.1933.XI. AC, report to the Council on the work of the sixteenth session held at Geneva from 15 to 31 May 1933, 13.

33. BL, LN, SPR Mic. B. 23/12, C.598.M.278.1933.XI. AC, summary of illicit transactions and seizures reported to the secretariat of the League of Nations between 1 July and 30 September 1933, 21.

34. BL, LN, SPR Mic. B. 23/12, C.661.M.316.1933.XI. AC, minutes of the seventeenth session, held at Geneva from 30 October to 9 November 1933, 50.

35. BL, LN, SPR Mic. B. 23/12, C.33.M.14.1935.XI. AC, minutes of the nineteenth session held at Geneva from 15 to 28 November 1934, 666.

36. The consignments into Iraq from Syria suggest that Russell's action in prompting the French authorities there to prevent supplies making their way to Egypt had simply resulted in their diversion to new markets. BL, LN, SPR Mic. B. 23/12, C.3.M.3.1934.XI. AC, summary of illicit transactions and seizures reported to the secretariat of the League of Nations between 1 October and 31 December 1933, 17–19.

37. BL, India Office Library (IOL) L/E/9/739–40. Report by the representative of the Government of India on the eighteenth session of the Opium Advisory Committee, 6.

38. BL, IOL L/E/9/739–40. Telegram from Government of India to Secretary of State for India, 1 January 1934.

39. BL, LN, SPR Mic. B. 23/12, C.33.M.14.1935.XI. AC, minutes of the nineteenth session held at Geneva from 15 to 28 November 1934, 22–31.

40. BL, LN, SPR Mic. B. 23/12, C.25.1935.XI. AC, report on the work of the nineteenth session between 15 and 28 November 1934, 5.

41. BL, IOL L/E/9/739–40. Report by the representative of India on the nineteenth session of the Opium Advisory Committee, 3.

42. BL, LN, SPR Mic. B 23/12, C.290.M.176.1936.XI. Annex 2 Progress Report by the Secretary in AC, minutes of the twenty-first session 18 May to 5 June 1936, 146.

43. BL, LN, SPR Mic. B 23/12, C.285.M.186.1937.XI. AC, report to the council on the work of the twenty-second session 24 May to 12 June 1937, 15.

44. France, the Netherlands, Poland, and Spain were also present on the Sub-Committee.

45. BL, LN, SPR Mic. B 23/12, C.253.M.125.1935.XI. AC, report to the council on the work of the twentieth session 20 May to 5 June 1935, 32–4.

46. BL, LN, SPR Mic. B 23/12, C.278.M.168.1936.XI. AC, report to the council on the work of the twenty-first session 18 May to 5 June 1936, 31–2.

47. BL, LN, SPR Mic. B 23/12, C.285.M.186.1937.XI. AC, report to the council on the work of the twenty-second session 24 May to 12 June 1937, 34–6.

48. BL, LN, SPR Mic. B 23/12, C.237.M.136.1938.XI. AC, report to the council on the work of the twenty-third session 7 to 24 June 1938, 9 and 26–7.

49. The questionnaire can be found in BL, IOL L/E/9/740.

50. BL, LN, SPR Mic. B 23/12, C.202.M.131.1939.XI. AC, report to the council on the work of the twenty-fourth session 15 May to 12 June 1939, 36–7.

51. BL, LN, SPR Mic. B 23/12, C.209.M.136.1939.XI. AC, minutes of the twenty-fourth session, 15 May to 12 June 1939, 32.

52. BL, LN, SPR Mic. B 23/12, C.125.M.114.1940.XI. AC, report to the council on the work of the twenty-fifth session 13 to 17 May 1940, 17.

53. BL, IOL L/E/9/740. From W. W. Nind to B. Renborg 9 November 1940.

54. Report of the Indian Hemp Drugs Commission 1893–1894 (Simla: Government Central Printing House, 1894), iii. 359.

55. R. N. Chopra, The Present Position of Hemp Drug Addiction in India (Calcutta: Thacker, Spink and Co, 1939), 33.

56. BL, IOL V/25/323/6–8. Memorandum on Excise (Hemp Drugs) Administration in India Series for 1930–6.

57. Ibid.

58. BL, LN, SPR Mic. B 23/12, C.345.M.193.1933.XI. AC, report to the council on the work of the sixteenth session held at Geneva from 15 to 31 May 1933, 4.

59. BL, IOL M/3/381. Summary of report by the Government of Burma on the Illicit Traffic in Dangerous Drugs for the calendar year 1939.

60. BL, IOL M/3/381. From E. G. S. Apedaile (Dep Sec to Gvt of Burma—Defence Dept) to Under Sec of State for Burma 30 January 1940.

61. BL, IOL M/3/381. From Burma Office (A. F. Morley) to Home Office (Drugs Branch) 5 April 1940; From Secretary, Burma Office (A. F. Morley) to Secretary Economic and Overseas Department 13 December 1939.

62. BL, IOL M/3/381. From E. G. S. Apedaile (Dep Sec to Gvt of Burma—Defence Dept) to Under Sec of State for Burma 30 January 1940.

63. BL, IOL M/3/381. Speech of the Hon the Minister for Finance on introducing the budget proposals for 1939–40 in the House of Representatives.

64. BL, IOL M/3/381. From Burma Office (D. T. Monteath) to H. H. Craw (ICS) 22 August 1940.

65. BL, IOL M/3/381. From W. H. Coles (Home Office) to W. D. Tomkins (India Office) 12 April 1940.

66. BL, IOL M/3/381. From Home Office (Drugs Branch) to A. F. Morley (Burma Office) 21 November 1939.

67. Mills, *Cannabis Britannica*, 47–68.

68. R. N. Chopra, *Opium Habit in India* (Calcutta: Thacker, Spink and Co, 1927).

69. BL, IOL L/E/9/740. India Office to Financial Dept (Central Revenues) 14 June 1929.

70. 'Notes from India', *The Lancet*, 1 (1929), 519.

71. BL, League of Nations Opium Advisory Committee Document Series OC 1542, 23 May 1934, 5. This document was circulated to the AC in the discussions that led to the formation of the Sub-Committee on cannabis.

72. Unlanced capsules of *Papaver somniferum*, consumed in a beverage and largely confined to consumers in the Punjab.

73. See Mills, *Cannabis Britannica*, 51–68, 105–21.

74. BL, League of Nations Opium Advisory Committee Document Series O.C.1542, 23 May 1934, 17.

75. Ibid. 20.

76. Ibid. 17.

77. Ibid. 20. The authors noted that the popularity of 'boja' was in decline and only one shop in the district now sold it.

78. Ibid. 105.

79. See Mills, *Cannabis Britannica*, 42–3, 114–15.

80. BL, League of Nations Opium Advisory Committee Document Series O.C.1542, 23 May 1934, 17.

81. Ibid. 107.

82. Ibid. 108.

83. Ibid. 109.

84. Ibid. 112.

85. Ibid. 115.

86. Ibid. 118.

87. Chopra, *The Present Position of Hemp*, 51.
88. Ibid. 3.
89. Ibid. 6.
90. Ibid. 102.
91. Ibid. 71.
92. Ibid. 74.
93. Ibid. 103.
94. Ibid.
95. Ibid.
96. Ibid. 96.
97. Ibid.
98. Ibid. 89.
99. Ibid. 104.
100. BL, IOL L/E/9/740. Answers to the Questionnaire of League of Nations regarding chronic cannabis intoxication by R. N. Chopra, expert appointed by the Government of India.
101. BL, IOL L/E/9/740. Government of India Finance Department to Economic and Overseas Department, 23 April 1940.
102. Chopra, *The Present Position of Hemp*, 51.
103. Ibid. 118.
104. Ibid. 32.
105. V. Berridge, *Opium and the People* (London: Free Association Books, 1999); G. Harding, 'Constructing Addiction', *Sociology of Health and Illness*, 8 (1986), 75–85; T. Parssinen and K. Kerner, 'Development of the Disease Model of Drug Addiction in Britain 1870–1926', *Medical History*, 24 (1980), 275–96; D. Peters, 'The British Medical Response to Opiate Addiction in the Nineteenth Century', *Journal of the History of Medicine and Allied Sciences*, 36 (1981), 455–88; H. Kushner, 'Taking Biology Seriously: The Next Task for Historians of Addiction and What to Do about It', *Bulletin of the History of Medicine*, 80 (2006), 115–43.
106. For more on Victorian responses to cannabis, see Mills, *Cannabis Britannica*, 69–92.
107. Such a fleeting reference hardly does justice to the extensive body of work dedicated to tracing the nature of colonial discourse. Following Said, however, researchers in this field have stressed that imperialism is as much a work of the imagination as it is the business of armies and administrators. The construction of the foreign either as enticing and desirable or as dark and dangerous justifies both invasion and domination. See e.g. J. Codwell and D. Macleod, *Orientalism Transposed: The Impact of the Colonies on British Culture* (Aldershot: Ashgate, 1998); R. Inden, *Imagining India* (Oxford: Blackwell, 1990); J. Majeed, *Uncovered Imaginings: James Mill's The History of British India and Orientalism* (Oxford: Clarendon Press, 1992); M. McLaren, 'From Analysis to Prescription: Scottish Concepts of Asian Despotism in Early

Nineteenth-Century British India', *International History Review*, 15/3 (1993), 469–501; B. Moore-Gilbert, *Postcolonial Theory: Contexts, Practices, Politics* (New York: Verso, 1997).

CHAPTER 4

1. National Archives (NA), HO 344/32. Minister's Case, Clement Attlee, Home Office 15 December 1949.
2. P. Addison, *No Turning Back: The Peacetime Revolutions of Post-War Britain* (Oxford: Oxford University Press, 2010), 7–132; D. Kynaston, *Austerity Britain, 1945–1951* (London: Bloomsbury, 2007); D. Kynaston, *Family Britain, 1951–1957* (London: Bloomsbury, 2009); K. Morgan, *Britain since 1945: The People's Peace* (Oxford: Oxford University Press, 2001), 1–194.
3. NA, HO 344/32. D. Bamuta, Report of an investigation into conditions of the coloured people in Stepney, 2.
4. Ibid. 3.
5. Ibid. 4.
6. Ibid. 5.
7. Ibid. 6.
8. Ibid. 4.
9. Ibid. 9–10.
10. NA, HO 344/32. From C. R. Attlee to Basil Henriques, undated.
11. NA, DPP 2/2130. Metropolitan Police Report 201/52/4, 12.
12. NA, DPP 2/2130. Central Criminal Court 18 March Session 1952 Notice of Further Evidence.
13. NA, DPP 2/2130. This account is taken from Statements of Witnesses called at Magistrates' Court and the Statements of Witnesses not called at Magistrates' Court.
14. NA, CRIM 1/2206. Part 1. HM Prison Brixton 25 February 1952.
15. NA, DPP 2/2130. This account is taken from Statements of Witnesses called at Magistrates' Court.
16. NA, DPP 2/2130. Metropolitan Police Report 201/52/4, 49.
17. NA, DPP 2/2130. Statements of Witnesses called at Magistrates' Court, 3–6.
18. NA, DPP 2/2130. Transcript of the shorthand notes from Reg vs. Backary Manneh, 24 March 1952, 6.
19. Ibid. 129.
20. For a critique of this book, see E. Goode, *The Marijuana Smokers* (New York: Basic Books, 1970), ch. 9.
21. NA, DPP 2/2130. Transcript, 129–31.
22. D. McIntosh Johnson, *Indian Hemp: A Social Menace* (London: Christopher Johnson, 1952). The copy presented at court is contained in NA, CRIM 1/2206, part 1.

23. NA, DPP 2/2130. Transcript, 172.

24. Ibid. 173.

25. Ibid. 176.

26. Ibid. 195.

27. Ibid. 206-8.

28. NA, DPP 2/2130. 'Notice of Appeal' 1 April 1952.

29. D. McIntosh Johnson, *A Doctor Regrets* (London: Christopher Johnson, 1949), 234.

30. D. McIntosh Johnson, *Bars and Barricades* (London: Christopher Johnson, 1952), 256-74.

31. D. McIntosh Johnson, *A Doctor Returns* (London: Christopher Johnson 1956), 11-29.

32. Ibid. 39.

33. Ibid. 98.

34. D. McIntosh Johnson, 'A Visit to Pont St. Esprit', *The Lancet*, 1 (1952), 820.

35. Headlines from 29 and 31 March 1952 reproduced in McIntosh Johnson, *A Doctor Returns*, 124.

36. Johnson, *Indian Hemp*, 45-9.

37. Ibid. 108.

38. Johnson, *A Doctor Returns*, 125.

39. NA, HO 344/32. The illicit traffic in Indian hemp in Great Britain since the war, Home Office Drugs Branch, 4 February 1947.

40. NA, HO 344/32. Dangerous Drugs, Metropolitan Police, CID, 25 January 1950.

41. NA, HO 344/32. The illicit traffic in Indian hemp in Great Britain since the war, Home Office Drugs Branch, 4 February 1947.

42. NA, HO 344/32. Dangerous Drugs, Metropolitan Police, CID, 25 January 1950.

43. NA, HO 344/32. The illicit traffic in Indian hemp in Great Britain since the war, Home Office Drugs Branch, 4 February 1947.

44. NA, HO 45/24948. F. Thornton to J. Walker, 14 March 1951.

45. NA, HO 45/24948. Dangerous Drugs Branch, Annual Report 1951.

46. NA, HO 45/24948. J. H. Walker, 3 July 1952.

47. NA, CO 1028/19. From W. I. J. Wallace, Colonial Office to Sir Hugh Foot, Governor of Jamaica.

48. NA, HO 344/32. The illicit traffic in Indian hemp in Great Britain since the war, Home Office Drugs Branch, 4 February 1947.

49. NA, HO 45/24948. Dangerous Drugs Branch, Annual Report 1951, 1.

50. NA, HO 45/24948. Dangerous Drugs Branch, Annual Report 1950, 6.

51. NA, HO 45/24948. Dangerous Drugs Branch, Annual Report 1951, 9. The Roebuck is now The Court, 108a Tottenham Court Road.

52. NA, CO 1028/19. From W. I. J. Wallace, Colonial Office to Sir Hugh Foot, Governor of Jamaica.

53. NA, HO 45/25245. Commonwealth Immigrants. Discrimination against coloured persons: representations and reports of incidents.
54. NA, HO 45/25124. Standing Committee B, Thursday 20 March 1952.
55. NA, CUST 49/4406. Smuggling of cannabis by two Jamaicans.
56. NA, CUST 49/4813. Seizure of car carrying cannabis and detention of uncustomed cigarettes: car seized, but covered by hire purchase agreement.
57. NA, HO 344/32. Indian Hemp in the UK 1947–8, Home Office Drugs Branch November 1948.
58. NA, HO 344/32. The illicit traffic in Indian hemp in Great Britain since the war, Home Office Drugs Branch, 4 February 1947.
59. NA, HO 45/24948. Dangerous Drugs Branch, Annual Report 1951, 8.
60. Ibid.
61. NA, MEPO 2/10167. R. J. Guppy, Assistant Under Secretary of State, Home Office, to R. L. Jackson, 25 October 1962.
62. NA, HO 319/5, DDA 59/70/1/22. Note of a meeting at the Home Office on 19 November 1962.
63. For a view of the contemporary situation in the West Indies, see A. Klein, M. Day, and A. Harriott (eds.), *Caribbean Drugs: From Criminalization to Harm Reduction* (London: Zed, 2004).

CHAPTER 5

1. 'Control of Drug Addiction', *The Lancet*, 1 (1952), 1026.
2. See Ch. 2.
3. For more on these nineteenth-century discussions about cannabis as a treatment for mental illness see J. Mills, *Cannabis Britannica: Empire, Trade and Prohibition, 1800–1928* (Oxford: Oxford University Press, 2003), 73–6.
4. 'A New Euphoriant for Depressive Mental States', *British Medical Journal* (*BMJ*), 2 (1947), 918–22.
5. 'Treating the Symptoms of Depression', *BMJ* 2 (1947), 933.
6. C. Parker and F. Wrigley, 'Effects of Cannabis', *The Lancet*, 2 (1947), 223.
7. C. Parker and F. Wrigley, 'Synthetic Cannabis Preparations in Psychiatry: Synhexl', *Journal of Mental Science* (1950), 276–9.
8. D. Pond, 'Psychological Effects in Depressive Patients of Synhexl', *Journal of Neurology, Neurosurgery and Psychiatry* (1948), 271–9.
9. 'Drugs in the Treatment of Depression', *The Lancet*, 1 (1955), 1065.
10. For more on British drugs research in this period see J. Slinn, 'Research and Development in the UK Pharmaceutical Industry from the Nineteenth Century to the 1960s', in R. Porter and M. Teich (eds.), *Drugs and Narcotics in History* (Cambridge: Cambridge University Press, 1996), 168–86.
11. See D. Healy, *The Antidepressant Era* (Cambridge, Mass.: Harvard University Press, 1999); D. Healy, *The Creation of Psychopharmacology* (Cambridge, Mass.:

Harvard University Press, 2002); A. Tone, *The Age of Anxiety: A History of America's Turbulent Affair with Tranquilizers* (New York: Basic Books, 2009).

12. 'Traffic in Dangerous Drugs', *The Lancet*, 2 (1946), 279.

13. J. Fraser, 'Withdrawal Symptoms in Cannabis-Indica Addicts', *The Lancet*, 2 (1949), 747–8.

14. 'Hemp', *The Lancet*, 2, (1949), 757–8.

15. 'Drug Addiction in America', *The Lancet*, 1 (1951), 1356–7.

16. 'Indian Hemp', *The Lancet*, 1 (1952), 1096.

17. D. McIntosh Johnson, *Indian Hemp: A Social Menace* (London: Christopher Johnson, 1952).

18. 'Indian Hemp', *BMJ* 2 (1952), 28.

19. 'Indian Hemp', *The Lancet*, 1 (1952), 1096.

20. 'A Visit to Pont St Esprit', *The Lancet*, 1 (1952), 820. This was an abridged version of his travels in France which are related in more detail in his books. See Ch. 4 for more on Donald McIntosh Johnson and his ideas about cannabis.

21. 'Narcotic Control', *BMJ* 1 (1956), 104.

22. 'Drug Addiction', *BMJ* 2 (1957), 210.

23. 'Addiction to Drugs', *BMJ* 2 (1959), 48.

24. 'Hemp from Budgerigar Seed', *BMJ* 2 (1959), 764. While the evidence only allows speculation, Tiger Bay was an area of Cardiff that included a significant proportion of Commonwealth migrants and as such the two accused in this case may well have been members of that group.

25. 'Home-grown Indian Hemp', *BMJ* 2 (1961), 1440.

26. 'Control of Narcotic Drugs', *BMJ* 1 (1962), 934.

27. National Archives (NA), MH 58/564. Report of Departmental Committee on Morphine and Heroin Addiction, 24.

28. NA, MH 58/564, DDA 2/12/1 16 November 1956.

29. NA, HO 319/1. Report of Interdepartmental Committee on Drug Addiction, 1.

30. Ibid. 4. These definitions were based on those provided by the World Health Organization published in its seventh report of 1957.

31. NA, HO 319/1, DA/59/48. Further Memorandum from the Home Office. Cannabis (Indian Hemp).

32. NA, HO 319/1. Minutes of Meeting held on 13 October 1959.

33. NA, HO 319/1, DA/59/48. Further Memorandum from the Home Office. Cannabis (Indian Hemp).

34. NA, HO 319/1, DDA 2/12/13. Minutes of Meeting held on 9 February 1960, 3.

35. NA, HO 319/1, DDA 2/12/13. Minutes of Meeting held on 27 April 1960, 1.

36. NA, HO 319/1, DDA 2/12/13. Second Draft Report 27 May 1960, 14.

37. Honnor and Goulding were both civil servants from the Ministry of Health. Goulding was a medically qualified pharmacologist.

38. NA, MH 58/571. Minutes of Meeting held on 7 June 1960, 1.

39. NA, HO 319/1, DDA 2/12/15, 9. Report of Interdepartmental Committee on Drug Addiction.

40. NA, FO 371, U1288. Future of International Control (Narcotic Drugs), Reconstruction File 23, 4 February 1946.

41. NA, FO 371, U5569. Establishment of Commission on Narcotic Drugs, Reconstruction File 23, 27 May 1946.

42. British Library (BL), UN Documents Collection (UN), E/34 27 February 1946.

43. *The UN and Narcotic Drugs: Half a Century of Successful Struggle against Crime, Disease and Social Affliction* (New York: UN Office of Public Information, 1960), 12–17.

44. A. Lande, 'The Single Convention on Narcotic Drugs, 1961', *International Organization*, 16/4 (1962), 782.

45. BL, League of Nations Collection (LN), Advisory Committee on Traffic in Opium and Other Dangerous Drugs (AC), SPR Mic. B 23/12, C.237. M.136.1938.XI. AC, report to the council on the work of the twenty-third session 7 to 24 June 1938, 9 and 26–7.

46. BL, UN, E/CN.7/196. UN Economic and Social Council 21 June 1950, Progress report on the work of the division of narcotic drugs for the period 16 May 1949 to 31 March 1950, 43.

47. BL, UN, E/1673. UN Economic and Social Council 27 April 1950, Procedure regarding draft single convention on narcotic drugs, 1.

48. BL, UN, E/CN.7/AC.3/3. Draft of the Single Convention, 27 February 1950, 32–5.

49. W. McAllister, *Drug Diplomacy in the Twentieth-Century: An International History* (London: Routledge, 2000), 156–7.

50. BL, UN, E/CN.7/SR.117. Commission on Narcotic Drugs Fifth Session Summary Record of the Hundred and Seventeenth Meeting 10 December 1950, 7–9.

51. BL, UN, E/CN.7/216. Report of the Commission on Narcotic Drugs (Fifth Session), 38.

52. Ibid. 25.

53. BL, UN, E/CN.7/256. The Problem of Indian Hemp, Note by the Secretary-General 19 March 1953, 3.

54. NA, HO 45/24948. Note by J. H. Walker, 3 July 1952. It is worth noting that the only other evidence of an urgent problem with cannabis consumption produced by the Secretariat in its report was the annual reports of the USA for 1936 and 1937 and P. Wolff's book *Marihuana in Latin America: The Threat It Constitutes* (Washington: Linacre, 1949). It may be recalled that the reliability of the latter was called into question at the trial of Backary Manneh discussed in Ch. 4.

55. BL, UN, E/CN.7/262. Commission on Narcotic Drugs Report of the Eighth Session, 16.

56. BL, UN, E/CN.7/276. The Problem of Cannabis, Note by the Secretary-General 22 March 1954, 1.

57. WHO, *Expert Committee on Drugs Liable To Produce Addiction, Third Report* (Geneva: WHO Technical Report Series no. 57, 1952), 11.

58. BL, UN, E/CN.7/262. Commission on Narcotic Drugs Report of the Eighth Session, 16.

59. The WHO representative was Pablo Osvaldo Wolff. See n. 54.

60. Anslinger remains a controversial figure in the history of drugs. See W. McAllister, *Drug Diplomacy in the Twentieth-Century: An International History* (London: Routledge, 2000), 89.

61. This account taken from BL, UN E/CN.7/SR231 Commission on Narcotic Drugs Summary of the Two Hundred and Thirty-First Meeting, 22 April 1954, 5–6.

62. Union of South Africa, *Report of the Inter-Departmental Committee on the Abuse of Dagga* (Pretoria: Government Printer, 1952).

63. See J. Mills, *Cannabis Britannica: Empire, Trade and Prohibition, 1800–1928* (Oxford: Oxford University Press, 2003), 160–2.

64. This account taken from BL, UN, E/CN.7/SR231. Commission on Narcotic Drugs Summary of the Two Hundred and Thirty-First Meeting, 22 April 1954, 7–12.

65. BL, UN, E/CN/7/L.92. The Question of Cannabis, Note by the representative of Greece.

66. BL, WHO/APD/56. The Physical and Mental Effects of Cannabis, Additional Study, 17 March 1955, 32.

67. See n. 54.

68. See R. Bonnie and C. Whitebread, *The Marihuana Conviction: A History of Marihuana Prohibition in the United States* (Charlottesville: Virginia University Press, 1974), 154–74; J. Mills, 'Colonial Africa and the International Politics of Cannabis: Egypt, South Africa and the Origins of Global Control', in J. H. Mills and P. Barton (eds.), *Drugs and Empires: Essays in Modern Imperialism and Intoxication, c.1500–c.1930* (Basingstoke: Palgrave, 2007), 178–82.

69. BL, UN, E/CN.7/SR 266. Commission on Narcotic Drugs Tenth Session Summary of the Two Hundred and Sixty-Sixth Meeting 20 April 1955, 14.

70. BL, UN, E/CN.7/SR 267. Commission on Narcotic Drugs Tenth Session Summary of the Two Hundred and Sixty-Seventh Meeting 21 April 1955, 4.

71. Commission on Narcotic Drugs, *Report of the Tenth Session* (New York, 1955), 12.

72. BL, UN, E/CN.7/SR 267. Commission on Narcotic Drugs Tenth Session Summary of the Two Hundred and Sixty-Seventh Meeting 21 April 1955, 6.

73. See J. Mills, *Cannabis Britannica*, 174.

74. BL, UN, E/CN.7/SR 270. Commission on Narcotic Drugs Tenth Session Summary of the Two Hundred and Seventieth Meeting 22 April 1955, 3–5.

75. BL, UN, E/CN.7/333. Report to the Economic and Social Council on the twelfth session of the Commission on Narcotic Drugs, 81.

76. BL, UN, E/CN.7/SR.286, 12.

77. By 1960 replies were circulated from the Union of South Africa, Basutoland, Bechuanaland, Swaziland, Northern Rhodesia, Southern Rhodesia, Brazil, Angola, Mozambique, Morocco, India, Pakistan, Italy, Egypt, Costa Rica, Burma, Lebanon, Mexico, USA, Jamaica, Cuba, the Dominican Republic, Haiti, and Greece.
78. BL, UN, E/CN.7/286/Add.8. Survey of the situation in Brazil, 19 April 1955, 8–17.
79. BL, UN, E/CN.7/286/Add.7. Survey of the situation in Southern Rhodesia, 30 March 1955, 4.
80. BL, UN, E/CN.7/286/Add.11. The cannabis situation in the Scherifian Empire (French Zone), 20 April 1956, 12.
81. Ibid. 10–11.
82. BL, UN, E/CN.7/286/Add.8. Survey of the situation in Brazil, 19 April 1955, 14.
83. BL, UN, E/CN.7/286/Add.7. Survey of the situation in Southern Rhodesia, 30 March 1955, 9.
84. BL, UN, E/CN.7/286/Add.12. Survey of the situation in India, 30 April 1956, 26–9.
85. BL, UN, E/CN.7/324. The Question of Cannabis, Note by the Secretary-General, 26 April 1957, 11.
86. BL, UN, E/CN.7/SR.342. Commission on Narcotic Drugs Twelfth Session Summary of the Three Hundred and Forty-Second Meeting, 6 May 1957, 5.
87. BL, UN, E/CN.7/L.212. The Question of Cannabis, 30 April 1959.
88. For more on the origins and impact of antibiotics in this period see R. Bud, *Penicillin: Triumph and Tragedy* (Oxford: Oxford University Press, 2007).
89. BL, UN, E/CN/7/SR.422. Commission on Narcotic Drugs, Fourteenth Session, Summary of 421st Meeting, 4 May 1959, 3–13.
90. BL, UN, E/CONF/34/5. The Merits of Antibiotic Substances obtainable from Cannabis Sativa, 2–3.
91. BL, UN, E/CN.7/399. Annex, The Question of Cannabis, Note by the Secretary-General, 5 December 1960, 9.
92. BL, UN, E/CN.7/399. The Question of Cannabis, Note by the Secretary-General, 5 December 1960, 7.
93. BL, UN, E.CN.7/AC.3/9. The Single Convention on Narcotic Drugs (Third Draft), 11 September 1958, 55.
94. BL, UN, E/CONF.34/1. Compilation of comments on the Single Convention (Third Draft), 40.
95. Ibid., India on Schedule IV.
96. Ibid., Iran: amendment to the redraft of article 39.
97. BL, UN, E/CONF.34/24. UN Conference for the Adoption of a Single Convention on Narcotic Drugs, Summary Records of Plenary Meetings, Thirty-Third Plenary Meeting 20 March 1961, 154.

98. BL, UN, E/CONF.34/24. UN Conference for the Adoption of a Single Convention on Narcotic Drugs, Summary Records of Plenary Meetings, Thirteenth Plenary Meeting, 8 February 1961, 58–62.

99. BL, UN, E/CONF.34/12. UN Conference for the Adoption of a Single Convention on Narcotic Drugs, Ad Hoc committee to deal with article 39, 23 February 1961, 2.

100. BL, UN, E/CONF.34/24/ADD.1. Ad Hoc Committee on Article 39 of the Third Draft, Tuesday 21 February 1961, 274.

101. BL, UN, E/CONF.34/12. UN Conference for the adoption of a single convention on narcotic drugs, Ad Hoc Committee to deal with article 39, 23 February 1961, 2.

102. BL, UN, E/CONF.34/24. UN Conference for the Adoption of a Single Convention on Narcotic Drugs, Summary Records of Plenary Meetings, Thirty-Fourth Plenary Meeting, 20 March 1961, 156.

103. BL, UN, E/CN.7/324. The Question of Cannabis, Note by the Secretary-General, 26 April 1957, 11.

104. Perhaps the high point of this 'empire-building and territory-claiming' came in the early 1950s when Leon Steinig, head of the UN's Division of Narcotic Drugs, proposed that he would head up a world monopoly on opium, which he later sought to extend to cover nuclear material too. He was removed in 1952. For more on this, and for a full account of the politics of the international drugs bureaucracies in this period, see W. McAllister, *Drug Diplomacy in the Twentieth-Century: An International History* (London: Routledge, 2000), 156–211.

CHAPTER 6

1. M. Booth, *Cannabis: A History* (London: Doubleday, 2003), 270–2; a more extensive and similarly excited account can be found in J. Green, *All Dressed Up: The Sixties and the Counterculture* (London: Pimlico, 1999), 173–202.

2. M. Booth, *Cannabis*, 272. In 2006 John Jiggens claimed that 3,000 people had attended (*Social History of Medicine*, 20/1 (2007), 180). By 2010 the Tate Liverpool website that accompanied their 'Summer of Love: Art of the Psychedelic Era' exhibition claimed that 5,000 people had been there; www.tate.org.uk/liverpool/exhibitions/summeroflove/timeline.shtm# accessed 3 November 2010. Steve Abrams, a founder of the Society of Mental Awareness in 1967, claimed that 10,000 people had attended (see S. Abrams, 'Soma, the Wootton Report and Cannabis Law Reform in Britain during the 1960s and 1970s', in S. Sznitman, B. Olsson, and R. Room (eds.), *A Cannabis Reader: Global Issues and Local Experiences* (Lisbon: European Monitoring Centre for Drugs and Drug Addiction, 2008), 45).

3. National Archives (NA), MEPO 2/10463. Report for Purpose of Reviewing Drug Trafficking. Metropolitan Police, CID, 4 October 1961.

4. NA, MEPO 2/10463. Report for Purpose of Reviewing Drug Trafficking. Metropolitan Police, CID, 18 April 1961.

5. NA, MEPO 2/10463. Report for Purpose of Reviewing Drug Trafficking. Metropolitan Police, CID, 13 January 1961.

6. For various recollections by those that considered themselves members of an 'alternative society' (x) in this period, see J. Green (ed.), *Days in the Life: Voices from the English Underground, 1961–1971* (London: Pimlico, 1998).

7. 'Obituary: Faris Glubb', *The Guardian*, www.guardian.co.uk/media/2004/may/17/pressandpublishing.guardianobituaries posted 17 May 2004, accessed 21 October 2010.

8. J. Green (ed.), *Days in the Life*, p. x.

9. 'Drugs Call by "Flower-Children"', *The Times*, 17 July 1967, 2

10. C. Coon, 'We Were the Welfare Branch of the Alternative Society', in H. Curtis and M. Sanderson (eds.), *The Unsung Sixties: Memoirs of Social Innovation* (London: Whiting and Birch, 2004), 195.

11. J. Green, *Days in the Life*, 202.

12. Ibid. 201.

13. C. Coon and R. Harris, *The Release Report on Drug Offenders and the Law* (London: Sphere, 1969).

14. Interview conducted by author with Caroline Coon, 3 March 2008. See also A. Mold, 'The Welfare Branch of the Alternative Society? The Work of Drug Voluntary Organisation Release, 1967–1978', *Twentieth-Century British History*, 17/1 (2006), 50–73.

15. J. Green, *Days in the Life*, 192.

16. J. Green, *All Dressed Up*, 188.

17. J. Green, *Days in the Life*, 192.

18. NA, HO 287/451. Drug offences: reports by chief constables on drug availability. Northampton and County Constabulary, 2 February 1968, 1–2.

19. NA, HO 287/451. Drug offences: reports by chief constables. Derby County and Borough Constabulary, 10 February 1968, 1.

20. NA, HO 287/451. Drug offences: reports by chief constables. Swansea Borough Police, 5 February 1958, 2.

21. NA, HO 287/451. Drug offences: reports by chief constables. Southend-on-Sea Constabulary, 31 January 1968, 1.

22. NA, HO 287/451. Drug offences: reports by chief constables. Coventry City Police, 6 February 1968, 1.

23. NA, HO 287/451. Drug offences: reports by chief constables. West Mercia Constabulary, 8 February 1968, 4.

24. NA, HO 287/451. Drug offences: reports by chief constables. Lincolnshire County Constabulary, 8 February 1968, 1.

25. NA, HO 287/451. Drug offences: reports by chief constables. Wakefield City Police, 8 February 1968, 1.

26. NA, HO 287/451. Drug offences: reports by chief constables. Warrington County Borough Police, 6 February 1968, 1.

27. NA, HO 287/451. Drug offences: reports by chief constables. Newcastle Upon Tyne City Police, 2 February 1968, 1.

28. NA, MEPO 2/10463. Report for Purpose of Reviewing Drug Trafficking. Metropolitan Police, CID, 3 July 1962.

29. NA, HO287/249. Drug offences: Dangerous Drugs Bill 1967; proposals for legislation; National Drug Squad Conference. The Drug Problem, by the chief constable of Brighton, 7 April 1967, 4.

30. NA, HO 287/451. Drug offences: reports by chief constables. Cardiff City Police, 6 February 1968, 2–3.

31. NA, HO 287/451. Drug offences: reports by chief constables. Hampshire Constabulary, 30 January 1968, 2.

32. NA, HO 287/451. Drug offences: reports by chief constables. York City Police, 30 January 1968, 1.

33. NA, HO 287/451. Drug offences: reports by chief constables. Surrey Constabulary, 2 February 1968, 1.

34. NA, HO 287/451. Drug offences: reports by chief constables. Lancashire County Police, 9 February 1968, 2–3.

35. NA, HO 287/451. Drug offences: reports by chief constables. Cardiff City Police, 6 February 1968, 2–3.

36. NA, HO 287/451. Drug offences: reports by chief constables. Birmingham City Police, 7 February 1968, 2.

37. NA, HO 287/451. Drug offences: reports by chief constables. Gwent Constabulary Report, 31 January 1968, 3.

38. NA, HO 287/451. Drug offences: reports by chief constables. Hampshire Constabulary, 6 February 1968, 5.

39. NA, HO 287/451. Drug offences: reports by chief constables. Bristol Constabulary, 6 February 1968, 2.

40. NA, HO 287/451. Drug offences: reports by chief constables. Essex County Constabulary, 1 February 1968, 4.

41. NA, HO 287/451. Drug offences: reports by chief constables. Sheffield and Rotherham Constabulary, 6 February 1968, 2.

42. NA, HO 305/10. Meeting with police; criticism of Metropolitan Police report on drugs situation in London. CID Central Officer's Special Report, 18 July 1966.

43. NA, HO 305/10. Meeting with police. Clipping from Evening Standard, 6 July 1966.

44. NA, HO 287/451. Drug offences: reports by chief constables. Birmingham City Police, 7 February 1968, 1.

45. NA, HO 287/451. Drug offences: reports by chief constables. West Midlands Constabulary, 7 February 1968, 1.
46. NA, HO 287/451. Drug offences: reports by chief constables. Bucks County Constabulary, 8 February 1968, 1.
47. NA, HO 287/451. Drug offences: reports by chief constables. Northallerton Constabulary, 5 February 1968, 1.
48. NA, HO 287/249. Drug offences: Dangerous Drugs Bill 1967; proposals for legislation; National Drug Squad Conference. Report on National Conference of Drugs Squad Officers, 17–19 October 1969, appendix L.
49. J. Mills, 'Globalising Ganja: The British Empire and International Cannabis Traffic, c.1834–1939', in J. Goodman et al. (eds.), *Consuming Habits: Global and Historical Perspectives on How Cultures Define Drugs* (London: Routledge, 2007), 66–88. See also Ch. 4 in this book.
50. NA, HO 287/451. Drug offences: reports by chief constables. Suffolk Constabulary, 6 February 1968, 1
51. NA, HO 287/451. Drug offences: reports by chief constables. Hampshire Constabulary, 30 January 1968, 3.
52. NA, HO 287/451. Drug offences: reports by chief constables. Sussex Constabulary, 29 January 1968, 1.
53. NA, HO 287/451. Drug offences: reports by chief constables. Mid-Anglia Constabulary, 7 February 1968, 1.
54. NA, HO 287/451. Drug offences: reports by chief constables. Oxfordshire Constabulary, 9 February 1968, 1.
55. NA, HO 287/451. Drug offences: reports by chief constables. Bristol Constabulary, 6 February 1968, 1.
56. NA, HO 287/451. Drug offences: reports by chief constables. Leicester and Rutland Constabulary, 31 January 1968, 2.
57. NA, HO 287/451. Drug offences: reports by chief constables. Lincolnshire County Constabulary, 8 February 1968, 2.
58. NA, HO 287/451. Drug offences: reports by chief constables. Dorset and Bournemouth Constabulary, 9 February 1968, 1.
59. NA, HO 287/451. Drug offences: reports by chief constables. Hampshire Constabulary, 2.
60. NA, HO 287/451. Drug offences: reports by chief constables. Norfolk Joint Police, 6 February 1968, 1.
61. NA, HO 287/451. Drug offences: reports by chief constables. Hertfordshire Constabulary, 7 February 1968, 2.
62. NA, MEPO 2/10463. Report for Purpose of Reviewing Drug Trafficking. CID Central Officer's Special Report, 24 February 1965.
63. NA, HO 287/451. Drug offences: reports by chief constables. Oxford City Police, 30 January 1968, 1–2.
64. NA, HO 287/451. Drug offences: reports by chief constables. Mid-Anglia Constabulary, 7 February 1968, 1.

65. C. Coon, 'We Were the Welfare Branch of the Alternative Society', 190.

66. A letter in 1972 noted that 'during 1954 a Detective Sergeant and Detective Constable were deputed to the specific job of handling drug enquiries'. NA, MEPO 2/10167. Meetings at Home Office on the increasing use of dangerous drugs. CID, 11 February 1972.

67. See handwritten sleeve notes on NA, HO 319/5. Dangerous Drugs Branch: co-operation with Metropolitan Police Dangerous Drugs Squad.

68. NA, MEPO 2/10463. Report for Purpose of Reviewing Drug Trafficking. CID, 13 January 1961.

69. Ibid.

70. NA, MEPO 2/10463. Report for Purpose of Reviewing Drug Trafficking. CID, 3 July 1962.

71. NA, MEPO 2/10463. Report for Purpose of Reviewing Drug Trafficking. CID, 9 October 1962.

72. E. Cooke, 'The Drug Squad', *Journal of the Forensic Science Society*, 3/1 (September 1962), 43–8.

73. NA, MEPO 2/10167. Meeting at Home Office re. increase in the use of dangerous drugs etc. Clipping from *The Times*, 29 September 1962.

74. NA, MEPO 2/10167. Meeting at Home Office re. increase in the use of dangerous drugs etc. Clipping from *Evening Standard*, 5 October 1962, 8.

75. NA, MEPO 2/10167. Meeting at Home Office re. increase in the use of dangerous drugs etc. Clipping from *Evening Standard*, 1 October 1962, 8.

76. NA, MEPO 2/10167. Meeting at Home Office re. increase in the use of dangerous drugs etc. Clipping from *Evening Standard*, 2 October 1962, 8.

77. NA, MEPO 2/10167. Meeting at Home Office re. increase in the use of dangerous drugs etc. Clipping from *Evening Standard*, 5 October 1962, 8.

78. NA, MEPO 2/10167. Meeting at Home Office re. increase in the use of dangerous drugs etc. Home Office, 25 October 1962.

79. Ibid.

80. Richard Davenport-Hines, 'Brooke, Henry, Baron Brooke of Cumnor (1903–1984)', *Oxford Dictionary of National Biography* (Oxford: Oxford University Press, 2004), http://www.oxforddnb.com/view/article/37227, accessed 26 June 2007.

81. NA, MEPO 2/10167. Meeting at Home Office re. increase in the use of dangerous drugs etc. Commander C (through Deputy Commander C), 5 November 1962.

82. NA, MEPO 2/10167. Meeting at Home Office re. increase in the use of dangerous drugs etc. CID Central Officer's Special Report, 29 November 1962.

83. NA, MEPO 2/10167. Meeting at Home Office re. increase in the use of dangerous drugs etc. Home Office to Metropolitan Police, 25 October 1962.

84. NA, MEPO 2/10167. Meeting at Home Office re. increase in the use of dangerous drugs etc. Dangerous Drugs Office, C.O.C.1 Branch, 28 January 1963.
85. NA, MEPO 2/10167. Meeting at Home Office re. increase in the use of dangerous drugs etc. Metropolitan Police to Home Office, 18 April 1963.
86. NA, MEPO 2/10167. Meeting at Home Office re. increase in the use of dangerous drugs etc. CID Central Officer's Special Report, 8 June 1963.
87. NA, MEPO 2/10463. Dangerous drugs: quarterly returns of trafficking and use, 1961–4. CID Central Officer's Special Report, 11 November 1963.
88. NA, MEPO 2/10463. Dangerous drugs: quarterly returns of trafficking and use, 1961–4. CID Central Officer's Special Report, 24 February 1964.
89. NA, HO 319/5, DDA.59 70/1/22. Dangerous Drugs Branch: co-operation with Metropolitan Police Dangerous Drugs Squad. Note of a meeting at the Home Office on 19 November 1962.
90. The government drafted the necessary legislation and it was introduced into Parliament as a Private Member's Bill by Sir Hugh Linstead in January 1964 (see NA, HO 319/266, DDA.611/36/12, 15 April 1964). This Bill proposed the ratification of the 1961 UN Single Convention on Narcotic Drugs. It also proposed to make it an offence to cultivate cannabis or to permit premises to be used for the smoking of the drug. Linstead was a British pharmaceutical chemist who was also Conservative MP for Putney at the time. See *The Times*, 22 January 1964, 8.
91. *The Times*, 24 February 1966, 5.
92. *The Times*, 23 March 1968, 3.
93. *The Times*, 30 March 1968, 9.
94. Ibid.
95. *The Times*, 8 April 1968, 9.
96. *The Times*, 24 January 1969, 10.
97. R. Howells, 'Sweet v. Parseley and Public Welfare Offences', *Modern Law Review*, 32/3, (1969), 310.
98. *The Times*, 24 January 1969, 2.
99. Interview with Caroline Coon, 3 March 2008.
100. NA, DPP 2/5125/1. Director of Public Prosecutions: Case Papers, NS. Detective Inspector Kelaher and Others, Preliminary Advice, 7 September 1972.
101. Interview with Caroline Coon, 3 March 2008.
102. NA, MEPO 2/9733. Arrest of John Winston Lennon and Yoko Ono Cox on 18 October 1968 for drug offences.
103. 'Former Drug Squad Chief Cleared by Jury of Conspiracy', *The Times*, 15 November 1973, 4.
104. NA, DPP 2/5125/1. Director of Public Prosecutions: Case Papers, NS. A/D (C), 11 September 1972.
105. 'Police Constable Gets Four Years', *The Times*, 26 January 1963, 5.

106. NA, MEPO 31/2. Affray between black and white youths outside The Gun public house on 12 September 1969. A1(1) Branch, 17 April 1970.

107. NA, MEPO 31/2. OG1/69/1405A1, 19 June 1970.

108. 'Detectives plotted against immigrants, QC says', *The Times*, 6 October 1970, 3.

109. 'Three detectives are acquitted', *The Times*, 24 November 1970, 3.

110. C. Coon and R. Harris, *The Release Report on Drug Offenders and the Law* (London: Sphere, 1969). Reproduced on www.drugtext.org, accessed 10.11.2010.

111. NA, HO 287/451. Drug offences: reports by chief constables. Lancashire County Police, 9 February 1968, 2–3.

112. NA, HO 287/451. Drug offences: reports by chief constables. Middlesbrough Constabulary, 8 February 1968, 5.

113. NA, HO 287/451. Drug offences: reports by chief constables. Wigan County Borough Police, 7 February 1968, 1.

114. NA, HO 287/451. Drug offences: reports by chief constables. Surrey Constabulary 2 February 1968, 1; Essex County Constabulary, 1 February 1968, 1.

115. NA, HO 287/451. Drug offences: reports by chief constables. Birmingham City Police, 7 February 1968, 13.

116. NA, MEPO 2/10167. Meeting at Home Office re. increase in the use of dangerous drugs etc. Home Office, 25 October 1962.

117. NA, HO 287/249. Drug offences: Dangerous Drugs Bill 1967; proposals for legislation; National Drug Squad Conference. D. J. Trevelyan, 24 February 1967.

118. NA, HO 287/249. Drug offences: Dangerous Drugs Bill 1967; proposals for legislation; National Drug Squad Conference. Meeting of Chief Constables on Drugs, 20 April 1967.

119. NA, HO 287/451. Drug offences: reports by chief constables. Northampton and County Constabulary, 2 February 1968, 3.

120. NA, HO 287/451. Drug offences: reports by chief constables. Kent County Constabulary, 5 February 1968, 3.

121. NA, HO 287/451. Drug offences: reports by chief constables. Berkshire Constabulary, 7 February 1968, 1.

122. NA, HO 287/451. Drug offences: reports by chief constables. Wakefield City Police, 8 February 1968, 2.

123. NA, HO 287/451. Drug offences: reports by chief constables. County Borough of Halifax Police, 25 January 1968, 2.

124. NA, HO 287/249. Drug offences: Dangerous Drugs Bill 1967; proposals for legislation; National Drug Squad Conference. Association of Chief Police Officers (ACPO) Item, Note for Chairman, 20 October 1970, 1.

125. NA, HO 287/249. Drug offences: Dangerous Drugs Bill 1967; proposals for legislation; National Drug Squad Conference. Police Federation, 10 March 1970, 1.

126. NA, HO 287/249. Drug offences: Dangerous Drugs Bill 1967; proposals for legislation; National Drug Squad Conference. M. J. Addison (Police Department Home Office), 29 July 1970.

127. NA, MH 149/162. Advisory Committee on Drug Dependence: constitution. Minister of Health announces membership, 31 October 1966.

128. NA, MH 149/162. Advisory Committee on Drug Dependence: constitution. Submission by Home Office recommending reappointment of Advisory Committee on Drug Dependence, December 1969.

129. Wootton almost missed out on serving with the Committee at all. The Home Office had suggested replacing her with a journalist as the Home Secretary had already invited her to participate in another advisory council (12 August 1966 Philip Allen to Sir Arnold France in NA, MH 149/162). However it was pointed out that she had been suggested by Lord Brain himself and the matter was dropped (31 August 1966 Emery to Guppy in NA, MH 149/162).

130. NA, MH 154/364. Drug dependence: narcotic drugs; sub-committee reports and minutes of meetings. First draft of report on LSD and Cannabis, 22 May 1967.

131. NA, MH 154/364. Drug dependence. Minutes of the First Meeting of the LSD and Cannabis Sub-Committee, 11 May 1967, 3.

132. Dr E. G. Lucas and Mr D. G. Turner were named in the final report as Joint Secretaries to the Committee.

133. NA, MH 148/403. Proceedings, minutes and reports. Second Draft Report on LSD and Cannabis.

134. NA, MH 148/403. Proceedings, minutes and reports. Minutes of the Third Meeting of the LSD and Cannabis Sub-Committee, 8 June 1967, 2.

135. NA, MH 148/403. Proceedings, minutes and reports. Second Draft Report on LSD and Cannabis.

136. NA, MH 148/409. Hallucinogens Sub-Committee: agenda, minutes and evidence. Note of a meeting held 10 January 1968, 8–9.

137. NA, MH 148/409. Hallucinogens Sub-Committee. Note of a meeting held 10 January 1968, 14–15.

138. NA, MH 148/404. Proceedings, minutes and reports. From Michael Schofield to Lady Wootton, 5 September 1967.

139. NA, MH 148/403. Proceedings, minutes and reports. Report from Michael Schofield.

140. NA, MH 148/403. Proceedings, minutes and reports. Minutes of the fifth meeting, 8 November 1967, 2.

141. Schofield was not afraid to air his views in public. His activities led to William Deedes seeking his resignation from the Sub-Committee on Powers of Arrest and Search in April 1969, at one point with the support of Sir Edward Wayne. Schofield remained on the Committee. (See NA, MH 149/162 for details of this spat.)

142. NA, MH 148/409. Hallucinogens Sub-Committee. Paper by Sir Aubrey Lewis on Cannabis, 12–28.
143. Ibid. 30.
144. Ibid. 29.
145. Ibid., attached docket.
146. NA, MH 148/409. Hallucinogens Sub-Committee. Minutes of the eighth meeting, 28 February 1968, 3.
147. NA, MH 148/409. Hallucinogens Sub-Committee. First draft outline for report on cannabis.
148. NA, MH 148/409. Hallucinogens Sub-Committee. Statements by members regarding legislation of cannabis and LSD.
149. NA, MH 148/409. Hallucinogens Sub-Committee. Minutes of the ninth meeting, 22 March 1968.
150. NA, MH 154/3656. Drug dependence: narcotic drugs; sub-committee reports and minutes of meetings. Advisory Committee on Drug Dependence. Minutes of the eighth meeting, 28 June 1968, 2.
151. NA, MH 148/403. Proceedings, minutes and reports. Third Draft Report on LSD and Cannabis, 7.
152. NA, MH 149/162. Advisory Committee on Drug Dependence. Submission by Home Office recommending reappointment of Advisory Committee on Drug Dependence, December 1969, 1.
153. For more on these characters and organizations, see Ch. 4.
154. All quotes taken from Hansard, HC (series 5), vol. 776, cols. 947–1012 (1968–9).
155. NA, MH 154/365. Drug dependence. Advisory Committee on Drug Dependence nineteenth meeting, 1 December 1970, 2.
156. Hansard, HC (series 5), vol. 798, col. 1480 (1969–70).
157. NA, MH 154/365. Drug dependence. Advisory Committee on Drug Dependence twelfth meeting, 28 February 1969, 2–3.
158. NA, MH 154/365. Drug dependence. Advisory Committee on Drug Dependence thirteenth meeting, 4 July 1969, 2.
159. It should be noted, however, that this occurred in a wider context where a range of social problems and issues were made the responsibility of new offices or committees in this period. Virginia Berridge has described the 'raft of new expert committees which came into being in the 1970s and [which] provided a means of cementing communities of interest between government and public health-medical expertise' (282). Glen O'Hara's work on the emergence of the office of the ombudsman in British political life identifies a similar desire to establish 'disinterested, "apolitical" decision-making and scrutiny that took such a grip on public life among developed nations towards the end of the twentieth century'. What such moves in government in this period seem to reveal is a desire on the part of elected politicians to pass on responsibility for thorny political issues like smoking, cannabis consumption, and bureaucratic failure. See V. Berridge, *Marketing*

Health: Smoking and the Discourse of Public Health in Britain, 1945–2000 (Oxford: Oxford University Press, 2007), 282; G. O'Hara, 'Insanity, Transnationalism, Bureaucracy: The Origins of Britain's "Ombudsman" in the 1950s and 1960s', paper presented at the Centre for the Social History of Health and Healthcare (CSHHH) Glasgow 22 March 2011.

CHAPTER 7

1. 'Lord Hailsham Urges JPs to Have No Mercy for Offences Committed in Business for Profit', *The Times*, 13 October 1973, 3.
2. National Archives (NA), HO 319/172. Advisory Council on the Misuse of Drugs (ACMD): Working Group on Cannabis (CWG). From W. E. C. Robins, Camberwell Green Magistrates' Court to Home Office, 18 June 1975.
3. NA, HO 319/173. ACMD: CWG. Minutes of the 14th meeting, 2.
4. In 1973 and 1974 about 6 per cent of convictions for possession of cannabis received immediate custodial sentences. In 1973 and 1974 only 3 per cent of those dealt with for unlawful possession of cannabis were cautioned (NA, HO 319/173. Statistics of Cannabis Offences, 1). These cautions were usually given to women and juveniles (NA, HO 319/17. CWG Minutes of the 14th meeting, 2).
5. NA, HO 319/172. ACMD: CWG. Minutes of the 13th Meeting, 9 July 1975, 3. The sample was of 2,000 male offenders convicted of the offence of unlawful possession of cannabis during 1971.
6. NA, HO 319/337. ACMD. Statistics on the Misuse of Drugs in the United Kingdom 1979, Home Office Statistical Department, 12 August 1980.
7. NA, HO 319/338. ACMD. From D. H. Ward to D. Hardwick, 18 December 1980.
8. NA, HO 319/172. ACMD: CWG. Statistics on stops and searches by the Metropolitan Police during 1973.
9. *Stop and Search* (London: Release, 1977); see also, *Stop and Search: Special Report* (London: Release, 1980).
10. NA, HO 319/172. ACMD: CWG. Minutes of the 13th Meeting, 9 July 1975, 3.
11. NA, HO 319/172. ACMD: CWG. Summary of the work of the CWG to 31 December 1974, 2.
12. NA, HO 319/173. ACMD: CWG. CWG (2)/12. These cities had populations of between 700,000 and 850,000 people.
13. This is a simplified version. Two amendments were actually offered but it should be noted that most of the discussion in the House of Lords and at the ACMD was of the first amendment.
14. Interview conducted by author with Lord Gifford, 15 October 2008.
15. Hansard, HL, vol. 379, cols. 1345–7 (10 February 1977).
16. Ibid., cols. 1351–2.
17. Ibid., cols. 1353.

18. NA, HO 319/287. Criminal Law Bill 1976: implementation of Bill in relation to Misuse of Drugs Act 1971. From Miss Edwards to Mr Taylor, 15 February 1977.

19. NA, MH 149/1945. ACMD: joint meetings of the Legal and Administrative and Cannabis Working Groups. Amendments to the Criminal Law Bill in relation to Cannabis offences. Note by the Home Office, February 1977.

20. NA, HO 319/287. Criminal Law Bill 1976: implementation of Bill in relation to Misuse of Drugs Act 1971. From Miss Edwards to Mr Taylor, 15 February 1977.

21. NA, HO 319/179. ACMD: CWG. Minutes of the 19th Meeting, 28 February 1977, 7.

22. NA, HO 319/180. ACMD: CWG. Minutes of the 20th Meeting, 24 March 1977, 5.

23. Hansard, HL, vol. 381, cols. 652–6 (24 March 1977). This attitude to experiences in other countries was not unlike that of the ACMD as it regularly considered evidence from elsewhere without ever being convinced that any particular case study pointed the way for Britain. For example, in January 1978 the 6th Joint Meeting of the Legal and Administrative and Cannabis Working Groups was presented with a collection of papers on the US experience and the chairman concluded the discussion by stating that 'while the information from America had been most interesting, there were clearly many differences in procedures which made direct comparison impractical' (NA, MH149/1945. 6th Joint Meeting of the Legal and Administrative and Cannabis Working Groups, 18 January 1978, 6).

24. Hansard, HL, vol. 381, col. 658 (24 March 1977).

25. Ibid. 637.

26. Hansard, HC, vol. 935–1, col. 567–72 (13 July 1977).

27. Interview conducted by author with Lord Corbett, 28 October 2008.

28. NA, MH 149/1945. Minutes of a Joint Meeting of the Legal and Administration Working Group and the CWG, 6 April 1977, 3. Those for it were Bloomfield, Boden, Power, Searchfield, Hart, and Graham. Those against it were Bewley, Griffith Edwards, Myers, Robins, and Saunders.

29. Ibid.

30. NA, HO 319/183. ACMD/CWG. ACMD, 26 July 1977. The letter was produced as a Written Answer to a question by Jack Ashley MP on 24 June 1977.

31. Jo Richardson MP also withdrew her proposed amendments relating to cannabis (these were not debated). Among these proposals was the repeal of 'stop and search' powers under section 23 of the Misuse of Drugs Act. See Criminal Law Bill, Notes on Amendments NC45 (NA, HO 319/288. Criminal Law Bill 1976: 2nd Reading; Misuse of Drugs Act 1971) and House of Commons Official Report, Standing Committee E Criminal Law Bill (Lords), *Twelfth Sitting Thursday 30th June 1977* (London: HMSO 1977), 729–40.

32. Interview conducted by author with Caroline Coon, 3 March 2008.

33. NA, HO 319/167. ACMD: CWG. Office of Population Censuses and Surveys, September 1974. Even if the money had been available for this, there was not necessarily agreement at the ACMD that such a survey would be the best use of resources. When discussing the direction of research into prohibited drugs in 1977 Griffith Edwards stated that 'research funds are scarce in this country . . . it would be hard to justify a reduction of more important projects to make way for studies in the epidemiology of cannabis use'. He pointed out, as an example of the 'more important projects', that there was no accurate data on alcohol use in the UK. In D. J. West (ed.), *Problems of Drug Abuse in Britain* (Cambridge: Institute of Criminology, 1977), 122.

34. NA, HO 319/172. ACMD: CWG. Cannabis and the Criteria for Legalisation of a Currently Prohibited Recreational Drug: Groundwork for a Debate, 50.

35. NA, MH 149/1945. ACMD. Minutes of the 3rd Joint Meeting of the Cannabis and Legal and Administrative Working Groups held on Wednesday, 21 September 1977, 3.

36. NA, MH 149/1945. ACMD. Minutes of the 5th Joint Meeting of the Cannabis and Legal and Administrative Working Groups held on 23 November 1977, 5.

37. NA, MH 149/1945. ACMD. Minutes of the 10th Joint Meeting of the Cannabis and Legal and Administrative Working Groups held on 16 August 1978, 2.

38. NA, HO 319/180. ACMD: CWG. Minutes of the 20th meeting, 24 March 1997, 6.

39. NA, MH 149/1945. ACMD. Letter from Robert Bradlaw (Chair of the ACMD) to the Home Secretary, 15 January 1979, 3.

40. Ibid.

41. *Report on a Review of the Classification of Controlled Drugs and of Penalties under Schedules 2 and 4 of the Misuse of Drugs Act 1971* (London: Home Office, 1979), vii.

42. NA, MH 149/1945. ACMD. From Margaret Pearson (Department of Health and Social Security (DHSS)) to Mr Hale (DHSS), 31 October 1978.

43. NA, MH 149/1945. ACMD. D. A. Cahal (DHSS) to Margaret Pearson (DHSS), 1 November 1978.

44. *Report on a Review of the Classification of Controlled Drugs*, v.

45. NA, MH 149/1946. ACMD. Draft Press Notice (Home Office).

46. NA, MH 149/1945. ACMD. A. W. Glanville (Probation and After-Care Department) to Mr Raison, 21 May 1979.

47. *Trash Rehashed: A Reply to the Advisory Council on the Misuse of Drugs* (London: Legalise Cannabis Campaign, 1979), 5–7.

48. NA, MH 149/1945. ACMD. D. A. Cahal (DHSS) to Margaret Pearson (DHSS), 1 November 1978.

49. NA, MH 149/1945. ACMD. A. W. Glanville (Probation and After-Care Department) to Mr Raison, 21 May 1979.

50. NA, HO 319/180. ACMD: CWG. From Griffith Edwards to J. C. Bloomfield, 14 March 1977.

51. NA, HO 319/180. ACMD: CWG. Minutes of the 20th Meeting, Thursday 24 March 1977, 3.

52. NA, HO 319/325. Expert Group on the Effects of Cannabis Use. From Griffith Edwards to D. G. Turner, 18 December 1979.

53. NA, HO 319/325. Expert Group on the Effects of Cannabis Use. From Griffith Edwards to D. G. Turner, 16 November 1979.

54. NA, HO 319/325. Expert Group on the Effects of Cannabis Use. From Griffith Edwards to D. G. Turner, 18 December 1979.

55. *Report of the Expert Group on the Effects of Cannabis Use* (London: HMSO, 1982), 60.

56. Nahas was an anaesthesiologist and was appointed to the UN Narcotic Control Board in 1971 by Secretary General Kurt Waldheim. He remained an inveterate advocate of controls on cannabis and dedicated much of his career to publications that claimed to show its harmfulness. See e.g. G. Nahas, *Marihuana, Deceptive Weed* (New York: Raven Press, 1973); *Keep Off the Grass: A Scientist's Documented Account of Marijuana's Destructive Effects* (New York: Reader's Digest Press, 1976). Paton was professor of pharmacology at Oxford between 1959 and 1984, and served in a number of influential roles including chairman of the British Pharmacological Society between 1978 and 1982. See H. Rang, 'Paton, Sir William Drummond MacDonald (1917–1993)', *Oxford Dictionary of National Biography* (*ODNB*) (Oxford: Oxford University Press, 2004), http://www.oxforddnb.com/view/article/53130, accessed 24 November 2010.

57. Wellcome Trust Library (WT), PP/WDP/F/1/14. From G. G. Nahas to W. D. M Paton, 6 June 1977.

58. WT, PP/WDP/F/1/14. From W. D. M. Paton to G. G. Nahas, 28 May 1977.

59. G. G. Nahas and W. D. M. Paton (eds.), *Advances in the Biosciences*, vols. xxii and xxiii *Marihuana: Biological Effects* (Oxford: Pergamon Press, 1979), 738.

60. *Report of an Alcoholism and Drug Addiction Research Foundation (Ontario) and WHO Scientific Meeting on Adverse Health and Behavioural Consequences of Cannabis Use* (Ontario: Addiction Research Foundation, 1981).

61. *Journal of the American Medical Association*, 30 April 1973, 631.

62. NA, HO 319/325. Expert Group on the Effects of Cannabis Use. From Griffith Edwards to D. G. Turner, 18 December 1979.

63. NA, HO 319/325. Expert Group on the Effects of Cannabis Use. From J. D. P. Graham to D. G. Turner, 3 February 1980. Paton's position on cannabis was well known to Griffith Edwards. As early as 1975 they had both been asked to assess for the BBC a film on cannabis that was to be broadcast in the Horizon series. Neither had liked it and they had agreed that it was 'very loaded and selective'. WT, PP/WDP/F/1/14. From W. D. M. Paton to G. Nahas, 4 June 1975.

64. WT, PP/WDP/F/1/14. Clipping of the *Sunday Observer*, 11 May 1980.

65. H. Rang, 'Paton, Sir William Drummond MacDonald (1917–1993)', *ODNB*.

66. *Report of the Expert Group on the Effects of Cannabis Use* (London: HMSO, 1982), 1–4. For more on the significance of this report for the 'remedicalization' of cannabis in Britain see S. Taylor, 'Remedicalising Cannabis: Science, Medicine and Policy, 1973 to the Early Twenty-first Century' (unpublished thesis, London School of Hygiene and Tropical Medicine, 2010).

67. When asked why he had sought this amendment in 2008, Robert Kilroy-Silk replied 'I am afraid I will not be of much help—I can't remember it'. Email from Robert Kilroy-Silk to author, 1 October 2008.

68. NA, HO 319/666. ACMD. Criminal Policy Department, 6 June 1981.

69. Hansard, HL (series 5), vol. 428, col. 911 (22 March 1982).

70. NA, MH 149/1946. ACMD: Report of the Expert Group on the Effects of Cannabis Use, D. J. Hardwick (Secretary of the ACMD) to Members of the ACMD, 16 March 1982.

71. NA, MH 149/1945. ACMD. Mr M. J. Power in Minutes of the 3rd Joint Meeting of the Cannabis and Legal and Administrative Working Groups, 21 September 1977, 3.

72. NA, HO 319/338. ACMD. Speech by the Home Secretary, Thursday 9 April 1981.

73. NA, HO 319/337. ACMD. From D. G. Turner to Sir Robert Bradlaw, 30 September 1981.

74. NA, J 271/53. Charged with possession of cannabis at Bedford Crown Court. Probation Officer's Report, 8 May 1972, 2. Names removed for ethical reasons.

75. NA, J 271/53. Charged with possession of cannabis at Bedford Crown Court. Probation Officer's Report, 15 May 1972, 1.

76. NA, J 325/28. Charged with unauthorized possession of a dangerous drug, namely cannabis resin. Social Security Report to the Crown Court, Swindon, 26 January 1972. Name removed for ethical reasons.

77. NA, HO 319/338. ACMD. R. Ratcliff, 'Misuse of Drugs in Scotland 1977 to 1979', 2.

78. M. Plant, *Drugs in Perspective* (London: Hodder and Stoughton, 1987), 73–9.

79. See http://www.discogs.com/artist/Musical+Youth, accessed 8 November 2011; A. Petridis, 'The Story of The Specials', *Mojo*, 98 (2002), 76–81; A. Campbell and R. Campbell, *Blood and Fire: The Autobiography of the UB40 Brothers* (London: Arrow, 2006).

80. NA, HO 319/338. ACMD. Misuse of Drugs in the United Kingdom in 1980 (ACMD 81/2), 3.

81. Ibid.

82. NA, HO 319/323. Meetings of Central Drugs Intelligence Unit, Home Office Drugs Branch and Home Office Central Research Establishment. Minutes of meeting held at the Home Office Drugs Branch, 30 April 1981, 4.

83. NA, HO 319/337. ACMD. Minutes of the 29th Meeting, 17 April 1980, 6.

84. NA, HO 319/323. Meetings of Central Drugs Intelligence Unit, Home Office Drugs Branch and Home Office Central Research Establishment. Minutes of meeting held at the Central Research Establishment, 19 January 1983, 5.
85. Hansard, HC (series 6), vol. 172, col. 125 (9 May 1990).
86. Hansard, HC (series 6), vol. 201, col. 1093 (16 January 1992).
87. NA, HO 319/338. ACMD. Speech by the Home Secretary, Thursday, 9 April 1981. This speech was issued as a press release on 9 April 1981.
88. NA, HO 319/356. Resources for enforcing the control of drugs entering the UK: effects of Civil Service cuts. From William Whitelaw to Geoffrey Howe, 24 June 1982.
89. NA, HO 319/356. Resources for enforcing the control of drugs. From Geoffrey Howe to William Whitelaw, 22 July 1982.
90. Hansard, HC (series 6), vol. 33, col. 498 (8 December 1982).
91. Report of the Chief Constable of Strathclyde Police (Strathclyde Regional Council 1980), 8.
92. Report of the Chief Constable of Strathclyde (Strathclyde Regional Council 1983), 5.
93. Report of the Chief Constable of Strathclyde (Strathclyde Regional Council 1984), 5.
94. Hansard, HC (series 6), vol. 77, col. 14 (15 April 1985).
95. Hansard, HC (series 6), vol. 163, col. 623 (8 December 1989).
96. NA, HO 319/338. ACMD. From D. J. Hardwick to B. Bennett, 16 December 1980.
97. NA, HO 319/337. ACMD. Minutes of the 29th meeting, 17 April 1980, 6.
98. NA, HO 319/323. Meetings of Central Drugs Intelligence Unit, Home Office Drugs Branch and Home Office Central Research Establishment. Minutes of meeting held at the Central Drugs Intelligence Unit, 20 October 1982, 4.
99. NA, HO 319/323. Meetings of Central Drugs Intelligence Unit, Home Office Drugs Branch and Home Office Central Research Establishment. From H. B. Spear to T. Moffat (Central Research Establishment), 11 November 1983.
100. A. Mold, *Heroin: The Treatment of Addiction in Twentieth-Century Britain* (DeKalb: Northern Illinois University Press, 2008), 68.
101. Metropolitan Police, *The Principles of Policing and Guidance for Professional Behaviour* (London: Public Information Department, Metropolitan Police, 1985), 29–30. The preface noted that this was primarily intended for the 'new entrant' to the Metropolitan Police although it was recommended to all serving officers.
102. Ibid. 27.

103. NA, HO 319/144. Misuse of Drugs Regulations 1985. Draft letter from G. H. Phillips to Mr Jackson (Private Secretary to Home Secretary), 27 August 1980.

104. NA, MEPO 4/511. Report of the Commissioner of Police of the Metropolis to the Home Secretary (January 1984), 1.

105. *Police and People in London: A Group of Young, Black People* (London: Policy Studies Institute, 1983), 6.

106. NA, MEPO 4/511. Report of the Commissioner of Police of the Metropolis to the Home Secretary (January 1984), 13.

107. Hansard, HC (series 6), vol. 63, col. 1463 (13 July 1984).

108. MEPO 26/2. Cautions by police in criminal cases: Metropolitan Police policy. Police Order No. 14 of 17 September 1985; Police Order No. 10 of 30 October 1984; Home Office Circular No. 14/1985.

109. MEPO 26/2. Cautions by police in criminal cases: Home Office Circular No. 14/1985.

110. MEPO 26/2. Cautions by police in criminal cases: Special Police Order, 11 December 1984, 127.

111. Hansard, HC (series 6), vol. 25, col. 245 (15 June 1982).

112. Hansard, HC (series 6), vol. 67, col. 351 (15 November 1984).

113. Hansard, HC (series 6), vol. 77, col. 310 (22 April 1985).

114. Hansard, HC (series 6), vol. 237, col. 808 (16 February 1994).

115. Hansard, HC (series 6), vol. 163, col. 584 (8 December 1989).

116. Hansard, HC (series 6), vol. 236, col. 569 (31 January 1994). The figures related to 1992.

117. Ibid., col. 573.

118. Hansard, HC (series 6), vol. 237, col. 809 (16 February 1994); vol. 236, col. 569 (31 January 1994).

119. Hansard HC (series 6), vol. 201, col. 1093 (16 January 1992).

CHAPTER 8

1. Hansard, HC (series 6), vol. 296, col. 428 (24 June 1997).

2. See 'History of Release', http://www.release.org.uk/about/history-of-release/1960s, accessed 9 September 2011.

3. This account is based on information from the Legalise Cannabis Alliance website http://www.lca-uk.org/intro.php, accessed 13 January 2009.

4. 'Consuming Cannabis: A personal journey by Free Rob Cannabis', http://cannabis.uk.net/CHIC/Consuming%20Cannabis.htm, accessed 13 January 2009 (material no longer available online).

5. 'Campaigners Light Up in Cannabis Protest', Press Association, 28 September 1997.

6. My thanks to Free Love Cannabis (formerly Rob Christopher and Free Rob Cannabis) for information provided by email dated 17 January 2009 on his career as a cannabis activist.
7. 'Why we believe it is time to decriminalise cannabis', *Independent on Sunday*, 28 September 1997, Features, 1.
8. 'Pot Power; Thirty years after the first cannabis rally, veterans and new campaigners gathered to fight a law that has left two generations alienated and criminalised', *Independent on Sunday*, 29 March 1998, Features, 1.
9. 'Rosie Boycott's speech in Trafalgar Square 28th March 1998', Legalise Cannabis Alliance homepage http://www.ccguide.org.uk/rb_traf.php, accessed 12 January 2009.
10. 'High on Success from the Cannabis Campaign', *The Independent*, 3 November 1997, Media section, M8; 'Rosie Boycott: Skunk is Dangerous. But I still believe in my campaign to decriminalise cannabis', *The Independent* (online), Sunday, 18 March 2007, http://www.independent.co.uk/opinion/commentators/rosie-boycott-skunk-is-dangerous-but-i-still-believe-in-my-campaign-to-decriminalise-cannabis-440657.html, accessed 7 January 2009.
11. 'High on Success from the Cannabis Campaign', *The Independent*, 3 November 1997, Media section, M8.
12. This account is based on information from the Legalise Cannabis Alliance website http://www.lca-uk.org/intro.php, accessed 13 January 2009.
13. 'Free Cannabis Wishlist', http://www.cannabis.uk.net/CHIC/FREE%20CANNABIS%20WISH%20LIST.htm, accessed 19 January 2009 (material no longer available online).
14. 'Howard at Odds with Scottish Ministers over Cannabis Fines', *The Scotsman*, 14 February 1994.
15. 'Going to Pot: The Politicians' Line', *The Guardian*, 23 September 1994, T3.
16. 'Short's Puff for Cannabis Sends Labour Reeling', *The Independent*, 30 October 1995, 1.
17. Ibid.
18. Hansard, HC (series 6), vol. 296, col. 428 (24 June 1997).
19. 'The Time is Right to Decriminalise Cannabis', *The Independent*, 28 September 1997, i. The idea that the change of government brought with it a sense of new possibilities for policy was reflected in related fields. Virginia Berridge noted 'the excitement among public health activists at an early conference on smoking in that year' (1997) in *Marketing Health: Smoking and the Discourse of Public Health in Britain, 1945–2000* (Oxford: Oxford University Press, 2007), 279.
20. T. May, M. Duffy, H. Warburton, and M. Hough, *Policing Cannabis as a Class C Drug* (York: Joseph Rowntree Foundation, 2007), www.jrf.org.uk/publications/policing-cannabis-class-c-drug, accessed 28 April 2009.
21. 'Chief Justice Urges Debate on Cannabis', *The Times*, 9 October 1997, 7.

22. *Therapeutic Uses of Cannabis* (Amsterdam: BMA/Harwood Academic Publishers, 1997): C. H. Ashton, 'Cannabis: Clinical and Pharmacological Aspects', *British Journal of Psychiatry*, 178 (2001), 101–6; A. Johns, 'Psychiatric Aspects of Cannabis Use', *British Journal of Psychiatry*, 178 (2001), 116–22; P. Robson, 'Therapeutic Aspects of Cannabis and Cannabinoids', *British Journal of Psychiatry*, 178 (2001), 107–15; 'Decriminalise Cannabis: Lords Cannabis Inquiry', *The Independent*, 11 February 1998, 1; Academy of Medical Sciences, *The Use of Cannabis and Its Derivatives for Medical and Recreational Purposes* (London: The Royal Society, 1998).

23. G. Hayes and H. Shapiro, *Drug Notes: Cannabis* (London: Institute for the Study of Drug Dependence, 1998).

24. HL, *Select Committee on Science and Technology, Ninth Report 1997–8, Cannabis: The Scientific and Medical Evidence; Report of the Independent Inquiry into the Misuse of Drugs Act 1971* (London: Police Foundation, 2000).

25. 'Labour peer joins cannabis debate', *The Times*, 16 October 2000, 5.

26. 'Monitor: Mo Mowlam and Cannabis', *The Independent*, 22 January 2000, 6.

27. 'Mowlam Cannabis Hints Cause a Stir', *Birmingham Evening Mail*, 6 November 2000, 5.

28. 'Full text of Ann Widdecombe's speech', guardian.co.uk, Wednesday 4 October 2000, (accessed 19 January 2009).

29. 'We Took Drugs Say Seven Top Tories', *Mail on Sunday*, 8 October 2000, 1.

30. 'Talking Tough yet Tender, Portillo Steals the Show', *Daily Mail*, 4 October 2000, 5.

31. For more on the strife between Widdecombe and Portillo at this time see 'Widdecombe is Left Fuming over "Cannabis Plot"', *The Times*, 9 October 2000; S. Walters, *Tory Wars: The Conservatives in Crisis* (London: Politicos, 2001).

32. 'Mo Mowlam: Obituary', *The Independent*, 20 August 2005, 40–1.

33. 'Mo, Smart, Funny and Brave but Forever on the Run from Her Demons', *Daily Mail*, 20 August 2005, 4–5.

34. 'Kennedy Call to Rethink Drug Law: Lib Dem Leader Seeks Royal Commission on the Legalisation of Cannabis', *The Observer*, 15 August 1999, 1.

35. Ibid.

36. 'Greens Sell Drugs Books on Website', *The Independent*, 9 September 1999, 2.

37. 'Delegates Defy Senior Figures on Drugs Policy', *Western Mail*, 21 September 2001, 10.

38. K. Hellawell, *The Outsider: The Autobiography of One of Britain's Most Controversial Policemen* (London: HarperCollins, 2002), 324.

39. Ibid. 357.

40. S. Pollard, *David Blunkett* (London: Hodder and Stoughton, 2005), 270.

41. Ibid. 274.

42. Ibid. 306.

43. Ibid. 307.

44. D. Blunkett, *The Blunkett Tapes: My Life in the Bear-Pit* (London: Bloomsbury, 2006), 309.

45. HC, *Select Committee on Home Affairs, Minutes of Evidence*, Examination of Witnesses (questions 1–19), 23 October 2001, www.publications.parliament. uk/pa/cm200102/cmselect/cmhaff/302/1102302.htm, accessed 27 April 2009. Blunkett almost had it right as the Advisory Council on the Misuse of Drugs (ACMD) had recommended recategorization in its published report of 1979. This had been rejected by the government in 1982. See Ch. 7.

46. ACMD, *The Classification of Cannabis under the Misuse of Drugs Act 1971* (London: Home Office, 2002), http://drugs.homeoffice.gov.uk/publication-search/acmd/cannabis-class-misuse-drugs-act?view=Binary, accessed 27 April 2009.

47. HC, *Select Committee on Home Affairs, Third Report*, 9 May 2002, http://www. publications.parliament.uk/pa/cm200102/cmselect/cmhaff/318/31802.htm, accessed 27 April 2009.

48. M. Fuller and S. Dark, *The Lambeth cannabis warning pilot scheme* (MPS Drugs Directorate, 2002) on www.mpa.gov.uk/committees/mpa/2002/020926/17/, accessed 28 April 2009.

49. B. Paddick, *Line of Fire* (London: Simon and Schuster, 2008), 141.

50. D. Blunkett, *The Blunkett Tapes*, 273.

51. HC, *Select Committee on Home Affairs, Third Report*, para 117, http://www. parliament.the-stationery-office.co.uk/pa/cm200102/cmselect/cmhaff/318/ 31808.htm#n116, accessed 17 February 2009.

52. B. Paddick, *Line of Fire*, 145.

53. Blunkett's wider ambitions to change the way in which the police acted culminated in the Police Reform Bill of 2002.

54. B. Paddick, *Line of Fire*, 142.

55. K. Hellawell, *The Outsider*, 324.

56. T. May, H. Warburton, P. Turnbull, and M. Hough, *Times They Are A-Changing: Policing of Cannabis* (York: Joseph Rowntree Foundation, 2002), pp. vii–ix.

57. Ibid., p. vi.

58. B. Paddick, *Line of Fire*, 144.

59. An amendment to the Police and Criminal Evidence Act (PACE) made possession of a Class C Drug an arrestable offence in 2003. The Criminal Justice Act 2003 preserved the arrest powers (see M. Duffy et al., *'It's a social thing': Cannabis Supply and Young People* (York: Joseph Rowntree Foundation, 2008), 4). Indeed, the purpose of the reclassification of cannabis to Class C, which was to ensure that possession was not an arrestable offence, was further undermined by the Serious Organised Crime and Police Act of 2005. This was a wholesale rationalization of the law which deemed that all offences could be arrestable provided that the arrest is necessary and proportionate to the

circumstances. In effect this represented a further extension of police discretion. See T. May et al., *Policing Cannabis as a Class C Drug*, 50.

60. T. May et al., *Policing Cannabis as a Class C Drug*, accessed 28 April 2009.
61. Association of Chief Police Officers of England, Wales and Northern Ireland (ACPO), *Cannabis Enforcement Guidance* (London: ACPO, 2003).
62. T. May et al., *Policing Cannabis as a Class C Drug*, accessed 28 April 2009.
63. 'Doctor acquitted of supplying cannabis to sick daughter; Dr Anne Biezanek', *The Times*, 20 October 1993, 6.
64. Interview in *The Guardian*, 23 October 1993, 27.
65. Taken from her own account published on www.cannabis-med.org/board-directors.htm, accessed 24 April 2009.
66. 'Upfront: Going to Pot—The Health Aid', *The Guardian*, 23 September 1994, 2.
67. Alliance for Cannabis Therapeutics, http://marijuana-as-medicine.org/alliance.htm, accessed 24 April 2009.
68. 'Ads Call for Legal Hashish', *The Mirror*, 4 April 1997, 2.
69. Taken from her own account published on www.cannabis-med.org/board-directors.htm, accessed 24 April 2009.
70. S. Crowther, L. Reynolds, and E. Tansey (eds.), *The Medicalization of Cannabis: The Transcript of a Witness Seminar held by the Wellcome Trust Centre for the History of Medicine at UCL, London, on 24th March 2009* (London: Wellcome Trust Centre for the History of Medicine at UCL, 2010), 36–7.
71. 'Cannabis Campaign: When Straw Compared Pot to Thalidomide', *Independent on Sunday*, 25 January 1998, Features, 1.
72. Biz Ivol, an MS sufferer who was prosecuted for medical cannabis use in Orkney, took to sending cannabis laced home-made chocolates to fellow MS sufferers. See 'Bitter Sweet End for Cannabis Candies', *Scotland on Sunday*, 4 November 2001, 10.
73. Interview with David Watson and Rob Clarke of HortaPharm, conducted by author on 9 June 2005.
74. Patient groups elsewhere similarly championed herbal cannabis in this period. For details of the US context see W. Chapkis and R. Webb, *Dying to Get High: Marijuana as Medicine* (New York: NYU Press, 2008).
75. ACMD, *Further consideration of the classification of cannabis under the Misuse of Drugs Act 1971* (London: Home Office, 2006), 6. Sinsemilla is the dried, seedless flower clusters of female cannabis plants.
76. *The Observer*, 13 June 2004, 3.
77. *The Express*, 11 March 2005, 12.
78. *Daily Telegraph*, 18 January 2005, 2.
79. ACMD, *Further consideration of the classification of cannabis*. From Home Secretary to Sir Michael Rawlins, 18 March 2005, 28–9.
80. Hansard, HC, 18 January 2005, col. 702, www.parliament.uk, accessed 12 May 2009.

81. 'Cannabis Arrests Fall under Softly Softly Law', *The Independent*, 29 January 2005, 9.

82. Hansard, HC, 19 January 2006, col. 984, www.parliament.uk, accessed 18 May 2009.

83. Ibid., col. 993, www.parliament.uk, accessed 18 May 2009.

84. ACMD, *Cannabis: Classification and Public Health* (London: Home Office, 2008), 3.

85. Hansard, HC, 25 April 2007, col. 942 www.parliament.uk, accessed 11 August 2009.

86. ACMD, *The Classification of Cannabis under the Misuse of Drugs Act*, 8; ACMD, *Further Consideration of the Classification of Cannabis*, 11; ACMD, *Cannabis: Classification and Public Health*, 16.

87. Hansard, HC, 18 January 2007, col. 1012, www.parliament.uk, accessed 11 August 2009.

88. ACMD, *The Classification of Cannabis*, 8; ACMD, *Further Consideration of the Classification of Cannabis*, 9.

89. Hansard, HC, 18 July 2007, col. 268, www.parliament.uk, accessed 11 August 2009.

90. ACMD, *Cannabis: Classification and Public Health*, 1.

91. From Sir Michael Rawlins to Susie Clark, Drug Strategy Consultation 2008, 19 October 2007. The letter included a summary of the ACMD discussion of the Home Office Consultation document that had taken place on 14 September 2007. http://drugs.homeoffice.gov.uk/publicationsearch/acmd/acmdconsultresponse.pdf?view=Binary, accessed 12 August 2009.

92. F. Elliot and R. Ford, 'Brown Planning Clampdown on Cannabis over Health Concerns', *The Times*, 9 January 2008, 5.

93. A. Porter, 'Brown Will Move to Reclassify Cannabis', *Daily Telegraph*, 9 January 2008, 15.

94. 'Clampdown on Cannabis', *The Express*, 9 January 2008, 8.

95. ACMD, *Cannabis: Classification and Public Health*.

96. Hansard, HC, 7 May 2008, col. 705, www.parliament.uk, accessed 12 August 2009.

97. Ibid.

98. ACMD, *Cannabis: Classification and Public Health*, 27.

99. Ibid. 32.

100. See e.g. 'Immigrants Jailed for "Cannabis Factory" Work', *The Scotsman*, 16 October 2007.

101. 'ACPO Supports Cannabis Reclassification', ACPO Press release 7 May 2008, http://www.acpo.police.uk/, accessed 24 August 2008.

102. Hansard, HC, 7 May 2008, col. 710, www.parliament.uk, accessed 25 August 2009.

103. 'Cannabis to be made Class B by Brown U-turn', metro.co.uk, 29 April 2008, accessed 25 August 2009.

104. Steve Rolles, 'Millions quit cannabis following reclassification', posted 7 May 2008, Transform Drug Policy Foundation http://transform-drugs.blogspot.com/2008/05/millions-quit-cannabis-following.html, accessed 25 August 2008.

105. J. Laurance, 'Exaggerated Claims are No Basis for Policy', *The Independent*, 4 April 2008, 18.

106. Hansard, HC, 7 May 2008, col. 707, www.parliament.uk, accessed 25 August 2009.

107. ACMD, *Cannabis: Classification and Public Health*, 8.

108. Taken from S. Blackman, *Chilling Out: The Cultural Politics of Substance Consumption, Youth and Drug Policy* (Maidenhead: Open University Press, 2004), 80–1.

109. ACMD, *MDMA ('ecstasy'): A Review of Its Harms and Classification under the Misuse of Drugs Act 1971* (London: Home Office, 2009), 13.

110. M. Duffy et al., 'It's a social thing', 13.

111. M. Melrose et al., *The Impact of Heavy Cannabis Use on Young People: Vulnerability and Youth Transitions* (York: Joseph Rowntree Foundation, 2007), 57.

112. M. Duffy et al., 'It's a social thing', 14.

113. Melanie Phillips, 'Cannabis Caused a 14-Year-Old to Kill. Yet Still They Say It's Harmless', *Daily Mail*, 14 February 2005, 10.

114. Jamie Doward and Tom Templeton, 'Hippie Dream, Modern Nightmare', *The Observer*, Features pages, 4 May 2008, 4.

115. This argument has two strands. The first is the idea that the violent and murderous cannabis user initially became established in British culture when the Victorians circulated stories about the 'hashassins'. Drawn from North African cultures, the figure of the 'hashassin' was a warrior crazed by cannabis consumption into acts of violence. The idea that cannabis could incite its consumers to murderous acts was reproduced in accounts of the 1857 Indian Uprising against British rule although the Indian Hemp Drugs Commission of 1893/4 pointed out that its properties rendered it unlikely to have this effect. It hypothesized that if those intent upon violence did use cannabis then it was more likely to be as a form of 'Dutch courage' in the same way that alcohol might be used to numb anxieties or doubts. For more see J. Mills, *Cannabis Britannica: Empire, Trade and Prohibition, 1800–c.1928* (Oxford: Oxford University Press, 2003), 69–123. The second strand of this argument is that English-language newspapers had been inventing stories about drug-fuelled violence since the start of the twentieth century in order to explain away troubling social phenomena or to justify measures against them. This has been demonstrated most vividly in the case of cocaine in the USA where Spillane has argued that journalistic accounts of cocaine-fuelled violence and mental illness by African Americans do not tally with actual instances of crime or asylum admissions of the period. Instead, he argues, these journalistic myths justified repressive measures on the part of the white authorities against

African Americans, particularly in the Southern states. See J. Spillane, *Cocaine: From Medical Marvel to Modern Menace in the United States, 1884–1920* (Baltimore: Johns Hopkins University Press, 2000), 119–22.
116. M. Duffy et al., 'It's a social thing', 45.

CHAPTER 9

1. The account above is drawn from J. Mills, *Cannabis Britannica: Empire, Trade and Prohibition, 1800–1928* (Oxford: Oxford University Press, 2003).
2. For a good summary of the evolution of the 'British system' of dealing with addiction and the controversies about its nature see A. Mold, 'The "British System" of Heroin Addiction Treatment and the Opening of Drug Dependence Units, 1965–1970', *Social History of Medicine*, 17 (2004), 501–17.
3. This conclusion was a bold attempt to break the historical association between cannabis and opiates which had lingered for over a century since the time that William Caine and others had bundled them together in the campaign for the Royal Opium Commission. See J. Mills, *Cannabis Britannica*, 96–104.
4. For a recent account of the place of evidence in policy-making on cannabis see M. Monaghan, 'The Complexity of Evidence: Reflections on Research Utilisation in a Heavily Politicised Policy Area', *Social Policy and Society*, 9/1 (2010), 1–12.
5. See L. Iversen, *The Science of Marijuana* (Oxford: Oxford University Press, 2000).
6. N. Rose, *The Politics of Life Itself: Biomedicine, Power and Subjectivity in the Twenty-First Century* (Princeton: Princeton University Press, 2007), 187–223.
7. A. Offer, *The Challenge of Affluence: Self-control and Well-being in the United States and Britain since 1950* (Oxford: Oxford University Press, 2006), 358.
8. E. Temple, R. Brown, and D. Hine, 'The "Grass Ceiling": Limitations in the Literature Hinder Our Understanding of Cannabis Use and Its Consequences', *Addiction*, 106 (2011), 238–44; J. Macleod and M. Hickman, 'How Ideology Shapes the Evidence and the Policy: What Do We Know About Cannabis Use and What Should We Do?', *Addiction*, 105 (2010), 1326–30.
9. V. Berridge, 'Illicit Drugs and Internationalism: The Forgotten Dimension', *Medical History*, 45/2 (2001), 282–8.
10. For a similar discussion on the interplay of national and international contexts from the US perspective see W. McAllister, 'Habitual Problems: The United States and International Drug Control', in J. Erlin and J. Spillane (eds.), *The Evolution of Federal Drug Policy* (Binghamton, NY: Haworth Press, 2004); W. McAllister, 'The Global Political Economy of Scheduling: The International-Historical Context of the Controlled Substances Act', *Drug and Alcohol Dependence*, 76/1 (2004), 3–8.

11. A thoughtful article along these lines is J. Richardson, 'Government, Interest Groups and Policy Change', *Political Studies*, 48/5 (2000), 1006–25. For a perspective from a historian's point of view on concepts such as 'policy community', 'interest group', or 'network theory', see the introduction in V. Berridge (ed.), *Making Health Policy: Networks in Research and Policy after 1945* (Amsterdam: Rodopi, 2005).

12. For an example see M. Jay, *High Society: Mind-Altering Drugs in History and Culture* (London: Thames and Hudson, 2010).

13. Alison Ritter has pointed out that there are multiple models of regulation available that could be applied to substances currently considered to be 'illicit drugs' and that the 'command control' model adopted almost a century ago is only one among a number of alternatives. See A. Ritter, 'Illicit Drugs Policy through the Lens of Regulation', *International Journal of Drug Policy*, 21 (2010), 265–70.

Bibliography

UNPUBLISHED SOURCES

British Library (BL)

IOL   India Office Library, Records and Private Papers.
LN   League of Nations Documents and Microfilm Collection.
UN   United Nations Documents Collection.

National Archives (NA)

ADM   Records of the Admiralty, Naval Forces, Royal Marines, Coastguard, and related bodies.
CO   Records of the Colonial Office, Commonwealth and Foreign and Commonwealth Offices, Empire Marketing Board, and related bodies.
CRIM Records of the Central Criminal Court.
CUST Records of the Boards of Customs, Excise, and Customs and Excise, and HM Revenue and Customs.
DPP   Records of the Director of Public Prosecutions.
FO   Records created or inherited by the Foreign Office.
HO   Records created or inherited by the Home Office, Ministry of Home Security, and related bodies.
MEPO Records of the Metropolitan Police Office.
MH   Records created or inherited by the Ministry of Health and successors, Local Government Boards and related bodies.

Wellcome Library

PP/WDP   Sir William Drummond MacDonald Paton Collection.

Interviews and private correspondence

Interviews with Caroline Coon (3 March 2008), Robin Corbett (28 October 2008), Anthony Gifford (15 October 2008), David Watson and Rob Clarke (9 June 2005).

Emails with Free Love Cannabis (17 January 2009), and Robert Kilroy-Silk (1 October 2008).

PUBLISHED REPORTS

Advisory Council on the Misuse of Drugs (ACMD), *The Classification of Cannabis under the Misuse of Drugs Act 1971* (London: Home Office, 2002).

—— *Further Consideration of the Classification of Cannabis under the Misuse of Drugs Act 1971* (London: Home Office, 2006).

—— *Cannabis: Classification and Public Health* (London: Home Office, 2008).

Academy of Medical Sciences, *The Use of Cannabis and Its Derivatives for Medical and Recreational Purposes* (London: The Royal Society, 1998).

Association of Chief Police Officers of England, Wales, and Northern Ireland (ACPO), *Cannabis Enforcement Guidance* (London: ACPO, 2003).

British Medical Association, *Therapeutic Uses of Cannabis* (Amsterdam: Harwood Academic Publishers, 1997).

Coon, C., and Harris, R., *The Release Report on Drug Offenders and the Law* (London: Sphere, 1969).

Duffy, M., et al., *'It's a social thing': Cannabis Supply and Young People* (York: Joseph Rowntree Foundation, 2008).

Hayes, G., and Shapiro, H., *Drug Notes: Cannabis* (London: Institute for the Study of Drug Dependence, 1998).

House of Commons (HC), *Select Committee on Home Affairs, Minutes of Evidence*, 23 October 2001, http://www.publications.parliament.uk/pa/cm200102/cmselect/cmhaff/302/1102302.htm

—— *Select Committee on Home Affairs, Third Report*, 9 May 2002, http://www.publications.parliament.uk/pa/cm200102/cmselect/cmhaff/318/31802.htm

House of Lords (HL), *Select Committee on Science and Technology, Second Report 1998–99, Cannabis: Government Response* (London: The Stationery Office, 1999).

—— *Select Committee on Science and Technology, Second Report 2000–01, Therapeutic Uses of Cannabis* (London: The Stationery Office, 2001).

—— *Select Committee on Science and Technology, Ninth Report 1997–8, Cannabis: The Scientific and Medical Evidence* (London: The Stationery Office, 1998).

May, T., Duffy, M., Warburton, H., and Hough, M., *Policing Cannabis as a Class C Drug* (York: Joseph Rowntree Foundation, 2007), http://www.jrf.org.uk/publications/policing-cannabis-class-c-drug.

—— Warburton, H., Turnbull, P., and Hough, M., *Times They Are A-Changing: Policing of Cannabis* (York: Joseph Rowntree Foundation, 2002).

Melrose, M., et al., *The Impact of Heavy Cannabis Use on Young People: Vulnerability and Youth Transitions* (York: Joseph Rowntree Foundation, 2007).

Metropolitan Police, *The Principles of Policing and Guidance for Professional Behaviour* (London: Public Information Department, Metropolitan Police, 1985).

Official Report of Parliamentary Debates (Hansard).

Police and People in London: A Group of Young, Black People (London: Policy Studies Institute, 1983).

Report of the Independent Inquiry into the Misuse of Drugs Act 1971 (London: Police Foundation, 2000).

Report of the Indian Hemp Drugs Commission 1893–1894 (Simla: Government Central Printing House, 1894).

Report on a Review of the Classification of Controlled Drugs and of Penalties under Schedules 2 and 4 of the Misuse of Drugs Act 1971 (London: Home Office, 1979).

Report of an Alcoholism and Drug Addiction Research Foundation (Ontario) and WHO Scientific Meeting on Adverse Health and Behavioural Consequences of Cannabis Use (Ontario: Addiction Research Foundation, 1981).

Report of the Expert Group on the Effects of Cannabis Use (London: HMSO, 1982).

Stop and Search (London: Release, 1977).

Stop and Search: Special Report (London: Release, 1980).

The UN and Narcotic Drugs: Half a Century of Successful Struggle against Crime, Disease and Social Affliction (New York: UN Office of Public Information, 1960).

Therapeutic Uses of Cannabis (Amsterdam: BMA/Harwood Academic Publishers, 1997).

Trash Rehashed: A Reply to the Advisory Council on the Misuse of Drugs (London: Legalise Cannabis Campaign, 1979).

Union of South Africa, *Report of the Inter-Departmental Committee on the Abuse of Dagga* (Pretoria: Government Printer, 1952).

World Health Organization, *Expert Committee on Drugs Liable To Produce Addiction, Third Report* (Geneva: WHO Technical Report Series no. 57, 1952).

WEB RESOURCES

Alliance for Cannabis Therapeutics, http://marijuana-as-medicine.org/alliance.htm

Free Love Cannabis, http://cannabis.uk.net

International Association for Cannabinoid Medicines, http://www.cannabis-med.org/index.php?lng=en

Legalise Cannabis Alliance, http://www.lca-uk.org/intro.php

Release, http://www.release.org.uk/

Transform Drug Policy Foundation, http://www.tdpf.org.uk

ARTICLES AND PAPERS

Where details of author are not available the article is listed in alphabetical order by title.

'A Case of Cannabis Intoxication', *The Lancet*, 1 (1935), 811.

'Addiction to Drugs', *British Medical Journal (BMJ)* 2 (1959), 48.

'Ads Call for Legal Hashish', *The Mirror*, 4 April 1997, 2.

'A New Euphoriant for Depressive Mental States', *BMJ* 2 (1947), 918–22.

'A New Way of Smuggling Narcotics', *The Lancet*, 1 (1940), 464.

Berridge, V., 'Illicit Drugs and Internationalism: The Forgotten Dimension', *Medical History*, 45/2 (2001), 282–8.

'Bitter Sweet End for Cannabis Candies', *Scotland on Sunday*, 4 November 2001, 10.

'Campaigners Light Up in Cannabis Protest', *Press Association*, 28 September 1997.

'Cannabis Arrests Fall under Softly Softly Law', *The Independent*, 29 January 2005, 9.

'Cannabis Campaign: When Straw Compared Pot to Thalidomide', the *Independent on Sunday*, 25 January 1998, Features 1.

'Cannabis Indica', *BMJ* 1 (1938), 1058.

'Cannabis Indica', *The Lancet*, 2 (1943), 296.

'Cannabis Indica for Herpes Zoster', *BMJ* 2 (1939), 431.

'Cannabis Law Sends "Wrong Signal"', http://news.bbc.co.uk

'Chief Justice Urges Debate on Cannabis', *The Times*, 9 October 1997, 7.

'Clampdown on Cannabis', *The Express*, 9 January 2008, 8.

Coles, W. H., 'A Case of Cannabis Indica Intoxication', *The Lancet*, 1 (1935), 1301.

——'Cannabis Indica', *The Lancet*, 1 (1935), 904.

'Control of Drug Addiction', *The Lancet*, 1 (1952), 1026.

'Control of Narcotics', *BMJ* 2 (1943), 718.

'Control of Narcotic Drugs', *BMJ* 1 (1962), 934.

Cooke, E., 'The Drug Squad', *Journal of the Forensic Science Society*, 3/1 (September 1962), 43–8.

'Dangerous Drug Traffic in Egypt', *The Lancet*, 1 (1932), 1372.

Davenport-Hines, R., 'Brooke, Henry, Baron Brooke of Cumnor (1903–1984)', *Oxford Dictionary of National Biography* (Oxford: Oxford University Press, 2004), http://www.oxforddnb.com/view/article/37227.

'Delegates Defy Senior Figures on Drugs Policy', *Western Mail*, 21 September 2001, 10.

'Detectives Plotted Against Immigrants, QC Says', *The Times*, 6 October 1970, 3.

'Doctor Acquitted of Supplying cannabis to Sick Daughter; Dr Anne Biezanek', *The Times*, 20 October 1993, 6.

Doward, J., and Templeton, T., 'Hippie Dream, Modern Nightmare', *The Observer*, Features pages, 4 May 2008, 4.

'Drug Addiction', *BMJ* 2 (1957), 210.

'Drug Addiction in America', *The Lancet*, 1 (1951), 1356–7.

'Drug Addiction in Egypt', *The Lancet*, 1 (1931), 713.

'Drugs in the Treatment of Depression', *The Lancet*, 1 (1955), 1065.

'Egypt: Appeal Without Standing', *Time*, 2 December 1935.

Elliot, F., and Ford, R., 'Brown Planning Clampdown on Cannabis over Health Concerns', *The Times*, 9 January 2008, 5.

'Former Drug Squad Chief Cleared by Jury of Conspiracy', *The Times*, 15 November 1973, 4.

Fraser, J., 'Withdrawal Symptoms in Cannabis-Indica Addicts', *The Lancet*, 2 (1949), 747–8.

Gaoni, Y., and Mechoulam, R., 'Isolation, Structure and Partial Synthesis of an Active Constituent of Hashish', *Journal of the American Chemical Society*, 86/8 (1964), 1646–7.

'Going to Pot: The Politicians' Line', *The Guardian*, 23 September 1994, T3.

'Greens Sell Drugs Books on Website', *The Independent*, 9 September 1999, 2.

'Home-grown Indian Hemp', *BMJ* 2 (1961), 1440.

'Lord Hailsham Urges JPs to Have No Mercy for Offences Committed in Business for Profit', *The Times*, 13 October 1973, 3.

Haagen-Smit, A. J., et al., 'A Physiologically Active Principle from Cannabis Sativa (Marihuana)', *Science*, 91 (1940), 602.

Harding, G., 'Constructing Addiction', *Sociology of Health and Illness*, 8 (1986), 75–85.

'Hemp', *The Lancet*, 2 (1949), 757–8.

'Hemp from Budgerigar Seed', *BMJ* 2 (1959), 764.

'High on Success from the Cannabis Campaign', *The Independent*, 3 November 1997, Media section M8.

'Howard at Odds with Scottish Ministers over Cannabis Fines', *The Scotsman*, 14 February 1994.

Howells, R., 'Sweet v. Parseley and Public Welfare Offences', *Modern Law Review*, 32/3 (1969), 310.

'Indian Hemp', *BMJ* 1 (1941), 676.

'Indian Hemp', *BMJ* 2 (1952), 28.

'Indian Hemp', *The Lancet*, 1 (1952), 1096.

'Immigrants Jailed for "Cannabis Factory" Work', *The Scotsman*, 16 October 2007.

Jacob, A., and Todd, A., 'Cannabidiol and Cannabol: Constituents of Cannabis Indica Resin', *Nature*, 145 (1940), 350.

Johnson, D. McIntosh, 'A Visit to Pont St. Esprit', *The Lancet*, 1 (1952), 820.

'Kennedy Call to Rethink Drug Law: Lib Dem Leader Seeks Royal Commission on the Legalisation of Cannabis', *The Observer*, 15 August 1999, 1.

Lande, A., 'The Single Convention on Narcotic Drugs, 1961', *International Organization*, 16/4 (1962), 782.

Laurance, J., 'Exaggerated Claims Are No Basis for Policy', *The Independent*, 4 April 2008, 18.

'Lebanon and Hashish', *The Lancet*, 2 (1943).

Loewe, S., 'Marihuana Activity of Cannabinol', *Science*, 102 (1945), 615.

McAllister, W., 'The Global Political Economy of Scheduling: The International-Historical Context of the Controlled Substances Act', *Drug and Alcohol Dependence*, 76/1 (2004), 3–8.

MacDonald, A., 'The Actions and Uses of Hemp Drugs', *Nature*, 147 (1941), 168.

McLaren, M., 'From Analysis to Prescription: Scottish Concepts of Asian Despotism in Early Nineteenth-Century British India', *International History Review*, 15/3 (1993), 469–501.

Macleod, J., and Hickman, M., 'How Ideology Shapes the Evidence and the Policy: What Do We Know about Cannabis Use and What Should We Do?', *Addiction*, 105 (2010), 1326–30.

'Marihuana', *The Lancet*, 2 (1939), 567.

Mold, A., 'The "British System" of Heroin Addiction Treatment and the Opening of Drug Dependence Units, 1965–1970', *Social History of Medicine*, 17 (2004), 501–17.

——'The Welfare Branch of the Alternative Society? The Work of Drug Voluntary Organisation Release, 1967–1978', *Twentieth-Century British History*, 17/1 (2006), 50–73.

Monaghan, M., 'The Complexity of Evidence: Reflections on Research Utilisation in a Heavily Politicised Policy Area', *Social Policy and Society*, 9/1 (2010), 1–12.

'Monitor: Mo Mowlam and Cannabis', *The Independent*, 22 January 2000, 6.

'More Light on Marihuana', *The Lancet*, 2 (1940), 370.

'Mo Mowlam: Obituary', *The Independent*, 20 August 2005, 40–1.

'Mo, Smart, Funny and Brave But Forever on the Run from Her Demons', *Daily Mail*, 20 August 2005, 4–5.

'Mowlam Cannabis Hints Cause a Stir', *Birmingham Evening Mail*, 6 November 2000, 5.

'Narcotic Control', *BMJ* 1 (1956), 104.

'Notes from India', *The Lancet*, 1 (1929), 519.

'Obituary: Faris Glubb', *The Guardian*, http://www.guardian.co.uk

O'Hara, G., 'Insanity, Transnationalism, Bureaucracy: The Origins of Britain's "Ombudsman" in the 1950s and 1960s', paper presented at the CSHHH Glasgow, 22 March 2011.

Parker, C., and Wrigley, F., 'Effects of Cannabis', *The Lancet*, 2 (1947), 223.

——————'Synthetic Cannabis Preparations in Psychiatry: Synhexl', *Journal of Mental Science* (1950), 276–9.

Pedersen, S., 'Back to the League of Nations', *American Historical Review*, 112/4 (2007), 1091–1117.

Peters, D., 'The British Medical Response to Opiate Addiction in the Nineteenth Century', *Journal of the History of Medicine and Allied Sciences*, 36 (1981), 455–88.

Petridis, A., 'The Story of The Specials', *Mojo*, 98 (2002), 76–81.

Phillips, M., 'Cannabis Caused a 14-Year-Old to Kill: Yet Still They Say It's Harmless', *Daily Mail*, 14 February 2005, 10.

'Police Constable Gets Four Years', *The Times*, 26 January 1963, 5.

Pond, D., 'Psychological Effects in Depressive Patients of Synhexl', *Journal of Neurology, Neurosurgery and Psychiatry* (1948), 271–9.

Porter, A., 'Brown Will Move to Reclassify Cannabis', *Daily Telegraph*, 9 January 2008, 15.

'Pot Power: Thirty Years After the First Cannabis Rally, Veterans and New Campaigners Gathered to Fight a Law that Has Left Two Generations Alienated and Criminalised', *Independent on Sunday*, 29 March 1998, Features, 1.

Powell, G., et al., 'The Active Principle of Marihuana', *Science*, 93 (1941), 522.

'Prevention and Treatment of Drug Addiction', *BMJ* 1 (1931), 495.

Richardson, R., 'Government, Interest Groups and Policy Change', *Political Studies*, 48/5 (2000), 1006–25.

Ritter, A., 'Illicit Drugs Policy through the Lens of Regulation', *International Journal of Drug Policy*, 21 (2010), 265–70.

'Short's Puff for Cannabis Sends Labour Reeling', *The Independent*, 30 October 1995, 1.

'Talking Tough Yet Tender, Portillo Steals the Show', *Daily Mail*, 4 October 2000, 5.

Temple, E., Brown, R., and Hine, D., 'The "Grass Ceiling": Limitations in the Literature Hinder Our Understanding of Cannabis Use and Its Consequences', *Addiction*, 106 (2011), 238–44.

Todd, A., 'Chemistry of the Hemp Drugs', *Nature*, 146 (1940), 830.

'The Active Principle of Cannabis Indica', *BMJ* 2 (1938), 40.

'The Anti-Narcotic Campaign in Egypt', *BMJ* 2 (1945), 612.

'The Campaign against Dangerous Drugs in Egypt', *BMJ* 1 (1935), 1274.

'The Drug Traffic in Egypt', *BMJ* 2 (1940), 21.

'The International Traffic in Dangerous Drugs' *BMJ* 1 (1930), 560.

'The Time is Right to Decriminalise Cannabis', *The Independent*, 28 September 1997, T1.

'Three Detectives Are Acquitted', *The Times*, 24 November 1970, 3.

'Traffic in Dangerous Drugs', *The Lancet*, 2 (1946), 279.

'Treating the Symptoms of Depression', *BMJ* 2 (1947), 933.

'Upfront: Going to Pot—The Health Aid', *The Guardian*, 23 September, 2.

'Useful Plants in India', *BMJ* 2 (1925), 963.

'We Took Drugs Say Seven Top Tories', *Mail on Sunday*, 8 October 2000, 1.

'Widdecombe Is Left Fuming over "Cannabis Plot"', *The Times*, 9 October 2000.

'Why We Believe It Is Time to Decriminalise Cannabis', *Independent on Sunday*, 28 September 1997, Features, 1.

BOOKS

Addison, P., *No Turning Back: The Peacetime Revolutions of Post-War Britain* (Oxford: Oxford University Press, 2010).

Berridge, V., *Opium and the People* (London: Free Association Books, 1999).

——*Marketing Health: Smoking and the Discourse of Public Health in Britain, 1945–2000* (Oxford: Oxford University Press, 2007).

——(ed.), *Making Health Policy: Networks in Research and Policy after 1945* (Amsterdam: Rodopi, 2005).

Blackman, S., *Chilling Out: The Cultural Politics of Substance Consumption, Youth and Drug Policy* (Maidenhead: Open University Press, 2004).

Blunkett, D., *The Blunkett Tapes: My Life in the Bear-Pit* (London: Bloomsbury, 2006).

Bonnie, R., and Whitebread, C., *The Marihuana Conviction: A History of Marihuana Prohibition in the United States* (Charlottesville: Virginia University Press, 1974).

Booth, M., *Cannabis: A History* (London: Doubleday, 2003).

Borowy, I., *Coming to Terms With World Health: The League of Nations Health Organisation 1921–1946* (Frankfurt: Peter Lang, 2009).

Bud, R., *Penicillin: Triumph and Tragedy* (Oxford: Oxford University Press, 2007).

Campbell, A., and Campbell, R., *Blood and Fire: The Autobiography of the UB40 Brothers* (London: Arrow, 2006).

Campos, I., *Home Grown: Marijuana and the Origins of Mexico's War on Drugs* (Chapel Hill: University of North Carolina Press, 2012).

Chapkis, W., and Webb, R., *Dying to Get High: Marijuana as Medicine* (New York: NYU Press, 2008).

Chopra, R. N., *Opium Habit in India* (Calcutta: Thacker, Spink and Co, 1927).

——*The Present Position of Hemp Drug Addiction in India* (Calcutta: Thacker, Spink and Co, 1939).

Codwell, J., and Macleod. D., *Orientalism Transposed: The Impact of the Colonies on British Culture* (Aldershot: Ashgate, 1998).

Courtwright, D., *Forces of Habit: Drugs and the Making of the Modern World* (London: Harvard University Press, 2001).

Crowther, S., Reynolds, L., and Tansey, E. (eds.), *The Medicalization of Cannabis: The Transcript of a Witness Seminar Held by the Wellcome Trust Centre for the History of Medicine at UCL, London, on 24th March 2009* (London: Wellcome Trust Centre for the History of Medicine at UCL, 2010).

Curtis, H., and Sanderson, M. (eds.), *The Unsung Sixties: Memoirs of Social Innovation* (London: Whiting and Birch, 2004).

Daly, M. (ed.), *The Cambridge History of Egypt: Modern Egypt, from 1517 to the End of the Twentieth Century* (Cambridge: Cambridge University Press, 1998).

Dikötter, F., Laaman, L., and Xun, Z., *Narcotic Culture: A History of Drugs in China* (London: Hurst, 2004).

Erlin, J., and Spillane, J. (eds.), *The Evolution of Federal Drug Policy* (Binghamton, NY: Haworth Press, 2004)

Fuller, M., and Dark, S., *The Lambeth Cannabis Warning Pilot Scheme* (London: MPS Drugs Directorate, 2002).

Goode, E., *The Marijuana Smokers* (New York: Basic Books, 1970).

Goodman, J., et al. (eds.), *Consuming Habits: Global and Historical Perspectives on How Cultures Define Drugs* (London: Routledge, 2007).

Green, J. (ed.), *Days in the Life: Voices from the English Underground, 1961–1971* (London: Pimlico, 1998).

——*All Dressed Up: The Sixties and the Counterculture* (London: Pimlico, 1999).

Grinspoon, L., *Marihuana: The Forbidden Medicine* (London: Yale University Press, 1993).

Grivas, K. (trans. D. Whitehouse), *Cannabis, Marihuana, Hashish* (London: Minerva Press, 1977).

Harrison, M., *Medicine and Victory: British Military Medicine in the Second World War* (Oxford: Oxford University Press, 2004).

Healy, D., *The Antidepressant Era* (Cambridge, Mass.: Harvard University Press, 1999).

——*The Creation of Psychopharmacology* (Cambridge, Mass.: Harvard University Press, 2002).

Hellawell, K., *The Outsider: The Autobiography of One of Britain's Most Controversial Policemen* (London: HarperCollins, 2002).

Herer, J., *The Emperor Wears No Clothes: Hemp and the Marijuana Conspiracy* (Van Nuys, Calif: Queen of Clubs Publishing, 1992).

Inden, R., *Imagining India* (Oxford: Blackwell, 1990).

Jay, M., *High Society: Mind-Altering Drugs in History and Culture* (London: Thames and Hudson, 2010).

Jiggens, J., 'Marijuana Australiana: Cannabis Use, Popular Culture and the Americanisation of Drugs Policy in Australia, 1938–1988' (PhD thesis, Queensland University of Technology, 2004).

Johnson, D. McIntosh, *A Doctor Regrets* (London: Christopher Johnson, 1949).

——*Bars and Barricades* (London: Christopher Johnson, 1952).

——*Indian Hemp: A Social Menace* (London: Christopher Johnson, 1952).

——*A Doctor Returns* (London: Christopher Johnson, 1956).

Klein, A., Day, M., and Harriott, A. (eds.), *Caribbean Drugs: From Criminalization to Harm Reduction* (London: Zed, 2004).

Kohn, K., *Dope Girls: The Birth of the British Drug Underground* (London: Granta, 1992).

Kozma, L., 'The League of Nations and the Debate over Cannabis Prohibition', *History Compass*, 9/1 (2011), 61–70.

Kushner, H., 'Taking Biology Seriously: The Next Task for Historians of Addiction and What to Do about It', *Bulletin of the History of Medicine*, 80 (2006), 115–43.

Kynaston, D., *Austerity Britain, 1945–1951* (London: Bloomsbury, 2007).

——*Family Britain, 1951–1957* (London: Bloomsbury, 2009).

McAllister, W., *Drug Diplomacy in the Twentieth Century* (London: Routledge, 2000).

Mack, A., and Joy, J., *Marijuana as Medicine?* (Washington: National Academy Press, 2001).

Majeed, J., *Uncovered Imaginings: James Mill's The History of British India and Orientalism* (Oxford: Clarendon Press, 1992).

Martel, M., *Not This Time: Canadians, Public Policy and the Marijuana Question* (Toronto: University of Toronto Press, 2006).

Matthews, P., *Cannabis Culture: A Journey through Disputed Territory* (London: Bloomsbury, 1999).

Mills, J., *Cannabis Britannica: Empire, Trade and Prohibition, 1800–1928* (Oxford: Oxford University Press, 2003).

——and Barton, P. (eds.), *Drugs and Empires: Essays in Imperialism and Intoxication, c.1500–1930* (Basingstoke: Palgrave, 2007).

Mold, A., *Heroin: The Treatment of Addiction in Twentieth-Century Britain* (Champaign: Northern Illinois University Press, 2008).

Moore-Gilbert, B., *Postcolonial Theory: Contexts, Practices, Politics* (New York: Verso, 1997).

Morgan, K., *Britain Since 1945: The People's Peace* (Oxford: Oxford University Press, 2001).

Nahas, G., *Marihuana, Deceptive Weed* (New York: Raven Press, 1973).

——*Keep Off the Grass: A Scientist's Documented Account of Marijuana's Destructive Effects* (New York: Reader's Digest Press, 1976).

——and Paton, W. D. M. (eds.), *Advances in the Biosciences*, vols. xxii and xxiii, *Marihuana: Biological Effects* (Oxford: Pergamon Press, 1979).

Nelson, R., *Hemp & Health* (1999), http://www.rexresearch.com/hhusb/hmphlth.htm

Offer, A., *The Challenge of Affluence: Self-Control and Well-Being in the United States and Britain Since 1950* (Oxford: Oxford University Press, 2006).

Paddick, B., *Line of Fire* (London: Simon and Schuster, 2008).

Parssinen, T., and Kerner, K., 'Development of the Disease Model of Drug Addiction in Britain 1870–1926', *Medical History*, 24, (1980), 275–96.

Plant, M., *Drugs in Perspective* (London: Hodder and Stoughton, 1987).

Pollard, S., *David Blunkett* (London: Hodder and Stoughton, 2005).

Porter, R., and Teich, M. (eds.), *Drugs and Narcotics in History* (Cambridge: Cambridge University Press, 1996).

Prain, D., *Report on the Cultivation and Use of Ganja* (Calcutta: Thacker and Spink, 1893).

Rang, H., 'Paton, Sir William Drummond MacDonald (1917–1993)', *Oxford Dictionary of National Biography* (Oxford: Oxford University Press, 2004), http://www.oxforddnb.com/view/article/53130

Rose, N., *The Politics of Life Itself: Biomedicine, Power and Subjectivity in the Twenty-First Century* (Princeton: Princeton University Press, 2007).

Rubin, V., *Cannabis and Culture* (Paris: Mouton, 1975).

Rudgeley, R., *The Alchemy of Culture: Intoxicants in Society* (London: British Museum Press, 1993).

Russell Pasha, T., *Egyptian Service 1902–1946* (London: Murray, 1949).

Said, E., *Orientalism* (London: Vintage Books, 1978).

Sloman, L., *The History of Marijuana in America* (New York: Bobbs Merill, 1979).

Spillane, J., *Cocaine: From Medical Marvel to Modern Menace in the United States, 1884–1920* (Baltimore: Johns Hopkins University Press, 2000).

Sznitman, S., Olsson, B., and Room, R. (eds.), *A Cannabis Reader: Global Issues and Local Experiences* (Lisbon: European Monitoring Centre for Drugs and Drug Addiction, 2008).

Taylor, S., *Remedicalising Cannabis: Science, Medicine and Policy, 1973 to the Early Twenty-First Century* (unpublished thesis, London School of Hygiene and Tropical Medicine, 2010).

Tone, A., *The Age of Anxiety: A History of America's Turbulent Affair with Tranquilizers* (New York: Basic Books, 2009).

Trocki, C., *Opium, Empire, and the Global Political Economy: A Study of the Asian Opium Trade, 1750–1950* (London: Routledge, 1999).

Walker, W., *Opium and Foreign Policy: The Anglo-American Search for Order in Asia, 1912–1954* (Chapel Hill: University of North Carolina Press, 1991).

——*Drugs in the Western Hemisphere* (Wilmington, Del.: Scholarly Resources, 1996).

Walters, S., *Tory Wars: The Conservatives in Crisis* (London: Politicos, 2001).

Walton, S., *Out of It: A Cultural History of Intoxication* (London: Hamish Hamilton, 2001).

West, D. J. (ed.), *Problems of Drug Abuse in Britain* (Cambridge: Institute of Criminology, 1977).

Wolff, P., *Marihuana in Latin America: The Threat It Constitutes* (Washington: Linacre, 1949).

Zheng, Y. *The Social Life of Opium in China* (Cambridge: Cambridge University Press, 2005).

Index

United States of America (*cont.*)
  Air Force 78 108, 126
  Bureau of Narcotics 3
  Columbia University 31
  Cornell University 31
  Detroit 42
  Marihuana Tax Act 3, 101
  National Research Council, National
    Academy of Sciences 148
  New York 43, 44, 88, 89, 96
University of Algiers 47
University of Bristol 63
University of Illinois 31
University of Manchester 31

Vauxhall Motors 172
Vaille, Charles 103
Veeraswamy's restaurant 66, 67
Viniegra, Salazar 48

Wakefield 121, 140
Walker, William 2
Warneford Hospital 72
Warnock, John 103
Warrington 122
Warwickshire 121
Wayne, Edward 141, 149
Weitzman, David 152
Wellingborough 121
Wellington School 118
Wells, H. G. 28
Wesleyan Methodist School, Lagos 66
West Indies 5, 6, 19, 51, 63, 65, 90, 93,
    119, 127, 147, 174, 175, 219, 223
Whitelaw, William 171, 175

Whittingham Hospital,
  Lancs 86, 87
Widdecombe, Ann 192–3
Wigan 139
Wilson, Richard 196
Windsor, Ontario 42
Wolff, Pablo Osvaldo 69, 88, 102–3,
  107, 150
Woodstock 71
Wootton, Barbara 8, 142–154, 155,
  159, 179, 184
Wootton Committee, *see* Advisory
  Committee on Drug Dependence
World Health Organization (WHO) 7,
  69, 95–115 passim 150, 168, 201,
  219, 228
  Expert Committee on Drugs Liable to
    Produce Addiction 79, 100, 102,
    109, 110
  *The Merits of Antibiotic Substances
    Obtainable from Cannabis Sativa* 109
  *The Physical and Mental Effects of
    Cannabis* 102
World This Weekend, The 191
Wrigley, Fred 86

Xun, Zhou 3

Yates, Gilbert 103
York 123
Yorkshire 180
Young Vigilantes 124, 125
Yugoslavia 104

Zheng, Yangwen 3